Erotics of
Deconstruction

For 'the library angel who looks after people
who write and read books'
(Geoff Ryman)

Erotics of Deconstruction

Auto-Affection After Derrida

Edited by Lynn Turner

EDINBURGH
University Press

Edinburgh University Press is one of the leading university presses in the UK. We publish academic books and journals in our selected subject areas across the humanities and social sciences, combining cutting-edge scholarship with high editorial and production values to produce academic works of lasting importance. For more information visit our website: edinburghuniversitypress.com

© editorial matter and organisation Lynn Turner, 2024
© the chapters their several authors, 2024

Grateful acknowledgement is made to the sources listed in the List of Illustrations for permission to reproduce material previously published elsewhere. Every effort has been made to trace the copyright holders, but if any have been inadvertently overlooked, the publisher will be pleased to make the necessary arrangements at the first opportunity.

Edinburgh University Press Ltd
13 Infirmary Street
Edinburgh EH1 1LT

Typeset in 11/13pt Bembo
by Cheshire Typesetting Ltd, Cuddington, Cheshire, and
printed and bound in Great Britain

A CIP record for this book is available from the British Library

ISBN 978 1 3995 3973 9 (hardback)
ISBN 978 1 3995 3975 3 (webready PDF)
ISBN 978 1 3995 3976 0 (epub)

The right of Lynn Turner to be identified as the editor of this work has been asserted in accordance with the Copyright, Designs and Patents Act 1988, and the Copyright and Related Rights Regulations 2003 (SI No. 2498).

CONTENTS

List of Illustrations	vii
Notes on Contributors	viii
Acknowledgements	xii

Lapping It Up: An Introduction *for* these Erotics of Deconstruction *Lynn Turner*	1

Part I: Procreativity

1.	Derrida's Tongues *Elissa Marder*	17
2.	Spoonful: The Dorsal Deconstruction of Eroticism *David Wills*	35
3.	Two Pirouettes: The Politics of Spoiling (for) Fun in Preciado's Revolutionary Vitalism and Derrida's Death Drive *Eszter Timár*	53
4.	Double Blind Date *Naomi Waltham-Smith*	72
5.	Postscript: Deconstruction and Love *Nicholas Royle*	91

Part II: Vulnerability

6.	Sanguine Resistance: Dreaming of a Future for Blood *Lynn Turner*	113
7.	Touch, Flesh, Wound and the Caress of the Screen *Elizabeth Wijaya*	134

8. No Deconstruction Without Pleasure: Openings, Tunnels and Holes 153
Quinn Eades

9. Bodies in E-motion: Kofman and Cixous Encountering Rembrandt 170
Lenka Vráblíková

10. Voice and Sextuality 188
Anne Emmanuelle Berger

Part III: Panthropology

11. The Masturbating Animal: The Auto-hetero-affection of the Living 217
Nicole Anderson

12. Playing the Field: Non-nonbinary Promiscuity 236
Vicki Kirby

13. 'Gene for Gene': Cloning, 'Sexiness' and the (Post) Maternal in Carola Dibbell's *The Only Ones* 256
Naomi Morgenstern

14. Erotics of Decomposition: Cells and their Oceans 275
Elina Staikou

Index 296

Illustrations

0.1   Sharon Kivland, from the series *Mes Liseuses*, 2015. Ink and gouache on paper from vintage French school exercise book   11

6.1   Jenny Holzer, *Lustmord*, on the cover of *Süddeutsche Zeitung*, 19/11/1993 Magazin No. 46   115

6.2   Jenny Holzer, *Lustmord*, detail on the cover of *Süddeutsche Zeitung*, 19/11/1993 Magazin No. 46   121

6.3   Jenny Holzer, *Lustmord*, one from the series. Ink on skin: Cibachrome print. Photo: Alan Richardson   125

7.1   Light on a corridor. *Lan Yu*, dir. Stanley Kwan, Hong Kong, 2001   138

7.2   The shadow of a bruise on Lan Yu's face before the embrace with Handong. *Lan Yu*, dir. Stanley Kwan, Hong Kong, 2001   140

7.3   The contours of a body under the covers and the truncated announcement of 4 June. *Lan Yu*, dir. Stanley Kwan, Hong Kong, 2001   141

7.4   Handong and Lan Yu in the last scene before the end-credits. *Lan Yu*, dir. Stanley Kwan, Hong Kong, 2001   147

9.1   Rembrandt, *The Anatomy Lesson of Dr. Nicholas Tulp*, 1632, Mauritshuis, The Hague   174

9.2   Rembrandt, *Bathsheba at her Bath*, 1654, Louvre Museum, Paris   180

Notes on Contributors

Nicole Anderson is Professor of Media and Cultural Studies at Macquarie University, Sydney, Australia and Professor Honoris Causa for the International Institute for Hermeneutics at Warsaw University, Poland. She publishes on animal studies, ethics, cultural studies, biopolitics, poststructuralism and posthumanism. The author of *Derrida: Ethics Under Erasure* (2012), she is writing a second book on Derrida. She is the founding editor of the *Derrida Today* journal (Edinburgh University Press) and the Executive Director of the aligned conferences. She is the co-author of *Cultural Theory in Everyday Practice* (2008), and co-produces an ongoing podcast series for PBS USA: https://futuresofdemocracy.com/.

Anne Emmanuelle Berger is Professor Emerita of French Literature and Gender Studies at Paris 8 University, France and Edith Kreeger Wolf Distinguished Visiting Professor of French at Northwestern University, US. Her books include *Algeria in Others' Languages* (2002), *Scènes d'aumône. Misère et Poésie au XXe siècle* (2004) *Demenageries, Thinking (of) Animals After Derrida* (co-edited with Marta Segarra, 2011), *Genre et Postcolonialisme. Dialogues transcontinentaux* (co-edited with Eleni Varikas, 2011) and *The Queer Turn in Feminism: Identity, Sexuality and the Theater of Gender* (2014). She is working on a book entitled *The End of Sexuality*.

Quinn Eades is Senior Lecturer in Creative Writing at The University of Melbourne, Australia. A writer, researcher, editor and award-winning poet, Quinn is the author of *all the beginnings: a queer autobiography of the body* (2015) and *Rallying* (2017). He is working on two volumes: an essay collection titled *Collaboration as Love*, and *is the body home*, a trans autobiography.

CONTRIBUTORS

Vicki Kirby is Visiting Professorial Fellow, Institute of Art and Architecture, Academy of Fine Arts, Vienna, Austria, and Emeritus Professor of Social Sciences, The University of New South Wales, Australia. Her books include *What if Culture was Nature All Along?* (edited, 2017), *Quantum Anthropologies: Life at Large* (2013), *Judith Butler: Live Theory* (2002) and *Telling Flesh: The Substance of the Corporeal* (1997). She is a member of the *Terra Critica* international think-tank and holds a Peek Grant through the Academy of Fine Arts, Vienna that brings research in human cognition into conversation with plant sciences.

Elissa Marder is Professor of French and Comparative Literature at Emory University, US. Her publications include *Dead Time: Temporal Disorders in the Wake of Modernity* (Baudelaire and Flaubert) (2001), *The Mother in the Age of Mechanical Reproduction: Psychoanalysis, Photography, Deconstruction* (2012), *Time for Baudelaire* (Poetry, Theory, History), eds E. S. Burt, Elissa Marder, Kevin Newmark, *Yale French Studies* 125/126 (2014); *Literature and Psychoanalysis: Open Questions*, ed. Elissa Marder, *Paragraph* 40.3 (2017). Her work engages with texts that challenge traditional conceptions of temporality, birth, technology, sexual difference and the limits of the human.

Naomi Morgenstern is Professor of English and American Literature in the Department of English at the University of Toronto, Canada. Specialising in psychoanalytic and poststructuralist critical theory and gender studies, she is the author of *Wild Child: Intensive Parenting and Posthumanist Ethics* (2018) as well as essays on a range of writers (Herman Melville, Toni Morrison, David Mamet, Alice Munro, among others). She is currently working on reproductive ethics and maternal sovereignty in contemporary literary and cinematic narratives.

Nicholas Royle's books include: *Telepathy and Literature* (1991), *After Derrida* (1995), *Deconstructions: A User's Guide* (as editor, 1999), *Jacques Derrida* (2003), *The Uncanny* (2003), *In Memory of Jacques Derrida* (2009), *Quilt: A Novel* (2010), *Veering: A Theory of Literature* (2011), *An English Guide to Birdwatching: A Novel* (2017), *Hélène Cixous: Dreamer, Realist, Analyst, Writing* (2020), *Mother: A Memoir* (2020), *An Introduction to Literature, Criticism and Theory* (6th edn) (with Andrew Bennett, 2023) and *David Bowie, Enid Blyton and the Sun Machine* (2023). He is an editor of the *Oxford Literary Review* and director of *Quick Fictions* (quickfiction.co.uk).

Elina Staikou teaches philosophy and is currently Dean of Students and Chair of Dissertation Committees at the Institute for Doctoral Studies in the Visual Arts in Maine, US. She is the author of *Deconstruction at Home, Metaphors of Travel and Writing* (2011) and of numerous articles in the field of deconstruction and decomposition. She is an Associate Editor of *Derrida Today*.

Eszter Timár is Assistant Professor at the Department of Gender Studies, Central European University, Vienna, Austria. Her research focuses on queer theory, deconstruction and feminist new materialism. Her articles have been published in *parallax*, *Derrida Today*, *Postmodern Culture*, *Angelaki* and the *Oxford Literary Review*.

Lynn Turner is the author of *Poetics of Deconstruction: On the Threshold of Differences* (2020), co-editor, with Undine Sellbach and Ron Broglio, of *The Edinburgh Companion to Animal Studies* (2018), editor of *The Animal Question in Deconstruction* (2013), and co-author, with Astrid Schmetterling, of *Visual Cultures As … Recollection* (2013). One of the associate editors of *Derrida Today*, she is a Reader in Visual Cultures at Goldsmiths, University of London, UK.

Lenka Vráblíková is Lecturer in both Visual Cultures and Art at Goldsmiths, University of London, UK. A co-founder of ن يوس ةال قرائی تا ش ب ك ة/Feminist Readings Network, her work lies at the intersection of visual culture with transnational feminisms, political ecology, critical university studies and feminist deconstruction. She has published essays in *Australian Feminist Studies*, *Feminist Encounters*, *Gender and Education*, *parallax* and *Journal of International Women's Studies*.

Naomi Waltham-Smith is Professor at the University of Oxford, UK and Douglas Algar Tutorial Fellow at Merton College. Interested in the politics of listening, she works at the intersection of sound studies with continental philosophy, decolonial theory and Black radical thought. She is the author of *Music and Belonging Between Revolution and Restoration* (2017), *Shattering Biopolitics: Militant Listening and the Sound of Life* (2021), *Mapping (Post)colonial Paris by Ear* (2023) and *Free Listening* (2024). She has been awarded fellowships at the Price Lab for Digital Humanities, Akademie Schloss Solitude, and the Hanse-Wissenschaftskolleg.

Elizabeth Wijaya is an Assistant Professor of East Asian Cinema in the Department of Visual Studies at the University of Toronto (Mississauga) and Graduate Faculty at the Cinema Studies Institute at the University of Toronto (St. George) in Canada. She is the Director of the Centre for Southeast Asian Studies at the Asian Institute, Munk School of Global

Affairs and Public Policy, a co-founder of E&W Films and Associate Producer of *Taste* (Dir. Lê Bảo, Special Jury Award, Encounters Competition, 2021 Berlinale Film Festival). She has published in the edited volume *Ecology and Chinese-Language Cinema*, and in the journals *Discourse*, *Derrida Today* and *parallax*.

David Wills is Professor of French Studies at Brown University, US. He is author of six books including *Killing Times* (2019), *Inanimation* (2016), *Dorsality* (2008) and *Prosthesis* (25th anniversary edition, 2021). He has translated six works by Jacques Derrida, including, with Geoffrey Bennington, a new version of *Glas*, now published as *Clang* (2021).

ACKNOWLEDGEMENTS

Many contributors have been lively interlocutors during the development of this volume, none more so than Elissa Marder, the veritable sounding board for the whole journey. Eszter Timár, Elina Staikou and Nicole Anderson deserve special mention along with Jennifer Bajorek, Katie Chenoweth, Kyoo Lee, Thomas Clément Mercier, Elizabeth Rottenberg and Elizabeth A. Wilson. Huge thanks to Carol Macdonald for supporting the volume with Edinburgh's Philosophy list and to the reviewers whose enthusiasm ensured the contract. Deep gratitude to Sharon Kivland for the cover image and the inspiration of her work. Thank you to the Jenny Holzer Studio, Esther Dörring at Sprüth Magers Gallery, Berlin, and DACS for supplying the images and permissions for Holzer's work. Thank you to Killian O'Dwyer for compiling the index. Lastly, I thank my dear co-Head of Department of Visual Cultures, Astrid Schmetterling, for her sense of knowing when and when not to send a message.

Lapping It Up: An Introduction *for* these Erotics of Deconstruction

Lynn Turner

Autobiography, the writing of the self as living, the trace of the living for itself, being for itself, the auto-affection or auto-infection as memory or archive of the living, would be an immunizing movement (a movement of safety, of salvage and salvation of the safe, the holy, the immune, the indemnified, of virginal and intact nudity), but an immunizing movement that is always threatened with becoming auto-immunizing, like every *autos*, every ipseity, every automatic, automobile, autonomous, auto-referential movement.

(Jacques Derrida)[1]

For her joyous benefit she is erogenous; she is the erotogeneity of the heterogeneous: airborne swimmer, in flight, she does not cling to herself; she is dispersible, prodigious, stunning, desirous and capable of others, of the other woman that she will be, of the other woman she is not, of him, of you.

(Hélène Cixous)[2]

If we 'must begin *wherever we are*' without any absolute justification, begin where we 'believe ourselves to be', then let's start with a scene that is not so much a screen that would veil an originary truth, nor a mirror that promises to reflect back a totality, even as a '*psyché*' of sorts is invoked.[3] While the latter names both a full-length mirror and the psyche, presumed to be *de facto* human, the work of Jacques Derrida invokes a '*psyché*' of a different colour, so to speak (close to, but not identical with, psychoanalysis). He does so at the point in *The Animal that Therefore I Am* by which the totalising gambit of any and all auto-biographical ambition is in question up to and including the historical juncture that aimed to weld the reference to oneself with the admission of sin and thus to solder autobiography to confession.[4] He does so, characteristically, without disavowing but by multiplying every incidence of auto-affection. No more the one-to-one correspondence of self and its reflected or inscribed impression. Our opening scene, then, is organised through the mnemonic iterations of a kind of mystic writing pad.[5]

* * *

If no chaste girl has ever read novels, then we here assemble for no chaste girls.

When she asked me to write for her, I said yes. The invitation came with a drawing, with a series of drawings, and you have just noticed one on the cover of this book. Perhaps you are reading in bed, and this book too is red hot. Books, girls, laps, and – as the artist Sharon Kivland, advises in an account of her exhibition – the question of their coincidence. It is Rousseau's work on education that warns of this risk to the chastity of girls and thus provides the pithy title of Kivland's project.[6] In her capitals: JAMAIS FILLE CHASTE N'A LU DE ROMANS.[7] In his warning, reading *Julie, or the New Heloise* could not possibly cause feminine undoing (he exculpates himself, naturally). Thus, should she approach such a text regardless, 'the harm was already done'.[8] Kivland indexes French literature of the eighteenth and nineteenth centuries that similarly militates against the very idea of women reading or even learning to read in the name of maintaining their maidenhood. Amongst the various components that orchestrate her mixed-media forays into such archives – forays which read against their interdiction – are a suite of drawings of modern young women sitting in bed, book in hand, reading. In some drawings the book is held up and its red cover dramatically occupies the space approximating the same visual weight as her head. In others – such as the one on this volume – the red line of the jacket is just visible as it effectively doubles the red lines of her lips. On their laps, they are an object lesson in metonymy. The open books lap against their laps *and* their lips, immediately speaking of the play on lips and labia served by the same French noun, *lèvres*, in the writing of Luce Irigaray. With Kivland's visual prompt '*livres*' joins with *lèvres*: when our lips speak together; when our books speak together. This book holds a certain kind of wish to speak with other books, to set the pages of all the books in all the libraries pulsing. And while Irigaray's lips, when they are recalled today, are often truncated to the misleading conceptual clarity of the 'two lips', we should remember that her text supposed an occasion in which numbers, exact figures, remain uncounted, remain unaccounted for:

We are luminous. Neither one nor two. I've never known how to count. Up to you. In their calculations, we make two. Really, two? Doesn't that make you laugh? An odd sort of two. And yet not one. Especially not one. Let's leave *one* to them: their oneness, with its prerogatives, its domination, its solipsism: like the sun's. And the strange way they divide up their couples, with the other as the image of the one.[9]

We should also note that this uncountable 'we' resists the specular structure that only at first glance represents a 'couple', since it only renders the one and its negative inversion.

In her chapter for this book, Naomi Waltham-Smith muses 'When our erotic secrets are disclosed, is it day or night?' Orienting our attention to the bed, *le lit*, to literature and to the female reader or *liseuse* (also the name of the bedjackets that they wear, also the name of a little lamp for reading, also the title of the drawings themselves: *Liseuses de Capital*) Kivland affirms the book as the metonymy of carnal knowledge. Red: the colour of blood, alarm, a revolutionary flag. Hilariously this voluminous bedtime reading is Marx's *Capital*. Capital letters, capital punishment for reading, *Das Kapital* for political philosophy in her lap! It is quite the head rush. Other elements of Kivland's exhibition specified the first chapter of volume one of that title on the commodity form (*la marchandise*) as eight women friends of the artist transcribed that very word into schoolgirl *cahiers* using sanguine ink (and the lined pages of the now quaint *cahiers* provide the ground for the portraits of these *Liseuses*). A structure of reading and writing repeats with the risk, the danger, of schooling effects with timelines unknown: What will she have learnt? What will she form? With what figure? Again, these theoretical touchstones book Irigaray in the learning curve of my reverie and the overlap of political and sexual economies that she identifies between the commodity as that fetishistic structure of exchange instituting calculation with the position of women precisely as merchandise in a sexual economy.[10] I'm struck by the luck of reading such eccentric texts, however haltingly, as an undergraduate more or less by accident when the typographically striking volumes that are Irigaray's English translations published by Cornell University Press announced themselves on the library bookshelves to supplement those otherwise in my field of vision – catalogued by the iron logo of the Women's Press. I found Jacques Derrida in the same way, likely on the same day with the spine of *Writing and Difference* glowing on the shelves so as to solicit my hand rather than through the insistence of any reading list. Those first impressions of 'continental philosophy' usher another beginning for this book. Just as there is more than one beginning, *Erotics of Deconstruction* eschews the conceptual fix of the definite article.[11]

* * *

For Rousseau, in Derrida's account, the 'entire art of pedagogy is a calculated patience, allowing the work of Nature time to come to fruition, respecting its rhythm and the order of its stages'.[12] Education is a 'necessary evil' since Rousseau imagines Nature to constitute a pure originary plenitude that therefore should not lack for anything, yet the long immaturity of human childhood nevertheless requires a guiding hand. 'Without childhood', Derrida drily remarks, 'no supplement would ever appear in Nature.'[13] Should the touch of a hand imply the intimate auto-affection of masturbation, it is because the latter is decisive in Rousseau's account. Like 'writing' when construed in metaphysical fashion to be the secondary rendering of a lost presence, Rousseau's hand 'cheats' Nature, supplying the ungovernable lie of imaginary images in 'her' lieu.[14] Necessary but 'evil' education intervenes causing Rousseau to himself identify the 'dangerous' structure of supplementarity that subsequently organises Derrida's readerly attention. Inevitably, it bucks the pedagogic timetable and 'destroys very quickly the forces that Nature has slowly constituted ...'.[15] 'In anguish' Rousseau feels himself to be ruined – while still defending himself against having been the first cause of such depravity (naming it 'involuntary', he implies that matters were out of his hands).[16]

Critical of the specular imaginary of speculative dialectics as that which produces a monosexuality or '*hommo-sexualité*', Irigaray proposes a tactility that can also be understood as an originary auto-affection.[17] While she makes suggestive use of the reflexive verb '*se parler*', Irigaray's English translator somewhat loses the inference of a self-addressed envelope of lips speaking *to* themselves in falling rather more on the side of an amorous assembly speaking 'together'. The poetic form and focus of her text addressing this tactility, this labial slip between lips and lips, positions self-touching as always and already the case. In displacing the phallogocentric economy and imaginary she displaces the temporality (before/ after) and spatiality (inside/outside) of a 'rupture between virginal and nonvirginal'.[18] The other 'already affects you. It is inseparable from you' she says.[19] There are no chaste girls here, no untouched state. Rather, auto-affectionate, they are *in* touch.

The *autos* of auto-affection comes under pressure in the pages of *Erotics of Deconstruction*, indexed by the incantation of terms that it prefixes in my first epigraph ('automatic, automobile, autonomous, auto-referential movement'). This is magnified by the disorienting quandary of what it is to come 'after' another: *auto-affection after Derrida*. Nicholas Royle's eponymous book makes much of the peculiarity this ostensibly simple grammatical construction yet fosters, from being 'later than', to acting 'in light of', to the most eccentric implication that is 'going in search of'.[20] Like Royle, we remain after Derrida – and auto-affection after Derrida – 'not prior or in the past but rather in the future, still to be read, still to come'.[21] This is constitutively the case irrespective of the life or death of the author. It is also performatively the case – given the supplementarity of the event of any and all reading – and pedagogically so since, some forty-eight years after the first English translation of *Of Grammatology*, we still battle the sedimented intellectual and institutional legacies of the sign, of the dialectic and their 'carno-phallogocentric' habits of thought and exposition.[22] Still, Derrida is automatically read as affirming the very arguments he is at pains to displace. This is for at least two linked reasons: the counter-intuitive nature of his thought and the stylistic ambition of his texts. Derrida's writing substantially proceeds without the most familiar forms of argumentation that is frontal or oppositional (a classical mode which would repeat the dialectical form of battle that formally conducts the problem) but by rendering argument through other forms. Those other forms might more explicitly demand a poetic invention of the text, staged through unnamed but variously sexed speakers, or challenging expectations of formal composition, or more subtly insinuating an alternative but not oppositional posture by means of a conditional tense.[23] That double question demonstrates that the divide between philosophy and literature has only ever been a disciplinary fiction, and consequently the authors who agreed to write for this volume have undertaken that task through a variety of poetic means, woven through a variety of media. Hence, as Elizabeth Wijaya's chapter argues, '[f]lesh touches, virtually'.

* * *

As Gayatri Spivak phrases it in one of a series of essays on deconstruction and feminism, '[a]ffirmative deconstruction says "yes" to a text twice, sees complicity when it could rather easily be oppositional'.[24] While many of the chapters here conjure a ludic erotics, this volume is not utopian or naive. Eszter Timár engages with the death drive and the way that for psychoanalysis after Derrida, death 'is not beyond life or outside of life: it is a feature of life'; Lenka Vráblíková accounts for the aesthetic attempt to defend against this threat by projecting it onto feminised others. Quinn Eades, meanwhile, delivers a poetic working through of sexual assault – a working through that asks after transgression at all levels and inhabits the vicious and vernacular languages that mark such an extreme and conflicted point of experience. Deconstruction thus addresses the worst. How in hell do we think with and write with the worst?

Perhaps surprisingly, along with the logic of the supplement finding its occasion with Rousseau's anxiety regarding masturbation – even as this names the question of evil, Derrida's work directly addresses the problem of sexual violence. Indeed, it is in the seminars on *Pardon and Perjury*, in light of testimonies given during the Truth and Reconciliation Commission in South Africa, that he suggests that violence has a fundamentally sexual character, writing that 'rape is not just one form of violence among others'.[25] In the *Death Penalty* seminars Derrida finds a sexual logic at work in the history of punishment. This is not confined to the horribly common methods of torture and abuse, nor the juridical predicament of the punishment of so-called sex crimes (although the latter warrants lengthy consideration due to their problematic status in Kant's calculation of *lex talionis*). He finds a sexual formation interior to the imaginary of the penal code. Thus, the criminal is not simply subject to punishment but to a *chastisement*. As Derrida explores, these two terms are not synonymous but speak to different etymologies, with the former drawing on economies of retribution, while the latter, through

> the act of chastising (*castigare*), which means 'to impose a correction, to rebuke, to mortify, etc.,' maintains, unlike 'penalty' or 'punishment,' a kind of sexual family likeness, a sexual subconscious lodged in the word, given its reference to chastity or purity (*castitas; castus* is the pure, the untouched, the virtuous, the chaste, the pious, the religious, the saintly...).[26]

Moreover, in the juridical archives in which he intervenes, the one who castigates, who exerts punishment, has the restoration in view of 'a chastity that has been threatened, damaged, or corrupted'.[27]

If raised into a kind of formalism, the supplement or substitute 'remains intact'. Thus, any selective appropriation of deconstruction – if misconstrued as a theoretical 'toolbox' from which the supplement might be lifted to perform the same role in any given task – would purify the supplemental structure, cleaning away the context of its signature event. Expressing caution, Derrida remarks

> One can interpret substitution as what lends itself to calculation, par excellence, substitution as repetition, as the very element and condition of the calculable, of calculating and prosthetic formalization, the 'for:' one *for* one, an eye *for* an eye, a tooth *for* a tooth. But this logic of calculable equivalence can also be thwarted by

LAPPING IT UP

the substitution of the unique, the nonrepeatable, the irreplaceable, by another thinking of substitution, indeed by another thinking of blood.[28]

It is another 'thinking of blood' for which the *Death Penalty* seminars
plead. While this is precisely the matter that Turner's chapter explores,
the wider inference is the contact between body and word without a
phenomenological claim to presence or the sublation of the former by
the latter. Deciding how this 'for' operates – what it is for! – demarcates
the delicate work of the decision. Departing from the calculus of exchange
whose perfect execution demands a life for a life, Derrida, reading the
writing of his friend Cixous, finds the most affirmative 'for':

> As if it were necessary to think life, the mighty power [*puissance*]
> of life, from 'for' and not the reverse [...] It would therefore be
> necessary for us first to surrender to a subjunctive (*might*) and to a
> preposition (*for*) [...] This 'for,' this *pro-* would become the prole-
> gomenon of everything, it would be said before any logos, it goes
> in all directions [...] An absolute prerequisite, the *pro* of *for* thus
> pronames and prenames everything. [...]
> And this is why, up to the end, 'for life' has no end, it knows
> no end.[29]

Resisting both the sterilised output that the *'what is it?'* question form
would claim and the instrumentation of use that *'what is it for?'* would
recognise, the 'simple' proximity of writings on such a grave matter as
the death penalty with those on literature speak to the erotic touch of
deconstruction.[30]

* * *

While my intellectual life and times in the 1990s were dramatically
impelled by the effusion of what Anglophone universities called poststructuralist feminist theory and queer theory, *Erotics of Deconstruction* yet
holds the impression that, decades later, we have everything to invent
through reading the vast corpus of works signed 'Jacques Derrida'.
Timár's chapter comments on the curiously selective texts circulating as
'deconstruction' in the latter fields, largely to shore up what academics
might remember as the 'performativity' years.[31] Yet '[w]herever the sex
is to be found' as David Wills writes in his chapter, 'it will be, it will
have been indirect, over the phone or through the envelope; and its protagonists will be far from stable subjects'. Many chapters, and evidently
what is taking the place of an introduction, draw energy from a range of

Derrida's contemporaries, especially Hélène Cixous and Irigaray, as well as through critical conversations with recent feminist, black and trans scholarship. In so doing the book cultivates a certain kind of *jouissance* without that signalling a retreat to either a theological 'good' or an immediate and thus eternal 'presence'. Dispatching those twin temptations – as Kivland's *Liseuses* invite – allows for the feminine libidinal economies that they variously invoke to surface without the stable ground of identity or essence that the derogatory term 'essentialism' assumes. If Derrida's deeply critical relation to Nature in *Of Grammatology* is directed towards Rousseau's imagined state rather than any other thought of 'nature', perhaps we should not rush to assume that any invocation of the sexes of bodies serves to ground them in an unchanging hence untouched, condition.[32] Elina Staikou's chapter in this volume names 'erotics' 'as force ready to blast open any interpretation of biological destiny'. This does not equate to the supersession of biology as such nor bar Derrida and the legacy of his thought being brought to bear upon reproductive capacities – and in a way that cannot be contained as a form of ideology critique as Turner's, Staikou's and Naomi Morgenstern's chapters demonstrate (highlighting blood, mitochondria and cloning techniques respectively). Moreover, in Vicki Kirby's chapter, 'biology, a nature that was culture all along, constantly investigates and transforms itself'.

Touch does not ossify into identity. In ways that uncannily evoke without naming the labile texts of Irigaray, Derrida invites us to read Cixous out loud. One 'must' he says, on the edge of an ethical imperative, read aloud 'Savoir' to allow its recurrent labial consonant 'v' to render 'the lips at last visible *and* tangible'.[33] While he names 'visibility', it is not the specular ambition that shines an interrogative philosophical light upon all (the speculation dispatched by Irigaray). Rather visibility and tangibility are in touch, and it is the work of the essay that apparently names 'Knowledge' and 'Her Vision' in its title – 'Savoir' – to venture this transformation. Even in the face of the revelatory promise of the restoration of sight (through laser surgery) Cixous pronounces: 'She hadn't realized the day before that eyes are miraculous hands, had never enjoyed the delicate tact of the cornea, the eyelashes, the most powerful hands, these hands that touch imponderably near and far-off heres.'[34]

When Royle's chapter remarks '... language is a body thing, a scene of erotic play' do not mistake this for a certain kind of doxa (in which it is language or 'culture' that is sexy, set above mute, unchanging hence biologically determinist nature). If we can start again, start all over the text again, all over the body again – if those definite articles haven't just thrown us for a conceptual loop – we can now reconsider an affirmative body of work that does not assume a fundamental categorical divide

LAPPING IT UP   9

between Nature and Culture, or Humans and other Animals, or the Concept and the Sensible as its own benchmark. That body has been multiplying since Derrida's death due to the endeavours of the Derrida Seminars Translation Project, and many of the chapters in this book dilate upon these newly available resources.[35] Readers of this volume can thus refresh their sense of just what might have been at stake in such texts as *Of Grammatology* as well as embark upon an introduction to Derrida's deep engagement within the complex terrain bequeathed by our philosophical, juridical, biomedical and literary traditions as it is sifted, resisted and read in these seminars (without simplification or generalisation).

Drawing the outside inside in the time before time that ruins the sequential logic of an intact state transformed by subsequent intrusion or Fall, auto-affection posed in this volume is, in a stroke, *hetero-affective*. For Irigaray, the overwhelming direction of her thought is the transformation of sexual difference away from its near automatic repetition of the division into the fictive unity of a masculine authorial 'one' with the negated feminised other 'as the image of the one'. As we have gleaned, her poetics strive to invoke a heterogenous tactile feminine 'self'.[36] Derrida relatively rarely uses use the locution 'hetero-affection' since his solicitation of 'self-presence', of 'self-touching', should already transmute that paleonymic *auto-* into *hetero*-geneity. Its implications run throughout his work as Nicole Anderson's chapter elaborates, rendering, as she does, his every invocation of autobiography as 'auto-hetero-graphy'. Autobiography *would* be immunising, as my first epigraph implies, were it not for the other that is always already within.

We must also face the explicitly wider thought that prompts Derrida to so reorientate auto-affection as to invoke 'the living in general'. While this phrasing derives from the interview conducted with Derrida in 1985 by Jean-Luc Nancy called 'Eating Well' – an interview that made the stakes of what he was later to name the 'question of the animal' explicit – it is anticipated in *Of Grammatology*. Following the chapter that elaborates 'that dangerous supplement' as it necessarily spoils Rousseau's Nature, the next one on the *Essay on the Origin of Languages* indexes the entire problematic of the animal question as it is rehearsed in Rousseau's efforts to specifically articulate the time of music *as human*.[37] There, Derrida's alternate formulation runs: '[a]uto-affection is a universal structure of experience. All living things are capable of auto-affection [...] Auto-affection is the condition of an experience in general.'[38] It is 'another name for "life"'.[39] Life *for* life.

* * *

Trotting into one of my seminars on the question of what it is to end and more frontally counterposing the commitment to storytelling practised by Donna Haraway in the spirit of 'making kin not babies', with Lee Edelman's infamous charge of reproductive futurism against narrative as such exemplified by the capitalised figure of The Child, came the trojan horse of a relatively obscure conversation between Cixous and Derrida convened by Royle, innocuously titled 'On Childhood and Deconstruction'.[40] I let loose that text entirely to interpose the startling evocation of deconstruction therein. Perhaps the lessons of that text were biding their time for this moment. In an extraordinary reflection on what 'in experience, is not yet speaking', Derrida remarks that

> ... one of the monstrosities of the reception of deconstruction, notably in the United States, [is] that deconstruction passes for a kind of linguisticist mania, for which there is nothing outside of words, nothing outside of language [...] Deconstruction began by *suspecting the authority of language*, of verbal language, and even the trace, which is not yet, which is not language, which is not verbality, which is not human, so, the child, *infans*, is not man [...] Deconstruction is animal, from this point of view. It is childlike and animal-like.[41]

Stranger still vis-à-vis our more familiar logics, this move does not rebuff 'language' by means of a claim to 'origins': this is 'a childhood without origin'.[42] This child or *infans*, in their polymorphous perversity, 'sticks out his/her tongue from the place where there is not yet the tongue'.[43] While this figure with its Freudian resonance is invoked several times in their conversation, there is something irresistible to the alliterative 'pp' that also inserts itself into the complex itinerary of the pleasure principle that – in Derrida's hands – is rewired as a 'postal principle' elsewhere.[44] Moreover, rather than being seen as the defective weakness requiring the dangerous supplement of education (as in Rousseau), this polymorphously perverse impetus speaks to what Elissa Marder, in her chapter, glosses as 'a radical indeterminacy that traverses and undermines given divisions between body, thing, world, and language'. Lapping against the ears, appealing to the mouth, Anne Emmanuelle Berger's chapter pursues the voice in Derrida as that which so 'insistently' evokes pleasure that she provisionally calls it 'sexual'. Derrida summons this childlike, animal-like polymorphous perversity in the space of learning that is the university. If you aren't reading this book in bed, then you are probably doing so in a university. If we have reversed the ostensible ordering of childhood and education, the gesture is not a simple inversion nor a simple task.[45] He asks:

How is one to institute, in as refined a way as possible, the perverse polymorph that we all repress, in the university? That is, all the same, one gives pleasure [*donne à jouir*] not only with the eyes, the mouth, etc., but also total *jouissance*. How to introduce *jouissance* into the university? That's it. In an interdisciplinary manner. [*Laughter in the room.*]⁴⁶

Figure 0.1 Sharon Kivland, from the series *Mes Liseuses*, 2015. Ink and gouache on paper from vintage French school exercise book.

Inciting laughter in the room, after citing 'The Laugh of the Medusa' in all her heterogeneity in the second epigraph is, if not a 'good' place to start, one that is chased here. From the affirmative 'Procreativity' of the first section, to the constitutive 'Vulnerability' of the living invoked by the second, and the fantastical imagination of the ludically invented third, 'Panthropology' – titles that naturally bear some overlap – the fourteen chapters of *Erotics of Deconstruction* invite you to join this pursuit.

Notes

1. Jacques Derrida, *The Animal That Therefore I Am*, trans. David Wills (New York: Fordham University Press, 2008), 47.
2. Hélène Cixous, 'The Laugh of the Medusa', trans. Keith Cohen and Paula Cohen, in *Signs* 1.4 (1976), 889–90, trans. modified.
3. Jacques Derrida, *Of Grammatology*, [1967] trans. Gayatri Chakravorty Spivak (Baltimore, MD: Johns Hopkins University Press, 1997), 162, emphasis original.
4. Derrida, *Animal*, 21–2. The canonical *Confessions* of both Augustine and Rousseau are cases in point.
5. Derrida reworks Freud's 'mystic writing pad' in this text – which closes by calling for a 'new *psychoanalytic graphology*'. Jacques Derrida, 'Freud and the Scene of Writing', in *Writing and Difference*, trans. Alan Bass (Chicago: The University of Chicago Press, 1978), 231.
6. Jean-Jacques Rousseau, *Julie, or the New Heloise: Letters of Two Lovers Who Live in a Small Town at the Foot of the Alps*, trans. Philip Steward and Jean Vaché (Hanover, NH: Dartmouth College Press, 1997), 'Never did a chaste maiden read Novels' (4).
7. Sharon Kivland, JAMAIS FILLE CHASTE N'A LUS DE ROMANS, Circuit, Centre d'Art Contemporaine, Lausanne, Switzerland, 2019.
8. Rousseau, *Julie*, 4.
9. Luce Irigaray, 'When Our Lips Speak Together', in *This Sex Which Is Not One*, trans. Catherine Porter (Ithaca, NY: Cornell University Press, 1985), 207.
10. Luce Irigaray, 'Women on the Market', in *This Sex Which Is Not One*, trans. Catherine Porter (Ithaca, NY: Cornell University Press, 1985), 170–91. While acknowledging Irigaray's direct address to the structures identified by both Marx and Claude Lévi-Strauss the reader might also juxtapose the supplement of black feminism variously articulating the qualitative difference between literal and symbolic exchange, from Hazel V. Carby, *Reconstructing Womanhood: The Emergence of the Afro-American Woman Novel* (New York: Oxford University Press, 1987) to Françoise Vergès, *The Wombs of Black Women, Race, Capital, Feminism*, trans. Kalama L. Glover (London: Duke University Press, 2020).
11. Compare Jacques Derrida, *Politique de l'amitié* (Paris: Éditions Galilée, 1994), translated as *Politics of Friendship*, trans. George Collins (London:

Verso, 1997). Various English reprints nevertheless imported the expected article. We might recall that the infamous declaration that there is no 'outside-text' in *Of Grammatology* did not use any article to describe 'text', definite or indefinite (158).

12. Derrida, *Grammatology*, 151.

13. Ibid., 147.

14. Ibid., 152.

15. Ibid.

16. Ibid., 150.

17. Luce Irigaray, *Speculum of the Other Woman*, trans. Gillian C. Gill (Ithaca, NY: Cornell University Press, 1985), 10. Her specific intervention should not be mistaken for homophobia.

18. Irigaray, 'When Our Lips Speak Together', 211.

19. Ibid.

20. Nicholas Royle, *After Derrida* (Manchester: Manchester University Press, 1995).

21. Ibid., 4.

22. 'Carno-phallogocentrism' was first named here: Jacques Derrida, '"Eating Well" or the Calculation of the Subject', [1985] in *Points ... Interviews 1974–1994*, ed. Elizabeth Weber (Stanford, CA: Stanford University Press, 1995), 280.

23. I remark on Derrida's cautionary use of the conditional as a guide to elucidating his own argument beyond that from which he takes leave in my *Poetics of Deconstruction: On the Threshold of Differences* (London: Bloomsbury, 2020), 107–8.

24. Gayatri Chakravorty Spivak, 'Feminism and Deconstruction, Again', in *Outside in the Teaching Machine* (New York and London: Routledge, 1993), 129.

25. Jacques Derrida, *Perjury & Pardon*, vol. II, trans. David Wills (Chicago: University of Chicago Press, 2023), 75.

26. Jacques Derrida, *The Death Penalty*, vol. II, trans. Elizabeth Rottenberg (Chicago: Chicago University Press, 2014), 167.

27. Ibid.

28. Ibid., 241.

29. Jacques Derrida, *H. C. for Life, That Is to Say ...*, trans. Laurent Milesi and Stefan Herbrechter (Stanford, CA: Stanford University Press, 2006), 86–88. Thomas Clément Mercier drew attention to these pages in his paper 'Power Failures and Im-possible Lives: Against the Politics of Pure Potentiality' at the *Derrida Today* 7 conference, University of Arizona, Washington campus, US, 2022.

30. See Jacques Derrida, '*Che cos'è la poesia?*', [1988] in *Points ... Interviews 1974–1994*, ed. Elizabeth Weber (Stanford, CA: Stanford University Press), 288–99, and Hélène Cixous, 'From my Menagerie to Philosophy', in *Resistance, Flight, Creation: Feminist Enactments of French Philosophy*, ed. Dorothea Olkowski (Ithaca, NY: Cornell University Press, 2000), 44.

31. See also Christian Hite, ed. *Derrida and Queer Theory* (Santa Barbara, CA: Punctum, 2017).
32. Anne Emmanuelle Berger brilliantly exposes misguided readings of Irigaray that bypass her appropriation of Heidegger's understanding of both poetics and nature. See her 'Irigaray's Breath, or Poetry After Poetics', in Ranjan Ghosh, ed., *Philosophy and Poetry: Continental Perspectives* (New York: Columbia University Press, 2019).
33. Jacques Derrida, 'A Silkworm of One's Own', in Hélène Cixous and Jacques Derrida, *Veils*, trans. Geoff Bennington (Stanford, CA: Stanford University Press, 2001), 49, emphasis added.
34. Hélène Cixous 'Savoir', in Hélène Cixous and Jacques Derrida, *Veils*, trans. Geoff Bennington (Stanford, CA: Stanford University Press, 2001), 9.
35. For the full list of seminars and publication timeline, see: https://derridase minars.org/volumes.html (accessed 15/01/2024).
36. The English translation uses 'self-affect' for '*s'auto-affecter*'.
37. See Lynn Turner, 'Voice', in Lynn Turner, Undine Sellbach, Ron Broglio, eds, *The Edinburgh Companion to Animal Studies* (Edinburgh: Edinburgh University Press, 2018), 519, 527–8.
38. Derrida, *Grammatology*, 165.
39. Ibid.
40. Donna J. Haraway, 'The Camille Stories: Children of Compost', in *Staying with the Trouble: Making Kin in the Chthulucene* (Durham, NC: Duke University Press, 2016), 134–68; Lee Edelman, 'The Future is Kid Stuff', in *No Future: Queer Theory & the Death Drive* (Durham, NC and London: Duke University Press, 2004), 1–31; Hélène Cixous and Jacques Derrida, 'On Deconstruction and Childhood', trans. Peggy Kamuf, in *Oxford Literary Review*, 41.2 (2019), 149–59.
41. Derrida, 'On Deconstruction and Childhood', 154, emphasis original.
42. Ibid., 156.
43. Ibid.
44. Jacques Derrida, 'Envois', in *The Post Card: From Socrates to Freud and Beyond*, trans. Alan Bass (Chicago: Chicago University Press, 1987), 113, 159.
45. Derrida specifies this move as 'a double gesture, a double science, a double writing, practice an *overturning* of the classical opposition *and* a general *displacement* of the system'. See 'Signature Event Context', in *Margins of Philosophy*, trans. Alan Bass (Chicago: University of Chicago Press, 1982), 329, emphasis original.
46. Derrida, 'On Deconstruction and Childhood', 157.

Part I
Procreativity

1

Derrida's Tongues

Elissa Marder

For it is when the mouth starts opening, when a tongue licks the word on the other's tongue, that Derrida approaches the shores of the Shakespearian idiom.
(Hélène Cixous)[1]

1. Arche catachresis: confusion of tongue

Tongue. The word is scandalously improper. It designates both the flexible fleshy organ that navigates the porous borders between self and world through touching, tasting, licking and kissing as well as also being a word for the signifying structure we call language. Moreover, tongue is both an organ of the body, prior to language, outside of language, but also an organ *in* the body: a quasi-prosthetic instrument for making sound and song as well as making meaning.[2] The word tongue exposes a confusion at the origin of language. The rhetorical name for that primal confusion is 'catachresis'.[3]

From its first publication in 1974 onward, Derrida's book *Glas* (*Clang*) has generated bewilderment and fascination due to its striking formal structure and its scandalous language play.[4] *Clang* is composed of two columns – one devoted to the motif of the family in G. W. F. Hegel and the other to a reading of Jean Genet. Derrida's two-column work was in part inspired by Jean Genet's earlier two-column work 'Ce qui est resté d'un Rembrandt déchiré en petits carrés bien réguliers, et foutu aux chiottes' ('What Remains of a Rembrandt Torn into Four Equal Pieces and Flushed Down the Toilet') which was first published in *Tel Quel* in 1967.[5] The two-column structure of *Clang* places readers in a double bind as the text both demands that one read both columns at once and makes it impossible to do so. The pairing of Hegel with Genet produces a relation that cannot be accounted for through dialectical opposition or negation.

Clang both implicitly obliges the reader to choose between the language of philosophy and the material word play of Genet's queer literary language and refuses to allow the reader to make that choice. The clanging of the tongue reverberates between and across both columns of Derrida's text. In the opening pages of *Clang* (*Glas*), in what is the first insert in the Jean Genet column, Jacques Derrida inserts a definition of 'catachresis' in which the word 'tongue' figures, not surprisingly, as the first example:

> Catachresis, n. 1. Trope by which a word that has been diverted from its proper sense is accepted into everyday usage to designate something else that retains an analogical relation with the first object. For example, tongue, because the tongue is the principal organ of articulated speech. (*Littré*, qtd in *C*, 8)

As the very name for the improper name of language, tongue is not merely one example of catachresis among others. It exposes the potential impropriety of all language and the impossibility of determining where language begins and ends.

Thus far, I have written 'tongue' rather than 'the tongue' to underscore that the underlying indeterminacy of the tongue resists being contained by any ontological unity. There is always more than one tongue, and the tongue is not one. The irreducible undecidability of the tongue has troubled philosophy ever since Aristotle pointed out that even when considered uniquely from the perspective of its practical function and purpose as a bodily organ, the tongue defies clear classification:

> [T]he tongue is used for both tasting and articulating; in that case, of the two functions tasting is necessary for the animal's existence (hence it is found more widely distributed), while articulate speech serves its possessor's well-being […] What can be tasted is always something that can be touched, and just for that reason it cannot be perceived through an interposed foreign body, for no more is it so with touch.[6]

The tongue not only is shared by two distinct senses (taste and touch) but is also used as an organ of speech. As an organ of taste and touch, the tongue creates a link between humans and a whole host of other animals whereas as an organ of articulated speech, the tongue appears to set humans apart from other animals. In its basic functions, it therefore embodies that which brings humans closest to and farthest from animal worlds.[7] In this regard, the tongue occupies a place analogous to that of sexuality.[8] It is therefore already marked erotically.

DERRIDA'S TONGUES

Even at the level of its function as a bodily organ, the tongue is radically undecidable because the tongue is always other than itself. In its very activity, the tongue confounds the distinction between auto- and hetero-activity. Oscillating between the inside and the outside of the body, the tongue is active and passive, penetrating and receptive. Its activities always involve both an element of auto-affectivity (the tongue enables the self to touch itself in tasting or talking) as well as a medium for touching some other being in the world through tasting, licking, caressing, kissing.

When deployed as an organ of speech, the tongue engages in itera-tion and imitation because spoken sounds must be recognisable repeti-tions to become intelligible elements of a shared tongue. In this sense, every speaking tongue belongs both to the particular speaker and to the community of speakers who share that common tongue. This irreduc-ible alterity recalls Derrida's haunting refrain about the politics of lan-guage in *Monolingualism of the Other*. 'Je n'ai qu'une langue, ce n'est pas la mienne.'[9] Although this sentence has been translated into English as 'I have only one language and it is not mine', the word 'langue' here – as always in Derrida's corpus – retains a trace of a non-verbal remain-der that cannot be subsumed under the term 'language'. Heard in this way, Derrida's refrain takes on a slightly different timbre: 'I have only one tongue; it is not mine.' In uttering, a tongue opens itself up to its underlying multiplicity as it disperses itself into incalculable variations of possible sounds, rhythms and audible expressions. Every tongue contains every other tongue within it. Each tongue is potentially all tongues, human or otherwise. Arche catachresis, tongue is never simply either bodily organ *or* articulated speech. This fundamental and irreducible confusion means that my tongue is not uniquely mine; even within my mouth, it is also the tongue of the other.

Anxiety about tongues proliferates in the Christian theological writings.[10] In 1525, the influential humanist Dutch philosopher, the-ologian and satirist Erasmus wrote a tome devoted to the dangerous and awesome excesses of the tongue.[11] In the work called *Lingua, The Tongue*, Erasmus declares that the tongue, akin to a *pharmakon*, is 'both deadly poison and a life-giving remedy'.[12] Rather than exemplifying that which is essentially proper to the human, the tongue's hyperbolic powers of mimicry undermine the very notion of the human by its promiscu-ous communication with an entire world of non-human creatures and modes of expression:

> Nature gave each creature its special cry, but man and only man
> can mimic the sounds of them all with the plectrum of his tongue,

doing it so exactly that if you only overheard the mimic you would think a child was crying, a pig grunting, a horse whinnying, a wife nagging her husband, or the cuckoo competing against the nightingale. Just count up the varieties of letters, syllables, and words, the pauses, clashes, and hisses peculiar to each of the languages. That single plectrum forms all those varied noises and produces them in the many languages of different nations.[13]

The diabolical single plectrum not only contains multitudes, it violates all boundaries that would separate beings according to species, age, sex or language. Associated indiscriminately with *phonè* and *logos*, infancy, animality, *and* articulated language, speech *and* writing, this bit of flexible flesh defies all regulation of the proper. This tongue blurs the possibility of establishing any clear distinction between nature and culture.[14] Even when deployed in its ostensibly 'natural' function, it usurps and surpasses the power of all other technical instruments:

Although musicians achieve this by means of different instruments, the plectrum of the tongue unaided produces the pitch and timbre of them all. For war it becomes a trumpet or bugle, but can call a retreat at will; it is a flute for festivity, a lyre for sensual enjoyment, and yet can utter a funeral dirge if it chooses. Why are we amazed at the remora, which, despite its tiny body, can bring to a standstill a ship in full sail, when we feel no surprise that the tongue, which is not much bigger than this fish, can summon or recall so many thousands of men wherever it chooses, and can arouse or lull them and provoke not just a war between states, but a continental war of Africa, Asia, and Europe. Well now, what is more successful or powerful than this organ? But then, what can be more destructive?[15]

The tongue is here depicted as a delivery device for all aspects of culture ranging from aesthetics, erotic activity and mourning to global war. It is both passive and active, human and animal, body and instrument. The tongue's flexibility, passivity, receptivity, affect, animality and femininity appear to enhance the pseudo-phallic superpower of this 'most destructive organ'.

In calling the tongue the 'most destructive organ', Erasmus draws upon a long tradition of Christian writings that attempt to reckon with and counteract the potentially disturbing moral and ethical implications of Aristotle's depiction of the tongue as an organ with dual (and implicitly duplicitous) functions. In the thirteenth century, John of Wales wrote

DERRIDA'S TONGUES

a treatise, *De lingua*, that describes how the slippery nature of the tongue both facilitates speech and promotes a vast panoply of sins including lying, gluttony, slander and blasphemy. Unlike other organs (such as the ears and the eyes), God warned humans against the potentially sinful activities of the tongue by locking it up in a double closure consisting of teeth and lips.[16] In Erasmus's vibrant riff on this traditional motif, Nature, in her infinite wisdom, prophylactically designs the morphology of the mouth as a means of containing and restraining the tongue's dangerous proclivities:

> Again, Nature covered the eyes with nothing but a frail membrane, suited only for sleep, but buried the tongue virtually in a dungeon, and bound it by many bonds – above, near the back of the palate, again on either side at the opening of the throat, and finally with cables stretching down into the chest-cavity. It is tied underneath to the lower jaw right up to the rampart of the teeth. This part is called *hypoglottis* 'undertongue' by the Greeks, and is so tightly attached that some men need surgery to enable them to speak clearly. In fact Varro thinks the word *lingua* 'tongue' comes from *ligare* 'to bind'. Then Nature sets in its path the double rampart and barrier of the thirty-two teeth. Homer implies a great deal when he speaks of 'the rampart of the teeth', since the tongue can be disciplined by a bite or wound of the teeth if it disobeys reason … Nature also set in its path the double doors of the lips, to show, I suppose, that we have a valuable treasure in the tongue, since she has hidden it away so thoroughly, but also showing the great danger of using it carelessly or out of season; hence although it is held down by many cables, she has enclosed it within a double palisade, to prevent that unbridled licence which is not a matter of uttering words, but of blurting out whatever comes into one's head.[17]

Uncontrollable, unruly, uncontainable. From Aristotle onwards, the tongue has been associated with sin, excess, madness, foolishness, femininity, duplicity, rage and desire.

Precisely because it is nothing properly in itself, the tongue is a principle of self-difference and relation. Metaphor of all metaphors, the tongue also resides in the heart. Erasmus writes 'the heart too has its tongue, that is, thought, by which a man speaks to himself'.[18] By translating the language of the heart into thought, Erasmus depicts the tongue as nothing in itself, but rather as the very medium of communication between heart, body, and mind without which self-reflection and auto-affectivity would be impossible. At the heart of thought, then, we find the tongue. Belonging neither to body nor language but as the very articulation of what resists being known as body or language, the tongue opens up the field of the erotic.[19]

The tongue's relation to erotics in general and sexuality in particular is everywhere and nowhere in Erasmus's treatise and in the Aristotelian tradition more generally. Even from the limited perspective of a bodily function, it bears remarking (precisely because it appears to have been forgotten by that tradition) that the tongue is not merely an organ of touch, taste and speech. It can also function as a non-sexed sexual organ. The tongue is both a primordial organ for pleasure in infancy (sucking at the breast involves the tongue) and an expression of adult sexuality. The erotic tongue has no proper place or function: kissing, licking and sucking are not limited to any one bodily zone, age or sex. The tongue expresses itself erotically in many ways: it can simultaneously perform the actions of a tongue and serve as a substitute for a hand or a penis. Put another way, whereas a tongue can take the place of a hand or a penis, a penis or hand can't as easily take the place of a tongue. Erotic kissing, in this sense, is an expression of the tongue. Is a kiss erotic without the plastic play of the tongue?

2. Deconstruction is an erotics of the tongue

In a famous passage from 'What is a Relevant Translation' Derrida expresses his 'passion for translation' as an erotic encounter involving the tongue and the body of the word:

> I believe I can say that I love the word, it is only in the body of its idiomatic singularity, that is, where a passion for translation comes to lick it as a flame or an amorous tongue might: approaching as closely as possible while refusing at the last moment to threaten or to reduce, to consume or consummate, leaving the body of the other, in the flame's flicker or through a tongue's caress.[20]

The translating tongue licks and caresses the body of the word in a sexual act which goes beyond the human. The tongue inflames and consumes the body of the translated word like a tongue of fire. The expression 'tongue of fire' is itself a catachresis. Neither literal nor figurative, this fiery tongue is the tongue of tongues: the very tongue of language.[21] In 'licking the word' like 'a flame or amorous body', the tongue touches the word at the very outer limits of language and between languages. The amorous encounter is tactile, passionate, active, passive, and almost

DERRIDA'S TONGUES

all-consuming. In the transfer from one language, that is, from one tongue to another, a touched word exposes itself as a bodily being that gives itself over to the other tongue while also resisting being entirely subsumed by the act. Translation exposes the body of the word in its vulnerability, its force, its radical singularity and its porosity, as it both submits to and resists being possessed by the tongue of the other. While it is no accident that Derrida explicitly thematises the erotic force of the tongue in a text devoted to translation, the erotic activity of the tongue is at work in all his writings.

Eroticised tongues are everywhere in Derrida's writings. In virtually every work, Derrida plays with the tongue. He sticks out his tongue at the history of philosophy by calling philosophers out for having systematically denied and repressed the irreducible confusion that the tongue poses to the very language of philosophy. As he points out throughout his corpus, although philosophy aspires to be a 'neutral' language that bypasses the contingencies and limitations of an idiomatic, vernacular tongue, philosophical texts and concepts do not stand above or outside the language in which they are written. Like all other writings, philosophical works are indelibly marked by the tongue that they receive and that they cannot completely control or master. Unlike most other philosophers, who – consciously or not – attempt to circumvent or deny the effects of the idiomatic tongue on thought, Derrida thinks *about* the tongue and *with* the tongue. In thinking with the tongue, he challenges the foundational axioms according to which Western philosophy recognises itself as philosophy. Thinking with the tongue entails thinking about pleasure, language, invention, writing, sexuality, sexual difference and childhood. Children play with words and with their tongues.

In a conversation with Hélène Cixous and Nicholas Royle in 2003 about childhood, Derrida points out that the Greek word *problema* means 'shield' – that which protects – and declares that because 'the problem is always reassuring', 'deconstruction does not even let itself be problematised … [it]is not a problematic'.[22] He then proposes that 'if there is something like deconstruction, it is the exposure to risk that leaves us without assurance, and without defence, thus without problematising mastery'. As the risk invoked here turns out to be intimately bound up with reconfiguring pleasure, desire and the impossibility of determining fixed boundaries between any supposed self and its presumed others, this designation recasts deconstruction as inextricably bound up with erotics. In the ensuing discussion, Derrida relates Freud's writings on children's play, creative writing and the 'polymorphously perverse' dimension of infantile sexuality to his own thinking about writing as a childish pleasurable bodily engagement with the other and with language. He writes:

... Everything we were talking about a moment ago, it's a childish manner, which is to say, in the strict sense of the term, perverse and polymorphous – the child is the perverse polymorph, no? To whom everything is allowed. Who does not want to renounce anything of all possible pleasures [*jouissances*]. And thus writing ... it's also simply a bodily engagement [*un corps à corps*] with the other. In any case, the bodily engagement with language in writing, is a bodily engagement that does not renounce any pleasure, thus any meaning. That is to say, *the whole body*. [He laughs.] The mouth, the eyes, etc. the sex, from all sides: perverse polymorph.[23]

Like the polymorphously perverse child who takes pleasure from 'the whole body', Derrida finds pleasure everywhere in writing's bodily engagement with language. By using the term 'perverse polymorph', Derrida opens up a channel of communication between Freud's conception of sexuality as the mark of a primordial inscription on and in the body prior to any determination of genital sexuality or gender identity and his own generalised eroticisation of writing. Creative writers, he says, are 'perverse polymorphs' who, in a 'state of childhood', experience in writing '[m]ore jouissance, there, phantasmatically, than what is commonly called "sexual pleasure" in the literal sense [laughter] so to speak. There is more pleasure with the letter than in literal sexual pleasure.'[24] The encounter with the body of the other in language is itself already an erotic contestation of the authority of phallogocentrism as it exposes the self to the dangers of pleasures that undermine and scramble the predetermined categories that regulate knowledge, meaning and identity. For Derrida, the intensity of the pleasures generated by writing attest to the fact that sexuality cannot be confined to contact between sexed bodies or even between human subjects, but rather is diffused and disseminated in a radical indeterminacy that traverses and undermines given divisions between body, thing, world and language. This erotic polymorphous language play is in fact a deadly serious matter for Derrida as it communicates with everything that the philosophical tradition attempts to repress, manage, disavow including the feminine, the body, the child, the animal, and a conception of sexual difference that would not be grounded in hierarchical opposition or any kind of ontological identity.

This description of writers as childish perverse polymorphs leads Derrida to speak about his own erotic play with the tongue in *Glas*.

And it is not by chance that, among all the polymorphous drives, perverse polymorphs that I evoked a moment ago, there is that of the *infans*, of the child who finds him/herself there, before language, who learns the language and learning the tongue, sticks out his/her tongue from the place where there is not yet the tongue. My interest, as far as my own little work is concerned, in both the child and in death led me to privilege literal pre-verbal formations such as syllables like gl, tr, pr, where it is not yet words. And where all the work, in books like *Glas* is organised around a certain pre-verbality: gl, +r. +l. That is what *Glas* is, a child playing with syllables that don't yet form a language. And then, next, naturally, one forms a language, since one is very old, very very old, *Glas* is a book of a very old man. It's someone who has read Hegel.[25]

[Et ce n'est pas par hasard que, parmi toutes les pulsions polymorphes, perverses polymorphes que j'ai évoquées tout à l'heure, il y a celle de infans, de l'enfant qui se trouve là, devant la langue, avant la langue, qui apprend la langue, tire la langue depuis là où il n'y a pas encore la langue.][26]

In the original French text, the word 'langue' appears five times in the first sentence of this passage. In the interest of rendering the sentence intelligible, the English translation of this sentence translates two occurrences of the word 'langue' as 'language' and the other three as 'tongue'. While the translation accurately conveys the meaning in each case, the translation inevitably underplays how Derrida plays with the word 'tongue' to express how the *infans* tongue resists being mastered by language. The child at the threshold of language takes pleasure in the tongue's unruly transgressive and sensuous refusal to be taken into the realm of language. Something of the verbal play of the tongue remains unaccounted for by speech.

In *Glas* (retranslated as *Clang* in 2021), Derrida reads Hegel and Jean Genet with his tongue. The tongue not only plays a pivotal (albeit different) role in each column of the text, but also serves as the oscillating clapper through which their undecidable relation to one another resounds. As Derrida indicates in the opening pages of the Genet column, the tongue is the very instrument – the organ – that must be put to work so that the primordial pre-linguistic reverberations of embodied bits of language can be heard and read:

Concerning what clangs here – and decomposes the corpse of the word (balc, talc, alga, brilliance [éclat], ice [glace], etc.) in all senses – this is the first and last time that, to make an example, you are here as if forewarned by this text. You'll have to do the rest of the work alone and blame yourself, like him, like one who writes, in your tongue. At least. 'Perhaps I wanted to accuse myself in my own tongue'. You will also have to work with the word 'tongue' as does an organist. (*C*, 9)

What does it mean to work (with) the word tongue? The tongue is both a word for language and the organ that decomposes the word into the remnants of its pre-/non-linguistic expressions. *Clang* puts the word tongue to work by playing with its catachrestic qualities. In the Hegel column, Derrida works with the word 'tongue' by exposing how Hegel represses and disavows his idiomatic relationship to his own language, the German tongue. In the Genet column, Derrida shows how Genet's writings expose the polymorphous sexuality of the tongue by decomposing words into preverbal secretions, excretions and spittle.

3. Eating tongues

Derrida begins his reading of the concept of the family in Hegel by calling attention to the fact that Hegel's philosophical conceptual vocabulary (as in the term *Sittlichkeit* for example) is bound up with the question of language in general and the family's relation to language in particular:

> Hegel did not skirt the problem of philosophical language. Is it a natural language or a philosophical language? It matters here that Hegel did not separate this question from a family question. I begin by summing up the results of his analysis: the family speaks and does not speak; it is a family from the moment it speaks – passing from *Klang*, if you will, to *Sprache*, from resonance to language – but it destroys itself *qua* family as soon as it speaks and abandons the *Klang*. (*C*, 14)

The term *Klang* here designates something like a familial dialect, an expressive idiomatic tongue. *Sprache*, on the other hand, is the language that brings the family into relation with the larger community. To the extent that the family expresses itself by *Klang*, it remains outside the movement of Spirit by being arrested at the level of materiality, the body and its own singular existence. In this sense, the family does not and cannot speak, as it has no relation to the community beyond itself. In its transformation from familial private tongue (*Klang*) to meaningful speech (*Sprache*), everything of the natural 'tongue' in language is sublated as meaning leaves the materiality of language behind by becoming concept. Paradoxically, therefore, once a spoken language becomes

DERRIDA'S TONGUES

language it no longer speaks in its own tongue. Likewise, once the family becomes the family it is no longer familial. As soon as a given spoken tongue 'posits itself' as a language, it universalises itself into a conceptual system and, in so doing, destroys its status as a natural language.

In a striking verbal image, Derrida redescribes Hegel's account for how natural language becomes concept as follows: 'The dialectic of language is dialectophagous.' 'La dialectique de la langue est dialectophage' (G, 15). By playing with his (French) tongue, Derrida calls attention to the way that Hegel's very conceptualisation of the dialectic – as a process of the destruction/preservation of the particular – necessitates that the dialect, the natural tongue, be eaten, consumed and swallowed up by the concept. Through this formulation, Derrida would seem to imply that the dialectical movement whereby natural language becomes language by consuming the tongue is not merely one example of the dialectic among others, but is its very founding principle. In other words, the dialectic only becomes dialectic in its overcoming of the tongue. The tongue is what must be swallowed in order for any universalising movement to take place.[27]

In this one poetic formulation, 'the dialectic of language is dialectophagous', Derrida condenses his entire reading of Hegel in *Clang*. By alluding to the fact that the words 'dialectic' and 'dialect' share a common Greek root, *dialegesthai* (to converse), he shows that Hegel both severs the trace of the speaking tongue in the word 'dialectic' and swallows the tongue of the dialect in the becoming conceptual language of language. Derrida glosses his own formulation as follows:

> Without this overflow of language that swallows and eats itself, which also vomits up a natural remainder – its own – that it can neither assimilate nor equate with the universal potency of the concept, language would not be language – living language, that is – it would not be what it is in itself, in conformity with its concept (*Begriff*) … . (C, 15–16)

> [La dialectique de la langue est dialectophage.
>
> Sans ce débord de la langue qui s'avale et se mange elle-même, qui vomit aussi un reste naturel – le sien – qu'elle ne peut ni assimiler ni égaler à l'universelle puissance du concept, la langue ne serait pas la langue – la langue vivante s'entend –, elle ne serait pas ce qu'elle est en soi, conformément à son concept (*Begriff*).]

Although the dialectic only becomes dialectic by eating its own tongue, the tongue cannot be entirely digested and metabolised. Because the tongue is catachresis (suspended in an undecidable oscillation between its bodily form and its capacity for meaning), it can never be completely subsumed by the system. The tongue that cannot be swallowed up into a universal concept or eaten is ejected as vomit.

It is no accident that Derrida derives his overall argument about Hegel's dialectic by generating an original scene in which the tongue both swallows itself and returns as vomit. The figure of vomit, that which cannot be assimilated by the system, is a guiding thread in Derrida's reading of Hegel in *Clang*. At a critical juncture in the text, he famously describes Hegel's fascination with Antigone's (feminine) role as sister in a brother/sister relation as 'the vomit of the system' (*C*, 183). In the section on Antigone, he points out that the 'vomit of the system' is not simply excluded from the system. Instead, 'the unassimilable, the absolutely undigestible' plays a fundamental, abyssal founding role in the system. The system constitutes itself with its vomit, that is, what it cannot assimilate. In Derrida's reading of Hegel, the tongue is the site of the original scene for the production of vomit. As arche catachresis, the tongue is thus linked to everything that the conceptual system cannot assimilate, including, notably, sexual difference and feminine desire.

If, in the Hegel column of *Clang*, Derrida focuses on how the language of philosophy founds itself by swallowing its tongue and repressing the body of language, in the Genet column he exposes the tongue as working on language before, beyond, and outside the bounds of meaning. *Clang* clangs with the tongue of language. It is language sounding its own death knell. The tongue is the organ that produces the death knell, the clang, the resounding *glas* of the text. As the editors/translators of *Clang* explain in their introduction:

> *Clang* translates the French *glas* [glɑ], a masculine noun referring to the fact, event and performance of a bell ringing: a clang, knell, peal, toll or chime. The word conveys the initial violence of the sounding of the bell, its echoing or resounding effects, and its fade to silence; and it speaks to the short life of that sound, whereby its ringing – like every such sound – is also its own death knell. Like the event it refers to, when the word *glas* is pronounced it begins as a guttural, quasi-metallic, perhaps even industrial clamour or pure noise, and ends in a type of crystalline vocalic sonority or music. (*C*, xvi–xvii)

The tongue works over the remains of the body of language. As such, it plays a pivotal role in the work of mourning: 'It also comes down to knowing how to have done with what one eats. The work of mourning

DERRIDA'S TONGUES

as work of the tongue, teeth, and saliva, of swallowing also, assimilation, and belching' (*C*, 40). The letters 'gl' are decomposed bits of the tongue.

Throughout *Clang*, Derrida plays with variations on the Greek word for tongue: *glôssa*. The opening insert in the Genet column includes three definitions from *Littré* that function like tattoos or peepholes in the text: *Catachresis*, *Catafalque* and *Cataglossism*. The third word, '*Cataglossism*', announces the insistent 'gl' activity of the tongue that punctuates the text. From the opening pages onward, errant '*gls*' loosen the tongue of the language of *Clang*. Cut off from the tongue, *gl* is a bit of the tongue for which there is no word and, because it remains outside of known definitions and categories, *gl* works to undo marks of identity, sex and gender:

GL

I don't say the signifier GL, or the phoneme GL, or the grapheme GL. 'Mark' would be better if one were to hear that word carefully, or open one's ears to it; not even 'mark' then. It is also imprudent to advance or set going le or la GL, to write it in capitals. It has no identity, no sex, no gender, makes no sense; it is neither a definite whole or the detached part of some whole

gl remains gl. (*C*, 137)

Gl is what the tongue does to the word. 'The tongue makes every word slide over its moist surface' (*C*, 159). Writing about Genet's *Our Lady of the Flowers*, Derrida focuses his attention on Genet's description of a tongue caressing itself against the roof of the palate of the mouth as it ejaculates spittle from the mouth's ambiguously genital-like inner organs. The text is made of what the tongue secretes and excretes:

In the middle of this floating side, at the entrance to the gullet, there hangs the fleshy appendage called the uvula, like a small grape. The text is spat out. It is like a discourse whose units mould themselves in the manner of an excrement or secretion. And since we are here concerned with a glottic gesture, the work of the tongue upon itself, its element is the saliva that also glues one unit to another. Association is a sort of gluey continuity, never reasoning or symbolic appeal; sense is made by the glue of chance, and progress has for rhythm little staccato jerks, clutching and suction, veneering – in every sense – and slippery penetration. Into the embouchure or along the column. (*C*, 161)

The erotic activity of the tongue is auto-/hetero-affective and polymorphously perverse. It has no sex nor gender. Derrida is most interested in the erotic ramifications of its undecidable, oscillating movement of rhythmic difference from itself. Derrida associates the rhythmic sounds produced by the tongue as it moves around in the mouth with the tolling of the bells in Edgar Allan Poe's 'The Bells'. In English, the clapper of a bell is also called a tongue. Derrida then relates the moaning and groaning made by the oscillating movement of the bells to the question of sexual difference, species difference and the definition of the human:

> What one would be tempted to isolate as galactic segment (moon, tocsin, a breast that swells, heaves or palpitates – twice – pouring out, etc.) does not even constitute a semantic or thematic chain, whether apparent or hidden. That chain is carried off into indecision through the suspended swinging or beating, the oscillation of the clapper (the 'true' impossible theme of the piece) being remarked or reverberating in the neither-nor of the ghouls (between man and woman, human and inhuman, language and non-language, etc.). Semantic sense is struck by the rhythm of its other, exposing itself there, open, offered in its very hiatus. (C, 178)

According to the *Oxford English Dictionary*, the word 'hiatus' derives from the Latin word for a gap, chasm or gaping aperture.[28] The hiatus Derrida invokes above exposes the action of the tongue. The suspended tongue, the oscillating clapper, is the organ for undoing and loosening relations between sexuality and (self) difference. A few pages later, in a gloss on Ivan Fonagy's reading of poetic sound and Genet, Derrida writes: 'The pendulum movement that brings with it all these "objects", themselves split, between one value and the opposing one, is also a movement of the tongue, mouth, glottis.' (C, 181)

The tongue is the organ of undecidable oscillation. Its rhythmic beating is what makes it possible for Derrida to play Hegel off against Genet and vice versa. The work of the tongue reverberates in both columns of *Clang* and establishes the undecidable relation between them. The tongue is also pivotal in Derrida's discussion of Freud's 'Fetishism' essay. Like the tongue, which Derrida works on through both Hegel and Genet, Derrida discusses fetishism as a principle of substitution in both columns. The specific reading of Freud's 'Fetishism' establishes a point of contact between them. In the Hegel column, Derrida credits Freud with imagining the possibility of a 'concept' of the fetish that would 'no longer be contained in the space of truth, in the opposition *Ersatz/non-Ersatz* at all' (C, 234–5). He is particularly interested in

DERRIDA'S TONGUES   31

Freud's presentation of the case of a man with a 'girdle' which 'covered
up his genitals entirely and so concealed the distinction between them'
(*C*, 236). The two opposed psychic operations (disavowal and affirmation of castration) in this case constitute what he calls an 'economy of
the undecidable' (*C*, 235). Roughly ten pages later, but this time in the
Genet column, Derrida returns to the 'argument of the girdle [*gaine*]' in
Freud's 'Fetishism' essay. Derrida prefaces his continued commentary on
the girdle by playing with the thought that once the fetish is no longer
conceived as a covering or stand-in for a hidden truth, the very phallocentric concept of 'truth' begins to tremble: 'Once the thing itself, in its
unveiled truth, is already found to be involved in the unveiling itself, in
the play of supplementary difference, then the fetish no longer has any
rigorously decidable status. Knell of phallogocentrism' (*C*, 252).

In the pages that follow, Derrida dwells on what he calls the 'consequences' of the 'logic of the girdle'. After remarking that the solidity
and consistency of the fetish derives from its 'being doubly linked to
contraries' he affirms that

> [t]he economy of the fetish is more powerful than that of the
> truth – which is decidable – of the thing itself, or than a discourse
> deciding castration (*pro aut contra*). The fetish is not opposable. It
> oscillates like the clapper of a truth that rings hollow [*qui cloche*].
> Like the tongue [*batail*] in the throat, in other words in the chasm
> of a bell. (*C*, 254)

Derrida compares the fetish that derives its power – more powerful than
the truth – from its undecidability, to the tongue in the throat or the
hollow sound made by a clapper that rings a bell. The tongue/clapper
hides no other thing. Its ringing sound is made, like the play of a tongue,
from the way it oscillates and resounds by touching and being touched.
Derrida writes:

> Headstock pendulum, the fetish oscillates – like the clapper of a
> truth that tilts, that cl – [comme le battant d'une vérité qui penche,
> qui cl –]. The undeniable is the uncastratable. That doesn't mean
> that there is no castration but that this *there is* has no place to take.
> The fact that one [*il y a qu'on*] cannot come down in favour of
> one or the other of the two contrary functions recognised in the
> fetish, no more than can one choose between the thing itself and
> its supplement. No more than one can between two sexes.
> The tongue remains in the sheath [*la langue reste dans la gaine*].
> (*C*, 255–6)

The final line of this passage, 'the tongue remains in the sheath' clangs like the punchline for the entire book. The image itself is highly erotic. As Derrida himself points out, the word *gaine* (or sheath) derives from the Latin word 'vagina', meaning sheath. The oscillating undecidability of the tongue conjures up the possibility of an erotic act of cunnilingus. 'The tongue that remains in its sheath' both hides and exposes the possibility of another thinking of sexuality, that would emerge from the body of language.

Derrida displaces the scene of Freud's argument of the girdle by putting his tongue in place of the fetish. Where the fetish still potentially speaks about castration and stands for a missing penis, the tongue is radically undecidable. Touching itself by touching the other, the tongue calls for another thinking of sexuality.

Notes

1. Hélène Cixous, 'Derrida Ghosting Shakespeare', in *Oxford Literary Review* 34.1 (2012), 3.
2. For a related discussion of the originary prosthetic qualities of the tongue, see Katie Chenoweth, *The Prosthetic Tongue: Printing Technology and the Rise of the French Language* (Philadelphia: University of Pennsylvania Press, 2019). Chenoweth writes: 'There is something "prosthetic" about the tongue from the start, insofar as prosthesis implies an intimate conjunction or articulation (*articulus* also means "joint") of nature and technē, speech and writing, human and machine, life and death' (40). 'The prosthetic tongue thus allows us to see that every tongue is caught up from the start in a movement of repetition and reproduction' (41).
3. Lee Edelman has written about catachresis as a way of thinking about the constitutive non-being of race, sex and queerness. A full engagement with his use of the term exceeds the scope of this essay. Lee Edelman, *Bad Education: Why Queer Theory Teaches Us Nothing* (Durham, NC: Duke University Press, 2022).
4. Jacques Derrida, *Glas* (Paris: Galilée, 1974); Jacques Derrida, *Clang*, trans. Geoffrey Bennington and David Wills (Minneapolis: University of Minnesota Press, 2021). Hereafter *G* and *C*.
5. This text has been reprinted and translated in Jean Genet, *Rembrandt* (Madras: Hanuman Books, 1988).
6. Aristotle, 'On the Soul', *The Complete Works of Aristotle: The Revised Oxford Translation*, vol. 1, ed. Jonathan Barnes (Princeton, NJ: Princeton University Press, 1984), 669, 671.
7. For a provocative discussion of the wide range of expressive qualities of animal voices that do not rely on the tongue as the organ of articulation, see Lynn Turner's chapter 'Voice' in *The Edinburgh Companion to Animal Studies*, eds Lynn Turner, Undine Sellbach and Ron Broglio (Edinburgh: Edinburgh University Press, 2018), 518–32.

DERRIDA'S TONGUES

8. For a more sustained discussion about how sexuality functions simultaneous as a link to animality and a separation from it, see my 'The Sexual Animal and the Primal Scene of Birth' in *The Mother in the Age of Mechanical Reproduction: Psychoanalysis, Photography, Deconstruction* (New York: Fordham University Press, 2012), 53–76.

9. Jacques Derrida, *Le Monolinguisme de l'autre, ou, La Prothèse d'origine* (Paris: Galilée, 1996); Jacques Derrida, *Monolingualism of the Other, or, The Prosthesis of Origin* (Stanford, CA: Stanford University Press, 1998).

10. For a good recapitulation of some of the major figures in this tradition, see Edwin D. Craun, 'Aristotle's Biology and Pastoral Ethics: John of Wales's De Lingua and British Pastoral Writing on the Tongue', *Traditio* 67 (2012), 277–303.

11. Desiderius Erasmus. *Collected Works of Erasmus: Literary and Educational Writings* 7, ed. Elaine Fantham (Toronto: University of Toronto Press, 1989). I discovered Erasmus's text *Lingua* from Emily Butterfield's book, *The Unbridled Tongue: Babble and Gossip in Renaissance France* (Oxford: Oxford University Press, 2016).

12. Erasmus, 'Lingua, The Tongue' in *Collected Works*, 262.

13. Ibid. 267.

14. Chenoweth, *The Prosthetic Tongue*, 12-47.

15. Erasmus, 'Lingua, The Tongue' in *Collected Works*, 268.

16. Medieval theologians grappled with the disturbing ramifications of Aristotle's depiction of the tongue as an organ with dual (and implicitly duplicitous) functions. In the thirteenth century, John of Wales wrote a treatise, *De lingua*, that discussed how the slippery nature of the tongue both facilitates speech and promotes a vast panoply of sins including lying, gluttony, slander and blasphemy. Unlike other organs (such as the ears and the eyes), God warned humans against the potentially sinful proclivities of the tongue by locking it up in a double closure consisting of teeth and lips. See Craun, 'Aristotle's Biology and Pastoral Ethics', 277–303.

17. Erasmus, 'Lingua, The Tongue' in *Collected Works*, 268–9.

18. Ibid., 333.

19. For a related discussion of the erotics of the tongue and the body of language in Hélène Cixous's 'Laugh of the Medusa', see my 'Force of Love' in *Oxford Literary Review* 40.2 (2018), 206–20.

20. Jacques Derrida, 'What is a "Relevant" Translation?', trans. Lawrence Venuti, in *The Translation Studies Reader: Second Edition*, ed. Lawrence Venuti (New York and London: Routledge, 2004), 424. I discuss this passage elsewhere. See: 'Kindling; or, Suicide by Fire', in *Desire in Ashes*, eds Simon Wortham and Chiara Alfano (London: Bloomsbury, 2015), 93–102, and 'Force and Translation; Or, The Polymorphous Body of Language', *philoSOPHIA* 3.1 (2013), 1–18.

21. Derrida's use of the expression 'tongue of fire' alludes in part to the Biblical reference in Acts 2:1–4 to the manifestation of the Holy Spirit: 'When the day of Pentecost came, they were all together in one place. Suddenly a

sound like the blowing of a violent wind came from heaven and filled the whole house where they were sitting. They saw what seemed to be tongues of fire that separated and came to rest on each of them. All of them were filled with the Holy Spirit and began to speak in other tongues as the Spirit enabled them.'

22. Jacques Derrida and Hélène Cixous, 'On Deconstruction and Childhood', *Oxford Literary Review*, 41.2 (2019), 149–59.

23. Derrida, 'On Deconstruction and Childhood', 156–7.

24. Ibid., 152.

25. Ibid., 156–7.

26. Hélène Cixous and Jacques Derrida, 'Bâtons rompus', in Thomas Dutoit, ed., *Derrida d'ici, Derrida de là* (Paris: Galilée, 2009), 213, emphasis added.

27. For a related discussion of sound and tongue in *Glas*, see Naomi Waltham-Smith, *Shattering Biopolitics: Militant Listening and the Sound of Life* (New York: Fordham University Press, 2021).

28. *Oxford English Dictionary*, s.v. 'hiatus (n.), Etymology', July 2023: https://doi.org/10.1093/OED/4799937402.

2

SPOONFUL: THE DORSAL
DECONSTRUCTION OF EROTICISM

David Wills

About nine tenths of the way through *Derrida*, the 2002 documentary film by Kirby Dick and Amy Ziering Kofman, Kofman decides to ask Derrida what he would like to see in a documentary about a philosopher such as Heidegger, Kant or Hegel. After pausing for ten seconds to scratch his ear, stare into space, and draw his hand down across his cheeks and mouth, Derrida replies that he would like to see consideration of 'their sex lives [*leur vie sexuelle*]'. He adds to the quip somewhat glibly – 'if you want a quick answer, okay?' – before expanding upon it more seriously:

> That they talk about their sex lives ... or that [in the film] one talks about their sex life ... Because it's what they don't talk about. I'd like them to talk about what they don't talk about. Why are these philosophers presented as asexual [*asexués*] in their work? Why have they erased their sexual life from their work, and why have they never taken into account their private lives – when I say 'sex life' I mean 'private', their private lives? There is nothing more important in private life than love ... I want them to talk about the part played by love in their private life.

And in response to the follow-up question concerning whether he would like to be asked to do the same in the documentary being filmed, he replies that he didn't say he would answer such a question, but:

> There are in the texts I have published quite a few things; they are also disguised [*dissimulées*] of course, but I haven't practiced the same type of dissimulation as ... the great philosophers you have just named. I've dissimulated of course, I've dissimulated like everybody else, but not in the same way ... I talk about it when I want to, and when I can.[1]

The sequence ends with Derrida asking the filmmakers what they are going to do with all of this, how their editing will determine what to keep in the film, which is tantamount to asking how much of the back and forth just recorded will be added to the archive, to the text and discourse of philosophy. As I read it, we can take advantage of this juxtaposition, of Derrida's double desire – on the one hand to have philosophers and philosophy speak of the sex, love and intimacy they avoid, and, on the other, to know what, in the same general context, the film he is in will keep in or leave out – to reflect on the erotics of deconstruction in terms of everything that that thinking does with the play of presence and absence, with what falls in or out of the space that is opened by every utterance in its essential iterability. For, if every utterance is a repetition even as it presents itself as something original, then every utterance, in so doing, opens space between what it is heard to say and what it is heard not to say; every utterance speaks through a type of structural *double entendre*.

The sex lives that philosophers don't talk about, the 'quite a few things' that the philosopher Derrida claims conversely to have spoken about, are therefore not simply functions of the connotations that this or that philosopher decides, or decides not, to 'allow' in his writing; they are not simply functions of this or that practice of dissimulation. Rather, the possibilities of dissimulation and *double entendre*, of expression and repression, are 'allowed' by the essential iterability just referred to: the understanding of differance we owe to Derrida means that utterance is conceived simultaneously as self and other, as sameness and difference. For that reason, the utterances of philosophy are neither transparent nor self-evident, debate may take place about what they mean, contradictions may be revealed between what a given philosopher writes in one place and in another. For the same reason, this or that philosopher may presume that their sex life does, or does not, belong in their discourse, whereas another one may decide that it does, but in a dissimulated way; yet also, still for the same reason, irrespective of this or that choice by this or that philosopher, their utterances will go about their own business of doubling, as it were on those utterances' own initiative.

Derrida's periphrastic explanation of the 'sex lives' he wants to hear about from philosophers ('I mean "private" [lives] … the part played by love') demonstrates the difficulty of determining what constitutes the erotic: where sex begins and ends, how it does or doesn't relate to love, to what extent it should be understood as private. The erotic, from that point of view, has its own particularly complex version of generalised or essential iterability, its own special negotiation of the space opened by its utterances or practices. Roland Barthes – a somewhat or sometime kindred thinker to Derrida – gave to erotic space the name 'intermittence':

SPOONFUL   37

> Is not the most erotic portion of a body where the garment
> gapes? ... It is intermittence ... which is erotic: the intermit-
> tence of skin flashing between two articles of clothing ...; it is
> this flash itself which seduces, or rather: the staging of an appear-
> ance-as-disappearance.[2]

Without ignoring the distinctions – virtual or actual – between private
or sex(ual) life and eroticism, one might set about tracking, from end
to beginning of the discourse of deconstruction, a series of versions of
erotic intermittence; spaces where the discourse with which Derrida's
philosophy clothes itself gapes to reveal some skin.

For example, backwards, decade by decade, one might cite these
cases, selected among various other possibilities. In 2003, in the second
year of his final seminar, *The Beast and the Sovereign*, Derrida sets out
a principle of intermittence when, discussing his disjointed comparative reading of Heidegger and Defoe, he argues that his practice of the
seminar requires 'a certain number of leaps, certain new perspectives
... another view of the whole, like for example when you are driving a
car on a mountain road, a hairpin or a turn, an abrupt and precipitous
elevation gives you in an instant a new perspective'. For he adds, within
telling parentheses, '(it goes without saying that each of my choices and
my perspectives depend broadly here, as I will never try to hide, on my
history, my previous work, and my way of driving, driving on this road,
on *my drives, desires and phantasms* [*mes pulsions, désirs et fantasmes*], even
if I always try to make them both intelligible, shareable, convincing and
open to discussion)'.[3] In 2000, in *On Touching – Jean-Luc Nancy*, almost
at the end of a long book that I'll find cause to return to, a book in
which one thematic thread is that of kissing eyes, he writes this: 'The
principle of philosophy is not philosophy ... [which] might therefore
consist in no more than a frenzied forgetting of the first kiss. I, the philosopher, hypothetically, run to catch the recollection of the first kiss.'[4]
Continuing, more quickly: in 1998, in 'A Silkworm of One's Own [*Un
ver à soie*]' a first person narrator recounts the childhood experience of
an 'orifice you had to imagine to be at the origin of their silk, this
milk become thread ... the extruded saliva of a very fine sperm, shiny,
gleaming, the miracle of a feminine ejaculation ... which I drank in
with my eyes';[5] in 1985, in *Right of Inspection*, looking into looking at a
photographic text involving, among other things, women making love,
one of the unidentified and ungendered voices says: 'I was saying that
the question of genre poses and develops sexual difference in its most
undecided and unstable form, precisely as a difference that trembles';[6] in
1974, he published *Clang*, with its polymorphous perversion of texts by

Hegel through association with, and contamination by, texts by Genet, two erections or columns that continue for 274 pages without touching, unless it be that they do nothing but that, nothing but caress, embrace and penetrate each other across, and in the blank space between them;[7] and, of course, in 1967 *Of Grammatology* had already staged the now famous analytical scene of Rousseau's supplementary sex, his recourse to masturbation as the 'dangerous supplement [that] breaks with nature'.[8]

Indeed, beyond the sexuality that haunts Rousseau according to Derrida's analysis, one should understand the more general concept of auto-affection to be operating as the originary 'trace' or 'differance' to which it is related, there and elsewhere,[9] functioning as something like the *beginning itself* of deconstruction. It also describes the *beginning itself of life*, of the animate: 'auto-affection is the condition of an experience in general ... another name for "life"'.[10] In examples that extend from the formal development of auto-affection as hearing-oneself-speak in *Voice and Phenomenon* (1967), to the autobiography of *The Animal That Therefore I Am* thirty years later, where it is described as 'the trace of the living for itself, being for itself, the auto-affection or auto-infection as memory or archive of the living',[11] Derrida describes the opening of self-sameness to otherness without which, one might say, nothing *gets going* at one end, or nothing *gets off* at the other. That is for him a function of 'every *autos*, every ipseity', and by means of it auto-affection becomes an 'automatic, automobile, autonomous, auto-referential movement'.[12]

Auto-affection is also, in many respects, another word for iterability: as I just made clear, every auto-affection is a hetero-affection, an originary othering of the self, and is to that extent an *iteration* of the self as other; I don't mean that every iteration is in opposition to the previous one, but rather that the possibility of iteration – a necessary possibility, not one that can ever be reduced – includes every possibility of othering including what I'll call inversion, for example that of the *autos* into *heteros* (or *allos*). Such is the problematic of Rousseau's dangerous supplement, the fact that it works or threatens to supplant the natural act inasmuch as it repeats or simulates it. Rousseau has recourse to it in the absence of Maman, cognisance of which brings her back as participant in it, however fantasmatic or hallucinatory her participation be; and, conversely, whenever her participation is real, she is both present and absent, and he is both receiving pleasure from her and giving pleasure to himself. There can be no original proffering, or act, either of the self or of the utterance: whatever the self does to 'get going' – as I just characterised it – and whatever it utters, is performed as a supplement to, a repetition as differance of, the absent original; it occurs in the absence of any pure autonomous self (*autos*) or purely invented utterance (*logos*).

SPOONFUL 39

This automatic *double entendre* means that even without the specifics of Rousseau's masturbation melancholy, auto-affection in all its guises will share its structure with eroticism, it will be both the operation of *touching on*, as it were in all innocence, the otherness in the self, and of *touching*, through every imaginable experience, the self and whatever the self takes as other. Anywhere anything begins, it begins as auto-affection, and functions as the self-stimulation that can be heard in the term, functioning coextensively, therefore, with what we understand as eroticism.

* * *

The discussion that follows will find an emblem of deconstructionist eroticism in Derrida's *The Post Card*. I'll call it an erotic coat of arms, and in discussing this scene of heraldry I'll come to concentrate especially on the escutcheon at its centre. An 'escutcheon', as Webster has it, is a 'defined area on which armorial bearings are displayed', described more precisely by the *OED* as 'the shield or shield-shaped surface on which a coat of arms is depicted; also in wider sense, the shield with the armorial bearings; a sculptured or painted representation of this'. A coat of arms, also called a heraldic *achievement*, is always figural, like the eagle bearing an olive branch in its right talon and arrows in its left, in the Great Seal of the United States, whose achievement bespeaks might and peace, with a supposed preference for the latter determined by the eagle's head being turned to the right. The escutcheon in this US example is the centre-piece shield containing a modified flag with alternating white and red stripes, representing the thirteen original colonies. The arms and escutcheon that I'll draw from *The Post Card* will also be primarily figural, and figurative.

The word 'escutcheon', *écusson* in French, comes up early in *Clang*, via a quote from Genet's *Funeral Rites*, serving as the pretext for both a figural and literal imposition of Derrida's signature upon the work of Genet. As Derrida writes:

One would have to dig into what is arbitrary about this name – Gallien – not to mention these initials, J. G. And if this chance pseudonym were to form the first name matrix of the text? As for initials, in *Funeral Rites* it is J. D., Jean D. 'The escutcheon [*écusson*] with a capital D embroidered in silver ...'.[13]

In referring to a name by its initials the word connects Derrida (J. D.) to Genet (J. G.), and to Genet's eroticism, which *Clang* celebrates in almost Bataillean fashion, even if that is far from all that *Clang* does. But one could argue that part of what fascinates Derrida in this celebration is

Genet's mobilisation of a complex system of ritual to support his erotic edifice, through reference to the coat of arms here, and through a whole heraldic or chivalric symbolism that turns around tattooing, as developed in particular in *Miracle of the Rose*.[14] I do not think it is exaggerating to say that a type of ritual functions in Derrida's philosophical practice, the repeated elaboration, even *intonation* of a single and singular idea – here, auto-affection. Similarly, ritual is never absent from eroticism, as I hope to demonstrate in the escutcheon I am about to emblematise.[15]

My erotic escutcheon, emblem or figure is this, from 'Envois', the major text in *The Post Card*: 'And after the telephone call', Derrida's narrator writes, 'I will turn my back to you to sleep, as usual, and you will cling up against me, giving me your hand, you will envelop me.'[16] Since the first time I read them, some forty years ago, I have been obsessed by those lines, by the type of fracture that they produce in the text of philosophy. I remember them as offering a form of entry into Derrida's text that was neither philosophical nor literary, neither erotic nor romantic, in any simple sense. If the words made me want to cry, I wasn't sure if I would be crying out of emotion or out of ecstasy.

The sentence presents no *double entendre* in the simple sense; on the surface level there is nothing sexual implied; it is not as if the narrator says something non-sexual while allowing or encouraging something sexual. Yet at the same time, it opens the text on two principal fronts: in the first place, it functions both constatively – 'you will do such and such, I understand or imagine you to be doing such and such' – and performatively, as invitation from the narrator to their lover to indulge in the acts or actions described. My reading of the escutcheon will work within that undecidable margin of this particular lover's discourse, between what this fragment from 'Envois' states and what it performs, increasingly as we approach the two figures lying at its centre. In the second place, the chosen sentence introduces a fruitful but potentially troubling undecidability concerning what constitutes the erotic, what distinguishes sex from love or intimacy, concerning what sex is and what sex this is, who is doing it. More specifically, as I will discuss, the utterance goes to the very heart of touching.

In the background of the escutcheon's elements as I shall read them is an idea I developed previously under the name of 'dorsality'.[17] In that discussion – one of whose epigraphs is precisely the quote in question – the dorsal is presented as a *technological* inversion of the frontal, which is not the same as an inversion of the frontal *by technology*; it is not the performance of a technological contrivance, not some natural frontal being turned around by the intervention of technology. Rather, the hypothesis of dorsality is this: what we presume to be a *natural* human is always already *technological*, such that the human relations – ethical, political, sexual – that traditionally depend on frontality, on some form of face to face, are subjected to, indeed make the *deviation* that I call the 'dorsal turn'. The first step in the development of the hypothesis involves locating human technology 'in the back' by arguing for its having originated in the bipedal upright stance, in the readjustment of the spinal column that freed the hands for manipulation of tools; technology in this interpretation is understood to reside behind or before the human, and, as just mentioned, the human is defined as *originarily* technological. The second step, that of introducing dorsality into human relations, promotes ideas of radical otherness, opening to what lies outside 'the frontal visual perspective of the knowable';[18] the dorsal, by definition, cannot be *fore*-seen, is a function of surprise, implies exposure to vulnerability.

In terms of ethical relations, the dorsal turn is indebted to Levinas while at the same time *controverting* his thinking in two ways. First, by emphasising what Levinas writes concerning the dissymmetry of the face-to-face encounter (referred to sometimes as a 'curvature'[19]) and its distinction from any simple reciprocal visuality, dorsality reconfigures the ethical relation as face-to-back. Second, by reading the values of nudity, passivity, vulnerability and destitution, which are in Levinas consistently and explicitly feminine (and sometimes infantile or animal[20]), in conjunction with the priority given to that same feminine in the 'concretisation' of the house, dorsality uncovers the primordial operation of technology in the Levinasian construction of interiority, and the ethics based on it.[21]

A dorsal conception of the political draws on Carl Schmitt's insistence on a confrontation of enemies across a front line or frontier – 'the friend, enemy and combat concepts'[22] – as fundamental to his definition of the political. But it finds Schmitt's elaboration of those concepts doubly problematised by what backs up the front, that is to say the presumed homogeneous national mass of citizen-friends whose soldier-representatives face a public, not a private, enemy across a line of demarcation that is also a line of contamination, a contamination that conversely reaches back to confound that presumed homogeneity of the nation. In more general terms, though, dorsality analyses mechanisms of political inversion: for example, what takes place between political theory and practice, the presumed realist application of one to the other through which a political plan will be implemented, whether by reform or by revolution; or the extent to which revolt, or revolution, or any supposed transformative politics, is beholden to a logic of transgression.[23]

A dorsal sexuality is inseparable from the ethics and politics just described; less because the sexual necessarily implicates the ethical and political, either in the ways that consume us in our current historical moment, or in the general sense of relations to another and to the collective, than because the technological specificity of dorsal inversion involves turning or opening towards an other that surprises to the extent of being inanimate. Within the dorsal relation – ethical, political or sexual – we are called on to deal not only with what escapes the visual perspective of the knowable, but also with an unknowability about *what* constitutes the other approaching from behind. The dorsal relation can therefore also be called 'prosthetic', in the sense of relating to what is as radically other as steel is to flesh, and reawakening what is human in us to its irrecuperable technological otherness. My aim here, however, is not to repeat the implications of dorsal eroticism that I have inventoried in detail elsewhere,[24] but rather to read what I find figured in the words I have taken as emblem, and described as escutcheon: 'and after the telephone call, I will turn my back to you to sleep, as usual, and you will cling up against me, giving me your hand, you will envelop me [*et après le coup de téléphone, je te tournerai le dos pour dormir, comme d'habitude, et tu te colleras contre moi, en me donnant la main, tu m'envelopperas*]'. The central clause, which Alan Bass justifiably translates literally as 'you will paste yourself against me', resonates with the enveloping of the final clause: I turn my back, you cling to me, you adhere to me, sticking, pasted or glued like a postage stamp, you wrap me up. Within the seal of the United States referred to earlier, the thirteen white and red stripes of its escutcheon stick to each other back to front, nestling against each other, adhering like a stack of stripes, thirteen canned sardines.

In American English, one would say that the two characters in the quotation are 'spooning'. The *OED* also has 'to spoon' as a verb (both transitive and intransitive), citing late nineteenth-century American examples:

4. a. intransitive. To lie close together, to fit into each other, in the manner of spoons.
1887 *Harper's Mag.* Apr. 781/2 Two persons in each bunk, the sleepers 'spooning' together, packed like sardines.
1894 *Outing* 24 343/2 The precision with which we could 'spoon' that sad night was truly beautiful to behold.
b. *transitive*. To lie with (a person) spoon-fashion.
1887 *Harper's Mag.* Dec. 49/2 'Now spoon me.' Sterling stretched himself out on the warm flag-stone, and the boy nestled up against him.

In spooning, two bodies borrow the same form, the one behind shaping itself to the (presumed) curvature of the other's back, adopting the

SPOONFUL   43

appearance of nestling spoons, performing a dorsal snuggle. Yet that supremely human, or animal, gesture finds its figure in the stacking of everyday utensils, in an impersonal multiplicity of utilitarian objects that seem far from suggesting the tender intimacy of two bodies lying in harmonious togetherness, perhaps in the afterglow of an act of love. Now, no objection can be made to that from a rhetorical point of view; there is no particular dehumanising effect intended by this analogy between bodies and spoons; figurative language performs such gestures all the time. Spooning occurs as eminently human, even if the sense of sight and vision lose the reciprocity that love demands, for one spoon(er) looks into emptiness, one is touched more than touching, one spoon is full of the other, and both resort or regress delicately into animality, into scent and nuzzling, coupling *a tergo*.

There are therefore two spoons in the centre of my escutcheon. On one side and the other of those spoons there appear a telephone and an envelope; the syntax of the sentence puts the spooning within the double thematic of the telephone and the envelope. Now, 'between phone and envelope' might be heard to mean between voice (*phonē*) and letter (*grammē*). But although that is how the syntax is heard or read at first sight, understanding it in that way would mean ignoring the extent to which the voice is already *telephonised*, diverted into technological space. The voice is spoken as if live, but its life is detoured through telephone lines; it performs the oxymoron of a live relaying or recording.[25] In Derrida's terms as developed extensively through *The Post Card*, the message conveyed by the voice gets posted; it necessarily has recourse to a system of messaging – transporting, sorting, distributing – that involves multiple effects of distancing, relay and delay. One can address one's message as clearly and explicitly as one wishes, cup one's hands like two facing spoons and utter directly into the ear of the other whom one is spooning, but the message will still have to travel, one will still have to entrust it to a postal system – however minute one suppose the space of transmission to be – within which everything that happens is outside one's control. So, it is as if the voice were uttering its message into a slit in a postbox; in speaking, as in writing, one is effectively mailing a postcard. The phone and envelope of the escutcheon operate through what *The Post Card* analyses as postal space.

The spooning is said to follow a telephone call, *le coup de téléphone*. The most straightforward reading of that would be that I spoke on the phone and then we spooned (more precisely, that after I will have spoken on the phone we will spoon); but it is complicated from a number of perspectives. Most importantly, it is complicated from the sexual perspective: one wants to know where the sex is. The spooning to come seems post-coital – I will turn my back to you to sleep. But the full performativity of that utterance comes into play once we infer that it is you that I will have been speaking to on the phone. We infer that the conversation took place between you and me because nothing indicates anything different. The previous parts of this letter from 24 September 1977 talk about letters that I write and post to you, leading the reader to presume that they are separate, as indeed they always are. 'I' will therefore having been speaking to an absent 'you' before I turn my back. As for telephoning, it happens in various places throughout the text; two days previous there is a parenthesis within which 'we were telephoning each other' (107). Hence, although I will continue to infer a sexualisation of the spooning scene, a certain logic here determines that the sex is first found on or in the telephone, that there is phone sex, after which we will spoon. I say that for reasons I'll come to in a moment, but it is also said somewhat disingenuously, based as it is on thinking that they were closer, as if together, when they spoke on the phone whereas they will be apart when they spoon. If you wish: I just imagine that I will turn my back to you to sleep and we will spoon; that is how it usually is, my habit [*comme d'habitude*], when we are together making love. So, the disingenuousness of saying they have phone sex derives from recourse to a presumption about the speaking voice being more present when the contrary argument has just been made: the voice is precisely telephonised, technologised, consigned to the postal principle; the phone signifies absence as much as does the envelope.

My saying there is phone sex is justified differently; it is based in the first place on a series of sexual usages of *coup* in French. To remain with the most crass: *tirer un coup* means 'to get it off, hook up, get laid'; *tirer son coup*, 'to shoot one's load', 'to climax'. By extension, after the *coup de téléphone* may be interpreted as 'following our phone sex'. But even there, calling it 'phone sex' is only a manner of speaking. The idea that the sex these spoons will have been indulging in occurs as a telephone *coup* or call doesn't in fact make the telephone call a euphemism for sex, or make it phone sex – a mutual stimulation by means of the voice, an *oto-affection* – in the usual sense. Rather, it amounts to saying, according to the logic of 'Envois', that the only sex there can ever be involving these two lovers will have to take place over the phone, over the ocean, through the mail: as I have just stated, the protagonist lovers never meet in the sense that we normally understand as *real*; they are never together in the 'present' space of the text itself. 'Envois' is entirely epistolary, a series of unidirectional postcards, and any termination of the distance that separates them – it is suggested[26] – would mean the end of their relation. So, there is only indirect contact, only post cards; they

SPOONFUL 45

meet only in the postal – or in this case telephonic – space of multiple relays. In that space – fictive space, if you wish – they have sex. Hence, telephone and envelope, and spooning, share the same structural space within the erotic escutcheon, the space of what will not have taken place. In the final analysis, therefore, I really have no idea what is going on in what I'll call this spoonful. From phone call to envelope, let alone in the spooning itself, I cannot account for all the organs, or their organisation. Yet even if it is only my drive, desire or phantasm at work, I will continue to read this escutcheon as if the spoons in it are sexually involved, having sex, albeit in the sense of having had sex.

Wherever the sex is found to be, it will be, it will have been indirect, over the phone or through the envelope; and its protagonists will be far from stable subjects. Readers of 'Envois' are warned of indirection from the first moment of the Preface, upon being told that what they are about to read is to be read as 'the preface to a book that I have not written' (3); a couple of pages later they will be further confounded upon learning 'that the signers and the addressees are not always ... identical from one *envoi* to the other, that the signers are not inevitably ... the senders, nor [are] the addressees ... the receivers, that is ... the readers' (5). The 'Envois' are thus a prefatory explanation of what the narrator planned to say, or would have said had 'he' remained constant from one instance to the next, or had he known that his addressee remained constant, or had he been able to prevent the reader from butting in; in short, he would have gone straight to it had there not been indirection. However, there is indirection, necessarily; the reader necessarily butts in, and as a result the 'Envois' have had to be redacted (perhaps even burned), so that what we read is only the 'remainders of a recently destroyed correspondence' (3). The redactions are indicated by a contrivance, a standard 52-character space irrespective of the volume of the redaction. There is an instance of such an abyssal space – as narrow as a punctuation point, as wide or as deep as one wants to imagine – immediately prior to the heraldic scene in question, which is therefore post-abyss, a fragment of text about spooning found teetering, risking falling backwards, disaster-film-like, into that yawning chasm.

Our spooning event comes after a colon and a 52-character abyss, and its first word is 'after'. From the first word, then, even before it, we are in the moment and under the regime of the 'post'. There is no sense to 'back' without an idea of 'after'; we call it 'back' because it comes after a 'front' presumed to be be*fore*. And yet to accept that idea is to subvert the order implied by every logical apparatus of the Western episteme. For the logic of 'back' being 'after', following a preceding or forerunning 'front', is this: 'back' comes after 'front' only to the extent that it is defined from the perspective of (another) 'front', which 'back' is in front of; hence the 'back' that is after 'front' is before 'front' (and for 'front' we could also say 'face', which would take us back to Levinas). Derrida is at pains to explain, and subvert, that logic that in 'Envois', inspired by the accident of Matthew Paris's tinted drawing, the chance inversion that has Plato dictating to Socrates, and, as a result, necessarily spooning him to the extent of buggering, coming into him from behind.

According to the same logic, 'back', or 'behind', is interpreted as 'before'. Such an interpretation is explicitly authorised, encouraged or even required. If Plato comes after Socrates historically, Socrates is before Plato, but seen from here Socrates is behind Plato; in Matthew Paris, Plato is behind Socrates, but we find that unusual only because (we know that) he comes after him, which is to say that he should be depicted in front of him, before him. Derrida wants to problematise order – basically, what it means to say something comes first – but beyond that, he wants to call into question the spatial or temporal senses of 'after' by relating them to the matter of the postal. The very paradoxes that I have just outlined are at work because of the abyss that gapes, the bottomless mailbox that opens as one posts a letter; an abyss wherein there is not only detour and delay, indirection and redirection, but also – because it involves a radical interruption, indeed rupture, at the heart of the system – inversion, back-to-frontness, that is to say, a turning around, but also, as in our escutcheon, spooning.

If, as the narrator will write two paragraphs from the end of the text, 'I will always ask myself what *to turn around* has signified' (256), the spooning concerning us here will in a sense be the answer he has already given himself; what he asks at the back of the text sends him back toward its front; between the two he will have turned his back on you to sleep, as usual, you will cling, or glue yourself (*tu te colleras*) like a stamp to my back, and there will be only spooning. The order – who spoons whom – matters as little as do the genders: you glue yourself to me, which would make me the envelope, but you *envelop* me as though you were the wrapper. From front to back it will have all been back to front; when the final postcard is addressed, stamped and posted, it will have been all back, there will have been only spooning. Throughout 'Envois' there is, we are told, 'not a word that would not be ... programmed on the back [*au dos*] ... In a word there will be only back [*du dos*]' (187); and we have already heard 'another voice in the same book sa[y]: everything is connoted in *do*, it's only the backs [*il n'y a que les dos*] that count, look back over the entire scansion (not the *das* as in *fort/da* or derrida, but also the most drawling *dos* ...), then one has to start everything over [*tout reprendre*] once more' (78).

SPOONFUL

Telephone, envelope, stamp, two spoons: these are the elements figured in this dorsal erotic escutcheon, the coat of arms of the postal system. Once 'everything become[s] a post card again' (80),[27] once the fact and threat of spacing haunts every message, infecting and invading every communication, but also inhabiting it, structurally, from the beginning, then the postal effect abounds. The spoons nestle within that postal effect: however snug they be, however much one touches the other, however much one takes the other inside itself, they nevertheless communicate across the space between them. *Without* that postal space, there would be no communicating, no need or possibility of it; yet, *because of* that space, there is necessarily delay and deferral, the necessary possibility of detour and diversion, return and inversion, turning back and turning around. Postal space, the space of every touch and contact, which we might now call spooning space, is the space of differance: 'Without this differance', Derrida writes in *On Touching*, 'there would be no contact *as such* ... but with this differance, contact never appears in its full purity.'[28]

* * *

Between telephone and envelope, then, falls the spooning; yet even between the spoons falls the postal abyss. An abyss is commonly found in the center of a coat of arms, placed in its escutcheon, a shield within a shield, one bigger escutcheon spooning another. For that we borrow the French term *mise en abyme*, or use our own, 'inescutcheon'. For example, during the Commonwealth, Cromwell had his lion rampant *en abyme* in the coat of arms of the Commonwealth (1655–9); similarly, the United Kingdom of George III had first the Elector, then the King of Hanover as inescutcheons from 1801–20. Every escutcheonal spooning harbours or accommodates the possibility of an inescapable inescutcheonal abyss; the spooned spoon leans back into the spooning spoon as if, at the risk of, falling into such an abyss. It is in response to, or for fear of that, that you give me your hand: I turn my back, you spoon me, clinging to me, I feel the abyss at or in my back, you give me your hand. In or across the abyssal inescutcheon of spooning, between me and you, between us and the abyss, there is – happily, it seems – your given hand.

The hand therefore appears as an inescutcheon, in abyss, between the spooning spoons. But I am not at all sure that it appears on this heraldic achievement, that it can be figured there, for it is something of a spectral hand. It wants to appear, to be found and held there. The heteroaffirmativity of this moment and this gesture – 'giving me your hand' – would promise the cadence and repose of harmonious love that we always were seeking; the fulfilment of a love threatened by the abyss of separation. The letter of 24 September 1977 ends on that note, with the spooning quote and its seemingly reassuring consummation: warm dorsal embrace, hand touching hand; I give you my back, you give me your hand. With this explicit touching, we are in the heart of eroticism, and in the private love life of philosophy. Now, it might be objected that there has been nothing but touch at work in this scene, that everything I have said about spooning is determined by touching, reinforced by clinging and enveloping. But the hand foregrounds touch in a different way, or foregrounds a different understanding of touching, and by means of this hand that you give me the abyssal rupture that structures spooning, and which I have tried to describe, far from being resolved, comes back into focus.

The hand returns us to the question raised in the earlier part of this essay, that of auto-affection as originary trace or differance, developed in the context of Rousseau's recourse to the 'dangerous supplement'. In giving himself his hand in the absence of Mme de Warens, he was still having her touch him, albeit phantasmatically. He was in fact giving her his hand to touch him; or at least, in her absence, she came to him bringing her hand to take his hand to give to him to pleasure himself. As we have consistently seen, the self-caress, like hearing-oneself-speak, cannot function without opening a space within that self, the same structural space within which an other operates; caressing even oneself means opening oneself to another. The mechanics of that auto-hetero-affection, developed by Derrida from his earliest writings, is again under the microscope in *On Touching*, the book-length analysis inspired by the work of Jean-Luc Nancy, first published in 2000 (its first form dates from 1992). 'Even when we are in (*self*)-touch', Derrida writes, 'or when the touching ones touch *themselves*, they are in touch with something other than themselves and are touched by something other than the same self that touches.'[29] The 'something other' mentioned here reintroduces the dorsal logic I described earlier: auto-affection opens a structure of self-othering that goes all the way to reversibility, so that whereas I think I am facing myself to touch myself, I am in fact creating another self whom I turn around to face and touch me; but also, or instead, whereas I think I am facing myself to touch myself, I am in fact spooning, or am spooned by another who, adhering symmetrically back against me, touches me, having me think or feel that I am touching myself.

What *On Touching* also makes abundantly clear is that this reversal, whereby I produce and set to work another to have me feel I touch myself, amounts to a *technological* inversion or reversal of the frontal. Derrida credits Nancy with being the thinker who insists above all that

SPOONFUL

the other I turn around to touch myself even as I think I am self-caressing, is an other*ness*, a *what* as much as a *whom*; the originary opening of differance is the 'ageless intrusion of technics, which is to say of transplantation [*greffe*] or prosthetics [*prothèse*]'.[30] In the terms of our escutcheon: not only do the spoons come to interrupt the sex or lovemaking taking place between telephone and envelope, not only do they figure the cold steel of the inanimate within the supposed living communication of the voice or even of the letter that is presumed to have transcribed that voice, but in their very spooning, as it were between the spooners nestling snugly, one curving to the fit of the other, in the space or abyss of their touching, *in their very contact*, there occurs the rupture that I mentioned earlier, referred to by Derrida as 'a differance in the very inside of the haptic'.[31] In spooning there is produced a space that suffers the intrusion of prosthetic otherness such that these spoons or spooners perhaps cannot even be said to touch:

> Isn't it necessary that this spacing open up the place for replacement, and that it make room for the substitute, for the metonymical supplement, and for technicity? ... I wonder whether there is any pure auto-affection of the touching or the touched, and therefore any pure, immediate experience of the purely proper body, the body proper that is living, purely living.[32]

Without differance or spacing there can be no affection, nothing touches anything, the spoons are all fused. But once there is the spacing of – the spacing making provision for, allowing – auto-affection, then there is also, necessarily, within the structural constitution of auto-affection, enabling of hetero-affection, an opening of the door to every heterogeneity, including prosthetic intrusion. Continuing the passage just quoted, Derrida asks whether the experience of touching 'is at least not already *haunted*, but *constitutively* haunted, by some hetero-affection related to spacing ... where an intruder may come through'.[33] To repeat: for Derrida, no one like Nancy insists on the 'essential and necessary originarity'[34] of this technological intrusion, of the general prostheticity or 'technical supplementarity' of the body, which permits but at the same time inverts or perverts touch as *interanimate* haptic affection: 'this supplementarity of technical prosthesis spaces out, defers, or expropriates all originary properness: there is no ... essentially originary touching before it, before its necessary possibility – *for any living being in general*'.[35] From the beginning, from what we might call the origin of life, nothing animate moves or self-affects without such a supplement, however dangerous, in this or that case, it come to be.

The hand you give me haunts in that way the abyssal centre of the erotic escutcheon: what consummates the spooning intrudes awkwardly upon the spooning. Though its reassuring touch seems to provide just the protection we need, it is a spectral hand, the hand of another, another hand given to me, but also *an other hand*, a hand of otherness, a supplementary hand, a substitute hand, a prosthetic hand. For it stands to reason: if you are able to give me your hand, it is because we have already given ourselves hands; we gave ourselves hands when we stood upright – in our paradigm self-technologising moment – giving ourselves the hands that would no longer simply carry us along on the earth, but would instead begin to function independently of the rest of the body, would be able to reach out and hold another hand, granted, but would also be able to reach out to hold something else, some thing. And if we could imagine giving ourselves hands, if we could invent such an idea and hatch such a plan, it was because we were already functioning within the differance of auto-affection, already schooled in giving ourselves to ourselves, even parcelling ourselves out to ourselves, already giving life to ourselves that way, from the beginning.

So, I'll end the telephone call, I'll turn and give you my back, and you will spoon me, giving me your hand. But in that spooning, the hand you give me, through which I feel myself touch you and myself, will be a hand whose relation to your body has had its 'properness' interrupted or ruptured; it will be a hand you have detached and given me, and it will touch me – whether my hand or my body more generally – as the hand of another, as a type of mechanical hand. As you put your arm around me, you'll put your hand to work and into circulation, and I'll take it, to use it as my own, to better feel the peel and press of your envelope.

Notes

1. Kirby Dick and Amy Ziering Kofman, *Derrida* (Zeitgeist Films, US, 2002). The sequence is at 1.14.04–1.16.55.
2. Roland Barthes, *The Pleasure of the Text*, trans. Richard Miller (New York: Hill and Wang, 1975), 9–10.
3. Jacques Derrida, *The Beast and the Sovereign*, vol. II, trans. Geoffrey Bennington (Chicago: University of Chicago Press, 2011), 206; *Séminaire: La bête et le souverain* (Paris: Galilée, 2010), 290.
4. Jacques Derrida, *On Touching – Jean-Luc Nancy*, trans. Christine Irizarry (Stanford, CA: Stanford University Press, 2005), 292; *Le toucher, Jean-Luc Nancy* (Paris: Galilée, 2000).
5. Jacques Derrida, 'A Silkworm of One's Own', in Hélène Cixous and Jacques Derrida, *Veils*, trans. Geoffrey Bennington (Stanford, CA: Stanford University Press, 2002), 88–9; *Voiles* (Paris: Galilée, 1998).

6. Jacques Derrida, *Right of Inspection*, trans. David Wills (New York: Monacelli Press, 1998), n.p.; Marie-Françoise Plissart, *Droit de regards*, avec une lecture de Jacques Derrida (Paris: Éditions de Minuit, 1985), x.

7. Jacques Derrida, *Clang*, trans. Geoffrey Bennington and David Wills (Minneapolis: University of Minnesota Press, 2021); *Glas* (Paris: Galilée, 1974).

8. Jacques Derrida, *Of Grammatology*, 40th anniversary edition, trans. Gayatri Chakravorty Spivak (Baltimore, MD: Johns Hopkins University Press, 2016), 165; *De la grammatologie* (Paris: Éditions de minuit, 1967).

9. Cf. Derrida, *Grammatology*, 179–82.

10. Ibid., 180.

11. Jacques Derrida, *The Animal That Therefore I Am*, trans. David Wills (New York: Fordham University Press, 2008), 47; first publication in Marie-Louise Mallet, ed., *L'animal autobiographique: autour de Jacques Derrida* (Paris: Galilée, 1999).

12. Derrida, *Animal*, 47 (I am interfering with Derrida's syntax here to make my point).

13. Derrida, *Clang*, 12 [*Glas*, 12].

14. See my discussion of Genet's interpretation of the tattoo as heraldry, in 'Effluvial Exhalations: Genet's Ontological Quandary', in *Tattooed Bodies: Theorizing Body Inscription Across Disciplines and Cultures*, ed. James Martell and Erik Larsen (London: Palgrave, 2022), 285–303. See also Jean Genet, *Miracle of the Rose*, trans. Bernard Frechtman (New York: Grove Press, 1966), 185–7.

15. A further reason for my attachment to the word 'escutcheon' is related to its etymology. As Webster tells us, it is derived from 'Middle English *escochon*, from Anglo-French *escuchoun*, from Vulgar Latin *scution-*, *scutio*, from Latin *scutum*, shield – more at ESQUIRE'. Like a coat of arms, a squire carries a shield, to protect from attack, to protect symbolically or actually the vulnerability of the flesh. But the squire I'm thinking of is the one nicknamed as such in the quintessential popular culture (or was it high culture?) skit from *Monty Python* ('Evening Squire ... know what I mean, know what I mean, nudge, nudge, know what I mean, say no more'), which stages so beautifully the operation of *double entendre* with erotic overtones.

16. Jacques Derrida, *The Post Card, from Socrates to Freud and Beyond*, trans. Alan Bass (Chicago: University of Chicago Press, 1987), 111. This, and other possible modifications of the Bass translation, are discussed below. Cf.: '*et après le coup de téléphone, je te tournerai le dos pour dormir, comme d'habitude, et tu te colleras contre moi, en me donnant la main, tu m'envelopperas*', Derrida, *La carte postale* (Paris: Aubier-Flammarion, 1980), 122. Further references to *The Post Card* will appear in the text.

17. Cf. David Wills, *Dorsality: Thinking Back Through Technology and Politics* (Minneapolis: University of Minnesota Press, 2008), esp. 3–16, 154–9, 197–202.

18. Ibid., 9.

19. Emmanuel Levinas, *Totality and Infinity*, trans. Alphonso Lingis (Pittsburgh, PA: Duquesne University Press, 1969), 86, 291.

20. Ibid., 259, 263.

21. For the reading of Levinas, see Wills, *Dorsality*, 42–63.

22. Carl Schmitt, *The Concept of the Political*, trans. George Schwab (Chicago: University of Chicago Press, 1996), 32. See my discussion in *Dorsality*, 133–7, further developed in Wills, *Inanimation* (Minneapolis: University of Minnesota Press, 2016), 179–90.

23. See Wills, *Dorsality*, 177–91.

24. Ibid., 158–9, 197–202.

25. The back/ground to everything developed here is a series of renditions of a blues song called 'Spoonful': as first recorded by Willie Dixon in 1960, then by Cream in 1968, and finally by the Kronos Quartet in 1993. They can be heard in any order, but in fact they are *heard* in competition with my *visual* reading of the escutcheon. Ideally, one would spoon the other; music nestling into writing. The lyrics begin like this: 'It could be a spoonful of coffee / It could be a spoonful of tea / But one little spoon / Of your precious love / Is good enough for me / Men lie about that spoonful / Some cry about that spoonful / Some die about that spoonful / Everybody fight about a spoonful / That spoon, that spoon / That spoonful ...'.

26. See repeated reference to her 'determination', and passages such as 175–6. I tried to account for the logic of this 'determination' in the context of 'adestination', in chapters 3 and 4 of Wills, *Matchbook: Essays in Deconstruction* (Stanford, CA: Stanford University Press, 2005); see especially 46–51, 61–8.

27. I am again taking a slight liberty with Derrida's syntax. The English translation has 'Let everything become a postcard again' (which could also be 'let everything revert to being a postcard'), for *que tout redevienne carte postale*, which has the sense of either the invocation chosen by Alan Bass, or the more straightforward subordination ('although everything may have reverted to being a postcard') that I am working from here. Cf. Derrida, *Carte postale*, 89.

28. Derrida, *On Touching*, 229. In quotes from *On Touching*, the translation is sometimes slightly modified.

29. Ibid., 245–6.

30. Ibid., 113. Incidentally, these lines follow two paragraphs where it is a question of 'the telephonic caress, if not the (striking) phone call' [*la caresse téléphonique, sinon du coup de téléphone*] (*On Touching*, 112–13; *Le toucher*, 130). The reference to an intruder – and Derrida's discussion more generally – alludes to Nancy's reflection on his heart transplant. See Nancy, *L'Intrus*, trans. Susan Hanson (East Lansing: Michigan State University Press, 2002); *L'Intrus* (Paris: Galilée, 2000).

31. Derrida, *On Touching*, 229.

32. Ibid., 179.

33. Ibid.

34. Ibid., 223.

35. Ibid., emphasis added.

3

Two Pirouettes: The Politics of Spoiling (for) Fun in Preciado's Revolutionary Vitalism and Derrida's Death Drive

Eszter Timár

Here, Freud pirouettes curiously.
(Jacques Derrida)[1]

Thanks to a facetious metaphysical pirouette, the dildo precedes the penis.
(Paul B. Preciado)[2]

Writing for a volume on erotics of deconstruction based in part on Derrida's engagement with *Beyond the Pleasure Principle* as marked by Freud's work of mourning over the loss of his beloved daughter, might, I fear, suggest that I'm into spoiling fun. This is especially in light of the fact that here I will consider 'To Speculate – On "Freud"' not so much as the text adjacent to the flaming hot 'Envois', in *The Post Card*, but more as the first missive from the material of Derrida's seminar, *Life Death* to the world of publications. In Derrida's reading, death and mourning weave through Freud's discussion of what might be outside of the limits hitherto marking the study of the psyche, the limits of pleasure. My other key text for this chapter is Paul B. Preciado's *Countersexual Manifesto*, a volume which appeared in French in 2000 and was published (based on the 2002 Spanish translation) in English almost twenty years later at Columbia University Press whose website characterises the volume as 'an outrageous yet rigorous work of trans theory, a performative literary text, and an insistent call to action'.[3] The introduction – written by Preciado for the English publication – provides the theoretical framework for the manifesto and places at its centre as the representative figure of revolutionary, progressive sexual politics, condensed in a queer visual joke, the figure of the pirouetting dildo. Importantly, the pirouette confers this revolutionary honour via

Preciado's deployment of Derridean supplementarity: the dildo is prosthesis incarnate.[4]

It is the figure of the pirouette that prompts this chapter because in 'To Speculate – On "Freud"', Derrida, in describing Freuds multilayered discourse of the return, offers the figure of a pirouetting Freud as he comments on Freud's introduction of the well-known scene of the *fort/da* featuring his grandson, Ernst, playing with a spool. I am interested in the ways these pirouetting figures, revolving around revolution, pleasure, questions of life, virility and death can tell us about our theoretical limits in thinking progressively about sexuality and in being affected by the deconstruction of life and death. In what follows, I will provide an exposition of Preciado's volume that shifts a gender revolution from the discourse of sexuality with ties to the dyke culture of Western modernity to claiming a trans revolution through the central figure of the dildo. After suggesting that the pirouetting dildo is a version of the Derridean marionette (a composite figure of anxieties concerning sovereignty), I will contrast it with Derrida's reading of Freud's theory of the death drive which draws on the biology of reproduction and death. My purpose will be to suggest that the celebration of the manifesto as a revolutionary text for trans theory relies on a contemporary tendency within feminist theory to embrace a certain vitalist discourse of affective ontology to distance itself from the linguistic turn. This celebration is based on a broader and earlier tendency of Anglophone feminist theory to draw on deconstruction only within certain limits: i.e. that deconstruction is useful for the gendered critique of patriarchy and its culture and language but that it has not much to offer when it comes to the thought of life in the conventional sense. Derrida's reading of Freud in 'To Speculate ...', on the contrary, provides a theoretically crucial deconstruction of the conventional opposition between life and death whose gendered aspects suggests that Freud's text, despite Preciado's claims that psychoanalysis is wholly inscribed in the logic of heteropatriarchy, is a resource for resisting this logic.[5]

Countersexual Manifesto is spun around the idea of the revolutionary dildo relying on the poststructuralist feminist queer theories at the time of its writing (Judith Butler, Donna Haraway, Monique Wittig) and framing its intervention as a Foucauldean resistance to 'the disciplinary production of sexuality in our liberal societies'.[6] Representing a theoretical-political (but proudly 'not academic') voice of the ongoing queer and trans revolution, its introduction routinely posits psychoanalysis as a homogenous discourse invested in the disciplinary production of sexuality. Psychoanalysis, a 'modern narrative of heterocapitalist colonialism',[7] is treated as a master discourse of gender oppression in the service of everything the

TWO PIROUETTES   55

revolutionary dildo is supposed to threaten. When Freud or Lacan are evoked, it is in order to refute them (even Butler is cited as if their work were in agreement with the simple refutation of Freud).[8]

The English translation shares important tendencies with some of contemporary cultural theory interested in what we could think of as Deleuze-inspired vitalism. I am thinking of strands of affect theory and feminist theory concerned with material immanence and a Spinozist conception of affect (embraced for its privileging affects increasing the capacity for action) according to a conventional concept of life that is self-evidently separable from death.[9] Indeed, its publication in Columbia University Press's 'Critical Life Studies' series places the volume in a certain scholarship on life associated with the theory of biopolitics or different engagements with the life sciences, including Darwin's work: what Elizabeth Grosz, a thinker whose work has consistently engaged with this legacy, refers to as 'the philosophy of life'.[10] Resonating well with these contemporary tendencies (taking hold around the time Preciado wrote the text) to prioritise affect increasing the potential to act, pleasure is the dildo's *raison d'être* and I am suggesting that this resonance does not only allow for the placement of the volume in the philosophy of life but also for its celebration of inciting a trans revolution. Its revolutionariness lies in part of what the dildo is doing to phallic pleasure: dismantling its hold on bodies. Countersexual practices reconfigure our bodies by creating new, countersexual pleasure centres while the 'genitals must be deterritorialized'.[11] The anus is such a centre: 'a "universal" erogenous center situated beyond the anatomical limits imposed by sexual difference', therefore outside of reproduction.[12] In Preciado's discourse, here more Deleuzean than Foucauldean in its rhetoric of vitalist, incessantly productive, immanent machinicity, the capacity for pleasure is considered a property of being a live body and the countersexual revolution harnesses this capacity in order to turn it against the tyranny of sexual difference. In the introduction, Preciado characterises his manifesto as 'the angry and impertinent response to the heterocolonial castration of the living being's radical multiplicity and forms of production of desire and pleasure'.[13]

At the same time, Derridean deconstruction plays an important role in Preciado's thinking in order to establish the dildo as a supplement that conceptually precedes anything that can be posited as the phallus. Preciado follows Judith Butler's interests in deconstruction in their early work on gender performativity: he cites several of those early texts by Derrida focusing on the deconstruction of the primacy of speech over writing ('... That Dangerous Supplement ...', 'Plato's Pharmacy', 'Signature, Event, Context') that have been cited in general in queer feminist theory when a certain indebtedness to deconstruction is expressed mainly because of the influence of the idea of performativity in this scholarship.[14] While this selection of texts does not always signal a concomitant resistance to psychoanalysis, as *Countersexual Manifesto* exemplifies, it can certainly function along with the political project of 'opposing psychoanalysis' as part of enacting revolutionary change committed to antipatriarchal struggle. Interestingly, what makes the manifesto's Derridean arguments on the prosthetic character of the dildo tolerable by the more vitalist parts of Preciado's toolkit is a certain consensus within feminist and queer theory about these texts in his theoretical combination that also includes Foucauldean and Deleuzean traits. According to this consensus, these texts, relevant for thinking about sex and gender, are about language and culture with no bearing for the thought about 'life' or the 'materiality' of embodiment.[15]

To be clear, I'm not interested here in scrutinising *Countersexual Manifesto* for the rigour of Preciado's treatment of any of the theories it shores up here in order to provide a political explanation for the hilarious pamphlet material within the manifesto: the countersexual contract and the sample exercises for bringing down colonial heteropatriarchal capitalism in the privacy of your home. Instead, I find it notable for its treatment of the lineage of texts it cites as being indebted to (Butler, Derrida, Foucault, Haraway, Wittig, even Deleuze[16]) as political resources, despite their argumentative-discursive differences: the fact that these 'authors', or rather, their texts, do not necessarily agree with each other is simply irrelevant here. We could consider this as part of the genre of manifestos as texts written to incite leaving the world of texts for engaging in action.[17] At the same time, we could also view this as the way in which these theoretical ('academic') texts may complement each other from the point of view of a feminism with a queer sensibility. Anglophone feminist theory since at least the 1990s has been engaging with theories of sexuality, and arguably the contributions of some of its most influential authors (such as Butler or Eve Sedgwick) have also greatly influenced queer studies. This queer feminist position seems to have shifted recently from a feminism with a sensibility for sexuality to a trans-friendly feminism (in other words, from a concomitant interest in sexual identity based on orientation to one in identification or what has been increasingly referred to as 'gender identity').[18] I am suggesting that the manifesto is a particularly salient textual example for both the terms for this shift and for orchestrating a version of this shift. In order to show this, I am drawing on what Robin Maltz – another queer feminist writer – called 'dyke discourse'. In Maltz's 'dyke discourse', 'daddy' is the same masculine figure as Butler's butch and Feinberg's stone butch: always

TWO PIROUETTES   57

in relation to a femme while in the same instance claiming to be the proper of dykeness.[19] Indeed, much of the queer feminist theoretical background Preciado places in action in his volume comes from Butler and Wittig.[20]

Dyke discourse is evoked in the manifesto in a number of ways. For a feminist readership with a keen interest in queer or trans politics, the figure of the dildo inevitably conjures scenes of dykedom and this is enhanced by Preciado's gesture of citing Wittig destabilising the conventional association between femaleness and lesbianism. 'I don't have a vagina', Preciado quotes Monique Wittig, who anecdotally said this at a feminist conference.[21] He also cites the well-known phrase from *The Straight Mind* – 'lesbians are not women' – and instead of addressing the relations between these formulations, he treats them as equivalent statements.[22] Could we read the complicated set of differences between these quotations as marking the shift I mentioned above from a feminism with a sensibility towards women's (homo)sexuality to a more trans-oriented theory? Consider for a second the shifts between state to possession, between a plural common noun and the first person singular, and between 'women' and 'vagina'. A vagina is something a dyke might say she/they(/he?) does not have and a dildo is something they might very much have. Dykes very much have dildos, it's theirs. But it's theirs as a dildo whose essence, so to speak, is a free detachability and attachability. The dildo is infinitely appropriable and therefore, according to Preciado, it represents everything that undermines the contemporary regime of phallic property.

Dyke discourse is also evoked by the second section of the book, 'Countersexual Reading Practices', featuring a poetic praise or hagiography of butchness entitled 'Prosthesis, Mon Amour' spanning the final eight pages before a quick author's note calling for a queer deconstruction of gender at the end of the volume. Although 'Prosthesis, Mon Amour' comes at the end of the book, it demonstrates very clearly that embracing the feminist valorisation of the butch as a seductive figure of innermost dissidence (as opposed to conceiving of the butch, as in the straight mind, as enacting a counterfeit performance emulating proper masculinity) provides Preciado with the stuff of his figure of the dildo. Consider the following series of citations from 'Prosthesis, Mon Amour' that show the indebtedness of this particular amalgam and suggest that the figure of the butch and the dildo may perhaps be interchangeable: 'Daughter of a postmetaphysical era, she became a technology thief when she realized that the gesture of the hand, the use of tools, and the knowledge of machines are not naturally linked to a single male or female essence', the 'butch made herself', and '[s]he is colder than war, harder than stone', while '[h]er body, both denied and magnified, is fucked without being penetrated and penetrates without fucking'.[23] Moreover, '[l]ike Monique Wittig, she had no vagina. Her sex was not genital. Her body was not the anatomical object of gynecology or endocrinology.'[24]

All this renders the butch radically transposable, which, in turn, guarantees her revolutionary status:

> At first, the butch was just an inversion of gender put in service of the femme (the butch was the 'perfect boyfriend,' the 'Prince Charming' all the girls dreamed of). Then she escaped the constraints of heterosexuality and pushed her transformation to its limit to liberate herself from her apparent telos: the male body.[25]

However, surprisingly, given the almost compulsory melancholic isolation suffusing the butch in much of 'dyke discourse' from Radclyffe Hall to Leslie Feinberg, Preciado's butch is full of productive life force:[26]

> That is the specificity of the butch: her productive desire, her spunk. When everything seemed to suggest that a tomboy was merely playing at masculinity, compensating for something that was 'lacking,' the butch takes the initiative and fabricates bodies.[27]

The politics of the dildo is elaborated in the first section entitled 'Theories', in the chapter on what Preciado names as 'Derridean' aspects of the dildo (also echoed in the title of the chapter on the butch). Here the dildo is considered as prosthesis in the supplementary sense of prosthetics: that is, as an imitation, the supplement both substitutes for and extends that which it is appended to or in place of. The 'normative referent' of the dildo is of course the 'erect penis' that gains the seal of authenticity of sex that is present by excluding other figures of embodied sexuality: 'Although the erect penis claims to be a self-presence that is immediate and authentic to itself, this self-identity is contaminated by what it tries to exclude: the flaccid penis, the clitoris, the vagina, the anus – and the dildo.'[28] This quotation prepares the claim that the dildo is an example of the Derridean 'dangerous supplement'. The deconstruction of the penis–dildo opposition will enable Preciado to suggest, as readers familiar with deconstruction in the wake of Butler's work are prepared to hear, that the derivative term conceptually precedes that which is posited as originary: writing, the mechanism of writing, the logic of the trace, is already 'present' in speech. According to the same logic of transposability, the dildo then will 'precede' the penis:

TWO PIROUETTES

The dildo adds only to replace. In the same way that the copy is the original's condition of possibility and that the supplement can supply only insofar as it produces what it is supposed to supplement, the dildo, the apparent plastic representative of a natural organ, retroactively produces the original penis ... Thanks to a facetious metaphysical pirouette, the dildo precedes the penis.[29]

However, as supplement (as copy and as condition of possibility), the dildo is not bound to the penis and within a few pages we read that 'anything can become a dildo. All is dildo. Even the penis.'[30]

As these examples show, the bond between the dildo and the penis is at least double: their likeness appears to be at the same time due to similarity and some sense of absolute opposition.[31] The dildo, as one of the 'excluded others' of figures of sexual embodiment, becomes the best revolutionary representative and most agential guerilla fighter upending the straight mind because of this privileged bond of multiple filiations between these two figures. All this is condensed in the hilarious image of the pirouetting dildo. The resonance between the manifesto's jacked-up butch and its dildo provides an air of avant-garde, indie, progressive buoyancy as the text performs the following double gesture: it renders the butch–dildo virile and lively while quasi-severing it from the rhetoric of femininity. After being liberated from her 'telos: the male body' as one of the quotes above suggests, the butch dildo is set free from femininity and dyke discourse as well.

Before I go on to pirouetting Freud, let me suggest here a link between Preciado's spunky butch dildo and Derrida's discussion of the marionette. Derrida's marionette, a figure that already appears in 'Typewriter Ribbon' and 'Faith and Knowledge', receives its most extensive treatment in the eighth session of *The Beast and the Sovereign Vol. I*, announcing a focus on the idea of the phallus, as a figure of sovereignty.[32] It is then immediately considered as at least a double figure comprising 'two arts of the marionette', where these arts are linked to sexual difference: inscribed in a general language of artifice and machinery, representing an uncanny hovering between animation and lifelessness, the marionette evokes the feminine in the figure of the figurine. Then, Derrida suggests that the 'phallus is itself originally a marionette'.[33] Taking as the point of departure the ancient Greek symbol of the ithyphallic symbol of power and autonomy carried around at public events, he discusses the phallus as the 'prosthetic representation of the penis in permanent erection, a penis that is hard, stiff, and rigid but detached from the body proper'.[34] Moreover, Derrida explicitly mentions that this is a 'male or female phallus'.[35] On the one hand perhaps because of the double nature of the marionette, on the other hand also because of this prosthetic detachability. Suggesting that erection, as that which the phallus represents in an image of eternal stiffness, is itself an automatic, machinic phenomenon outside the control of the subject (and thereby disallowing an interpretation according to which only the phallus but not the erect penis would be 'marionettiform'), Derrida asks:[36]

> if the phallus is automat and not autonomous, if there is something in its stiffness and hardness that is machinelike or mechanical, already in itself prosthetic, and that withdraws it from human responsibility, is it proper to man or else, already cut from man, is it a 'something,' a thing, an a-human, inhuman what, which is, moreover, scarcely more masculine than feminine?[37]

Clearly Preciado's dildo is very much like a marionette with its prosthetic, phallic stiffness, its detachability and machinic 'thingness'. Its manic spunk resonates with what Derrida calls the logic of sovereignty of reaching for a height superseding any conceivable high, 'toward the greatest and the highest but also, through a hyperbolic and irrepressible upping of the ante'.[38] This is because the essence of sovereignty is 'excess, hyperbole, an excess insatiable for the passing of every determinable limit'.[39] This excessive reaching beyond a certain limit is performed by severing the dildo's ties from dyke discourse but in this performance of severing, the connection is also necessarily affirmed. In other words, this gendered play of sexual difference is a necessary aspect of the dildo as a marionette.[40] There is more. When, a little earlier, Derrida enquired into the difference between the two marionettes, the '[feminine] beast and the [masculine] sovereign', and between the 'who and the what' of the marionette, and between the 'two arts' or the 'two fables' (reason and poetry) of the marionette, he says the following: 'The difference between the two would be, perhaps, almost nothing, scarcely the time or the turn of the breath, the difference of a breath, the turning of a scarcely perceptible breath.'[41] The turn of breath: the beginning and end of life suggests again that the marionette is a figure between life and death.[42] The prosthetic dildo is such a composite figure where the different positions in terms of sexual difference, the difference between it being a subject or an object, of being or not being animate (butch-dildo) and the difference between it belonging to the reason or the poetry of sovereignty (evoking also the difference between machine and event) are all pirouetting, turning over, 'breath'.[43]

The dildo as a pirouetting marionette and its being funny (dildo with a tutu?), is my cue to link 'To Speculate – on "Freud"'. While 'Freud's

TWO PIROUETTES   61

legacy' is not the only text where Derrida uses the term 'pirouette',
or even in *The Post Card*, the term here connects the two texts in an
uncanny way.[44] Here it is Freud who is pirouetting, who comes full circle
standing on one foot having raised the other in in anticipation of finding
a secure enough spot to advance his attempts at working out what we
might be able to know about the part of our psychic composition that
lies outside of what he considers the purview of the pleasure principle.
The 'pirouette' refers to Freud's decision to suddenly drop his preceding
hypotheses about dreamwork and traumatic neuroses and, in returning
to his point of departure, introduce his famous thoughts on children's
play. It is this pirouette that ushers in Ernst and the scene of the *fort/da*.

   The limits of the pleasure principle are in part introduced with the
help of this scene in which he observes his grandson Ernst playing with
a wooden spool, throwing it over his bed and retrieving it repeatedly
with the help of the string attached to it. As Freud explains, this is a
'complete' version of an activity Ernst frequently occupied himself with
in various forms. Freud here surmises that Ernst is compelled to throw
toys away in order to deal with the otherwise unexpressed distress felt
over his mother leaving home from time to time: to make the frustration
manageable, he designs an activity that helps him feel he controls the situation. Before inventing the game with the spool, Ernst throws his toys,
scattering them all over the place, but with no string to pull them back
with, he is relying on the adults around him to gather them. Freud points
out that this seems to betray the idea of playing with the toys, and later
with regards to the complete version with the spool, he remarks that this
was also not an ordinary game, since it was a compulsive activity with
a specific use. Apparently, the boy does not treat toys in the way that
deserves to be called a game; instead, he is after gaining a specific kind of
satisfaction inscribed in loss. And perhaps the most poignant passages of
'To Speculate …' are those in which Derrida, as mentioned above, listens
to *Beyond* as also inscribed in loss: the loss of Sophie, Freud's daughter
and Ernst's mother, who died a few years after we see Ernst throwing
his spool, at the time of finalising the manuscript of *Beyond*. As Derrida
points out, when Freud discusses Sophie's death (in a footnote in *Beyond*
or in private correspondence), he tends to hide or skip acknowledging their filial bond, thus repeating in a certain manner his grandson's
game with the spool. Sophie haunts *Beyond*, and a wish for her return,
both Ernst's and Freud's, renders it a text 'scanned by a rhetoric of the
"*zurück*"'.[45]

   To some extent, pirouetting Freud and the pirouetting dildo feel
funny in similar ways. They are animated by a certain carnivalesque the-
atricality of counterfeit performance (the dildo masquerading as the real

deal, and Freud unable to assume the mastery of the properly scientific theorist). But these pirouettes are also very different: Preciado's dildo is pirouetting as it is overflowing with irreverent spunk, its spin is full of life as well as machinic productivity. Freud's pirouette, however, serves to make space for death, loss and mourning as primary when thinking about life: what is beyond the pleasure principle is marked by loss both in terms of Freud's own work of mourning for the loss of his daughter Sophie, who is also Ernst's mother, and in terms of working towards the idea of the death drive.

The thought of the death drive is in part haunted by Sophie and indebted to her disappearance. Importantly for linking this thought to that of sexual difference and filiation, Sophie is not just an offspring or a parent, she is a daughter and a mother. As Derrida suggests, in some respects she also represented Freud's mother, based on the relational similarity between Ernst and Freud concerning their younger brothers. Freud's pain is rendered legible in Derrida's commentary on the textual choices he makes in discussing this loss. In *Beyond*, the personal relation to Ernst and Sophie and acknowledging Sophie's passing appear only in one footnote, and, similarly, in his private correspondence Freud subtracts his own filial relation to the deceased: 'snatched away from glowing health, from her busy life as a capable mother and loving wife, in four or five days, as if she had never been'.[46] 'There is a mute daughter', is Derrida's opening sentence at the beginning of the middle section in 'Freud's Legacy', and we can hear Freud's filial-affective relation being muted (even if her presence is in fact conjured in *Beyond* in the memory of Freud discussing Ernst's game with her in agreement).[47] 'Dead silence about death', opens the middle section in the next chapter, 'Paralysis', where Derrida is reading Freud's discussion of biology and death.[48] The affective-poetic charge resonating between these uncomplicated and punchy opening sentences suggest a link between the maternal/filial feminine and death.[49] The loss of the maternal feminine prompts and permeates the game of the *fort/da* in its complete (the spool) and incomplete (scattering toys) forms. Derrida also raises the possibility (even if he dismisses it at the same time) that the skirted bed as the hymen of the *fort/da* may also figure Sophie.[50] Her disappearance shapes both the game of *fort/da* and the final text of *Beyond*.[51] This loss is a painful case of the *usteron proteron* [sic], where the one who came after as the supplement in reproduction disappears first; where the child comes to haunt the mourning parent. It is in the same instance the loss of the favourite child and is a figural representation of the 'mid-mourning' that is the condition of possibility of filiation as such.[52] Filiation may in fact at least in part be the ongoing mid-mourning of the loss of the maternal feminine. In sum, Sophie is the maternal/filial

TWO PIROUETTES 63

feminine on the one hand and the death drive on the other, precipitating Ernst's desire to conquer feelings of loss conjuring the return on the one hand and the pleasure principle to ensure survival in the service of return. All the above is condensed in Freud's pirouette.

Importantly for an interest in 'critical life studies' or the philosophy of life, Freud's speculations about the life drives or the pleasure principle and the death drive very much engage with biology: 'To Speculate ...' reads Freud's *Beyond* as informing Derrida's analysis of François Jacob's theoretical work on biology, *The Logic of Life*, during the seminar on life death. For Freud, this engagement with biology helps construct his framework in which the counter-intuitively enigmatic death drive and the pleasure principle work in a tense tandem (and we see the similarly tense collaboration between the pleasure principle and the reality principle). Derrida emphasises that these nested antagonistic forces in Freud's text work together in a metaphorical discourse of the vesicle. The vesicle is a unit of life (not necessarily only biological but it is also the minimal structure of the idea of the biological organism), endowed with a birth and a death: 'the protoplasmic bulb, with its cortical layer, must protect itself against excitations coming from the outer world, must amortize them, sort out the messages –, filter them, limit their quantity of energy'.[53] Referring to biology, *Beyond* suggests that the return-bound struggle for survival is not to avoid death but to avoid death that is not proper to it. The pursuit of ongoing survival is finding one's own death. In other words, to be conceived of as an autonomous unit of life, the organism needs to be able to have its own proper death. Death here is not beyond life or outside of life: it is a feature of life. The pleasure principle in its heterogeneous entwinement with the reality principle will develop a stiffness in order to become more vivacious, more robust in fending off the other who brings death that is now one's own.[54]

While Freud and Preciado consider the living body in similar terms: being embodied means to have the capacity to be energised and the management of this energy, in a technical-chemical manner, will be guided by the aim of experiencing pleasure. In going beyond, however, Freud's speculations consider the binding that takes place in secondary processes as endemic to the development of the pleasure principle and further on still, the reality principle is considered as an auxiliary extension of the pleasure principle serving the purpose of the return to a state of energetic homeostasis. Even more perplexingly, the pleasure principle is conceived as a tendency working in the service of a return to a homeostatic state in the midst of ongoing excitations through their management. This, in turn, is a *telos* that represents another end: the return of organised life to an inorganic state:

We have found that one of the earliest and most important functions of the mental apparatus is to bind the instinctual impulses which impinge on it, to replace the primary process prevailing in them by the secondary process and convert their freely mobile cathectic energy into a mainly quiescent (tonic) cathexis ...

[...] The pleasure principle, then, is a tendency operating in the service of a function whose business it is to free the mental apparatus entirely from excitation or to keep the amount of excitation in it constant or to keep it as low as possible ... [It] is clear that the function thus described would be concerned with the most universal endeavour of all living substance namely to return to the quiescence of the inorganic world. We have all experienced how the greatest pleasure attainable by us, that of the sexual act, is associated with a momentary extinction of a highly intensified excitation. The binding of an instinctual impulse would be a preliminary function designed to prepare the excitation for its final elimination in the pleasure of discharge.[55]

I have selected this long excerpt in part as it helps illustrate several of the stakes of Preciado's text. To begin with, at the end of the passage we can see a nice formulation of what Preciado sends the dildo to fight off or dismantle. Positing orgasmic pleasure in phallic terms as the epitome of pleasure as such (where pleasure takes place always in the most intense manner in a singular or at least countable instance) is a particularly salient example of what the *Countersexual Manifesto* sets out to counter as a certain political (heteropatriarchal, colonial, biopolitical) organisation of pleasure. However, as the preceding parts of the excerpt suggest, the conceptual resources of psychoanalysis are not exhausted by this phallic aspect.

In order to make this point, I suggest we connect the term 'tonic' in the first sentence with the concluding image of pleasure as a final elimination of discharge. 'Tonic' in English, French and German has two currents of meaning, one sometimes considered musical, the other biological and medicinal. Within the latter, we can differentiate between two senses, stretched by the curious tension of Derrida's notion of life death. 'Tonic' can indicate a sense of quieting down and even dormancy (often associated with bouts of paralysis) as well as having an invigorating effect. So 'mainly quiescent (tonic) cathexis' can be read as both dormant (or stiff) cathexis and invigorating cathexis. It is almost as if Freud felt that cathexis needs to be stiff to be invigorating (quite like a marionette, perhaps), which, in turn, in one instance suggests that some figure of death is necessary for the ongoing survival of anything that is alive, that life becomes more alive via its being subjected to stricture while also repeating the gesture of designating life in phallic terms. Importantly though, the text of *Beyond* also disidentifies with these phallic terms. If the pleasure principle is constructed in these phallic terms as that which intensifies and consolidates by binding, the death drive appears to have issued it in the name of the return. In addition, the *telos* of a 'final elimination of excitation' served by the 'the pleasure of discharge' sounds quite chilling. In this imagery, the theory of the death drive stages a complexly gendered relationship between the death drive and the pleasure principle where the terms of the former are inscribed according to the link between feminine filiation and death I discussed above: the pleasure principle itself may be conceived of as borne by a prior commitment within life itself to return its matter to death. Some of Freud's formulations, in fact, evoke a certain queer negativity. For instance, in his treatment of the idea of the natural death of any organism he offers the example of conjugative plasmid transfer among bacteria, outlining a hypothesis according to which the 'union with the living substance of a different individual ... [introduces] fresh "vital differences" which must then be lived off'.[56] I find Freud's language here particularly melancholic: he is describing the idea of reinvigoration as an additional, almost unwanted, burden or even a penetrative intrusion the organism is too weak to fend off. This melancholy sense of the death drive offers something like a resistance to phallicity, although it is not the resistance of 'countering' by the pirouetting dildo's return to the erect marionette of the phallus in a breath. Derrida's name for this 'dissidence' throughout *The Beast of the Sovereign Vol. I* is detumescence, the involution of sovereign phallicity: 'fall, falling off, detumescence, fall back toward the low' refers to an undoing of the marionette's phallic tendency towards hyperbolic heights.[57] If we allow for the possibility of reading Freud's thoughts about binding pleasure with respect to its intensification not only as a discourse of maturation but also in terms of its innuendos, we arrive at a text governed by a certain melancholy queer leather aesthetic.[58]

'To Speculate ...' is a text that troubles both the convenient treatment of deconstruction as a merely linguistic enquiry uninterested in live embodiment and the convenient treatment of psychoanalysis as in complete identification with the discourse of phallic authority. It gives us a hesitatingly speculative Freud, pirouetting from the traumatised soldiers to the wounded ego of his grandson ending up with the death drive in a series of rhetorical constructions that feature the maternal-filial as both life-giving and associated with death, but then also introducing in the idea of tonicity as a certain figure of life death where these terms, life and death, are not in an opposition to each other and where phallicity and a certain resistance to its claim to sovereign dominance is necessarily intertwined.

I started this chapter with my worry about spoiling fun, and indeed spoiling fun provides it with something like a throughline: Ernst is spoiling fun by spooling according to his own compulsive game – instead of having real fun – and Freud is spoiling fun when he designates the seeking of pleasure in the service of a backward search for death as a primary force of life. Preciado is spoiling (heteropatriarchal) fun while also spoiling for the exuberant fun offered by the priapic dildo whose vitalist spunk ends up inflating the phallicity of the marionette with no relief of detumescence. I hope I have shown that the composite gesture of referring to deconstruction as a legitimising theoretical domain (according to a legacy of queer feminist theory which conceives of deconstruction as indifferent with regards to the question of the materiality of life, or the 'philosophy of life') and the rhetorical injection of vitality into the figure of the butch dildo run the risk of repeating what it sets out to counter.

Notes

1. Jacques Derrida, 'To Speculate – On "Freud"', *The Post Card: From Socrates to Freud and Beyond*, trans. Alan Bass (Chicago and London: Chicago University Press, 1987), 257–409, 297.
2. Paul B. Preciado, *Countersexual Manifesto*, trans. Kevin Gerry Dunn (New York, Columbia University Press, 2018), 67.
3. See http://cup.columbia.edu/book/countersexual-manifesto/978023117 5630 (accessed 22/12/2023).
4. Consider the title for Jack Halberstam's preface, 'We Are the Revolution! Or, the Power of the Prosthesis', ibid., ix.
5. 'To Speculate ...' is closely based on Derrida's seminar, *Life Death*, eds Pascale-Anne Brault and Peggy Kamuf, trans. Pascale-Anne Brault and Michael Naas (Chicago: University of Chicago Press, 2020). Dawn McCance introduces the notion of life death as follows: 'Derrida chooses the title La vie la mort ... not in order to suggest either that life and death are not two, or that one is the other, but rather that the difference at stake between the two is not of a positional (dialectical or nondialectical) order.' Dawn McCance, *The Reproduction of Life Death: Derrida's La Vie La Mort* (New York: Fordham University Press, 2019), 11–12.
6. Preciado, *Countersexual*, 21.
7. Ibid., 7.
8. This is, of course, not the case. See for example Judith Butler, *The Psychic Life of Power: Theories in Subjection* (Stanford, CA: Stanford University Press, 1997) or *Precarious Life: The Powers of Mourning and Justice* (London: Verso, 2004).

9. See works by Rosi Braidotti (such as 'Affirmation, Pain and Empowerment', *Asian Journal of Women's Studies* 14.3 (2008), 7–36) or Elizabeth Grosz, *Becoming Undone: Darwinian Reflections on Life, Politics, and Art* (Durham, NC: Duke University Press, 2011).

10. Grosz, *Becoming Undone*, 14.

11. Preciado, *Countersexual*, 71.

12. Ibid., 30.

13. Ibid., 5.

14. While Butler's early work on gender, which in part inspired Preciado's work, is very much interested in what Freudian psychoanalysis has to say, it is interesting that the texts they use from Derrida in these works are not considered as having anything specific to say about sexual difference or feminism: these 'early works' are consulted for their insights about language and the performative.

15. While the work of Elizabeth A. Wilson might be considered of the same kind, it is important to note that Wilson does use biology in ways that seem to resonate with this sense of vitalism, but her consistent reliance on psychoanalysis across her volumes makes this question in her case more complicated.

16. Despite the fact that it offers a queer critique of the valorisation of homosexuality in the Deleuzean oeuvre, the volume otherwise relies on the Deleuzo-Guattarian lexicon of assemblage and desiring machines.

17. Let me note the brilliant exception of Cixous's manifesto calling on women to write, i.e. to engage in the political action of entering the world of texts. Hélène Cixous, 'The Laugh of the Medusa', *Signs* 1.4 (1976), 875–93.

18. See for example the following cluster of recent scholarship on the question on gender identity. Elizabeth Barnes, 'Gender without Gender Identity: The Case of Cognitive Disability', *Mind* 131.523 (2022), 838–64; Robin Dembroff, 'Beyond Binary: Genderqueer as Critical Gender Kind', *Philosophers' Imprint* 20.9 (2019), 1–31; Anca Gheaus, 'Feminism Without "Gender Identity"', *Politics, Philosophy & Economics* 22.1 (2023), 31–54; Jennifer McKitrick, 'A Dispositional Account of Gender', *Philosophical Studies* 172.10 (2015), 2575–89.

19. Robin Maltz, 'Toward a Dyke Discourse', *Journal of Lesbian Studies* 3.3 (1999), 83–92. Maltz's purpose in the article is to counter queer theory's purported androcentrism with placing the focus on queered femininity. The figure of the dyke daddy here is melodramatised as a lonesome rogue runaway whose 'femininity' or non-maleness renders its masculinity or androgyny exempt from patriarchy. How fascinating that this consistent figure of the runaway butch can centre both Maltz's call for a gynocentric critique of heteropatriarchy (referring to Elizabeth Grosz's work) and Preciado's work as a salient piece of trans theory. For Butler's butch see 'Imitation or Gender Insubordination', in *Inside/Out: Lesbian Theories, Gay Theories*, ed. Diana Fuss (New York and London: Routledge 1991), 13–31.

20. Perhaps there is also a healthy dose of butchness in Haraway's cyborg in terms of its close association with (solid) masculinity through the idea of (hard) machine and the sense of profound outlaw/revolutionary character.

21. Preciado, *Countersexual*, 183, n.69. Wittig's *The Straight Mind* opens, in Louise Turcotte's prologue, with a reference to the 1978 annual MLA conference in New York as the original utterance of what became 'The Straight Mind' in the volume (32). See Monique Wittig, *The Straight Mind and Other Essays* (Boston, MA: Beacon Press, 1992), 8. I also heard a version of this from a professor of mine sometime in the early 2000s. According to them, the sentence goes, 'I am a body that occupies the space of lesbian', and it was voiced at the 1987 conference entitled 'The Homosexuality, Which Homosexuality?' Interestingly, the quote Preciado provides is in French, indicating the possibility of either a third conference perhaps in France or its fantasy. What an afterlife of a series of events where someone said something (although it is unclear what was being said) and different versions of it circulate to create a filial network of bonds in the academic-political communities organised around queer feminism since the 1990s.

22. Ibid., 77.

23. Ibid., 168, 169, 171.

24. Ibid., 171.

25. Ibid., 168.

26. For the constitutive melancholy of the butch, see Heather Love's work, especially the chapters on Willa Cather and Radclyffe Hall in *Feeling Backward: Loss and the Politics of Queer History* (Cambridge, MA: Harvard University Press), 2007.

27. Preciado, *Countersexual*, 171.

28. Ibid., 66.

29. Ibid., 67.

30. Ibid., 66.

31. While the introduction treats the two terms interchangeably: 'If the penis (phallus) is the organic embodiment of this hegemonic tradition, the dildo is its cyborg other' (9), in these examples Preciado's dildo counters not the phallus but the penis because the 'dildo is not the phallus and does not represent the phallus because the phallus ... does not exist. The phallus is nothing but the phantasmic and political hypostasis of the penis within heteronormative patriarchal culture' (63). In (yet another) turn, Derrida's discussion of the phallus as a marionette, the very phenomenon of penile erection, is conceived of as a phallic marionette.

32. Jacques Derrida, 'Faith and Knowledge: The Two Sources of "Religion" at the Limits of Reason Alone', in *Acts of Religion*, ed. Gil Anidjar (New York: Routledge, 2002), 40–101, 83–4, 86; 'Typewriter Ribbon: Limited Ink (2)', in *Without Alibi*, ed. and trans. Peggy Kamuf (Stanford, CA: Stanford University Press, 2002), 71–160, 87, 158; *The Beast and the Sovereign, Vol. I,*

eds Michel Lisse, Marie-Louise Mallet and Ginette Michaud, trans. Geoffrey Bennington (Chicago: University of Chicago Press, 2009). The first two sources are texts concerning Derrida's distinction between machine on the one hand and event or miracle on the other.

33. Derrida, *Beast I*, 222.
34. Ibid.
35. Ibid.
36. Ibid. Derrida uses the term 'marionettiform' (223).
37. Ibid., 222.
38. Ibid., 256.
39. Ibid., 257.
40. While the connection between being butch and being a girl may be contentious, Derrida's gesture of delineating the marionette first in terms of a virgin femininity suggests a connection here: 'the association of the name goes more spontaneously, from the start, to the figure or figurine of a girl, of a virgin, since the name marionette comes first from a miniature representation of the Virgin Mary of "mariolette," a diminutive of "mariole"'. Ibid., 188.
41. Ibid., 218.
42. A lengthier analysis of Preciado's dildo as a vitalist marionette would involve reading together the texts cited in note 29 above, which would throw the connections between the machine, the event, poetry and vitalism into sharp relief.
43. For a discussion on sexual difference and the marionette, see Kelly Oliver's *Technologies of Life and Death: From Cloning to Capital Punishment* (New York: Fordham University Press, 2013). For an argument on the necessary impossibility to delineating the difference between the two forms of the marionette, see Apple Igrek, 'Prosthetic Figures: The Wolf, the Marionette, the Specter', *Environmental Philosophy* 16.1 (2019), 181–99.
44. Derrida employs the term 'pirouette' in several other texts. In 'The Double Session' he discusses linguistic signification, taking Mallarmé's use of the term. The term also occurs in *Spurs* and in 'Envois', both times in a sense of return in discussions in relation to death (linking it to femininity in *Spurs*) or suicide (in 'Envois'). See 'The Double Session', in *Dissemination*, trans. Barbara Johnson (Chicago: University of Chicago Press, 1981), 240–1; *Spurs: Nietzsche's Styles*, trans. Barbara Harlow (Chicago: University of Chicago Press, 1979), 47–9; *The Post Card*, 15.
45. Derrida, 'To Speculate ...', 362. *Zurück*, an adverb, means back or backwards (in the sense of direction) in German.
46. Ibid., 329.
47. Ibid., 306.
48. Ibid., 353.
49. See Elissa Marder, *The Mother in the Age of Mechanical Reproduction: Psychoanalysis, Photography, Deconstruction* (New York: Fordham University Press, 2013).

50. Derrida, 'To Speculate ...', 316.

51. On the multiple ways in which Sophie shapes the writing of *Beyond* (both alive, as she died after Freud's writing first draft of the work, and as a ghost) see Elizabeth Rottenberg 'At Witz End: Theory in a Time of Plague', *Derrida Today* 13.2 (2020), 210–16. See also David Farrell Krell, 'Pulling Strings Wins No Wisdom', *Mosaic* 44.3 (2011), 15–42.

52. Derrida, 'To Speculate ...', 335, 340. The name of the rhetorical device *hysteron proteron* has an etymological link to ancient Greek *ústéra*, connecting this sense of latter-ness to the womb, a privileged site of filiation. 'Mid-mourning' is Derrida's term for the deconstruction of the opposition between introjection and incorporation in the psychoanalytic literature on mourning. See Jacques Derrida, '*Fors*: The Anglish Words of Nicolas Abraham and Maria Torok', trans. Barbara Johnson, *The Georgia Review* 31.1 (1977), 64–116.

53. Ibid., 347.

54. I have referred to Derrida's discussion of the *hysteron proteron* before. The most cited illustration of this device comes from the *Aeneid* of Virgil: '*Moriamur, et in media arma ruamus*' ('Let us die, and charge into the thick of the fight'). In the light of Derrida's linking the mid-mourning of filiation to this literary device, I find it striking that the paradigmatic example of the *hysteron proteron* concerns the ideal of meeting one's own death. Applying the device and thereby reversing the order of temporality suggests that the call to die is the primary force framing the subsequent call to plunge into fight. In turn, this latter call appears first of all as a call to describe the kind of death we intend to find for ourselves instead of a patriotic call to defeat an enemy. *Hysteron proteron* flips the most phallic and violent figure of aggressive virility (armed soldiers ready to charge) into the current of the death drive. See 'Hysteron-proteron', *Encyclopædia Britannica*, ed. Hugh Chisholm, vol. 14 (11th edn) (Cambridge: Cambridge University Press, 1911), 212.

55. Sigmund Freud, *Beyond the Pleasure Principle*, trans. James Strachey (New York: W. W. Norton, 1961), 56.

56. Freud, *Beyond*, 55.

57. Let me note the difference between Preciado's notion of the 'flaccid penis' mentioned earlier and Derrida's detumescence. While for Preciado the flaccid penis becomes one of the oppressed sexual figures (arguably, different marionettes of sovereignty) lead by the dildo in this sexual insurgency, detumescence for Derrida in the seminar session on the marionette does not divorce the lack of erection from the figure of the phallus. Rather detumescence is the negative foil against which sovereignty may be erected, arguably its condition of possibility and may be considered part of the off and on pulsing of what Derrida in the second volume of the seminar calls survivance. On survivance (and its difference from life death), see Kas Saghafi, 'Dying Alive', *Mosaic* 48.3 (2015), 15–26.

58. A more dykey version of this aesthetic resonates in Lacan's discussion of the death drive as what organises the affective impact of the Antigone in Sophocles's tragedy. Elissa Marder suggested that we read Antigone, figure of entombed feminine filiation, as a butch. See Elissa Marder, 'Anti Antigone', *Diacritics* 49.2 (2021), 13–22.

4

DOUBLE BLIND DATE

Naomi Waltham-Smith

There is in literature, in the exemplary secret of literature, a chance of saying everything without touching upon the secret ... when there is no longer even any sense in making decisions about some secret behind the surface of a textual manifestation (and it is this situation which I would call text or trace), when it is the call [*appel*] of this secret, however, which points back to the other or to something else, when it is this itself which keeps our passion aroused, and holds us to the other, then the secret impassions us.
(Derrida, 'Passions')

Amuse-bouche

The Italian comedy *Perfetti sconosciuti* (2016), translated as *Perfect Strangers* for English audiences, has a simple conceit, which perhaps explains why in 2019 it took the record for the most remade film.[1] At a dinner party, seven old friends – three couples and one man whose date is ostensibly a no-show for reasons to do with sex revealed later – reluctantly agree to play a game proposed by the psychoanalyst hostess Eva whereby they all put their phones in the centre of the table. They are to read out all texts or emails, show any images received, and answer any calls on speaker-phone. The result is a series of embarrassing and increasingly devastating revelations. One of the women has secretly obtained a quote to put her mother-in-law in a care home, the hostess is getting a 'boob job' with another cosmetic surgeon even though her husband does this for a living, while he, despite frequently ridiculing her profession, has not told her that he's been in analysis for the last six months. It seems he's learned something from the process when he takes a call from their teenage daughter and shows emotional maturity in giving her fatherly advice on how to decide whether that night should be her 'first time'. We learn

DOUBLE BLIND DATE

that he's given her a pack of condoms and is more attuned to his daughter's evolving parental needs than his wife – who had lost her temper when she had found them, having searched through her daughter's bag. Eva is only able to see her daughter's burgeoning sexual desires through a clinical lens and struggles to provide the trusted place of challenge of a mother against which her daughter can define herself. Sex remains a theorised object whose approach is fraught with doubt.

Trust, dis- and mistrust, secrecy, suspicion and jealousy are recurring themes as the evening reveals a series of online flirtations, sexual infidelities, secret sexualities and uncritical prejudices (the last two of which explain the no-show). Seeing hidden sides of one another, the friends become strangers or blind dates to one another. The only person whose secret is kept is the analyst's, whose lover is among the guests, but she must silently endure the cruelty of discovering that he's having multiple affairs. *Perfetti sconsciuti* is reminiscent of other disastrous dinner party films, including *Who's Afraid of Virginia Wolf?* (1966), *The Exterminating Angel* (1962) and *The Party* (2017). Paolo Genovese's lightweight confection shares with Sally Potter's black-and-white black comedy about a newly promoted British Health Minister and London elites the secrets, revelations affairs, perfidious text, complicated pregnancies, emasculated husbands, strained friendships and culinary upsets, but the latter and the secrets it uncovers are much darker, as hinted at when a Chekhovian gun appears in an early scene when the husband of the three-timing late-to-arrive guest snorts coke in the lavatory. The setting, however, in a single residence with claustrophobic domestic spaces, provides opportunities for overlooking other guests though a window or hatch, and the symbolism of food devoured or ruined are all cut from a similar cloth. Both films render sex as suspicious as it is desirable. In short, sex, insofar as it is a pleasure, is constitutively also a problem, and above all, perhaps, a problem for philosophy whose sex-aversion is seemingly indexed to the power of sex.[2] It is in this undecidability that the deconstruction of eroticism and the eroticism of deconstruction plays out, not entirely unlike a comedic screenplay. In my remake that unfolds in several courses over the coming pages, though, the cast of deconstructive thinkers for dinner guests will put some pressure on and transform the ways in which the films configure the relation between sex and thought and in constellation with notions of secrecy, blindness and jealousy.

Perfetti sconosciuti and its remakes are set on the occasion of a lunar eclipse, which is a visual metonym for hiddenness and secrecy and provides an explanation of sorts for the strange evening that unfolds. At the end of the film, after the eclipse has passed, we learn that its events were in an alternative fictional reality that did not in fact take place because the analysand had objected to playing the game. In the Italian original, the husband Rocco, denies he has anything to hide when Eva challenges him on why he insisted on not playing. 'Because we're break-able', he explains, 'all of us, some more than others.' The mobile phone has become a 'black box' too perilous to play with. The film is thus ret-rospectively interpreted as a cautionary fable in the mode of the 'as if'. Nonetheless, Eva offers that he may look at her phone; there's no pin code. He compliments her on her new earrings, and it's unclear whether he's aware that they were a gift from their friend with whom she's been having a secret affair. However, in the French remake by Fred Cavayé, entitled *Le Jeu* and translated as *Nothing to Hide* for English audiences, there is a slightly different emphasis that does not rely on the fragility of people or relationships. 'Too bad we didn't play that phone game. It could have been fun', Marie muses. 'Fun?' Vincent queries. 'I doubt that.' She scoffs. He goes on: 'I don't care what's in your phone. In love, as in friendship, some things are best kept secret.' She looks at him slightly nervously, then wordlessly walks back into the apartment and we see her remove the earrings. He watches her, then looks over the bal-cony to see her lover Thomas about to get into his car, smiles, and waves him off, but then he pulls a slight grimace, as if he might already suspect or know. He then catches sight of an elderly couple embracing tenderly on a balcony opposite and smiles knowingly to himself.

Hors d'œuvre

What is the moral of this tale for deconstruction and its curiosity for and suspicion of eroticism? Vincent speaks of the need for secrecy in love not so much because the truth might break us but – and this is why the early scene with the mother snooping on her teenage daughter is so instructive – because of the necessary degree of autonomy and differ-entiation in relationships. Demands for total transparency, by contrast, come from a place of anxiety and co-dependence which kills not only trust but sexual desire as well and from which stems the urge to act out via affairs and secret online activity in a hapless bid to evade emotional fusion. But what of sex and secrecy? Isn't sex the (fantasy of) ultimate no-holds-barred fusion? What credit does deconstruction instead give to what is kept hidden in eroticism? While one might try to interpret the Italian original within the framework of a bureaucratic, deterministic attachment theory with its demands for 'good (enough) mothering', the French remake rejects the hypervigilance and ocularcentrism of certain strands of psychoanalysis, which embrace everything that Derrida rejects in the conventional dialectic of censoring secrecy and authoritarian transparency in favour of the talking cure's aural attention to what is hidden and invisible in the psyche.[3] The deconstruction of psychoanalysis, though, will also entail recognising that what resists analysis is nonetheless appropriated to the sphere of (psychoanalytic) reason and made analysable and conceptualisable *as a secret*.

Even more passionately than Derrida, Anne Dufourmantelle's provocative *Défense du secret* has the psychoanalyst 'cross over to the side of the secret', which dispenses with the boundaries between 'the solar and the nocturnal, speech and silence, intimate friend and others' and thus with the dialectical oppositions in which philosophy has presented the secret to itself (private/public, concealed/revealed, blindness as castration/visionary insight, and so on).[4] The goal of telling all on the couch, though, is not self-transparency, she argues, but to imagine the possibility of living otherwise 'like two instruments in an orchestra listening to each other work through an unknown score' (*DS* 20/4). This demands more displacement than revelation to make room for an intimacy with oneself, with all one's unspoken fantasies, that the era of social media and platform surveillance threatens to drown out with noise and jealousy in relationships.

> To respect the intimate space of the other is to make an alliance with the night without wanting to put an end to it, to imagine that light isn't the opposite of the dark but its most secret ally, and to recognize in the secret ... the opposite of a threat, the very condition of relation. (*DS* 20–1/4)

For Dufourmantelle, the secret is a *pharmakon* (*DS* 49–50/25–6), both carrying a 'potential charge of violence' (*DS* 63/35) and resembling a secret garden that is the reserve of our freedom and creative power. Psychoanalysis for its part, if it was once the excavation of secrets in the face of bourgeois repression, has come to resemble the social norms of the day. Psychoanalysis invented the unconscious, as a secret place set apart, to make sense of the secret of our desire. 'The lifting of secrets is its backroom [*officine*] – its passion, in a way', as Eva/Marie represents, and yet as her husband enjoins, this approach towards self-knowledge 'does not mean to succumb to a tyrannical desire to know everything' (*DS* 40/20).

If 'the secret begins with the body' or with *jouissance* (*DS* 71/41), it is because it is marked by an originary alterity and differentiation of which deconstruction has made itself the witness or guardian. Inappropriable, unpresentable *jouissance*, with its resistance to phenomenality and totalisation, is, for Derrida, the secret 'élan' of philosophy, what it sets apart, encrypts, (p)reserves, and all the same what drives its desire and haunts it insofar as it comes from the other. Dufourmantelle might almost be writing of philosophy's encounter with sex when she argues trenchantly:

> In an amorous encounter, we don't know exactly where the other is: The one who holds us in their arms escapes us in their thought and their daydreams. They're never entirely ours. To want to know everything about the other is a sickness [*maladie*] that slowly kills what it wants most to protect. (*DS* 79/45)

Eroticism is a set of approaches to this secret of desire, but one should be careful how close one gets. Dufourmantelle observes that if psychoanalysis has liberated us from unknown shackles of the unconscious, it also developed the tools to impoverish the interior world. 'This desiccation', Dufourmantelle wryly observes, chiming with the moral of *Perfetti sconosciuti*, 'might even be one of the principal reasons for undertaking analysis' (*DS* 139/96). It is, in part, for this reason that deconstruction brushes right up against psychoanalysis but not without a certain resistance, if only because psychoanalysis leaves the secret as only provisionally resisted or hidden (insofar as it yet be heard or made present to conscious), whereas deconstruction ruins the *telos* of analysis in advance with a notion of the absolute or unconditional secret. Whereas in psychoanalysis, as in *Perfetti sconosciuti* and its remakes, there are either no secrets or secrets that are 'negotiable', deconstruction discerns at the heart of philosophy's desire 'a resistance to the daylight of phenomenality that is radical, irreversible'.[5] To the reduction of a *poleros* that looks to philosophical truth or analytic reason to lift the veil of the passions of resistance or at least to undo the entangled knot of multiple resistances, Derrida in *Résistances de la psychanalyse* will counterpose the 'secret of literature'. At the very site of resistance, literature – which can say everything and yet retains the right not to respond – perhaps makes psychoanalysis 'sing' because it 'prefers not to' play the metaphysical game of desiring either a straightforwardly originary indivisible presence or the dialectical oppositionality between presence and non-presence that will readily resolve into it, and accordingly literature prefers not to engage in the dialectic of resistance and non-resistance that animates psychoanalysis.[6] Deconstruction resists and radicalises (resistance to this) desire.[7]

L'entrée

Imagine a dinner party with a number of deconstructionist friends, in which they are rendered as strange to one another as blind dates.

Blind Date is the title of Dufourmantelle's 2003 book about the long scheduled yet continuously postponed or missed meet-cute between sex and philosophy.[8] Among her fellow travellers and dinner guests who have also reflected on these themes are Derrida, Jean-Luc Nancy and Hélène Cixous, but we might also imagine two other guests in a bid to set them up at last, Sex and Philosophy, together with their matchmaker Psychoanalysis. There is also an absent eighth guest whose identity remains secret for now. What follows is not so much a remake as a deconstruction, nor does it purport to make any personal revelations or to speak of these philosophers' private sex lives or fantasies, only to say something about the secret or unacknowledged liaisons, suspicions and jealousies in their interwoven philosophising about eroticism and hence about how these exchanges themselves in their (un)veiling and invisible seeing perform something like an erotics of deconstruction.

Like sex, dinner parties are in need of preliminaries: introductions for guests who do not know one another, an aperitif, starters or antipasti, degassing a bottle of biodynamic wine, or decanting a full-bodied red. The preliminary is also the index of a secret affinity. Jean-Luc studied Anne from across the room. Evidently, he knew her work well, intimately, yet his expression gave nothing of that away. A close acquaintance would have spotted it instantly. 'Preliminaries' – that, after all, was her word that he'd echoed – adoringly remembered? – in Sexistence fourteen years later.[9] In his opening chapter entitled 'Preliminaries' only a handful of women are referenced, credited – Shoshana Felman, Marie-Hélène Bohner-Cante, Claire Nancy – and Dufourmantelle's own third chapter of the same title receives no mention. Whether suppressed or repressed, the reverberation of her voice and the blind or unconscious contact between the two texts are nonetheless unmistakable. They are so close he daren't approach her, but he keeps his distance, eyeing the untouchable from afar.

The issue is how sex – having it or not – allows itself to be thought, or doesn't. Even to think about sex means recognising that sex (necessarily) has 'its philosophical preliminaries, its margins, its surroundings, its subterranean periphery, its steep slope, its white lines', its 'a priori' approach, even if the pair constantly miss each other like ships in the night (BD 16–17/4). Philosophy is what makes it possible to think sex, and yet it is constantly cofounded by the elusive eventuality of what it has approached time and time again and yet studiously not submitted to conceptualisation, instead preferring to gawp.

On the one hand Nancy's text tactfully brushes up against Dufourmantelle's, but on the other hand it devours, even cannibalises the words for which it hungers. Like sex and philosophy, it's as if these two writers 'have been deliberately avoiding each other forever, who knows why; perhaps because they are of the same nature?' – both 'dangerous ... inflammable, corrupting, and socially subversive' and both 'deflected [*détournés*]' where desire is turned towards other ends that they incessantly dodge (*BD* 14/3). Both Nancy and Dufourmantelle seek to conceptualise the tactful approach of preliminaries. He likens sex's (pre)liminaries to seductive blandishments in which 'one approaches, one considers, one scents, one lets oneself be approached, brushed, and stroked in the various senses of that word' (*Sex* 11/1). And philosophy, she tells us, is 'an art of touching', specifically insofar as it lacks a tactile surface or nerve endings, the 'art of touching concepts' (*BD* 28–9/9–10). For Dufourmantelle, sex remains philosophy's aporia, a blank or silent spot that is 'the locus of philosophy's obscure, nocturnal, indiscernible astonishment' (*BD* 29/9). And here we may recall the metaphor of the lunar eclipse in the film, an exceptional night within the night.

If for her, sex is 'an art of intelligence', pure intelligence of the other that becomes 'thought' precisely in that abandonment of self-belonging and of complete transparency of the self to the self (*BD* 28–9/9–10), for him sex 'knows so little of itself' (*Sex* 18/6) and is all the more powerful for it. In particular, while 'it is made of touch, through and through, and touch is all it does (tact, proximity, intimacy, dexterity, grazing, caress, thrill, tremor, trouble)', it knows 'nothing else' about touch besides 'élan, trust, itch, hunger, and appetite ... nothing except that it is agitated, animated, and excited' (*Sex* 17/6). To the extent that sex is the block or impasse 'it requires [philosophical] preliminaries to pass to the unknown' (*Sex* 18/5–6).

It can be no coincidence that both writers have recourse to a sonic metaphor in a bid to touch what philosophical concepts cannot touch. For her, philosophy touches in that it is like sound: 'a resonance' that marks the resistance of the material world in language (*BD* 27/9). Sex is for her the 'untouchable in the body' as 'pure resonance' (*BD* 29/9–10), while for him its fatality is a 'tone' where 'tension ... doesn't even know what it tends toward, what it wants to attain or touch – *contingere*: with what it wishes to meet up, against which it wishes to brush, to the contingency of what contact it aspires' (*Sex* 17/6).

One of the secret affinities, then, between Nancy and Dufourmantelle is that their haptocentric understandings of eroticism, of sex and philosophy, partake at once of the sonorous as a kind of spaced-out tactility. Each in their own way thinks a tactful touching that abstains from touching *too much* (however that limit might be defined, assuming any touching were itself already too much) and this requires a displacement across the sensorium to a mode characterised by touching over a distance. And yet

DOUBLE BLIND DATE

it is precisely on this point (which by its very nature refuses to be pinned down to a point of contact in space or in time, so already undoes the 'at once' of aural and haptic) that they subtly part ways. The multiple eroticisms of multiple deconstructions – and hence their mutual attraction and seduction as well as repulsion – emerge in this gaping space opened up by words as yet unuttered, for Nancy continues unseen to brush up against, graze and strike the odd glancing blow at Dufourmantelle, without perhaps quite seeing her and without her name coming to his lips.

To make sense of this scene one might recall that for Nancy, more than pleasure, sex is about a senseless sense that opens up from 'the secret or the mystery of intimacy'.[10] Fidelity as 'the force of attachment' comes from the surprise, even dizzying stupor, when two people share a 'mutual abandonment' of 'being-outside-of-oneself',[11] which has the character of a hunger to consume the other and be consumed by them. If sex tends to cultivate attachment or love, love cultivates sex not to spiritualise it but to intensify it 'like musical instruments intensify sounds'.[12] Hence a reader must hear in their inner ear a mute music that drives the unspoken intimacy and affection between these philosophies. Between the two of them, is a certain arhythmic rhythm, a syncopation – in Nancy's parlance a ravishing syncope in which the proper or self-identity undecides itself[13] – that turns on the musical. Her rhythm is that of 'a word wrenched from the body, reached by *jouissance*' where speech begins and ends (*BD* 111/47). His sex is a lyricist at or beyond the threshold of speech that 'wants to set words to its music ... its tension, its force, its energy' (*Sex* 48/27). Her philosophical touch, like that of a musician, sets in motion 'a precise virtuosic resonance' of mingling worlds and bodies (*BD* 29/10).

The musical or sometimes choreographical theme, while each puts forward bodies in desire, in motion, with their sounds and their scents, only goes so far. Unlike the mediation of music and dance, sex (like Dufourmantelle)

> remains, precisely, evoked: called from afar, entreated to come be done or be felt without thereby being presented. Nothing perhaps more than sex provides an occasion for allusion or evocation, for undertones and overtones, for the inaudible, the unheard of and the hint, for the well-nigh, for offering up to substitution, slippage – and thus also for joking, banter and licentiousness. (*Sex* 164/110)

Sex, though, withdraws from music insofar as it deforms forms, turns them inside out, 'ex-*peauses*' them, causing their skin to touch and their boundaries to evaporate; far from what is exposed, it is the name for what touches (on) this ex-peausition itself.[14] For Dufourmantelle, sex inhabits 'a musical scansion' philosophy can only envy, unable to join or stifle it (*BD* 112/47) since it too has its origins in this 'muted music' – a phrase Nancy uses in *À l'écoute*.[15] Philosophy remains in close proximity to this pulsation without, however – as Nancy suggests in a short text on *galant* music I have approached via the art of tactful touching that is translation – pushing or pressing, touching the heart without punching it in the gut.[16] This tact, this restraint, this asymptotic approach to the liminary that always leaves a minimal gap, this skipped heartbeat brings sound, sex and philosophy in step for a fleeting moment.

Le plat principal

If among the earliest scansions, as Dufourmantelle suggests, are 'silence/ noise [*silence, bruit*], light/darkness [*lumière, téneèbres*], I/you' (*BD* 113/148) in that moment of the hidden moon, is it day or night? The metaphor of night and darkness is prominent in the film, especially the exceptionally dark night on account of the lunar eclipse which is none-theless presented as a spectacle of visibility to be captured on their mobile phones with a selfie stick. In the extraordinary opening of his book on Nancy, *Le toucher*, Derrida receives an uninvited visitation from a per-plexing question that addresses itself to the syncope or a certain eclipse of the senses: 'When our eyes touch, is it day or is it night?' (*T* 11/2). This highly charged scene of eroticism sees Jacques approach his friend so closely that their eyes 'press together like lips' (*T* 12/2), 'a kiss of the eyes on the eyes of the other' (*T* 343/306).

The question, however, is whether what touches in this moment is two eyes or two gazes, the visible organ of sight or vision itself, or perhaps some mixture of the two. This conundrum gives rise to a certain irreducible blindness if one imagines Jacques's gaze refocus-ing between staring at Jean-Luc's eyes and meeting their gaze so that either vision or the visible must remain in obscurity. The question itself comes to Derrida unseen, as such pre-phenomenological in the night of the senses 'before the light of day' (*T* 11/1). In a lunar eclipse, one is not simply in darkness; the obscurity of the night and hence some-thing like the impossibility of seeing are rendered visible, hence why it becomes a strange time in which the very veiling and unveiling of the secret and thus its eroticism become discernible, albeit from the unseen place of a fable or dream whose operation is to keep secrets precisely by laying them bare in a test: *When our erotic secrets are disclosed, is it day or is it night?*

DOUBLE BLIND DATE 81

Where we are – this night – seems even darker, then. Don't we have to make a choice between looking or exchanging glances or meeting gazes, and seeing, very simply seeing? And first between seeing the seeing and seeing the visible? For if our eyes see what is *seeing* rather than *visible*, if they believe that they are seeing a gaze rather than eyes, at least to that extent, to that extent as such, they are seeing nothing, then, nothing that can be seen, nothing *visible*. Away from all visibility, they founder in the night. They blind themselves so as to see a gaze; they avoid seeing the visibility of the other's eyes so as to address themselves only to his or her gaze, to his or her sight that is merely seeing, to his or her vision. At this instant, here, is it daytime? ... Is it night? Would one have to *make* it night, make the night *appear* in order to see oneself looking at the other or see oneself beheld by the other? In order to see the other seeing us, that is, provided we'd no longer see the other's eyes' visibility, then, but only their clairvoyance? Is that what night is, our *first night*? ... The first for which we'd need a taste to hear it, before seeing or touching? (*T* 12/2–3)

This displacement or prosthetic substitution of the senses is worth observing. The reference to taste recalls that *Perfetti sconosciuti*, no less than *The Party*, turns on culinary misadventure, but unlike Sally Potter's coterie, which has chance to partake of little besides alcohol and drugs, the psychoanalyst's guests are seen devouring a cheese plate almost as a metonym for the taking into oneself of the other and of the secret in the transference of desire. Derrida will later accuse Levinas of being somewhat reckless to assume that eating and drinking, unlike volup-tuousness, are 'solitary pleasures' (*T* 92/77). This interiorisation of the other, of the secret, of the secreting of the other, will be of significance, but for now what matters is this deconstruction of philosophical intui-tionism, which, notwithstanding or precisely because of the privilege it accords to vision, necessarily reaches at the point of immediate presence a 'blind spot' where 'the eye *touches* and lets itself be touched by a ray of light, unless it is (more rarely, and more dangerously) by another eye, the eye of the other' (*T* 138/120). Derrida's argument in *Le toucher* is that metaphysical haptocentrism finds its exemplary expression in phe-nomenology, whose notion of optical intuition is nonetheless 'tactually filled-in' (*T* 185–6/161) so as to fulfil its fantasy of immediate, intimately proximate presence – an experience of smooth, uninterrupted contact that he describes as 'continuistic' since it admits of no spacing, no gap, no effraction of the other, and hence touches blindly since there is no room for the distance of sight.

It is the audacity of love (Derrida specifies love and not erotic desire) that as it were sees through the alternative between enlightenment and blindness – a mad love which consists precisely in refusing to choose between reason and madness, clarity and obscurity.

> But precisely, when my gaze meets yours, I see *both* your gaze *and* your eyes, love in fascination – and your eyes are not only *seeing* but also *visible*. And since they are visible (things or objects in the world) as much as seeing (at the origin of the world), I could precisely touch them, with my finger, lips or even eyes, lashes and lids, by approaching you – if I dared come near to you in this way, if I one day dared. (*T* 13/3)

Derrida returns to this scene of him and Nancy caressing and stroking one another's eyes and touching that look on his approach towards discussing Levinas's 'phenomenology of Eros' as profanation of the secret (*T* 90/75). At stake in Jacques's exchange of suspicious glances with Jean-Luc, in their face-off, is the possibility of a touch that goes beyond phenomenology and its continuism. That is precisely what Levinas seeks with his analysis of the caress that turns its back on the phenomenological to face the ethical – except that the limits of the ethical and the face will be precisely where Jacques thinks he has the upper hand over both his friends. That Levinas casts the caressed object of Eros's as feminine, passive, infantile, even animal puts it beyond responsibility. And it is surely felicitous that at this point Derrida fantasizes about a missed encounter (a blind date?) between a couple yet to meet, Levinas's Eros and Nancy's Psyche; their union must be shrouded in darkness after Venus, jealous of Psyche's limelight-stealing beauty, seeks to take her revenge via her son Eros who mistakenly pricks himself with an arrow intended for Psyche and, when he accordingly falls in love with her, must keep his face hidden from her during their trysts. The irreducible blindness of Eros is linked to an inviolable virginity of the caressed: 'Voluptuosity profanes; it does not see. *An intentionality without vision*, discovery does not shed light.'[17] But only a moment before Levinas speaks of 'the night of the erotic, behind the night of insomnia the night of the hidden, the clandestine, the mysterious, land of the virgin, simultaneously uncovered by *Eros* and refusing *Eros* – another way of saying: profanation' (*TI* 289/258–9).

Here, again, is one of the hallmarks of the deconstruction of eroticism in that it passes by way of a deconstruction of the secret, but it is, moreover, this undecidability of the patent or exposed secret that brings about an (erotic?) encounter between ethics and erotics. Where for Levinas the face is the precondition of the ethical relation to the other, for Derrida the erotic caress 'runs the risk of locking things up in secrecy, clandestinity, the asocial, but also in animality' (*T* 96/80).

> An exorbitant ultramateriality ... designates the exhibitionist nudity of an exorbitant presence coming as though from farther than the frankness of the face, already profaning and wholly profaned, as if it had forced the interdiction of a secret. *The essentially hidden throws itself toward the light, without becoming signification.* Not nothingness – but what is not yet ... In the effrontery of its production this clandestinity avows a nocturnal life not equivalent to a diurnal life simply deprived of light; it is not equivalent to the simple *inwardness* of a solitary and inward life which would seek expression in order to overcome its repression. It refers to the modesty it has profaned without overcoming. The secret appears without appearing, not because it would appear half-way, or with reservations, or in confusion. The simultaneity of the clandestine and the exposed precisely defines *profanation.*' (*TI* 286–7/256–7)

This secret is an 'obscure light coming from beyond the face' (*TI* 285/254) – from behind the shaded face of the moon perhaps. From Derrida's perspective, this is where Nancy differs (albeit not enough) from Levinas to 'send shivers [*faire frémir*]' down the spine of phenomenology and unnerve its idea of the caress as pure experience prior to conceptuality or the theoretical, grasping touch (*T* 98/82). By comparison, Levinas's 'beyond of the face' that 'filters' though the face remains still too much of 'the order of the face itself' (*T* 95/79), and hence of transparency, knowledge, mastery, of the performative's 'I can.' While Levinas gestures in this direction towards an eventality exceeding all anticipation, Derrida is at pains to uncover beyond (the beyond of) the face of his thought a more radical deconstruction of the distinction between ethics and erotics. The caressed is not consigned to an asociality, or at least mute sociality, misleadingly characterised and excluded by anthropocentric humanism as 'animal'. Rather, it is always already ethical, and the ethical is irreducibly profaned by perjury, treachery, indecency, by 'the shame of the profanation [that] lowers the eyes [*baisser les yeux*]' rather than scrutinise (*TI* 291/260). When Jacques stares into Jean-Luc's eyes, he wonders if his dear friend could forsake the very form of the alternative between day or night or if he, like Emmanuel, is still seduced by the infinite.

Le fromage

Nancy's postscript bids '*salut* to the blind we become' and to the manifest secret to which his recently deceased friend was so attracted.[18] It was only fitting perhaps that Hélène first set eyes on Jacques from behind, unseen, her gaze and his eyes unseen while he recounted a story of being blind,[19] though, unlike Sex and Philosophy who in Dufourmantelle's characterisation, 'have been deliberately avoiding each other forever' (*BD* 14/3), they do not stay apart for long but indeed would keep meeting on these blind dates over many years. Each blindness would find the other's but not without perhaps a measure of jealousy (which is blind) and its disavowal (which is doubly so and is the source of their mutual jealousy), as Anne would observe in the interactions between Sex and Philosophy (*BD* 81–3/33–4). The French remake of the film, *Le jeu*, makes much of characters looking, sometimes with ardour, other times with suspicion or jealousy, through Venetian blinds or their reflection from one space to another. 'Blinds', as Dufourmantelle notes, 'also means "shades," interior shutters – in French *jalousies* (jealousies)' (*BD* 83/34) which enable one to see without being seen, what are called 'stolen glances' which cannot be given or taken back. Philosophy is jealous of Sex's pure, 'blind' experience, the seeming instantaneity of its intuition, its abandonment to and possession of the truth, that in *jouissance* it 'surprises' the essence that remains for philosophy an untouchable object of desire. As Dufourmantelle warns, however, 'the "*jalousies*" that separate philosophy's windows from the pure essence of being and those that cover over the search for pure pleasure in the chiaroscuro [*clair-obscur*] of bedrooms do not filter the same light [*le même jour*]' (*BD* 90/37).

Cixous's 'Savoir' recounts the story of a woman who 'had been born with the veil in her eye [and] in her soul [*le voile dans l'œil*]' (Cixous herself, we learn from Derrida who was previously blind to her blindness even having known her for over thirty years).[20] Before she has surgery to correct her myopia, 'she could see that she could not see' (Sav 11/3) and afterwards, waking 'as night ended' and beginning to make out the patterns on the carpet, 'she could she herself see. She saw sight coming [*voyait venir la vue*]' (Sav 15/8). As if mirroring the scene in *Le toucher*, she 'touched the world with her eye', discovering what might be the 'supreme enjoyment' – and supremely tactile, if not erotic enjoyment – not of *coming* to see but of '*seeing-with-the-naked-eye*', of 'the delicate tact of the cornea, the eyelashes ... eyes are lips on the lips of God' (Sav 16/9–10).

Immediately, though, Cixous effects a displacement of the senses towards her hearing herself say, and the unheard-of as her secret veil

DOUBLE BLIND DATE

is lifted. Speaking of the woman's love for her myopia precisely in the moment her eyelids are physically relieved, Cixous writes in a sensory prostheticity: 'The joy of the unbridled eye: you can hear better like this. To hear you have to see clearly. Now she could hear clearly even without glasses' (Sav 18/12). Derrida, who for his part is fed up with and wants to be finished with the veil without finishing (with) it, to use a construction that recurs throughout *Le toucher* (touching without touching, and so on), who actually wants to be finished with *un*veiling, remarks on the substitution of hearing for sight, then touch for hearing, in what one might describe as a corporealisation, if not an incorporation, an eroticisation of sense. He then proceeds to take up the texture or weave of her writing with myriad 'invisible homonyms and apostrophes' (Ver 38/36) playing on the words *voile* (meaning 'veil' in the masculine and 'sail' in the feminine) and *ver* (meaning 'worm' but whose sound also resonates in *vert* (green), *vers* (verse), *verre* (glass), *vertu* (virtue) *verité* (truth), and so on). These quasi-homophones form a 'braid of phonemes [that] is not always invisible, but primarily it gives itself to be heard, it is knotted out of sight, becoming thus a thing of myopia and blindness' (Ver 55/56).

He himself confesses to a kind of blind voyeurism in his childhood (imagine it recounted as a dinner party story!) as he watches his child self watching silkworms in a shoebox, blind to their undecidable sexual difference. He is not coy. He makes a blindingly patent secret of a scene that could be an anecdote to which one is expected to attach little truth value or just as well a stand-in for another primal scene of initiation into sexuality (and artistic creativity). As in *Perfetti sconoscinti*, the scene is secreted in plain sight in a discursive structure where, as David Wills describes literature's secret, 'disbelief is willingly suspended to enable the gratuitous, the frivolous, the autobiographical, the fictional to be given free rein'.[21]

In 'Fourmis' Jacques is an onlooker to another fictional scene, a theatrical reading that he and Hélène play out on stage in front of the colloquium audience, he in the role of the man, she the woman.[22] They act out an interpretation of sexual difference 'in the sense that [they] are reading it, which is to say without seeing it' because, beyond anatomical fact and any opposition between nature and culture, sexual difference, never visible as such, gives itself only to be read and not to be known, perceived, seen or proven. Like the fable of sexual difference, her word *un fourmis* in the masculine (if the sex of *une fourmi* were not already imperceptible enough in the insect's blackness) comes to them 'at once removed from vision, doomed to the obscurity of blindness but promised in this way to reading' (F 72/19). Stressing the telephonic nature of their relationship, Derrida says that to interpret sexual difference requires a leap from seeing to reading involving an 'abocular moment' with or without a telephonic supplement (the phones on the dining table) but an act of faith nonetheless.

In the unseeing of this aural connection, sexual difference, ever the perfect stranger or blind date, is only to be witnessed 'in the absolute incommensurability or the *without-rapport* [*sans-rapport*] that marks all rapport with the other' (F 92/35) – which is say, the obscure night or secret of the other in erotic desire. Deconstruction, as multiple practices of reading finally, devours a body or corpus that is not at last *unveiled*, neither is it appropriated and introjected or reincorporated within a crypt, but is able to undo itself and untie itself from any dialectic of concealing and disclosure, of interiority and exteriority – of secreting. Therein lies the eroticism of deconstruction: an eroticism that it constructs conceptually, that it touches on, and just is in going 'outside itself in itself and near itself' (Ver 83/89).

Le dessert

The dinner party is haunted by the ghostly presence of another guest, an object of fascination provided they be shrouded in mystery but of cruel distrust the moment the secret is secreted, the secret of the secret no longer hidden away, the repression no longer suppressed, encrypted under the (pin) lock and key of a mobile phone or another game of deception and projection. She is born out of Sex's untouchability for Philosophy, the exile of thought's total eclipse (*BD* 228–9/101). Her name is Literature. Her enchantment is mistrusted, by Philosophy who fears lest her bedazzlement defeat sovereign reason and by Sex who fears a rival in ravishment whose magic blinds to the puppet strings that sex lays bare (*BD* 156–8/67–8). Both Sex and Literature deploy these shiny filaments in a bid to suspend death. While Philosophy conceptualises the world 'back to back with death', Sex may be our response to our fearful condition of mortality (*BD* 231–2/102–3). Literature is born to this couple on an 'indefinitely postponed blind date', born 'with hunger and astonishment', 'with sex and love of knowledge fastened tight to the body', and 'with desire and the whole history of philosophy in thin slices cut up raw' (*BD* 234/103).

In Hélène's hands, writing is to call (back) the beloved with monosyllabic injunctions on the telephone line or by a silvery wisp of hair. For Anne, meanwhile, insofar as, like Sex and Philosophy, it is horrified by crypts (*BD* 163/70), Literature is on the side of life, or more precisely knows no sides for it is an act of traversal, transfer, translation, prosthesis.

DOUBLE BLIND DATE   87

In slicing up desire and philosophy, there is a less a chiaroscuro-effect opposing light to darkness than a spacing out of the thin cuts of a Venetian blind. Literature's iterability detaches and re-grafts the secret away from its source, the displacement and replacement of words and letters seemingly impelled by, taking off from, the untranslatable idiom, and yet it is this very flight – the taking-place of replacement, the substitutability of literature's performative force – that is untranslatable and hence in some sense secret, hidden in plain sight.

Well, not quite *sight*. Literature's 'cryptography' (*HC* 11/4) is not of the order of the visual but the aural. For reasons that are not altogether clear, Dufourmantelle describes Sex's response to the anguish of death as 'an inaudible response, one never heard', except that it seems to have something to do with speed: instead of becoming audible, sex begins anew 'in an endless merry-go-round that keeps us alive, desiring' (*BD* 232/103). It is Hélène's speed that captivates Jacques. The magical might (*puisse*) of Literature in the inky blackness of her pen or the dazzling blindness of her white spaces – in touching the other at a speed 'faster than light', observes Jacques perhaps with a trace of jealousy or at least watching her from behind the blinds – this magical might '(sur)renders itself [*se rend*] blindly, without a necessary need for visibility, to the greatest possible distance, that of the other wherever he may be' before any phenomenality (*HC* 75/83–4), such that it is 'a question of speaking to the ear' (19/13).

Cixousian writing is a musical cord, a chant of enchantment, an amorous song of songs (*HC* 71–2/79), which Mireille Calle-Gruber suggests has the effecting of taking away visibility and hence readability to give instead what she describes as vision or revelation.[23] Calle-Gruber observes how vision lines (*doubler*) writing while writing overtakes (*doubler*) vision[24] – an erotic entanglement if ever there was one – but what she doesn't take to heart is the sonorous character of this affair. Derrida, by contrast, appreciates that what is pronounced 'before and beyond any visibility and therefore any readability ... is a question of speaking to the ear, and the ear alone' (*HC* 18–19/13). This distinctly audible enchanting passion of literature – inseparable from the power of sexual difference as the differantial generativity of power itself – is the blinding secret of deconstruction's eroticism. Hélène often speaks of her myopia, likening 'writing blind' to closing one's eyes when having sex so as not to divert the body from intimacy and to close off any distracting exterior and to be in the same Night together.[25] 'Behind my eyelids ... I become a thing with pricked-up ears', she writes. 'The blaze of day prevents me from hearing. From seeinghearing. From hearing myself. Along with me. Along with you. Along with the mysteries.'[26] She likes to say that literature is the pursuit of, a race towards, the secret, which might always outrun the secretary of the text. On one occasion when she mentions this idea in a dialogue with Jacques, he chimes in underscore that the secret 'is not only that which one hides' but 'existence itself'.[27] He continues: 'However close I am to the other, even in fusioning "communion" or erotic ecstasy, the secret is not revealed. The other is separated ... This interruption is not negative. It makes possible [*donne sa chance à*] the encounter, the event, love itself.' Whereas he emphasises the distance, the apartness of (sexual) *différance*, including of the other in me, she here highlights its proliferation. In exhuming secrets, Literature 'secretes secrets' and 'in a state of continual secretion, it constantly augments itself'.[28] With eyes that are also ears, the resonant amplification of everything that goes by the name of literature bears witness to all the missed encounters between Sex and Philosophy – blind dates perhaps, but not unheard.

Notes

1. '"Perfetti Sconosciuti" da Guinness, la commedia di Genovese è il film con più remake di sempre', *La repubblica*, 15 July 2019: https://video.repubblica.it/spet tacoli-e-cultura/perfetti-sconosciuti-da-guinness-la-commedia-di-genovese-e-il-film-con-piu-remake-di-sempre/339676/340267 (accessed 31/12/2023).
2. See, from a less deconstructive perspective, Oliver Davis and Tim Dean, *Hatred of Sex* (Lincoln: University of Nebraska Press, 2022).
3. On the ramifications of John Bowlby's preference for observation over listening, see ibid., 101–5. On Derrida's preference for the secret over the non-secret, even when distinguishing between the absolute secret of deconstruction and 'what is generally called secret', see Jacques Derrida and Maurizo Ferraris, *Il gusto del segreto* (Roma-Bari: Laterza, 1997), 53; *A Taste for the Secret*, trans. Giacomo Donis (Cambridge: Polity, 2001), 59.
4. Anne Dufourmantelle, *Défense du secret* (Paris: Payot & Ravages, 2015), 19; *In Defense of Secrets*, trans. Lindsay Turner (New York: Fordham University Press, 2021), 3. Hereafter cited in the text as *DS* with the French page numbers given first, then the English translation.
5. Derrida and Ferraris, *Il gusto del segreto*, 51–2/57–8.
6. Jacques Derrida, *Résistances de la psychanalyse* (Paris: Galilée, 1996), 38; *Resistances of Psychoanalysis*, trans. Peggy Kamuf, Pascale-Anne Brault and Michael Naas (Stanford, CA: Stanford University Press 1998), 24. On literature's non-response see *Passions* (Paris: Galilée, 1993), 66; 'Passions', trans. David Wood, in *On the Name*, ed. Thomas Dutoit (Stanford, CA: Stanford University Press, 1995), 3–31, at 29.
7. Derrida, *Résistances*, 42/27.
8. Anne Dufourmantelle, *Blind Date: sexe et philosophie* (Paris: Calmann-Lévy, 2003); *Blind Date: Sex and Philosophy*, trans. Catherine Porter (Urbana: University of Illinois Press, 2007). Hereafter *BD*.

DOUBLE BLIND DATE

9. Jean-Luc Nancy, *Sexistence* (Paris: Galilée, 2017); *Sexistence*, trans Steven Miller (New York: Fordham University Press, 2021). Hereafter *Sex.*

10. Jean-Luc Nancy and Irving Goh, *The Deconstruction of Sex* (Durham, NC: Duke University Press, 2021), 65.

11. Ibid., 65, 51.

12. Ibid., 67.

13. Most notably in *Le Discours de la syncope, 1. Logodaedalus* (Paris: Flammarion, 1976); *The Discourse of the Syncope: Logodaedalus* (Stanford, CA: Stanford University Press, 2008). On ravishment as syncope, see Peggy Kamuf, 'On the Subject of Ravishment (A même Jean-Luc Nancy)', *Paragraph* 16.2 (1993), 202–15, at 203.

14. Jean-Luc Nancy, *Corpus*, bilingual edition trans. Richard A. Rand (Fordham University Press, 2008), 32–7. See also Derrida, *Le toucher – Jean-Luc Nancy* (Paris: Galilée, 2000), 11; *On Touching – Jean-Luc Nancy*, trans. Christine Irizarry (Stanford, CA: Stanford University Press, 2005), 301/267 and 301n.2/366n.5 where he praises it as 'a magnificent and necessary word'. Hereafter *T.*

15. Jean-Luc Nancy, *À l'écoute* (Paris: Éditions Galilée, 2002), 47. *Listening*, trans. Charlotte Mandell (New York: Fordham University Press, 2007), 23.

16. Jean-Luc Nancy, '*Galant* Music' with translator's introduction by Naomi Waltham-Smith, in *The Oxford Handbook of Western Music and Philosophy*, ed. Tomás McAuley, Nanette Nielsen and Jerrold Levinson (New York: Oxford University Press), 1019–28.

17. Emmanuel Levinas, *Totalité et infini: Essai sur l'exteriorité* (Paris: Kluwer, 1990 [1961]), 291; *Totality and Infinity: An Essay on Exteriority*, trans. Alphonso Lingis (Pittsburgh, PA: Dusquesne University Press, 1969), 260. Hereafter *TI.*

18. Originally published in French as 'Salut à toi, salut aux aveugles que nous devenons', *Libération*, 11 October 2004, 3; reproduced in the English translation at 313–14.

19. Hélène Cixous, 'Je suis d'abord un auteur de textes qui n'ont pas de noms', interview with Marine Landrot, *Télérama*, 2974, 10 January 2007, 16.

20. Hélène Cixous, 'Savoir' and Derrida 'Un ver à soie (points de vue piqués sur l'autre voile)', both in *Voiles*, with drawings by Ernest Pignon-Ernest (Paris: Galilée, 1998) at 14 and 36 respectively; 'Savoir' and 'A Silkworm of One's Own', in *Veils*, trans. Geoffrey Bennington (Stanford, CA: Stanford University Press, 2002), 17–92, at 6 and 34. Hereafter Sav and Ver.

21. Ginette Michaud, 'On a Serpentine Note', in *Demenageries: Thinking (of) Animals after Derrida*, ed. Anne-Emmanuelle Berger (Amsterdam: Brill, 2011), 41–72, at 47. David Wills, 'Passionate Secrets and Democratic Dissidence', *Diacritics* 38.1/2 (2008), 17–29, at 23.

22. Jacques Derrida, 'Fourmis', in *Lectures de la différence sexuelle*, ed. Mara Negrón (Paris: des femmes, 1994), 69–102, at 96; 'Ants.', trans. Eric Prenowitz, *Oxford Literary Review* 24.1 (2002), 17–42, at 36. Hereafter F.

23. Mireille Calle-Gruber, 'La vision prise de vitesse par l'écriture', *Littérature* 103 (1996), at 79–93, at 82.
24. Ibid., 85.
25. Hélène Cixous, 'Writing Blind', trans. Eric Prenowitz, *TriQuarterly* 97 (1996), 7–20, at 16–17.
26. Ibid., 7.
27. Hélène Cixous and Jacques Derrida, 'From the Word to Life: A Dialogue between Jacques Derrida and Hélène Cixous', interview with Aliette Armel, trans. Ashley Thompson, *New Literary History* 37.1 (2006), 1–13, at 13.
28. Ibid., 12–13.

5

POSTSCRIPT:
DECONSTRUCTION AND LOVE

Nicholas Royle

P.S. I love you.

x

I was only five years old when I first heard Paul McCartney singing that song. It was the B-side of the Beatles' first single, 'Love Me Do', which came out on 5 October 1962 on Parlophone Records. I couldn't make much sense of the words. 'P.S.': that was beyond Latin to me. But I loved the voices (Paul with John and George) and the melody. *Remember that I'll always be in love with you.* And then there is the at-once quaintly plaintive and faintly demonic reverberation of *you, you, you …* What is it about the line, *Treasure these few words 'til we're together*? A madeleine one can taste, a photo one can see, an object one can touch, but with music everything seems already submerged, dissolving, echo.

x

Listening to music, Jacques Derrida suggests in an interview with Elisabeth Weber in 1990, is an experience of 'impossible appropriation'.[1] His concern is with a love of music and song, before it is a concern with literature or philosophy. As he declares in one of the 'Envois' (30 August 1977): 'Only the song remains, it is reborn each time, nothing can be done against it, and it is only it, within it, that I love.'[2] It has to do with the desire for idiom, the longing to make or morph into a musical signature. In another interview, in 1983, he tells Catherine David: 'You dream, it's unavoidable, about the invention of a language or of a song that would be yours, not the attributes of a "self", rather the accentuated paraph, that is, the musical signature, of your most unreadable history.'[3]

x

The P.S. is under way. It's about the love letter, the song as love letter, the poem, novel, post card, unidentifiable literary object, life-death writing or autobiothanatoheterography.

x

Michal Ben-Naftali says that 'Derrida demanded our love', where love is to be understood as 'not necessarily a personal love, based on acquaintance, but the love of the thinker he was'.[4] The word 'demand' makes the philosopher sound a bit coercive and imperious. But it is true that his work is a love thing. When Green Gartside sang 'I'm in love with Jacques Derrida', in 1981, he wasn't simply responding to a demand, he was doing something singular with voice and melody, he was countersigning through his music.[5] For me it was a beautiful statement of the obvious: that reading Derrida gives you (you, you, you) – everyone and each time unique – an invitation to invent, to respond in a singular way. Reading Derrida is dangerous. It involves your feelings as much as thoughts. It draws you into vertiginous places (the supplement is at the origin, there is unconditional hospitality, there is no atom, speed precedes you, there is the experience of the impossible), but if this process of being drawn in as a reader is akin to being seduced or falling in love, it also supposes new kinds of responsibilities concerning the self or *auto-*, narcissism and its aporias, the human and other animals, the dead and the unborn.

x

I declare. I do declare. These fragments seek to reckon with Peggy Kamuf's compelling and extraordinary remark that 'if we ceased [...] to be able to *declare* a love of texts, to renew and preserve the force of that declaration, then we would also have ceased being able to love anything or anyone at all'.[6]

x

I have always been writing about love and deconstruction, even if my first book *Telepathy and Literature* (1990) deliberately avoided talking about the latter. (It made a single passing reference to 'so-called American deconstruction'.)[7] The story of deconstruction (especially with a capital D or an 'ism' on the end) is not a love story. This might be illustrated by the case of J. Hillis Miller who, for many years an internationally respected theorist of deconstruction, eventually felt he had to dissociate himself from the word because it had become so toxic, such 'a spectacular example of a deeply rooted ideological distortion'.[8]

Like Derrida I have never been fond of 'deconstruction': it is, as he observed in 1980, 'a word I have never liked and one whose fortune

POSTSCRIPT 93

has disagreeably surprised me'.[9] I enjoy not speaking of it. Maximum pleasure (*jouissance*, ecstasy, bliss) without a word: 'Every time there is "jouissance" [...] there is "deconstruction" ... Deconstruction perhaps has the effect, if not the mission, of liberating forbidden *jouissance*.'[10]

x

I have written books and essays that make no explicit mention of deconstruction, while remaining passionately, lovingly deconstructive. But in 1998 I wrote a short text called 'What is deconstruction?'[11] This was a kind of love letter. It wasn't a full-out asking-for-the-moon love letter, like the one on poetry at the heart of *Telepathy and Literature*, a fragmentary telepathic lover's discourse that was in conversation, without saying as much, with the hilarity of Geoffrey Bennington's great essay 'Deconstruction and the Philosophers (The Very Idea)'.[12] No, this was a more conventional, formal-sounding missive addressed to the editor or editors of the *Chambers* dictionary.

'Dear Madam/Sir', it began, 'I love your dictionary.'[13] The 'Dear Madam/Sir' was intended to sound a bit funny. Androgynous, uncertain, mixing or crossing genders, playful. *I love your dictionary*. I was, in the moment of writing, conscious of the enunciation 'I love your dick', a fragment, a 'dictionary' cut off in its prime. The editor (be they he or she) would not have been likely to hear this, however, because the letter was never sent.

x

'What is deconstruction?' focused on the definition provided in what was then the dictionary's most recent edition (1998):

> **deconstruction** n. a method of critical analysis applied *esp* to literary texts, which, questioning the ability of language to represent reality adequately, asserts that no text can have a fixed and stable meaning, and that readers must eradicate all philosophical or other assumptions when approaching a text.[14]

Following a discussion of that definition, I went on to propose an alternative:

> **deconstruction** n. not what you think: the experience of the impossible: what remains to be thought: a logic of destabilisation always already on the move in 'things themselves': what makes every identity at once itself and different from itself: a logic of spectrality: a theoretical and practical parasitism or virology: what is happening

today in what is called society, politics, diplomacy, economics, historical reality, and so on: the opening of the future itself.[15]

And then the letter ended: 'That's it. I have to stop. It will be obvious to you by now that I cannot send this. I ask myself: What would it mean to suppose that a letter like this could reach its destination? I ask you, dear, anonymous reader.'[16]

This ending sought to recall an irreducible, even indestructible element in deconstructive thinking, namely the sense that writing is necessarily 'writing blind' (Hélène Cixous), that 'I do not know to whom I am addressing these words' (Derrida).[17] With the 'dear, anonymous reader', I wanted to affirm a sense of closeness and intimacy, along with strangeness and the unknown. I was imagining a reader who might hear here an echo of Derrida's '*Fors*', which is about the figure of the crypt, forms of foreignness in *you*. 'Fors' is a French preposition meaning 'save' or 'except', but it is also suggestive of what is outside, foreign (from Latin *forās, forīs*, out of doors). Derrida's text is about desire and idiom, about 'what is produced in speech or in writing by a *desire for idiom* or an *idiom of desire*'.[18] No matter what psychoanalysis (Freud, Abraham and Torok), neuroscience, totalitarian politics or AI may rumble to, there is 'a secret of "me" for "me"'.[19] Derrida concludes his exploration of the question 'What is a crypt?' with the strange verbless sentence: 'In you, anonymous reader in this much-sealed case.'[20]

x

It is perhaps tempting to read this postscript as a work of guilt and reparation. My bad for not sending the letter. This time, on the publication of Lynn Turner's *Erotics of Deconstruction*, I promise to send a copy (along with this postscript) to *Chambers*. Cross my heart.

x

'In poetry, you must love the words, the ideas and images and rhythms with all your capacity to love anything at all.'[21] This aphorism comes from Wallace Stevens.

Such heart-crossing passion concerns the writing of a critical essay, a piece of fiction or autobiography as much as a poem. That is, for me, what Jacques Derrida means by 'poetic thinking'.

An aphorism is a declaration. It is not surprising that aphorisms appealed to him. Or that one of his most sustained meditations on love takes the form of aphorisms.

'Aphorism Countertime' begins: 'Aphorism is the name.'[22] It is a text written in the name of love. It sets out an argument to be found in

POSTSCRIPT 95

many other texts, including the interview 'Passages – From Traumatism to Promise': 'The name is *necessary* [*Il* faut *le nom*], love consists perhaps in giving a name.'[23] *Call me but love*: Romeo's words in Shakespeare's play constitute 'the common law of love'.[24] Love here shimmers as what Derrida elsewhere calls, in a rather beautiful crazy phrase, a 'temporary proper name'.[25]

Aphorisms gathered together: so many dreamed declarations of independence.

x

My love of *Chambers* dictionary has to do with my love of words, with the depths and riches, the compendious nature of this single-volume work, its special attentiveness to history and literary meanings, its concision, care and (sometimes) wit. The entry for 'deconstruction' remains a lamentable, small yet telling detail – a dismal aberration on the part of its editor or editorial team. I would not be writing about it again here if it weren't for the fact that *Chambers* is *still* promulgating this terrible definition, twenty-five years later, in print and online, virtually unchanged.[26]

Deconstruction 'asserts that no text can have a fixed and stable meaning', says *Chambers*. But for all its attentiveness to language, deconstruction isn't and never was just about (or even primarily about) *texts*. It remains, as much as ever, a way of getting at the 'experience of the impossible', the unthought, and 'what is happening today'. Nor is deconstruction particularly concerned to 'assert' anything: it's more about exploring the uncertain, the undecidable, the *perhaps*. And then perhaps the most woeful bit of all: 'readers must eradicate all philosophical or other assumptions when approaching a text'. More alarming than approaching a highly poisonous frog or a radioactive leak, this sounds like a guaranteed life-changing traumatic encounter. It's a terrifying diktat. Who in their right mind would be interested in doing something like that? Or: how could anyone *be* in their right mind and still know that they were 'approaching a text'? The dictionary here resembles a Dalek (a few pages earlier pleasingly defined as 'a mobile mechanical creature with a harsh staccato voice. (Created for the BBC television series *Dr Who.*)'): *Eradicate all assumptions! Eradicate! Exterminate! Exterminate!*

x

Among other things, my alternative dictionary entry for 'deconstruction' made no explicit reference to love or the erotic. Hence these fragments in the form of a postscript.

x

The P.S. is supplementary but necessary. There must always be space and time for a P.S. for deconstruction.

x

I've always felt a sense of the postscript or afterword, of coming after as well as what comes after, what is still to come, in my reading of Jacques Derrida. I knew his writings before I met him. We corresponded and got to know one another in some respects through letter-writing, before we met 'in person'.[27] I translated his work on telepathy and his aphorisms about love in Shakespeare's *Romeo and Juliet* before we became friends. I had already published *After Derrida* (1995), a book that circles around the aphorism: 'Deconstruction is love.' I'd heard him say this at a seminar in London in 1985 and wrote asking if it was okay to quote him. We both knew it was a funny request. I quoted the letter (dated 13 December 1991) in which he 'authorize[s] me with all [his] heart to cite this unpublished phrase'.[28]

At the same time there was something uncanny about our friendship, as if it had always already begun. His longest letter of a more formal kind (15 September 1990) was a response to my posing a series of questions around the notion of afterword, in particular 'What is an afterword?' and 'Can deconstruction have an afterword?' Published under the title 'Afterw.rds' (where the dot might indicate an 'o' and/or an 'a' and/or a way of inventing a new non-synonymous substitution for 'deconstruction'), Derrida's letter explores what he calls the 'affinity' between deconstruction and 'the strange experience of the afterword'.[29]

The *afterword*, as he elaborates it, 'signals towards what comes *after* the order, meaning and authority of the question "what is?"'.[30] One cannot speak of what deconstruction 'is', because the *is* is what is *in deconstruction*. As he observes: 'You know that "deconstruction", writing of a deconstructive style, the experience of deconstruction do not lend themselves to [some] totalization or post-totalization and cannot be punctuated by the full-stop after which a "post-word" could be written.' What's maddening but also loving about deconstruction is 'the supplement':

> deconstruction *must* have the afterword that it *cannot* have. For, always incomplete, of an incompletion which is not the negativity of a lack, it is interminable, an 'interminable analysis' ('theoretical and practical', as we used to say). As it is never closed into a system, as it is the deconstruction *of* the systemic totality, it needs some supplementary afterword each time it runs the risk of stabilizing or saturating into a formalized discourse (doctrine, method,

POSTSCRIPT

delimitable and canonised corpus, teachable knowledge, etc.). It *must* be what it both is and is not in itself: an effect of after the event, a sort of afterword to 'all', this 'all' that cannot totalize itself, the 'all' of philosophy, this 'all' of western culture, or rather the infinite idea of totality, wherever and in whatever form it can *present* itself.[31]

There is always a chance of 'the *experience of the impossible*'. This is the phrase that constitutes, in his view, 'the least bad definition of deconstruction, the most "necessary", the most necessary here no longer contradicting the impossible'. Deconstruction, he observes, '"lives" on this "contradiction"' [*'vit' de cette 'contradiction'*].[32]

Deconstruction involves 'having to be what one cannot be'.[33]

As he suggests elsewhere: 'To be is to be queer.'[34] This would be another of Derrida's aphoristic prompts for starting to ruminate on *erotics of deconstruction*.

Queerness, seduction, chase and desire – it's an unending carry on: 'The afterword runs after, never stops getting out of breath *running after* what is in front of it [*L'Afterword court après, comme on dit en français, il ne finit jamais de s'essouffler à* courir après *ce qui se trouve devant lui*].'[35]

x

Don't stop, never stop, can't stop. *I'll always be in love with you.*

x

Sudden erection fall in the midst, I was saying – following the fourth syllable of *I love your dictionary*.

Love of the penis is not a standard position from which to write about love: I associate it with Leo Bersani who, in his book *A Future for Astyanax: Character and Desire in Literature* (1976), provided one of the earliest accounts of the deconstructive erotic. He touched on 'love of the cock' perhaps most directly in the later book *Homos* (1995), but arguably it's everywhere, in everything he wrote. Consider these two sentences from *Homos*:

> In masturbation the boy's body, more specifically the penis, disciplines the hand that would rule it. If it is time to sing the praise of the penis once again, it is not only because a fundamental reason for a gay man's willingness to identify his desires as homosexual is love of the cock (an acknowledgement profoundly incorrect and especially unpopular with many of our feminist allies), but also because it was perhaps in early play with that much-shamed

organ that we learned about the *rhythms* of power, and we were or should have been initiated into the biological connection between male sexuality and surrender or passivity – a connection that men have been remarkably successful in persuading women to consider nonexistent.[36]

Persuading women, one wants to add, but also (in so many ways and so much of the time) persuading *themselves*. This passage from *Homos* is part of a querying (and a queering) of masturbation, of the question who one is when one masturbates, and is contributory to a more general affirmation of 'unidentifiability'.[37] I admire Bersani's writing for its intellectual energy, but also for how this is inseparable from the words, tone and syntax. It's about manifest embodiments, how the prose presses, the singular flux of attunement and ramifying. There are correspondences here with Derrida's consistent association of invention with passivity, as well as with Cixous's conception of masturbation as (in Elissa Marder's phrase) 'the royal road to the invention of new aesthetic forms'.[38]

x

No one said *royal rod*.

x

Paul de Man notes: 'Words have a way of saying things which are not at all what you want them to say. You are writing a splendid and coherent philosophical argument but, lo and behold, you are describing sexual intercourse.'[39] The writer must always be on the watch for the embarrassing, laughable or distasteful possibilities of innuendo. But if Deconstruction were a person (androgynous, uncertain, mixing or crossing genders, polysexual), practically the first thing they would say, after giving you the eyes, is that language is a body thing, a scene of erotic play.

There is, Derrida suggests, the 'flame' or 'amorous tongue' of 'desire for the idiom'.[40] It's a matter of lingophilia, that is to say 'a critical, amorous, deconstructive fascination with the tongue'.[41] There is love of words in speaking, the desire to sing and 'invent new orifices'.[42] All of this is caught up in what I call *the literary turn*.[43] This is not about the 'linguistic turn' or any kind of prioritising of language over life, the world, politics or anything else – in other words, any of that still widespread nonsense about Derrida as a 'linguistic philosopher' or deconstruction as a form of 'linguistic philosophy'. The literary turn has to do with the child or childlike. And by the same turn, *in* this turn, it is a way of seeing how deconstruction is 'a coming-to-terms with literature'.[44]

POSTSCRIPT   99

At a conference in Paris in March 2003 I asked Derrida and Cixous: 'In what ways is deconstruction childlike?'[45] Cixous speaks of the dream. 'The child is a dreamer', she observes, and at the same time the dreamer is a child: 'when one is an adult and one wakes up, one no longer has the rights of the dreamer and the child.' What is 'most forceful and most illuminating about the procedure of deconstruction', she says, has to do with 'the eternal child that you have the good fortune to be'.[46]

Like Cixous, Derrida does not conceive Eros in terms of lack or loss. As he says elsewhere: 'I rarely speak of loss [or] lack [...] I don't believe desire has an essential relation to lack. I believe desire is affirmation.'[47] Castration, lack, absence: these are not the stuff of deconstructive desire. Cixous and Derrida have no hankering to be associated with what she calls 'the spurious Phallocentric Performing Theatre.'[48] Rather, the child is key. Deconstruction, Derrida suggests, entails a reckoning with 'pre-linguistic experience', with 'what, in experience, is not yet speaking, has not yet submitted to the law of language'; and then also, necessarily, it is 'transgression of the law of language, out of love for language'.[49] Deconstruction, he proposes, 'is the genius of childhood'.[50]

x

Following the child ('the child that I am', 'that I follow', as Cixous elsewhere remarks, playing on *suivre*, and the animal that I am), Derrida conceives desire in terms of 'not want[ing] to renounce anything of all possible pleasures [*jouissances*]'.[51] He stresses the logic of the child as 'perverse and polymorphous', akin (as Freud recognised) to the creative writer. The writer, in Derrida's view, like the child, 'always wants more': 'the bodily engagement with language in writing, is a bodily engagement that does not renounce any pleasure'.[52] This leads him on (it's an instance, he intimates, not so much of 'invention' as of 'a passivity') – this is where he is led on – to make the arresting declaration: 'There is more pleasure in the letter than in literal sexual pleasure.'[53]

x

No one said 'royal rod', or indeed 'I love your dick' as such. These are examples of language working in ways perhaps more readily associated with poetry and literary fiction, jokes and dreams. Around the time I declared my love of *Chambers* I was completing a little book about E. M. Forster. Forster is deeply interested in how erotically playful language wants to be. As I tried to show in that book and in a later essay, 'Impossible Uncanniness: Deconstruction and Queer Theory', Forster's essays, novels and 'sexy stories' (as he called them) invite us into a verbal underworld of suggestive, shifting erotic possibilities, sexual identities and positions, pleasures and provocations to come.

Forster's essay 'Anonymity: An Enquiry' (1925), for example, argues that literature is characterised by a desire for anonymity and unidentifiability. He sees this in the writings of Dante, Shakespeare and Coleridge, among others.[54] 'Literature wants not to be signed', he contends.[55] Forster justifies this anthropomorphism by insisting that 'literature is alive', 'tenaciously' alive. Literature says, "'I, not my author, exist really'".[56] It has to do with what he calls 'the lower personality': the writer must 'let down buckets into [the] underworld' where names no longer signify; it is, he says, 'a very queer affair' down there.[57] And its effect, he argues, is to release the reader into a world of magical anonymity in turn. If deconstruction is a coming-to-terms with literature, Forster's essay encourages us to consider this in terms of a coming-to-terms with a queer underworld in which all names are made-up, temporary, dreamy instances of nicknaming.

I think of this underworld in terms of that remarkable creature of solitude, the mole. Forster was known to friends as *la Taupe* (the mole, in French, is feminine). The figure of the mole plays a small but integral role in the book *E. M. Forster*.

x

There was a ten-day 'Autobiographical Animal' conference around the work of Jacques Derrida at Cerisy in July 1997, at which I had the honour and pleasure of being able to deliver a paper called 'Mole'.[58] 'Mole' offered a reading of Kafka and Freud, *Spectres of Marx* and *Hamlet*, focusing especially on the figure of the Shakespearean ghost, the speaking mole who is a disturbing but also funny embodiment of secret and hidden subterranean activities, and who orchestrates things from a chthonic perspective. Derrida's *Politics of Friendship* sees no sharp distinction between friendship and love and speaks of a shared *aimance* ('lovingness'), but also insists on the uncanny: 'friendship would be *unheimlich*'.[59] The mole would be, perhaps, a figure of what remains uncanny, strange, crossing, out of reach in lovingness.

Just after speaking of this mole, I stood with Jacques outside the château, looking away across the green sward, and we laughed together, imagining that we could see it.[60]

x

Deconstruction is love. The refrain goes back and back. 'How to love anything other than the possibility of ruin?' asks a voice in *Memoirs of the Blind*. 'Love is as old as this ageless ruin – at once originary, an infant even, and already old.'[61] Shakespeare explores this in a sonnet about

POSTSCRIPT   101

decay, defacement, rising (and falling) sea-levels, as he invites us to see *ruin* in the word 'ruminate':

> Ruin hath taught me thus to ruminate,
> That time will come and take my love away.
> This thought is as a death, which cannot choose
> But weep to have that which it fears to lose.[62]

To think about deconstruction as love is to reckon with a sense of originary ruin, to acknowledge mortality as the condition of loving, to affirm a logic of mourning in thinking.

Shakespeare's words *inscribe* what they *describe*. The literal wandering of letters, whereby 'ruminate' carries 'ruin'(or 'ruine') within it, has affinities with Derrida's memorable phrase about the figure of 'death stroll[ing] between letters'.[63] The collapsed inscription of 'ruin' in 'ruminate' goes with the strange temporal twisting of the final line: to have to weep to have what we have to think we no longer have, a thought of having to be what one cannot.

'Ruminate' is remarkable, too, in suggesting the experience of an impossible space. You might hear *room* (the homophone), but there's no room of one's own here. It's more the space of an inhuman stomach. 'Ruminate' is one of those rare words – though it's intriguingly frequent in Shakespeare's work – that comes from the body of a non-human creature. As the *OED* puts it, in characteristically anthropocentric mode: 'Of an animal: to chew the cud; to chew again food that has been partially digested in the rumen. Also in figurative contexts.'[64] *Ruminate* pertains to something already swallowed. The time of rumination is in ruin.

Time will come and take my love away. You might miss it, the veering possibilities of 'time will come': sexual identity undecidable, the orgasm, the play on the poet's name. Sonnet 64, as Stephen Booth puts it,

> is full of words used with sexual connotations. No sexual sense is active at any given point in the poem, but the cumulative effect of the diction is to invoke a vague aura of reference to male helplessness to postpone the moment of sexual climax and the general collapse and sexual helplessness that follows sexual emission.[65]

Enough love of the diction. Enough too, perhaps, of the 'male helplessness'. Still, it's strange how the sonnets can be so redolently sexy, and so devoted to playing with the 'will', and yet remain so impersonal, so cool and detached.

x

Erotics of signature: where Forster sees writing's desire to be unsigned (literature is 'the spirit of life', a queer place not of 'reverence' but of 'imagination', welling up from an underworld in which 'there are no names' and 'no personality as we understand personality'), Derrida stresses the countersignature.[66] The writer, according to this perspective, wants to let the other sign, wants to be signed by the other. This is the focus of *Signsponge*, the poetic, strange, curiously erotic book about the French poet Francis Ponge and the concept of signature, in which Derrida suggests that 'it is the other, the thing as other, that signs'.[67] The signature only exists insofar as it is endorsed, countersigned. As he says elsewhere: 'it is the ear of the other that signs'.[68] A deconstructive desire for idiom, in this respect, would go along with a desire 'given over to idioms to come'.[69]

x

Deconstruction says *come*. But it is never just one voice that says it. It's come apart, a scatter. 'I cannot imagine a living bliss that is not plural, differential.'[70]

x

There is crossing, beings crossing, letters crossing, cutting across one another.

x

And it is about desire, the greatest possible enjoyment, in which the experience of a promise is embedded. As one of the voices puts it in *Right of Inspection*: 'Haven't you ever come on a promise, enjoyed it all the way? Have you ever enjoyed anything else?'[71]

An eroticising of the scene of signature is singularly evident in the workings of Ponge's poetry. As Derrida comments in the interview 'Counter-Signatures': 'something sexual happens [...] something happens to the body of language through the signature of the poet. To do [*Faire*] something to the language and in the name of the language: *faire l'amour, faire la vérité, make love, make the truth.*'[72] Already with these improvised remarks we may sense that Derrida is describing his own work as well as the poet's.

x

In the love-making of a writing or reading, there would be 'the momentary singularity of a certain coitus of signatures'.[73] I was and remain intrigued by this formulation. It is Derrida's conception (in perhaps more than one sense) of the event: 'the event is idiomatic every single

POSTSCRIPT   103

time, neither thing nor person is engaged beyond the momentary singularity of a certain coitus of signatures'.[74] At some point in 1991 I wrote to him and, *inter alia*, asked if he would say more about this strikingly sexual phrasing. At the end of his letter in response (dated 13 July), he added a postscript, in which he observed: '"Coitus", which can have the sense you know, signifies first of all the experience that consists in going (*ire*) towards the other, to the other, *with* the other. A coitus of signature signifies all that, in other words the crossing of this event crossed with the sense you know.'[75]

All living and all loving is *with* the other. Derrida affirms the sense of the Latin *coitus* (going together), from the verb *coīre* (to go together), while also insisting on a crossing.

x

Two days later, on his birthday (15 July 1991), he wrote a long letter to Francine, the widow of his friend Max Loreau, in which this figure of crossing comes back. After a mole-like progression, it is like a postscript to the postscript. It is about two who '*cross right by one another* [*se croiser*]', in other words

> passing, from afar, without any assured contact, without any assurance, 'crossing right by one another' in an improbable 'meeting', that is to say, without proof, forever intangible, intangent, and intact, without witness, the time of an interminable greeting to which each one alone and the others alone (all of them alone and each alone and without witnesses) will think they can bear witness, the 'crossing right by one another' of two at once finite and 'perpetual' arrivals [*venues perpétuelles*], perpetually finite, having come from who knows where and from a distance that remains unascribable by anyone.[76]

This figure of crossing, suggestively echoing the 'coitus of signatures' that Derrida had glossed a couple of days earlier, also resonates with what Jean-Luc Nancy says in 'Shattered Love': 'love is the impossible, and it does not arrive, or it arrives only at the limit, while crossing'; love, he declares, 'comes *across* and overtakes itself, being the finite touch of the infinite crossing of the other'.[77]

x

In the going together, 'towards the other, to the other, *with* the other', the together is to come, out of reach. This is the distance that Derrida evokes in 'Aphorism Countertime' when he declares:

I love because the other is the other, because its time will never be mine. The living duration, the very presence of its love remains infinitely distant from mine, distant from itself in that which stretches it toward mine and even in what one might want to describe as amorous euphoria, ecstatic communion, mystical intuition.[78]

Treasure these few words 'til we're together. In song, in memory, to come.

Everyone who was with me when I fell in love with 'P.S. I Love You' is dead: my grandfather, my mother, my father, my brother. In my mind's ear the 'together' vibrates, calls back and forward to Wallace Stevens's 'The Auroras of Autumn', especially the section of that great poem which evokes '[t]he mother's face', '[t]he purpose of the poem', a homely space of childhood where everyone is '[t]ogether, all together': 'The house will crumble and the books will burn.'[79]

x

In all of Shakespeare's sonnets, the word *together* appears only once, and even there it is not about journeys ending in lovers' meeting. It is futural. It is in the stars of your eyes: 'I read such art / As truth and beauty shall together thrive.'[80]

x

It's you – I'm hoping, I'm dreaming, it's you.

x

P.P.S. A few further additions, then, for the dictionary definition:

> **deconstruction** n. love: a loving transgression of the law of language: a coming-to-terms with literature: afterw.rds: having to be what one cannot be: the genius of childhood: the mole in life: coitus of signatures: that which says *come* in multiple voices.

Seaford, 15 July 2023

Notes

(I am very grateful to Elissa Marder for her astute comments on an earlier draft of this text and to Lynn Turner for further helpful suggestions.)

1. Jacques Derrida, 'Passages – from Traumatism to Promise', trans. Peggy Kamuf, in *Points ... Interviews, 1974–1994*, ed. Elisabeth Weber (London: Routledge, 1995), 395.

POSTSCRIPT

2. Jacques Derrida, 'Envois', in *The Post Card: From Socrates to Freud and Beyond*, trans. Alan Bass (Chicago: Chicago University Press, 1987), 43.

3. Jacques Derrida, 'Unsealing ("the old new language")', trans. Peggy Kamuf, in *Points … Interviews, 1974–1994*, ed. Elisabeth Weber (London: Routledge, 1995), 119.

4. Michal Ben-Naftali, '"I have an empty head on love": The Theme of Love in Derrida, or Derrida and the Literary Space', in *Deconstruction and the Survival of Love*, ed. Luke Donahue and Adam R. Rosenthal, special issue of *Oxford Literary Review* 40.2 (2018), 221–2.

5. Scritti Politti, 'Jacques Derrida', track three on *Songs to Remember*, Rough Trade Records, 1982, LP.

6. Peggy Kamuf, 'Deconstruction and Love', in *Deconstructions: A User's Guide*, ed. Nicholas Royle (Basingstoke: Macmillan, 1999), 158.

7. Nicholas Royle, *Telepathy and Literature: Essays on the Reading Mind* (Oxford: Basil Blackwell, 1990), 29.

8. Having declared 'I am not a deconstructionist', Miller goes on to say why he has given up on the term: 'the erroneous understanding of deconstruction, promulgated by the mass media and by many academics […] is almost impossible to correct, however carefully, patiently, and circumstantially, with many citations, you explain its wrongness'. See his 'Introduction Continued: The Idiosyncrasy of the Literary Text', in Ranjan Ghosh and J. Hillis Miller, eds, *Thinking Literature Across Continents* (Durham, NC: Duke University Press, 2016), 9–10.

9. Jacques Derrida, 'The Time of a Thesis: Punctuations', trans. Kathleen McLaughlin, in *Philosophy in France Today*, ed. Alan Montefiore (Cambridge: Cambridge University Press, 1983), 44.

10. Jacques Derrida, 'This Strange Institution Called Literature', trans. Geoffrey Bennington and Rachel Bowlby, in *Acts of Literature*, ed. Derek Attridge (London: Routledge, 1992), 56.

11. Nicholas Royle, 'What is Deconstruction?', in *Deconstructions: A User's Guide* (Basingstoke: Palgrave, 2000), 1–13.

12. Royle, 'A Letter on Poetry', in *Telepathy and Literature*, 121–41; Geoffrey Bennington, 'Deconstruction and the Philosophers (The Very Idea)', in *Oxford Literary Review* 10 (1988), 73–130.

13. Royle, 'What is Deconstruction?', 1.

14. Ibid.

15. Ibid., 11.

16. Ibid., 12.

17. Hélène Cixous, 'Writing Blind: Conversation with the Donkey', trans. Eric Prenowitz, in *Stigmata: Escaping Texts* (London: Routledge, 1998), 139–52; Jacques Derrida, 'My Chances/*Mes Chances*: A Rendezvous with Some Epicurean Stereophonies', trans. Irene Harvey and Avital Ronell, in *Psyche: Inventions of the Other*, vol. 1, ed. Peggy Kamuf and Elizabeth Rottenberg (Stanford, CA: Stanford University Press, 2007), 344.

18. Jacques Derrida, '*Fors*: The Anglish Words of Nicolas Abraham and Maria Torok', trans. Barbara Johnson, in Nicolas Abraham and Maria Torok, *The Wolf Man's Magic Word: A Cryptonymy*, trans. Nicholas Rand (Minneapolis: University of Minnesota Press, 1986), xlvi.

19. Jacques Derrida, in *Points ... Interviews, 1974–1994*, ed. Elisabeth Weber (London: Routledge, 1995), 149.

20. Jacques Derrida, '*Fors*', xlviii.

21. Wallace Stevens, *Collected Poetry and Prose* (n.p.: Library of America, 1997), 902.

22. Jacques Derrida, 'Aphorism Countertime', trans. Nicholas Royle, in *Acts of Literature*, ed. Derek Attridge (London and New York: Routledge, 1992), 416.

23. Derrida, 'Passages – from Traumatism to Promise', 390, translation slightly modified. Peggy Kamuf has: 'love consists perhaps in *over-naming*'. The original French verb here is *surnommer*: to give a name to, to dub, to nickname.

24. Derrida, 'Aphorism Countertime', 429.

25. Jacques Derrida, '*Istrice 2: Ick bünn all hier*', trans. Peggy Kamuf, in *Points ... Interviews, 1974–1994*, ed. Elisabeth Weber (London: Routledge, 1995), 302.

26. The wording of the 1998 edition is preserved in the most up-to-date print version (13th edition, 2014). The current online definition in *Chambers 21st Century Dictionary* is very similar: '**deconstruction** n. an approach to critical analysis applied especially to literary texts which asserts that it is impossible for any text to communicate a fixed and stable meaning, and that readers should leave behind all philosophical and other concepts when approaching a text'. https://chambers.co.uk/search/?query=deconstruction&title=21st (accessed 17/05/2023). The new and quite odd phrase 'philosophical and other concepts' would doubtless merit a fuller discussion. There are non-philosophical concepts? What are the editors referring to here? Concept albums? Concept films? Concept cars?

27. We did not meet 'in person' until September 1995. I describe that encounter and other meetings in greater detail elsewhere: see, in particular, *In Memory of Jacques Derrida* (Edinburgh: Edinburgh University Press, 2009) and 'On the Run (Imagining Derrida)', in *Derrida Today* 10.2 (2017), 125–41.

28. Nicholas Royle, *After Derrida* (Manchester: Manchester University Press, 1995), 140.

29. Jacques Derrida, 'Afterw.rds: or, at least, less than a letter about a letter less', trans. Geoffrey Bennington, in *Afterwords*, ed. Nicholas Royle (Tampere, Finland: Outside Books, 1992), 197–203, with French original and Finnish translation on facing pages thereafter (204–17).

30. Derrida, 'Afterw.rds', 198.

31. Ibid., 199.

32. Ibid., 200/210.

33. Ibid., 199–200.

34. Jacques Derrida, 'Justices', trans. Peggy Kamuf, in *Provocations to Reading:*

POSTSCRIPT

107

J. Hillis Miller and the Democracy to Come, ed. Barbara Cohen and Dragan Kujundzic (New York: Fordham University Press, 2005), 243.

35. Derrida, 'Afterw.rds', 201/214.

36. Leo Bersani, *Homos* (Cambridge, MA: Harvard University Press, 1995), 103. In the prologue to the book Bersani discreetly identifies 'love of the cock' with '[his] own sexual perspective' (8).

37. Bersani's contention that 'unidentifiability is an act of defiance' (*Homos*, 32) has affinities, I think, with Derrida's declaration: 'don't count me in'. See 'I Have a Taste for the Secret', in Jacques Derrida and Maurizio Ferraris, eds, *A Taste for the Secret*, trans. Giacomo Donis (Cambridge: Polity, 2001), 27.

38. On invention and passivity see, in particular, Jacques Derrida, 'Psyche: Invention of the Other', trans. Catherine Porter, in *Psyche: Inventions of the Other*, vol. 1, ed. Peggy Kamuf and Elizabeth Rottenberg (Stanford, CA: Stanford University Press, 2007); Elissa Marder, 'Force of Love', in *Deconstruction and the Survival of Love*, ed. Luke Donahue and Adam R. Rosenthal, special issue of *Oxford Literary Review* 40.2 (2018), 212.

39. Paul de Man, 'The Concept of Irony', in *Aesthetic Ideology*, ed. Andrzej Warminski (Minneapolis: University of Minnesota Press, 1996), 181.

40. Jacques Derrida, 'What Is a "Relevant" Translation?', trans. Lawrence Venuti, in *Critical Inquiry* 27.2 (2001), 175.

41. I contrast this fascination with the emergence of what I call lingophobia. See 'Lingophobia', in *French Thought and Literary Theory in the UK*, ed. Irving Goh (London: Routledge, 2020), 36, 38.

42. Jacques Derrida, 'The Rhetoric of Drugs', trans. Michael Israel, in *Points ... Interviews, 1974–1994*, ed. Elisabeth Weber, trans. Peggy Kamuf and others (London: Routledge, 1995), 245.

43. For more on this, see 'The Literary Turn', in Nicholas Royle, *Veering: A Theory of Literature* (Edinburgh: Edinburgh University Press, 2011), 92–118.

44. Jacques Derrida, 'Deconstruction in America: An Interview with Jacques Derrida', trans. James Creech, *Critical Exchange* 17 (1985), 9. Derek Attridge cites this formulation as an epigraph to 'Derrida and the Questioning of Literature', his excellent introduction to *Acts of Literature* (London: Routledge, 1992).

45. Hélène Cixous and Jacques Derrida, 'On Deconstruction and Childhood', trans. Peggy Kamuf, in *Oxford Literary Review* 41.2 (2019), 149–59.

46. Cixous, 'On Deconstruction and Childhood', 155.

47. Derrida, '"Dialanguages"', trans. Peggy Kamuf, in *Points ... Interviews, 1974–1994*, ed. Elisabeth Weber (London: Routledge, 1995), 143.

48. Hélène Cixous, 'Sorties: Out and Out: Attacks/Ways Out/Forays', in Hélène Cixous and Catherine Clément, *The Newly Born Woman*, trans. Betsy Wing (London: I. B. Tauris, 1996), 85.

49. Derrida, 'On Deconstruction and Childhood', 153.

50. Ibid.

51. Hélène Cixous, *Portrait of Jacques Derrida as a Young Jewish Saint*, trans.

Beverley Bie Brahic (New York: Columbia University Press, 2004), 53; Derrida, 'On Deconstruction and Childhood', 151.

52. Derrida, 'On Deconstruction and Childhood', 151–2.

53. Ibid., 151, 152.

54. Nicholas Royle, *E. M. Forster* (Plymouth: Northcote House, 1999); 'Impossible Uncanniness: Deconstruction and Queer Theory', in *In Memory of Jacques Derrida* (Edinburgh: Edinburgh University Press, 2009), 113–33. Oliver Stallybrass quotes Forster's use of the phrase 'sexy stories' in his introduction to *The Life to Come and Other Stories* (Harmondsworth: Penguin, 1989), 16.

55. E. M. Forster, 'Anonymity: An Enquiry' (London: Hogarth Press, 1925), 15, 22.

56. Forster, 'Anonymity', 15.

57. Forster, 'Anonymity', 16–17.

58. 'Mole', trans. Ian Maclachlan and Michael Syrotinski, in *L'Animal auto-biographique: Autour de Jacques Derrida*, ed. Marie-Louise Mallet (Paris: Galilée, 1999), 547–62; published in English in *The Uncanny* (Manchester: Manchester University Press, 2003), 241–55, and also in *The Animal Question in Deconstruction*, ed. Lynn Turner (Edinburgh: Edinburgh University Press, 2013), 177–91.

59. Jacques Derrida, *Politics of Friendship*, trans. George Collins (London: Verso, 1997), 178. 'Lovingness' is David Wills's suggestion for 'aimance'.

60. A photograph around this moment appears in Nicholas Royle, *In Memory of Jacques Derrida* (Edinburgh: Edinburgh University Press, 2009), 134.

61. Jacques Derrida, *Memoirs of the Blind: The Self-Portrait and Other Ruins*, trans. Pascale-Anne Brault and Michael Naas (Chicago: Chicago University Press, 1993), 68–9.

62. William Shakespeare, Sonnet 64, in *Shakespeare's Sonnets*, ed. with analytic commentary by Stephen Booth (New Haven, CT: Yale University Press, 1977), 56/57.

63. Jacques Derrida, 'Edmond Jabès and the Question of the Book', in *Writing and Difference*, trans. Alan Bass (London: Routledge and Kegan Paul, 1978), 71.

64. See *OED*, 'ruminate', 3a. I discuss the *OED*'s anthropocentric 'animal' usage more fully in 'Poetry, Animality, Derrida', in the *Blackwell Companion to Derrida*, ed. Zeynep Direk and Leonard Lawlor (Oxford: Wiley Blackwell, 2014), 525ff.

65. Booth, commentary in *Shakespeare's Sonnets*, 246.

66. Forster, 'Anonymity', 22–3.

67. See Jacques Derrida, *Signéponge/Signsponge*, trans. Richard Rand (New York: Columbia University Press, 1984), 54.

68. Jacques Derrida, *The Ear of the Other: Otobiography, Transference, Translation*, trans. Peggy Kamuf, ed. Christie V. McDonald (New York: Schocken Books, 1985), 51.

POSTSCRIPT 109

69. Derrida uses this phrase to describe the poetry of Michel Deguy: see 'How to Name', trans. Wilson Baldridge, in Michel Deguy, *Recumbents: Poems* (Middletown, CT: Wesleyan University Press, 2005), 192.

70. Derrida, '"Dialanguages"', 137.

71. Jacques Derrida, *Right of Inspection*, trans. David Wills, photographs by Marie-Françoise Plissart (New York: Monacelli Press, 1998), n.p.

72. Jacques Derrida, 'Counter-Signatures', trans. Peggy Kamuf, in *Points ... Interviews, 1974–1994*, ed. Elisabeth Weber (London: Routledge, 1995), 370.

73. Derrida, *Signéponge/Signsponge*, 50.

74. Ibid.

75. My translation. More fully, the wording of the postscript runs: 'P.S.: Bien sûr, vous pouvez me poser une question, celle-ci, et je vous réponds. "Coït", qui peut avoir le sens que vous savez, signifie d'abord l'expérience qui consiste à aller (*ire*) vers l'autre, à l'autre, *avec* l'autre. Un coït de signature signifie tout cela, c'est-à-dire le croisement de cet événement croisé avec le sens que vous savez' (Derrida's emphases).

76. Jacques Derrida, *The Work of Mourning*, ed. Pascale-Anne Brault and Michael Naas (London: Chicago University Press, 2001), 98–9.

77. Jean-Luc Nancy, 'Shattered Love', trans. Lisa Garbus and Simona Sawhney, in *The Inoperative Community*, ed. Peter Connor (Minneapolis: University of Minnesota Press, 1991), 99, 102.

78. Derrida, 'Aphorism Countertime', 420–1.

79. Stevens, *Collected Poetry and Prose*, 357.

80. Sonnet 14, in *Shakespeare's Sonnets*, 14/15.

Part II
Vulnerability

6

SANGUINE RESISTANCE: DREAMING OF A FUTURE FOR BLOOD

Lynn Turner

What is the meaning of cruelty?' Is it *blood*, a history of blood, as the etymology seems to indicate (*cruor* is red blood, blood that flows)? (Jacques Derrida)[1]

Blood pressure

She wasted their blood: when she could have saved lives with blood donations, she gave away the chance, using it for aesthetic purposes instead. Blood stains. Not merely a 'waste', then, a loss, but the selfish gesture of a self-aggrandising artist holding on to their blood, keeping it all to herself.[2] Blood count. Such commentary formed part of the heated public chastisement delivered to American artist Jenny Holzer in the German press in 1993. Blood pressure. It was almost as if Holzer was the guilty party, practically a thief. Blood loss. Whatever could have happened?

Exploring the incorporation of blood in Holzer's work for a volume named *Erotics of Deconstruction* begins rather surprisingly with the truly horrific terrain of systematic sexual violence in war time, with the brutalisation of the most intimate, with what Gayatri Spivak bluntly named the 'metonymic celebration of territory acquisition'.[3] Blood sports. Through this chapter however, I hope to both elaborate the complexity of the sexual politics at stake as they are deeply informed by philosophy and effect a shift, a change in the question, in the grounds, and, yes, in the erotics of a future for blood.

Blood type

The first edition of Holzer's *Lustmord* series was published in the Sunday magazine supplement of *Süddeutsche Zeitung*, a German newspaper given to showcasing artists' work at the weekend.[4] The first twenty-eight pages, printed at 'full-bleed', that is without a 'clean' border or frame but going up to the edge of each page, showed photographs of human skin in close-up, inscribed in capital letters with handwritten tattoo-like texts before abruptly returning to normal coverage such as advertisements for holidays. Attached to the cover of the magazine, however, was a white card reminiscent of a private view invitation printed with one of Holzer's texts, using blood incorporated into the red ink (with seven litres of ink in total, not the 90 litres of blood wholly concocted in the press).[5] This was the 'wastage' blotting out any other reading of the text which read 'I AM AWAKE WHERE WOMEN DIE'. The blood was donated by Bosnian women programmatically raped by Serbian men during the nationalism of the Bosnian War of 1992.[6] While this was hardly the first time that rape has been deliberately used as a military tactic, it was an historically significant event in that it led to mass rape being recognised and prosecuted as a war crime by an international criminal court.[7]

Diane Elam drew attention to Holzer's *Lustmord* series in her chapter on 'Feminism' in *Deconstructions: A User's Guide* published in 2000, largely focusing on it as a linguistic performance between senders and receivers.[8] Her chapter thus remains within the orbit of the received reception of Holzer from the 1980s onwards as an artist whose medium was 'language', without particularly questioning how that privileged term might be shifted through the more Derridean mainstays of either the text or of countersignature. Noting the three voices specified for the *Lustmord* texts – perpetrator, victim and witness – Elam acknowledges the consistent positioning of the victim as female. She adds that the perpetrator's sex is not specified and thus the possibility of women committing such violence is 'not ruled out'. Under the ugly sign of '*Lustmord*' however, and the post-Weimar aesthetic exploitation of the 'sex murder' of women by men in German art and literature, often linked to military contexts, the overwhelmingly gendered personae and the overwhelmingly gendered nature of the discourse and practice of sexual assault should not be downplayed.[9] Elam took note of the blood in the ink substantially in the context of its hypocritical reception: the German public recoiled from the impropriety of handling blood on the Sunday papers, not the systematic assault from which the series took leave. Like all extant art historical criticism regarding Holzer's work, blood enters the frame in a supporting role, something from which sense is made but which itself, taken to be 'literal', adds nothing.[10]

Between 1999 and 2001, Jacques Derrida's seminars focused on the death penalty. There the red thread of blood drew material, thematic, poetic and conceptual analysis. 'What is the meaning of cruelty?' Derrida

Figure 6.1 Jenny Holzer, *Lustmord* on the cover of *Süddeutsche Zeitung*, 19.11.1993 Magazin No. 46. © Jenny Holzer. ARS, NY and DACS, London 2023.

asked, 'Is it *blood*, a history of blood, as the etymology seems to indicate (*cruor* is red blood, blood that flows)?'[11] The cruelty of the technology of *making* blood flow floods the philosophical and literary archive investigated in the first volume of seminars to such an extent one might add it to the skills that *Homo Faber* fancies that he alone can execute. This was the skillset habitually entrenched under the sign of 'capacity' or 'ability' versus the animalised projection of 'privation' or lack of ability that drew Derrida's attention in *The Animal that Therefore I Am*.[12] With regard to the death penalty, this imagined capacity is tied not 'simply' to devising techniques of cruelty – of causing blood to visibly flow – but to the imagined ability to control finitude, enacted by means of calling time on the life of the condemned by ending it.[13]

The second volume of the *Death Penalty* provides a long sequence of sessions considering guilt and criminality signally in relation to psychoanalysis and haunted by the counter-intuitive Freudian implication that guilt precedes crime. The penultimate session, however, begins with the question 'How to conceive of blood?' subsequently repeating a refrain that asks after a possible future for blood.[14] If that possibility aims at 'clocking' blood – at knowing every drop without spilling one – it will fail: it will curtail any such future in the interests of consistency and of the self-same. Such was the totalising ambition to which the long shadow of Hegelian dialectics laid claim. Indeed, the 'absolute concept' is the 'end of blood' for Hegel, as Derrida puts it, 'in the double sense of [being] the term that puts an end to blood and the *telos* of blood spiritualised'.[15] In his book *Killing Times*, David Wills remarks that Hegel even makes a passing reference to that 'absolute concept' as the 'universal blood'.[16] The French homophony emblematises their transubstantiation – *sens* for *sang*, meaning for blood. Making blood flow thus ironically incorporates making blood disappear since 'No history of the death penalty will be possible without a history of blood' and, Derrida goes on to say, 'of the *sans sang*, the "without blood" of the Eucharist [...]'.[17] 'Christ's blood' as Wills glosses it, 'managed to flow as a result of his cruel execution, yet at the same time be sublated and invisibilized by the concept'.[18] Derrida also reminds us that this disappearing act also characterises the Virgin Mary's Immaculate Conception including the birth of Jesus. It is at one with the problematic psychoanalytic logic that mandates a sequential and orderly shift from the immediate sense-certainty of the mother (the bloody mother) to the judgement, sign and law of the father (the clean father).[19] The concept is thus the ideal means by which any otherwise unruly flow of blood is 'staunched' up to and including being made to flow in Derrida's arresting argument – and one from which he departs. His departure does not pierce the concept in a correspondingly cruel attempt to *draw* blood, 'like for like' in a parallel calculation to that performed by *lex talionis* (the legal retaliation that should strictly measure 'an eye for an eye'). In a striking and deeply idiosyncratic gesture that both avoids the ostensibly self-evident and absolute distinction between the permeable and the impermeable and also avoids declaring a brand-new concept, Derrida evokes 'a certain non-impermeablity [*non-étanchéité*] of seemingly impermeable concepts' as their general condition as the 'very place and work of deconstruction'.[20] The sheer oddity of this phrasing – the non-impermeable rather than the permeable – should give us pause. He further reminds us that all 'supposedly opposed concepts' – such as active *versus* passive or conceptual *versus* sensible – 'touch each other in their coupling'.[21] They touch each other 'in the action or activity of the act, [they] can no longer be distinguished from [their] opposite, the passion or the passivity of suffering or of desire'.[22] This tactile touchstone of deconstruction must be nurtured today.

This chapter returns to Holzer in affirmation of what Derrida often names his 'dreams' of opening paths that do not simply repeat the desire for mastery emblematised by the clean-up operation of the concept with the supportive legwork of the binary opposition. Two key instances of such dreams are that of 'an animal that doesn't intend harm to the animal'[23] and of a 'sexuality without number'.[24] The first case marks a distance from the work of the concept named in the definite article ('*the* animal') by means of the indefinite, and the second questions the very idea that sexuality can be counted in discrete taxonomic units. In the face of cruelties enacted in the extreme forms of rape and murder *and* the conceptual support of cruelty as making blood flow and/or absolutely staunching its flow, mindful of the obscene repetition of such acts at the time of writing by Russian troops against Ukrainian women[25] (up to and including the escape of some of those women to Poland, a country whose laws have recently made access to abortion all but illegal[26]), this chapter invokes Derrida, Hélène Cixous and Gayatri Spivak to dream of another future for blood and for sexual difference. Such a future, if there is one, must displace the moral calculus of waste versus proper usage. Without retreat to purity, to innocence, or to chastity, the difficulty and necessity of this path draws on what is most particular to the auto-affective force of deconstruction and to the erotics that it might affirm. Herein, I dream of a future for blood.

Blood stain

Beyond the elementary acknowledgement of blood donated by women including survivors of the nationalist assault that attempted to impregnate them with Serbian children and thereby shred their identification as Bosnian and as Muslim, no art historian specifically asked after the blood in Holzer's artwork. In all likelihood, it was obtained through a pin prick to the finger or a needle in the median cubital vein. In a sense it too was made to flow, but through a force moderated by invitation and by donation. Their donated blood also departed from the 'seat of life', hidden within the body.[27] The exposure of *this* blood, however, troubled the substitution of death for life, *cruor* for *sanguis* – the substitution that, in Hegel's hematological legacy, should have secured meaning.

While the metonymy of this blood given by women could not be staunched, it was met with conceptual reinforcements that still attempted to capture its flow. The disgust levelled against the contaminating proximity of that pressing red text could not exclude the abject force with which so many cultures persist in colouring menstruation. Joan Simon is the only art historian to allude to the 'archetypal fears' of 'women's bleeding' alongside the immediate traffic in blood in Germany at that time – fears regarding AIDS and a scandal over HIV infected blood supplies.[28] Sofia Kouloukouris noted that antiretrovirals were not in effective circulation until 1996 so perhaps the question of contamination was more prevalent in 1993.[29] To root the reaction to Holzer's work in a then more understandable fear of contamination misses the entire sense in which abjection – like other psychic processes – cannot be held to reason. Abjection has no truck with argument. Indeed, if one were to strictly invoke Julia Kristeva's work as the prism through which to theorise the appalling scapegoating of gay men during the AIDS crisis, one would nevertheless have to reckon with the animating force of maternal and animal abjection as that which perpetually haunts what psychoanalysis holds to be the symbolic order.[30]

Holzer's text, no matter how neatly printed, could not spiritualise the blood with which it was 'polluted' in the eyes of the reactive public of Germany, the very country whose twentieth-century history infamously trafficked in narratives of blood purity explicitly tied to a nationalist and racist imaginary.[31] Holzer's rubrication so disturbed this Christian country that even the Archbishop of Munich complained.[32] Blood *could* be construed to be a waste product, of sorts. She wasted their blood.

Wastage, however, does not just suggest a messy, unstaunched flow, or the failed idealisation of sublation, but ultimately signs a so-called 'pro-life' discourse. The red text awake where women die is the metonymy of blood that 'wastes', that washes out unfertilised ova in the ordinary yet seemingly forever uncanny monthly occurrence of menstruation. Such a description – she wasted their blood – speaks only to a prescription for perpetual pregnancy that is in utter disregard for menstruation as part of the self-regulating environment of the female reproductive system that must expel or 'waste' blood on a monthly basis in order to maintain a healthy and receptive endometrium.[33] This reception of *Lustmord* signs the death of women killed in the most terrifying and vile of contexts by stamping out the waste of *their* lives with the wasted opportunity to give birth.[34] Given the 'territory acquisition' at issue in the Bosnian War with 20–50,000 women having been raped, this point is all the more repulsive.[35]

In the theoretical archive of misread menstrual speech acts, the public reaction to Holzer's work is reminiscent of the account of the impossibility of hearing the suicide as speech act completed by Bhuvaneswari Bhaduri in Gayatri Spivak's foundational account of what, in 1988, she named the intersection of race, class and gender in 'Can the Subaltern Speak?'[36] There, in Calcutta in 1926, Bhaduri waited for her period to start before hanging herself in order to displace the default reading of her death as the shameful admission of sexual impropriety. She was not pregnant. In contrast to the Rani of Sirmur who appears 'only on call' in the colonial archives that Spivak searched, Bhaduri was a 'figure who intended to be retrieved, who wrote with her body […] rendering her body graphematic'.[37] She wrote with her blood, in other words, blood that was not made to flow. Red blood that was not read.[38] Never mind her radicalism and her difficulty, indeed refusal, to carry out a political assassination leading to her action, never mind her displacement of the widow's right to immolate herself only after the 'filth' of her period has finished, Bhaduri was nevertheless embalmed within the compulsory feminine figure of falling victim to 'illicit love' by Spivak's female interviewees (Bhaduri's ostensibly 'more emancipated granddaughters').[39]

The moral demand for Holzer not to waste blood but to save lives at first sounds like an appeal for a transfusion, a term which perhaps passes for the terms of a 'good' donation. That is what giving blood should entail – the secure passage from the interior of one into another! Should the survivors of sexual assault be tasked with giving blood for others? The very idea would be laughable had it not been the implication. And, since this is not blood 'in general', but blood donated by women survivors of assault, the appeal to 'wasted blood' resuscitates the ghost pregnancies or 'waste' of life to which they have said 'no'. One way to read this red text is at counterpoint to the illumination of the place where women die, is as a consanguineous affirmative refusal: No, we are not pregnant. We are not pregnant: we are bleeding and we are alive. We incorporate *cruor and sanguis*. We 'do not concept' perhaps, to quote Cixous's account of writing.[40] We cut loose from what Spivak elsewhere termed the 'uterine' economy of women's subjugation.[41]

Yvonne Volkart's catalogue essay for the subsequent *Lustmord* exhibition at the Kunst Museum Thurgau, Switzerland in 1996 carefully read the sequence of Holzer's texts and treated them as a poetic form, the structure of which deserved attention. Her reading, however, divorced Holzer's lines from the magazine print run and considered them prior to any 'artistic' 'contextualisation', prior then to any drop of blood.[42] It is in a long footnote, that by coincidence occupies the full width of the page in typographic echo of Derrida's 'Circonfession', that Volkart briefly indicates the complex address of the red text on the card composed with blood.[43] Having noted the three phases of Holzer's text that sequentially sign the text as perpetrator, then victim, then witness, Volkart recoils from the ostensible victim's claim to being awake where women die. She treats the presentation of that card as running counter to its ostensible statement and rather reads it as a condemnation or castigation in advance of the reception of such a declaration. This newspaper is not a 'red top' (like *The Sun* in the UK or *Bild Zeitung* in Germany). But Holzer's text spoke to the wider press context and what Volkart named the 'cynicism' of 'short, screaming, red headline[s]' in kitsch echo of rubrication in a legal document.[44] Tabloid media, she suggested, are the ones who are

> wide awake where women, and others, die so as to be the first to tell the world, but their telling is lecherous, and amounts to a lust-ful presentation of death to make it palatable. In fact, we are not at all awake where women die, but bored and indifferent [...].[45]

Read as an exposure of the cynical news cycle, read as a 'red top', the concept blots out the blood and reverts it to that which is made to flow as if it is impermeable to any other cause, to any other sense. A repeat-offender, relentless red tops reduce the alert: their attrition dampens the alarm call of seeing the colour red.[46]

By the end of her essay Volkart, like Elam, concedes to the posi-tionality of perpetrator, victim and witness as 'linguistic and ideological constructs' that rather underplays her own insight that the perpetrator's line 'I SING HER A SONG ABOUT US' could stand as a greedy metonymy for the entire sequence since we are drawn so powerfully into it and with such awful collusion.[47] Earlier, she had remarked on the impossibility for the victim to make a simple or constative accusation given the degree to which 'pornographic narratives' 'permeate' expres-sion to the extent where victims feel themselves to be complicit, taken in by the narratives of perpetrators: 'YOUR AWFUL LANGUAGE IS IN THE AIR BY MY HEAD'.[48] The awful language of *Lustmord*, of 'sex murder' aims to recruit every frame of reference. The habitual dom-inance of 'carno-phallogocentrism' consecrates its economy when fold-ing animalisation and feminisation into sacrificial identity: 'SHE ACTS LIKE AN ANIMAL, LEFT FOR COOKING'.[49]

Only Joan Simon's account of this work mentions the sucker punch coming should this 'private view invite' card be opened. Returning to

SANGUINE RESISTANCE 121

the convention of black ink, although still in a handwritten scrawl, the interior of this invitation card set out two more lines. The first is taken from the litany of the witness in evident intimate and horrible proximity to the victim: SHE FELL ON THE FLOOR IN MY ROOM. SHE TRIED TO BE CLEAN WHEN SHE DIED BUT SHE WAS NOT. The second – likely the last of the three texts to be read – both

Figure 6.2 Jenny Holzer, *Lustmord* detail on the cover of *Süddeutsche Zeitung*, 19.11.1993 Magazin No. 46. © Jenny Holzer. ARS, NY and DACS, London 2023.

announces the voice of the perpetrator and crystallises the misogyny and the murder invoked in this *Lustmord*: THE COLOR OF HER WHERE SHE IS INSIDE OUT IS ENOUGH TO MAKE ME KILL HER.

Drawn in by the plot of the perpetrator, lured inside, she is not clean. She is inside out, and her red text is on the outside. In this voice, her bloody exposure makes 'me' cruel. *Après-coup* readers are drawn into this world, and *après-coup* some of those readers, their guard let down, felt pressed into a proximity with that red event the guilt for which they projected onto Holzer.

Blood vengeance

'It's a shame we couldn't bleed the commanders and the soldiers who were involved', Holzer drily remarked in an interview, continuing: 'A few hundred thousand litres would have been great ... instead of the murderers, the women who still survive were asked and they volunteered their blood. I thank them for that.'[50]

Unsurprisingly in the *Death Penalty* seminars, the concepts of blood at stake are at one with a drive to purify: securitising, immunising, defensive. Whether in being made to flow or virtualised, the blood of castigation chastens, chastises. This concatenation linking castigation with chastity prompts Derrida to open the terrain of blood as it is stage managed by the death penalty to that of blood in Freud's account of virginity.

Red tops, headlines, capital letters, death by decapitation.

It may seem eccentric that Derrida berates Freud for only barely discussing the death penalty in 'The Taboo of Virginity', especially when that brief moment serves to reorient the essay around castration. Derrida is speaking, however, to a pernicious substitution that will render the question of the death penalty unthinkable. Its fleeting apparition comes when Freud invokes the story of *Judith and Holofernes*.[51] The specific text he invokes is Friedrich Hebbel's 1840 tragedy called only *Judith*; Holofernes having lost his name as well as his head in a neat condensation of the misogynist account of female ambition the play advanced. Hebbel rewrote the Biblical heroine as a resentful virgin left in this condition by her impotent first husband.[52] This 'Judith' subsequently takes her revenge upon his substitute, the Assyrian General Holofernes, by beheading him. Judith's ostensibly nationalistic defence of her homeland was, Freud tells us, merely a surrogate 'motive to conceal a sexual one' prompted by his invasive defloration of her body. 'Beheading', he continued, 'is well known to us as a symbolic substitute for castration.'[53] Judith thus did not kill Holofernes so much as castrate him. With this flourish, castration assumes central relevance. Derrida remarks, unhappily, that for Freud, therefore, 'Decapitation supplements castration: it is a figure for castration. *And not the reverse.*'[54] With this one-way ticket, Freud both upholds phallocentrism and depreciates the death penalty: the death penalty, like death, disappears as such. Thus, castration, to Derrida's consternation, assumes the inaugural status of 'the first violence, violence itself'.[55] This is all the more insidious given that Freud's title 'The Taboo of Virginity' cannot but recall his prior origin tale 'Totem and Taboo' in which the first violence was patricide, infamously committed by the band of brothers.[56] My purpose here is not to adjudicate as to which violence beat the other to first place. It is not to determine which criminal broke the first law that they then also founded. This would only remain trapped within the same logic. The 'Sanguine Resistance' of my title dreams of transforming the terms of the debate itself.

The lever that Freud uses to steer away from 'primitive' rituals with which to manage the flow of deflowering as well as that of menstrual bleeding comes from one of his patient's dreams: a young woman, he says, betrays her 'wish' not merely 'to castrate her young husband' but 'to keep his penis for herself'.[57] Judith, we can now surmise, did not merely avenge herself upon her rapist, did not merely castrate Holofernes, but robbed him.

At the beginning of the ninth seminar, Derrida wrote of the 'non-impermeability' of the concept as that which might let down the 'speculative Good Friday' that (ostensibly) raises blood above (mere) matter.[58] There he reminded us of the tactility between ostensible conceptual oppositions that 'touch each other in their coupling' and 'in the action or activity of the act, can no longer be distinguished from [their] opposite, the passion or the passivity of suffering or of desire'. Near the end of the seminar, to Derrida's evident exasperation with Freud's sexual politics, he finds those couples locked in hostility, resentment and revenge. Yes, *those couples.* It is not just a formal suite of binary oppositions. As Cixous puts it in an essay directed towards fighting for the '*Sorties*' or 'ways out': 'Always the same metaphor [...]' logocentrism is a phallogocentrism that reads sexual difference by 'coupling it with the opposition: *activity/ passivity.*'[59] This conceptual contract disavows contact. This ostensible couple – articulated as an opposition – for Derrida and for Cixous 'is the movement through which the couple is destroyed'.[60]

The point at which hostility gains ground in Freud comes through his appropriation of what Sándor Ferenczi floated as a 'paleo-biological speculation', in which the 'battle of the sexes' was embedded as a permanent war – *Eris* and not *Eros*, as Derrida remarks – and one 'waged by women'.[61] Since Freud construed this battle through wholly binary terms, it can admit no level of contact that could diminish their difference: the apparent contact of combat serves only to reverse but not to displace its terms. In this scene the inaugural crime is now hers: not having a penis of her own, she is perpetually hellbent on stealing his. In hock to her precisely ahistorical 'paleo-biological' 'natural' deficit, in this scene the stage directions position her alone as the one who 'become[s] passive and suffer[s]'.[62]

In the Death Penalty seminars, Derrida's critical resistance to the antagonistic form of the couple – in both senses – sits alongside his affirmation of psychoanalysis as that which can help us properly ask the question of what happens to us when we cry, blush, laugh. He does not launch a wholesale denunciation of the need for or practice of psychoanalysis. In a gesture that plainly invites a future analysis of 'the psyche' beyond the human, the Freudian corpus nevertheless helps us appeal to what he reframes as a 'phylogenetic psychoanalysis [...] of the living body in general'.[63]

Blood rites

Scanning between 'primitive' cultures and his own time, Freud goes to extraordinary lengths to refuse any notion of progress or alteration to the coupling of the couple. To do so would, minimally, admit something of history to the relations between the sexes. Indeed, Derrida suggests that what is at stake in here 'is nothing less than the question of history for Freudian psychoanalysis'.[64] The origin story of Ferenczi's 'paleo-biological speculation' is insufficient (for Freud), it requires the supplement of resentment born of penis envy and this must remain an eternal condition never to be surmounted as demonstrated within his own period.[65] Remarkably, Freud produces as evidence: 'the strivings and [...] the literary productions of "emancipated" women'.[66] The scare quotes belong to Freud. The force of accusation laid against women who write stunned this reader, as well as Derrida for several reasons articulated with notable precision in light of the accumulated seminars on the Death Penalty.[67] Flat out he asks 'Why would the appropriating castration of the penis be something feminist and literary par excellence?'[68] And, why have these 'spokeswomen' 'in fact been engaged in literature?'[69] Shifting the grounds of the question, Derrida responds that is not that Freud's 'targeting lacks insight', but that 'the phenomenon he has not failed to identify requires an interpretation about which psychoanalysis does not utter a word'.[70] Diverging from the letter of Freud, Derrida affirms what he acknowledges as the 'original and irreplaceable role of literature in the feminist

SANGUINE RESISTANCE   125

cause' and links it to the fact that it has been poets and writers generating abolitionist discourse – not philosophers 'or even politicians'.[71]

In such a gesture this 'J. D'., Jacques Derrida, implicates himself, his own work, and the thought and the risk of writing in deconstruction. Such an alignment does not simply affirm emancipated women in a magnanimous political claim of solidarity ('everyone is castrated'), nor

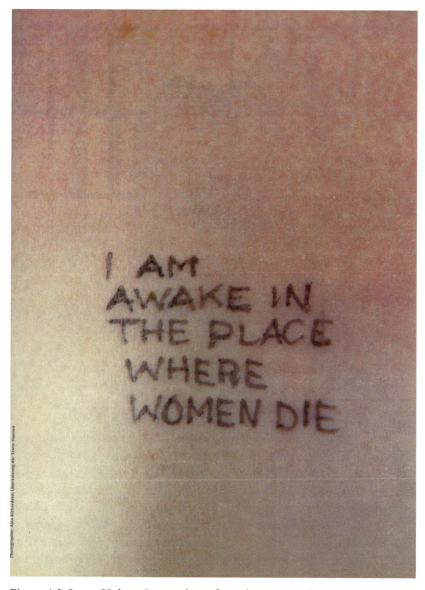

Figure 6.3 Jenny Holzer, *Lustmord* one from the series. Ink on skin: Cibachrome print. © Jenny Holzer. ARS, NY and DACS, London 2023.

does it fortify a politics in which those women can only be emancipated by assuming the impermeable sovereignty in which men encourage themselves to believe ('no one is castrated'). Rather, the vulnerability that strips Derrida down to his 'animal hairs' – affirmed in *The Animal That Therefore I Am* – comes to mind: the vulnerability of the living in general, the mortality of the living in general, the 'ability to suffer', the power to 'not be able', as well as the couples in contact in the *Death Penalty* seminar.[72]

Writing in a similar vein – and during that decade of notable French feminist literary flourishing that was the 1970s – Cixous does not address the death penalty in its narrow juridical sense, but she does indict the death struggle in its Hegelian and Lacanian dialectical legacies – in which the willingness to enter into a fight to the death will elevate 'lord' over 'bondsman'.[73] She too affirms the work of poets (but not novelists who she names the 'allies of representationalism').[74] In the same essay whose refrain repeatedly invokes the need for woman to 'write her self' and to 'bring women to writing' since they have been 'driven away as violently [from writing] as from their bodies', the Cixous of 'The Laugh of the Medusa' names poetry as that which feeds upon the unconscious – 'that other limitless country, [...] the place where the repressed manage to survive'.[75]

Blood donation

The blood that she wasted is construed to evidence violence. While we know that the work was made in proximity to bloody hell as the forced metonymy of nationalist misogyny, the reception of Holzer's *Lustmord* automatically reverted to something else. The automaticity is instructive.

This is a crime scene. Right? Right, but which one? Recalling Freud's indictment of writerly 'emancipated' women once more, and the entrenchment of a war of sexual difference (construed to be both singular and oppositional), he describes a 'phase' in the early life of little girls (although as Derrida points out this is hardly a phase when it is apparently dictates eternal relevance). Envious and hostile towards 'their favoured brothers', Freud writes that little girls 'even try to urinate standing upright'.[76] Parenthetically, he remarks that this envy is not so much to do with their *lack* of the 'sign of masculinity' but because of its 'diminished size'.[77] Never one to let a parenthesis pass by, I will return to Derrida's remarks on matters of size. In a devastating passage wrought by means of an escalating rhetoric of 'rection', Derrida elaborates the *mise en scène* of difference in Freud's script, writing:

SANGUINE RESISTANCE

> It is a question, then for these poor girls, in their virile protest, of standing upright so as to lay claim to their rights, their alleged rights. Such that between the rectitude of right (*Recht, droit*) and the rectitude of the erect body, there is an analogy, a common rection or direction that may lead one to think that the boy enjoys a natural right, so to speak, one which the girl tries vainly, and precociously to supplement by way of an artificial *mimesis*, of a non-natural right [...].[78]

Illegitimately keeping it to herself, building her 'House' upon it, bolstering her professional name as an artist and one 'who writes', there is something uncannily familiar about the hostile reception to Holzer's incorporation of the women's blood.[79] Blood banked: in this reception she stands accused of turning the gift into what Cixous calls a 'gift-that-takes', one that takes the credit.[80] The public exchange of Holzer for the war criminals vanishes the blood shed in pain in military rape camps. It attempts to staunch her incomprehensible gesture of *allowing* blood to flow without prefiguring its outcome. Rather than an introjection which would transmute blood into a sign or concept, she renders a variation on incorporation – one with an open crypt, so to speak.[81] The women's experience is entirely blotted out: they are transfigured into Holzer's victims rather than those with whom she is in consanguineous accord. History diminishes before the one crime. In echo of the vengeful woman's castration of her husband, invading General, or any other man (in this sea of ersatz equivalents), in order to steal the penis that she is otherwise naturally denied, this paleo-biological stop-clock inscribes Holzer as the one who 'makes bleed'. She did cause the women to be pricked with little needles after all (size matters, again). She wasted their blood. This ludicrous displacement of guilt takes advantage of the conceptual history of blood in which the threat of blood to life should it vacate the 'seat of life' internal to a presumed to be sealed body is stage managed by the vaunted impermeability of the concept. There is '[n]o future for blood' in the 1993 reception to *Lustmord*, only the repetition of the same.[82]

Rendering blood impermeable – making it 'hard' so to speak – recalls the blood integral to erection insofar as phallic erection is rendered in ideal form: solid, in disavowal of liquid variability, this ever-upright figure in a sleight of hand finesses the rectitude of right (*Recht, droit*).[83] This impermeable blood occupies its essential ideal form in the elevation of carno-phallogocentrism. Holzer is entitled to neither phallic erection nor symbolic endorsement. Hence, in the public's refusal to be touched by the blood that they nevertheless handled that Sunday morning, *she* was chastised.

128   LYNN TURNER

As readers will now recall, in the incarnadine light of the Death Penalty seminars, in echo of Derrida's treatment of so-called binary oppositions across his work, the concept articulates a certain 'non-impermeablity'. In deconstruction, 'touch is finitude itself' and it 'renders all couples of concepts non-impermeable'.[84] Blood may be historically hijacked into the work of transubstantiation, but it cannot achieve such transcendence. Taking that Freudian parenthesis regarding size in the direction it quietly concedes, Derrida suggests that rather than the blunt binary of presence or absence of the penis dictating an eternal law of penis envy, we 'should' be led to the literate *fort/da* of erection/detumescence. We would, then, address the matter of erection. Yet now, the shifting and vulnerable rhythm is rerouted without a conceptual brace. It is inherent, admitting what is effectively a deconstruction 'from the inside'. The rhythmic literacy of the body is internal to 'erection itself' 'in men and in women' as the septuagenarian Derrida insists.[85] As Man loses what Freud cathects as his 'natural standing' the entire ground in all of its anthropomorphism shifts. This loss could only be construed to be vindictive, damaging or illegal, within the very conceptual frame that Derrida and Cixous are at pains to displace.

In the essay called 'Castration or Decapitation' Cixous speaks, in the name of pleasure, to 'relieving man of his phallus'.[86] Yet her gesture is not a bloodletting, and neither is it a theft: it is generosity. She returns man to the lower case, to an 'erogenous field and a libido that isn't stupidly organised around that [phallic] monument, but appears shifting and diffused, taking on all the others of oneself'.[87] Shared grounds are not identical: they are mobile and heterogenous, 'just as much feminine as masculine': they are precisely improper.[88] If Cixous's and Derrida's couples sideline combat even as they proliferate contact, this cannot mandate a new norm in the form of a renewed Couple bent upon defending against counting beyond two. Adding more units, or types, or numbers that would leave each one intact would miss the point. It would be tactless, which is to say, untouched.

In the face of that red text where women die, that blood haunting the set text of misogyny in which women are made to die, where blood flow should signify their end, Holzer and the women who volunteered dispense with closure. Blood in excess of cruelty: yes, I hereby affirm, she wasted their blood. In her 'Sorties' Cixous writes:

> There is waste in what we say. We need that waste. To write is always to make allowances for superabundance and uselessness while slashing the exchange value that keeps the spoken word on its track. That is why writing is good, letting the tongue try itself

SANGUINE RESISTANCE
129

out – as one attempts a caress, taking the time a phrase or a thought needs to make oneself loved, to make oneself reverberate.[89]

If we now read the poetic practice of Holzer across media with the expansive 'writing' of Cixous and of Derrida, then we allow for a blood donation without combat, without contract. This tactic of the graphematic body, to echo Spivak, is not on the take.

Departing from extreme violence, she drew words with blood, dreaming of a sanguine resistance.

Notes

1. Jacques Derrida, *The Death Penalty*, vol. I, trans. Peggy Kamuf (Chicago: Chicago University Press, 2014), 96.
2. Noemi Smolik notes this reaction as indicative of a functionalist attitude in 'History Inscribed on Women's Bodies' in Jenny Holzer's exhibition catalogue, *Lustmord* (Kunstmuseum des Kantons Thurgau, 1997), 127.
3. Gayatri Chakravorty Spivak, *A Critique of Postcolonial Reason: Toward a History of the Vanishing Present* (Cambridge, MA: Harvard University Press, 1999), 300.
4. *Süddeutsche Zeitung*, 19/11/1993 Magazin No. 46.
5. An indicative press article was reproduced within the *Lustmord* catalogue with the headline: 'Drucken mit Blut: Künstlerin vergeudet 90 Liter Lebenssaft' ('Printing with Blood: Artist Wastes 90 Litres of lifeblood').
6. They also volunteered their skin for Holzer's photographs. See Sofia Kouloukouris, 'Text Performativity in the Work of Jenny Holzer: The Case of Lustmord', University of Geneva, available online: https://www.academia.edu/39828581/TEXT_PERFORMATIVITY_IN_THE_WORK_OF_JENNY_HOLZER_THE_CASE_OF_LUSTMORD (accessed 07/07/2023).
7. 'Landmark Cases' archived on the *United Nations International Criminal Tribunal for the former Yugoslavia* website: https://www.icty.org/en/features/crimes-sexual-violence/landmark-cases (accessed 07/07/2023).
8. Diane Elam, 'Deconstruction and Feminism', in Nicholas Royle, ed., *Deconstructions: A User's Guide* (Manchester: Manchester University Press, 2000), 83–104.
9. Marsha Meskimmon examines the German history of *Lustmord* works in 'Jenny Holzer's *Lustmord* and the Project of Resonant Criticism', in *n.paradoxa* 6 (2000), 12–21. The noun derives its conceptual status from German sexologist Richard von Krafft-Ebing, discussed in Amber Aragon-Yoshida, '*Lustmord* and Loving the Other: A History of Sexual Murder in Germany and Austria (1873–1932)', PhD thesis, Washington University in St. Louis, 2011. https://openscholarship.wustl.edu/etd/551/. Jovana Prisina notes the grim existence but comparative rarity of female perpetrators in 'Female War

Criminals: Untold Story of the Balkan Conflicts', on the *Balkan Transitional Justice* website, 30 November 2018: https://balkaninsight.com/2018/11/30/female-war-criminals-untold-story-of-the-1990s-conflicts-11-29-2018/ (accessed 07/07/2023).

10. Kouloukouri writes 'The reading is literal. We exit representation to enter presentation [...]', in 'Text Performativity'.

11. Derrida, *Death Penalty*, vol. I, 96.

12. Jacques Derrida, *The Animal That Therefore I Am*, trans. David Wills, ed. Marie-Louise Mallet (New York: Fordham University Press, 2008), 27.

13. Derrida, *Death Penalty*, vol. I, 257.

14. Jacques Derrida, *The Death Penalty*, vol. II, trans. Elizabeth Rottenberg (Chicago: Chicago University Press, 2014), 214.

15. Ibid., 215.

16. David Wills, *Killing Times: The Temporal Technology of the Death Penalty* (New York: Fordham University Press, 2019), 106.

17. Derrida, *Death Penalty*, vol. I, 191.

18. Wills, *Killing Times*, 92.

19. Derrida troubles this through the fascinating suggestion that even the 'sense-certainty' of the mother is in question, in Jacques Derrida and Elizabeth Roudinesco, *For What Tomorrow: A Dialogue* (Stanford, CA: Stanford University Press), 40–1.

20. Derrida, *Death Penalty*, vol. II, 217.

21. Ibid., 218.

22. Ibid.

23. Derrida, *Animal*, 62–4.

24. Jacques Derrida, 'Choreographies', interview with Christie McDonald. *Points. Interviews, 1974–1994* (Palo Alto, CA: Stanford University Press, 1994), 108.

25. See 9056th Meeting, 'Sexual Violence 'Most Hidden Crime Being Committed against Ukrainians'', Civil Society Representative Tells Security Council', archived on the *United Nations Meetings Coverage and Press Releases*, 6 June 2022: https://www.un.org/press/en/2022/sc14926.doc.htm (accessed 07/07/2023). By the time of manuscript finalisation, the disastrous relations between Israel and Palestine also repeat this violent situating of women as proxies in the battle over territory, see Gaby Hinsliff, 'Whatever your view of the Israel-Hamas war, rape is rape. To trivialise it is to diminish ourselves', in *The Guardian*, 1 December, 2023: https://www.theguardian.com/commentisfree/2023/dec/01/israel-hamas-war-rape-is raelis-palestinians (accessed 02/12/2023).

26. See Ari Shapiro, Ayen Bior, Matt Ozeg et al., 'This Secretive Network helps Ukrainians Find Abortions in Europe', 1 June 2022: https://www.npr.org/2022/06/01/1101473557/ukrainian-refugees-abortions-eu rope-poland-warsaw (accessed 07/07/2023).

27. Wills refers to the Biblical fratricide in which Abel's blood 'cries out from the ground', as a perversion of *sanguis* – of blood as the 'seat of life'

within the body rather than that which has been shed in cruelty. *Killing Times*, 113.

28. Joan Simon, 'No Ladders; Snakes: Jenny Holzer's *Lustmord*', in *Parkett* 40/41 (1994), 82.
29. Kouloukouri, 'Text Performativity'.
30. See Julia Kristeva, *Powers of Horror: An Essay on Abjection*, trans. Leon Roudiez (New York: Columbia University Press, 1982). Recent scholarship sheds light upon this double abjection of the feminine and the animal (substantially missed in the earlier reception of her work), see Lynn Turner, *Poetics of Deconstruction: On the Threshold of Differences* (London: Bloomsbury, 2020), 27–52.
31. See Rachel E. Boaz, *In Search of "Aryan Blood": Serology in Interwar and National Socialist Germany*. NED-New edition, 1 (Budapest: Central European University Press, 2012).
32. See Smolik, 'History Inscribed on Women's Bodies', 126.
33. Albeit a system that is now frequently biomedically supplemented with hormonal contraception as Preciado discusses. I await the supplemental theorisation of HRT with interest. See Paul B. Preciado, 'Pharmacopower', in *Testo Junkie: Sex, Drugs, and Biopolitics in the Pharmacopornographic Era* (New York: The Feminist Press, 2013), 173–235.
34. Thank you to Gil Anidjar for underlining this point in his feedback after this material was first presented at the 7th *Derrida Today* conference, University of Arizona campus, Washington, June 2022.
35. The unbearable details are reported in 'Sexual Violence in Bosnia' on the *Remembering Srebrenica* website: https://srebrenica.org.uk/what-happened/sexual-violence-bosnia (accessed 07/07/2023).
36. Spivak's 1988 essay was revised within the 'History' chapter of her subsequent book, *A Critique of Postcolonial Reason* from which citations are taken here.
37. Spivak, *Critique*, 246.
38. This red text was also read by Kyoo Lee in 'Just Throw Like a Bleeding Philosopher: Menstrual Pauses and Poses, Betwixt Hypatia and Bhubaneswari, Half Visible, Almost Illegible', in Helen A. Fielding and Dorothea E. Olkowski, eds, *Feminist Phenomenological Futures* (Indianapolis: Indiana University Press, 2017), 38.
39. Spivak, *Critique*, 300.
40. Hélène Cixous, 'Writing Blind: Conversation with the Donkey', trans. Eric Prenowitz, *Stigmata: Escaping Texts* (New York and London: Routledge, 1997), 144.
41. Gayatri Chakravorty Spivak, 'French Feminism in an International Frame', in *Yale French Studies* 62 (1981), 182–3.
42. Yvonne Volkart, 'I Sing her a Song about Us', in Holzer, *Lustmord*, 121.
43. Gil Anidjar gives specific treatment to 'Circonfession' in his '*Le Cru*: Derrida's Blood', in *theory@buffalo* 18 (2015), 8–22.
44. Oisin Keohane alerted me to the colour of ink in legal texts.

45. Volkart, 'I Sing her a Song about Us', 116.
46. See Tobias Menely, 'Red', in Jeffrey Jerome Cohen, ed., *Prismatic Ecology: Ecotheory beyond Green* (Minneapolis: Minnesota University Press, 2014), 24.
47. Volkart, 'I Sing her a Song about Us', 118.
48. See also 'Interview. Christian Kammerling and Jenny Holzer', in *Süddeutsche Zeitung* – reprinted in the *Lustmord* catalogue. In discussing the pornographic specificity of the texts Holzer remarks that documentary videos of the abuse of women in the former Yugoslavia were circulated as porn videos (122).
49. Jacques Derrida, '"Eating Well" or the Calculation of the Subject', in *Points … Interviews 1974–1994*, ed. Elizabeth Weber (Stanford, CA: Stanford University Press, 1995), 280.
50. Holzer, qtd in 'Interview', 123.
51. My related paper, 'Red Threads', expanding upon Artemisia Gentileschi's well-known painting of *Judith Beheading Holofernes* was presented at the Finissage of the exhibition *Guilty! Guilty! Guilty!: Towards a Feminist Criminology*, Kunstraum Kreuzberg, Berlin, February 2023. Incidentally, the German public also recoiled at the exhibition poster featuring this very painting for Wiesbaden museum. See 'German poster of Baroque old master "too disturbing"', on *BBC News* online, 16 November 2016: https://www.bbc.co.uk/news/blogs-news-from-elsewhere-38001010 (accessed 07/11/2023).
52. Elissa Marder points out the inexplicable elision of the mother among the substitutions in Freud's 'Virginity' essay – given his own prior insistence that the mother is the girl's first love object – in her 'Belladonna', in *Division: A Quarterly Psychoanalytic Forum* 17 (2017), 30–2.
53. Sigmund Freud, 'The Taboo of Virginity', [1917] in *On Sexuality*, vol. 7 in the Freud Library (London: Penguin, 1991), 207.
54. Derrida, *Death Penalty*, vol. II, 228, emphasis added.
55. Ibid.
56. Sigmund Freud, 'Totem and Taboo', [1913] in *Murder, Mourning and Melancholia*, trans. Shaun Whiteside (London: Penguin, 2001), 141.
57. Derrida, *Death Penalty*, vol. II, 230.
58. Derrida, 'Eating Well', 280.
59. Hélène Cixous, 'Sorties: Out and Out: Attacks/Ways Out/Forays', in Hélène Cixous and Catherine Clément, *The Newly Born Woman*, trans. Betsy Wing (London: I. B. Tauris, 1996), 63–4, emphasis added.
60. Ibid., 64.
61. Derrida, *Death Penalty*, vol. II, 233.
62. Ibid., 234.
63. Ibid., 225. He follows this by refusing to attribute such 'capacities' to the 'proper of man'.
64. Derrida, *Death Penalty*, vol. II, 235.
65. In parenthesis Derrida remarks that this attitude is 'contrary to what his heirs, claiming to be more subtle, assert in order to exempt him from accusations of organicism or biologism'; ibid., 232.

66. Freud, 'Taboo of Virginity', 279.
67. I have broached this stunning passage several times to date (this chapter being the most sustained). See my *Poetics of Deconstruction*, 3–4.
68. Derrida, *Death Penalty*, vol. II, 232.
69. Ibid., emphasis original.
70. Ibid.
71. Ibid., 232–3.
72. Derrida, *Animal*, 5.
73. See Alexandre Kojève, *Introduction to the Reading of Hegel*, [1947] trans. James H. Nichols Jnr (Ithaca, NY: Cornell University Press, 1980).
74. Hélène Cixous, 'The Laugh of the Medusa', trans. Keith Cohen and Paula Cohen, *Signs* 1.4 (1976), 875.
75. Cixous, 'Laugh of the Medusa', 875, 880.
76. Freud, 'Taboo of Virginity', 205.
77. Ibid., 204.
78. Derrida, *Death Penalty*, vol. II, 237. There is clearly more work to be done on the political and philosophical imaginary of fluids such as urine and sperm as Derrida indicates here.
79. Derrida positioned Freud's 'Beyond the Pleasure Principle' as a variety of autobiography that attempts to build his 'House', or the institution of Freudian psychoanalysis as such. See 'To Speculate – on "Freud"', in *The Post Card: From Socrates to Freud and Beyond*, trans. Alan Bass (Chicago: Chicago University Press, 1987).
80. Cixous, 'Laugh of the Medusa', 888.
81. I explore Derrida's deconstruction of the opposition between the ostensible failure to mourn that is 'incorporation' versus the ostensible success of 'introjection' in *Poetics of Deconstruction*, 15–24.
82. Derrida, *Death Penalty*, vol. II, 234. The future (*l'avenir*) for Derrida conveys a wildly different thought to the Lacanian frame famously refused by Lee Edelman in *No Future: Queer Theory and the Death Drive* (Durham, NC: Duke University Press, 2005).
83. Compare Luce Irigaray 'The "Mechanics" of Fluids', in *This Sex Which Is Not One*, trans. Catherine Porter (Ithaca, NY: Cornell University Press, 1985), 106–18.
84. Derrida, *Death Penalty*, vol. II, 218.
85. Ibid., 234.
86. Hélène Cixous, 'Castration or Decapitation', trans. Annette Kuhn, in *Signs* 7.1 (1981), 51.
87. Ibid.
88. Ibid.
89. Cixous, 'Sorties', 93.

7

TOUCH, FLESH, WOUND AND THE CARESS OF THE SCREEN

Elizabeth Wijaya

1. A wounded sky

Could there be a shared experience of a wounded sky? In *Elemental Passions*, Luce Irigaray writes: 'A wound may create the sky: that is so. But it is a sky which cannot be shared.'[1] In *Speculum of the Other Woman*, she asks: 'Could it be true that not every wound need remain secret, that not every laceration was shameful?' Irigaray performs an erotic, vulvic reading of Christ's side wound, showing that the wound could be an auto-erotic site of ecstatic desire allowing for a recognition of sexual difference.[2] This chapter is situated within the possibilities of the wound as the trace of fleshly trauma and also of transformative desire.

Irigaray and Jacques Derrida question how to share a world in the face of solitude, finitude and difference.[3] *The Beast and the Sovereign, Vol. II* begins on 11 December 2002 with three short sentences: 'I am alone. Says he or she. I am alone.'[4] Paul Celan's lines, 'Die Welt ist fort, ich muss dich tragen' ('The world is gone, I must carry you'), born of the wounds of the Second World War, resonate across the sessions. Three days after the Iraq War started on 20 March 2003, Derrida proposes that if *Die Welt ist fort*, there can only be two possibilities. First, 'Either carry the other out of the world, where we share at least this knowledge without phantasm that there is no longer a world, a common world.' Or, 'to carry you for a few moments', within a world that is destined to become trace but might still be temporally shareable: 'to do things so as to make as if there were just a world, and to make the world come to the world'.[5] This excerpt from Derrida's epic sentence conveys the urgency at the dawn of an armed conflict amid a time of climate crisis.[6] While the death of each, singular person is the end of a world unto itself, the apocalyptic end without remainder of the entire world is hardly far from Derrida's mind.[7] I propose that cinematic scenes could express this phenomenon of making the world tenable and touchable even as it is falling away. Considering the Greek root of *poiesis* as 'making', the gesture of making a finite, fictional world is not a turning away from the socio-political world but the activation of an intimate ethics of intensifying duration.[8]

The heart of this essay is an enigmatic scene of queer love in *Lan Yu* (2001), which occurs after a brief allusion to the 1989 Tiananmen Square protests and massacre – a time in which the sky and the sense of open, shared space is wounded and the promise of a space of appearance in a political world, is already disappearing. In *Literature in the Ashes of History*, Cathy Caruth references the forgetfulness of history and the disappearing grounds for memory and asks, 'How can we bear witness to such a disappearing history?'[9] Within the visible social and political world of their time, the bodies of Handong and Lan Yu undergo a double erasure where their sexualities and the historical event inciting their embrace are relegated to the shadows of history. Even if the imagined queer encounter in the aftermath of a massacre could be censored – a cinematic scene, broadly conceived, is itself a secret world with a time that is both real (the existing film) and imagined (the possibility of the imagined scene). Within the general possibility of cinematic scenes being archival fragile worlds with their own finitude, the queer, erotic scene in particular captures the ethical-erotic possibility of making a proximate, intimate world and placing it nearby, in abeyance, during precarious times. Margaret Hillenbrand writes on the open secret as a structuring force in China's disavowal of its troubled past, including the events of Tiananmen Square.[10] With its indistinct engagement with Tiananmen by turning it into the background of an erotic embrace and the film's mediatic history of censorship, piracy, re-editing, official video releases and restoration – *Lan Yu* is one example of making a world poetically appear under erasure.

2. Queerness as horizon and horizon of significance

Lan Yu is a queer film classic set and partially shot without permission in Beijing. The director, Stanley Kwan, made his gay sexuality public with a documentary *Yang ± Yin: Gender in Chinese Cinema* (1996). The producer of *Lan Yu*, Zhang Yongning recalls: 'since we knew that we couldn't show it there anyway, it gave us a strange sort of license to just shoot and see what happens'.[11] The film is adapted from a web novel, first published in Chinese on the internet in 1998 as *Beijing Story* by the author with the pseudonym of Beijing Comrade. In 2016, the English translation of the novel was published as *Beijing Comrades* and the translator notes that since its usage in the 1989 Hong Kong Lesbian and Gay Film Festival, the word 'comrade' (*tongzhi*) has also 'come to designate a subaltern sexual identity, similar in some ways to the English word *gay*'.[12] Bao Hongwei recalls that *Lan Yu*'s inclusion in the line-up contributed to the shutting down in December 2001 of what became the first Beijing Queer Film Festival.[13] The previous year, Li Yinhe's translation of queer theory (*ku'er lilun*) by writers including Teresa de Lauretis marked the emergence of the queer (*ku'er*) subject in China's social discourse.[14] Bao describes the proposed and actually used names of the festival from the China Comrade Cultural Festival (*Zhongguo tongzhi wenhuajie*), China Homosexual Film Festival (*Zhongguo tongxinglian dianyingjie*), Beijing Gay and Lesbian Film Festival (*Beijing tongxinglian dianyingjie*), Beijing Queer Film Forum (*Beijing ku'er dianying luntan*) to the current Beijing Queer Film Festival (*Beijing ku'er yingzhan*) as a reflection of the slippages of linguistic and cultural translation and the 'queer subjectivities these terms denote'.[15] My use of queer in this chapter acknowledges the importance of the term within debates on *Lan Yu*.[16] I am also inspired by José Esteban Muñoz's pronouncement that 'To see queerness as horizon is to perceive it as a modality of ecstatic time in which the temporal stranglehold that I describe as straight time is interrupted or stepped out of.'[17]

Major work on Irigaray and cinema has focused on questions of feminine cinematics, feminist experimental cinema and women's filmmaking.[18] Kwan's debut feature *Women* (*Nuren Xin*, 1985) has a literal translation of 'Women's Heart'.[19] Unlike most of Kwan's filmography, women do not take centre stage in *Lan Yu*. However, circumscribed possibilities of existence for women are in bound relation with the constraints that impede Lan Yu and Handong's prospects of finding a time and space for their gay love to flourish. Furthermore, I am considering an opacity to gender and sexuality that cannot be determined in advance, before each encounter between touching bodies, where 'the most intimate life is held in reserve'.[20] Bao observes that Lan Yu's character traits defy cultural expectations of 'the gender binary'.[21] It is explicit in the novel and implied in the film that Lan Yu only has sexual relations with men while Handong has sexual relations with men and women, but we never ascertain the configurations of their sexuality or what that could be. As Elizabeth Grosz ventures, 'one could read what Irigaray is asking as the question: "what would other relations of sexuality be like if and when there was a recognition of the existence of more than one?"'[22] In *An Ethics of Sexual Difference*, Irigaray calls for a 'revolution in thought and ethics' where 'We need to reinterpret everything concerning the relations between the subject and discourse, the subject and the world.'[23] Penelope Deutscher notes that the expanded possibility of sexual difference in *An Ethics of Sexual Difference* need not subordinate the differences of class, race, age and gender through which: 'One lives an inhibited embodiment marked by one's sense that a more diverse range of possibilities is prohibited in advance.'[24] Through *Lan Yu*, I consider horizons of possibility harboured within the worlds of death and mourning alongside Gail Weiss's exhortation that

> To the extent that Irigaray is suggesting that each of us should be a horizon of significance for the other, it is clear that this claim does not and should not apply only to relationships between the sexes. If we can extend this claim to characterize same-sex relations as well as relations between individuals of different races, ages, and social classes, her position becomes much more appealing and much more powerful.[25]

In *Lan Yu*, class, age, gender and sexual differences are entangled. The central relationship in *Lan Yu* is between Chen Handong and the titular character, Lan Yu. Handong is a businessman whose neoliberal instincts extend from his practice of crony capitalism to his attempts to purchase sexual gratification while, initially at least, insulating himself from emotional and personal vulnerability – to seek touch without being touched in reciprocal risk. Lan Yu is a working-class student who has migrated to the capital. Set over a decade from the late 1980s to the 1990s, in the transitional time after Deng Xiaoping's economic reforms, the film focalises on their periods of erotic connections and disconnections. Elliptically edited by William Chang, *Lan Yu*'s episodic construction leaves the audience always one step behind, catching up with the lovers and the changes in their lives, against the backdrop of political and societal change in Beijing.

The opening voiceover is narrated by Handong and played against a black background: '*Neitian zaoshang ni zoule yihou, wo yizhi wei ni xuanzhe xin, yizhi juede ni rengran zai wo shenbian, ni zhidao ma?*' On the Criterion-on-Demand website that streams the film distributed by Mongrel Media Inc, the subtitles provided read: 'I've thought of you every day. / It's as if you're always with me. / You know …'.[26] In my translation of this voiceover, I emphasise not only the sense but also the specific usage of terms: 'That morning after you left, for you, my heart was continuously suspended / I continue to feel that you are still by my side / Do you know?' The film begins with an apostrophe to the absent one, announcing a departure while holding on to the sense that the beloved still remains nearby. With the suspended heart of the lover mourning the beloved – before the first diegetic image of the film – we

Figure 7.1 Light on a corridor (*Lan Yu*, dir. Stanley Kwan, Hong Kong, 2001).

hear this sonic image of the proximity of life/death. The first image from the film world is a corridor where dim illumination from the window creates vertical shadows on the wall. It is only later in this film that we recognise that the film has started in Lan Yu's apartment, one of the interior spaces, including Handong's apartment and Handong's car, that function as spaces of queer intimacy. Here, right at the opening of the film, is a doubling of psychic and domestic interiority, the interplay of light and shadows, and the nearness of death in life and life in death.

Though this film is so much about Beijing's period of epochal change, we barely see outdoor scenes or know where recurrent spaces such as Handong's office are located in relation to the other spaces in the film. Frequently, the wider world is invoked through indirect means. The prelude to the 4 June 1989 massacre is suggested from the confines of Handong's office. Mixed within the whirring sound of the fan in the foreground, the flapping papers and conversations in the office, we hear the distant sirens of emergency vehicles, soon joined by rising and falling choruses of indistinct shouting mixed with bicycle bells. Handong peeps out of his window, but the camera remains fixed on the office space so we can only imagine the chaotic scene implied by the noises outside. Handong's employee and friend, Liu Zheng, confides to Handong that Liu's wife is hospitalised in a precarious state of labour and muses that 'in this world, he only has her'. After Liu leaves, a business associate, Luo Daning, arrives with a warning that 'they're clearing the Square tonight', 'Young people who want a future better stay home.' As a casual but loaded aside, Luo mentions that he saw Lan Yu keeping order in the crowd and eating a boxed meal by the roadside. This conversation

TOUCH, FLESH, WOUND AND THE CARESS OF THE SCREEN   139

suggests that Handong has not been in contact with Lan Yu for a while, though, characteristic of the time jumps in this film, we do not know how long their separation has lasted. Handong is shown to be affected by this news. After Luo leaves, Handong reflects by himself in the office, with a glance out of the window, as the voices and vehicle noises from outside the visual field of the film increase in intensity and volume. In this disjunct between the visible and audible in this scene, with the sound of political and policing activity, the audience is left to imagine the turmoil of the world outside, contrasting with the mundane hums of the office and Handong's growing unease. Even Liu Zheng's mention of his wife's perilous labour adds to the sense of life and futurity under threat.

Following the scenes of Handong's silent reflection at the office and in his apartment, the film cuts to a mostly black screen with bokeh effects in the right of the frame, which gradually reveal themselves to be bicycle lights riding towards the screen. In the next shot, framed by the view from the windshield, bicycles cross from the right of the screen to the left. This disorientation of directions is repeated with close-up shots of wheels and blurry bodies passing while faint gunfire punctuates the sound of bicycles, trishaws and general chaos. In this series of quick cuts, we see glimpses of Handong looking lost before parking his car in a quiet spot, a blurry unknown figure running away, and two shots of the surroundings before Lan Yu's hand is shown approaching Handong. In a sequence without dialogue, Lan Yu's hand is shown twice: the camera is placed at the exterior of the car, and we see Lan Yu's hand reaching into the car to touch the sleeping Handong before cutting to the interior of the car where we see Lan Yu withdrawing his hand. This truncated focus on hands and the belated revelation of Lan Yu's face continues in three shots that show an embrace: a close-up of Handong's hands over Lan Yu's torso; a close-up showing Lan Yu's head to the left and Handong's head and shoulder to the right of the frame; followed by a crossing of the 180-degree line, with Handong at the left of the frame and Lan Yu at the right of the frame, where we finally see Lan Yu's face before Handong pulls Lan Yu into an embrace. In each of these shots, shadows fall over their bodies and faces. It is only in this shot, lasting a few seconds, that we see a shadowy bruise on Lan Yu's left cheek. The scene cuts to an interior of Handong's bed, where the two lovers are shown embracing. The sound of Lan Yu's crying is layered over the two shots from the apartment: one showing Handong holding Lan Yu in bed while a vulnerable Lan Yu whose face is once again obscured, embraces Handong. Lan Yu's cries are layered over a wide shot of the bedroom framed by mirrored doors, where the contours of a body are barely visible underneath luxuriant sheets. The only speech in this scene is a dispassionate voice announcing the words 'at 4:30 am, on June 4 …', before a cut to black. So much goes unsaid and unseen in this scene, where the closed wound on Lan Yu's face becomes metonymous for the militarised violence of Tiananmen Square and the history that remains under state authoritarian control. The shadow of the exposure to death is intertwined with the shadow of bodily exposures and erotic vulnerability, recalling Derrida's thought on originary survival, where 'surviving is life beyond life, life more than life, and my discourse is not a discourse of death, but, on the contrary, the affirmation of a living being who prefers living and thus surviving to death, because survival is not simply that which remains but the most intense life possible'.[27]

Alongside Derrida's words in *On Touching*, where 'Touch, more than sight or hearing, gives nearness, proximity – it gives nearby', this chapter extends the caress between the bodies onscreen to the intersubjective possibility of caresses beyond the screen.[28] Cinema can take the form of desire for a caress beyond its diegetic world, reaching out towards the unknown and unknowable differences of the potential audience, who would see and hear the occluded scenes of history that dwell within the marks of wounded flesh. Lan Yu's wounded face becomes a surface where the worlds of prohibited sexual and political desires find a minimal dwelling, and the blurred scenes of history leave barely visible marks. In the novel, this post-Tiananmen scene is depicted with dialogue between the lovers, but in Kwan's adaptation, it is the relational flesh that speaks in tandem with Lan Yu's wails. Concluding the implied offscreen

Figure 7.2 The shadow of a bruise on Lan Yu's face before the embrace with Handong (*Lan Yu*, dir. Stanley Kwan, Hong Kong, 2001).

TOUCH, FLESH, WOUND AND THE CARESS OF THE SCREEN 141

Figure 7.3 The contours of a body under the covers and the truncated announcement of June 4th (*Lan Yu*, dir. Stanley Kwan, Hong Kong, 2001).

violence of the Tiananmen night with this scene of erotic desire and grief does not necessarily imply a dimming of political desire. By dwelling for this moment in a world of fleshly embrace, when a collective world of appearance has been crushed, Kwan makes a world where touch itself becomes a promise of desirous survival. What is Lan Yu lamenting in his cries as the two embrace? In this scene, we do not know where the political and the personal begin or end and there is a visual as well as symbolic opacity in the shadows that fall across their entwined flesh.

In the scene of intimacy in *Lan Yu*, which is born of and anticipates institutional forms of forgetting, fleshly forms of wounded memory intermix with the contours of an emerging post-Tiananmen world. In *Elemental Passions*, Irigaray speaks of the moment of emergence: 'The first outline of forms emerging. A world being born. Not yet caught within a defined horizon – that circle which condemns it to being endlessly repeated, governed by properties already fixed.'[29] Across the book, wounds, light and birth recur and reside in the remembering body:

> The memory of touching? The most insistent and the most difficult to enter into memory. The one that entails returning to a commitment whose beginning and end cannot be recovered. Memory of the flesh, where that which has not yet been written is inscribed, laid down? That which has no discourse to wrap itself in? That which has not yet been born into language? That which has a place, has taken place, but has no language. The felt, which expresses itself for the first time. Declares itself to the other in silence.[30]

In Irigaray's provocative reading, the memory of flesh touching is an originary, affective moment that precedes its entry into discourse and chronological time. The event occurs before the world has a language for it.[31] Recalling Muñoz on queer time as ecstatic time which interrupts the politics of the present, the disorienting, reticent scene of Handong and Lan Yu's embrace creates a queer world while the world is going or already gone. A world is born as a world dies, a world begins as it is dying, a world is dying as it begins. In Thomas Chen's reading of *Lan Yu*, the public square is the lost arena of possibility that is replaced inadequately by the private circle of desire and interests.[32] Chen focuses on *Lan Yu*'s depiction 'of the closure of mass activity, the replacement of revolution with romance'.[33] In my reading, shifting the focus from the defeat of public protest to an intensification of the bodily connections between Handong and Lan Yu is itself a revolutionary gesture of the erotic encounter as a form of sexual solidarity and worldmaking. Kwan is intentional about turning the military massacre into the background of a love scene: 'I was interested in how we could transform June 4 into the moment that Chen Handong commits to Lan Yu.'[34] Rather than a retreat into solipsistic romance, Kwan's multi-directional focus on the hands and torso of Lan Yu and Handong, without regard to the 180-degree line, shows the durational erotics of the flesh as an enduring practice. Beyond the sociality of the circle and the square, the cinematic displacement of public action and memory onto the wounded flesh of Lan Yu is a way of marking the political and ethical significance of queer intimacy. In *Lan Yu*, queer intimacy harbours emergent worlds of colliding differences.

The post-Tiananmen scene of embrace between Handong and Lan Yu constitutes the clashing of worlds old and new. In the novel's dialogue which Kwan excises in the adaptation, Lan Yu asks 'you really care for me that much?', and Handong's interior dialogue observes 'the word care comes out very quickly, as if he was somehow afraid to say it'.[35] Without the verbal articulation of care onscreen, the post-Tiananmen embrace captures the affective softness of flesh against flesh, against the display of hard military power offscreen that is neither unheard nor unfelt but unseen other than the glimpse of the small wound on Lan Yu's face. Michael Berry notes that Handong's name has the meaning of protecting Mao Zedong's thought, which 'recalls a dark era of political fanaticism and state violence', and Handong's father is a government cadre whose passing just before 4 June 'is a powerful foreshadowing of the imminent disaster and a sign of the failure of the old regime'.[36] In that moment, the embraces form a bulwark against an impoverished sexual and political existence facing forces of state and societal repression.

TOUCH, FLESH, WOUND AND THE CARESS OF THE SCREEN   143

David L. Eng argues that 'queerness in Kwan's film comes to function as a critical tool for organizing and evaluating not just the contemporary emergence of nonnormative sexualities and desires in (post) socialist China, but also, and more urgently, historical continuities and ruptures among China's (semi)colonial past, its revolutionary aspirations for a socialist modernity, and its contemporary investments in a neoliberal capitalist world order'.[37] Certainly, the film's narrative is organised around the meeting of oppositional forces, between past and present, rich and poor, heteronormative and queer, worldly and innocent, urban and country, with Handong on the side of the establishment and Lan Yu, with his untimely death, as the embodiment of a new generation of doomed youth. Yet, in the lacunas of the film and the intervening time between Lan Yu and Handong's encounters, the film is haunted by shadows of almost-possible configurations of existence.

In Kwan's film, the name Lan Yu stands in for 'Beijing' in the novel's title. This shift signals the power and seduction of this figure for Kwan's filmic world. Lan Yu's name carries the meaning of 'blue' *Lán* 蓝 'universe' *Yǔ* 宇. While Handong's name, as an imperative to protect Maoist thought, evokes a known statist ideology that has already unfolded in history, Lan Yu's name connotes a world of resistant mystery and the opacity of an unknowable universe. Since Handong's reflections constitute the narratorial voiceover, Lan Yu's interiority eludes the audience. In another scene from the novel that is excised in the film, when Handong discovers that Lin Ping, a woman he marries out of the desire to live a dutiful heteronormative life, has outed Lan Yu at Lan Yu's conservative workplace and caused Lan Yu's dismissal, Lin Ping resorts to a homophobic self-defence, 'Besides, people like that? What difference does it make if there's one less of them in the world?'[38] The film jumps in time from the photo shoot in preparation for Handong's and Lin Ping's wedding to a time when Handong is already divorced. In so doing, Kwan maintains the focus on Handong and Lan Yu, while also avoiding the novel's stereotypical portrayal of Lin Ping as the scorned, vengeful women. Though the lines dismissing Lan Yu's existence are not spoken in the film, in its sensuous focus on Handong and Lan Yu's intermittent and intense meetings, the film provides a sensory answer to a homophobic dismissal of queer life, that it indeed does make a difference if there's one less Lan Yu, one less singular universe of possibilities.

When societal and political conditions deny places of inhabitation for queer love caught up in a moment of historical protest that is also under the shadow of denial, could the cinema provide a durational world where the intertwined condition of sex, body and flesh may find a place of expression without essentialist, predetermined forms? In thinking of cinema and spectatorial relation, I turn to the radicality of the figure of the reciprocal caress via Irigaray's rewriting of Levinas. It would not be possible to think the radical possibilities of Levinas's 'Phenomenology of Eros' without Irigaray's intervention into the gendered phenomenology of the caress. 'Fecundity of the Caress' enacts the time of tenacity and non-appropriative alterity inaugurated by the caress where: 'Touch makes it possible to wait, to gather strength, so that the other will return to caress and reshape, from within and from without, a flesh that is given back to itself in the gesture of love.'[39] Gayatri Spivak argues that Irigaray 'undoes Levinas's sexism by degendering the active-passive division' and describes 'Fecundity of the Caress' as a text 'that assumes that both partners do things, and are not inevitably heterosexual'.[40] Tina Chanter reads Irigaray's refusal of Levinas's reduction of the feminine to the maternal as an opening 'to the possibility of homosexuality'.[41] Anne Berger emphasises that for Irigaray, it is the 'addressed other' that matters, 'thinking of sexual difference always means thinking of a/the relation between two, assessing the terms of their bonds, in other words, thinking of love or what may prevent it'.[42]

In *Irigaray and Politics*, Laura Roberts argues that criticisms of essentialism neglect that Irigaray's work poses 'an ontological challenge to the western tradition'. The crux of Roberts's argument is that Irigaray's work on sexual difference is 'connected to bodies which exist in the world in multiple incarnations'.[43] Penelope Deutscher reminds us of the idea of the 'sensible transcendental' in Irigaray's interest in situating divinity within the world of the senses.[44] With infinity in the finitude of the body and its contact with another infinite-finite body, the 'sensible transcendental' opens up gender and sexuality as an infinite possibility of transcendence. While the heterosexual example predominates in Irigaray's writing, in the potential for thinking the infinite relations of a person to a gender that is predeterminable as the negative of a man/woman binary, the relevance of the thought goes beyond heterosexual relations. By imagining the gendered pronouns in Irigaray's 'Fecundity of the Caress' in suspended ambivalence, without overdetermining what form of fleshly incarnations the pronouns assume, sexual difference on the ontological level need not presume the forms of appearance of sexual and gendered difference in lived experience. In holding on, via Irigaray, to the sense of the caress in *Lan Yu* as the birth of an indeterminate, intersubjective world, how could *Lan Yu* in turn caress and disorient Irigaray's world?

Alongside her committed practice of Yoga, Irigaray has written on the tropes of the East and West.[45] In *A New Culture of Energy*, Irigaray returns to the topic of the caress as 'the gesture that can give us back to ourselves after a neutralization or a loss of identity in living together or

TOUCH, FLESH, WOUND AND THE CARESS OF THE SCREEN   145

in the technical universe of work'.[46] Irigaray reminds us that the caress could be patriarchal and predatory or it could be an intimacy that is reciprocal and restorative, where 'the caress is a sort of exchanged speech that resituates the one and the other within the intimacy of his or her flesh'.[47] Despite her deconstructive tendencies, the binaries of East and West remain. The teachings of the East are sometimes cited as a site of edification and reparation for what is amiss in Western culture or marked off as a difference beyond comment. It occurs, for example, in *An Ethics of Sexual Difference*, when Irigaray describes a 'gesture often reserved for women (at least in the West)'.[48] The parenthetical aside leaves open the anthropological possibility of cultural and gendered differences in the West and non-West. This demarcation between the East and the West reappears when Irigaray claims belonging to both worlds:

> After ten years of practice, this culture and world had become mine and I could no longer tell if I belonged to the Western world or to the Eastern world where yoga was born. I belonged – I belong – henceforth to both.[49]

In Irigaray's biographical and historical appeal to the 'Western world' and 'Eastern world', what remains undeconstructed (but not undeconstructible) is the locus/orientation/histories of the 'East' and 'West' and the separation into distinct worlds. Even in Roberts's defence of multiple incarnations in Irigaray, there is the persistence of the marker of the 'western tradition'. There are resonances between my interest in touch and Laura Marks's thesis on haptic visuality, which also invokes the caress, though we differ with regards to the question of the 'West'.[50]

What happens if the promise of the fecundity of the caress is extended to thoughts of different provenance without deterministic appeals to the distinct worlds of East and West? Naoki Sakai reminds us of the histories of colonialism and structural racism condensed in the term 'the West'.[51] With *Lan Yu*'s cinematic caresses, the opacity and porosity of the touching of skin and shadow, skin and cloth, skin and light, creates an interstitial world for the visual and sonic image, distinct from geopolitically rendered, calculable, separable worlds. At a glance, reading *Lan Yu* alongside Derrida and Irigaray could be rendered as the meeting of Eastern and Western works or thoughts. Additionally, the narrative of the novel and film include elements of the putative West such as Lan Yu's abandoned plans for migration to America, Handong's import-export business and Lin Ping's work as a translator. However, rather than disentangling what belongs properly to the East or West in the inside or outside of the film, remembering the promise of the caress and the

146   ELIZABETH WIJAYA

scenes of embrace leads to a more radical disorientation. In writing on
Marie-Françoise Plissart's photography, Derrida notes: 'no caress can
close the distance or exceed the image, the distance of the image'.[52]
Beyond the oppositions of life or death, East or West, private or public,
past or present, something resistant, rather than nothing, survives. Right
till the final image of *Lan Yu*, the caress remains a suspended promise,
a provocation of the audience, that cannot be determinately possessed.

3. Suspended embrace and the distance of the image

In the coda of *Lan Yu*, the camera looks on from the interior of
Handong's car into the Beijing exterior. 'You know what?', the interior monologue begins in a voiceover as Handong drives, noting that
'Whenever I pass the site where you had the accident, I stop / But
my mind is at peace ... / Because I feel you are always with me.' In a
tightly composed shot, the side window of the car acts as a frame within
the film frame, providing an obstructed vision of Beijing. The scene
cuts briefly to a medium close-up shot of Handong in the driver's seat
before cutting to a wide shot of Beijing, as Taiwanese singer Huang
Pin-Yuan's plaintive Mandopop song 'How could you allow me to be
in sorrow' accompanies the scene. The image of the inscrutable heart is
sonically invoked. The popular song is from the album *Supporting Actor's
Heartfelt Voice (Nan Pei Jiao Xin Sheng)*, released in 1990 by the Taiwan-
headquartered company, Rock Records.[53] Though the lyrics do not
specify a gender for the addressee of the song, the official music video
suggests a heterosexual scene of lost love between a man and a woman.
Lan Yu's place in cinematic history has expanded the imaginative possibilities for the gender configuration of the song's lovers. As the song
plays on, the view of Beijing becomes increasingly obscured by the
blue fencing and concrete enclosing the sides of an overhead bridge. At
this point, the functions of the wide shot and close-up merge as we see
blurry washes of blue with indistinct glimpses of the urban setting. At
one point in the chorus of the song, which is not subtitled, the singer
laments the beloved leaving without saying a word and the longing to
see the beloved again. There is only a brief glimpse of traffic at a junc-
tion before a cut to black. The third minute of the song continues as,
for a few seconds, we see the final scene of the film. In a desaturated
medium close-up, the familiar figures of Handong and Lan Yu move
in slow motion as Handong embraces Lan Yu. With their faces buried
in each other, arms and hands become the sites of bodily expression of
desire. There are echoes of Handong and Lan Yu's prior reunion in Lan
Yu's apartment, but this scene is slower, and the framing is even tighter,

Figure 7.4 Handong and Lan Yu in the last scene before the end-credits (*Lan Yu*, dir. Stanley Kwan, Hong Kong, 2001).

showing only brief hints of the environment. Is this a flashback, flashforward, a memory, or imagination? In *On Touching*, variations of the question 'When our eyes touch, is it day or is it night?' recur.[54] Linnell Secomb reads this question as 'When our I's touch, there is the promise of day and night, the anticipation of life and death, that facilitates friendship and love, and the singular-plural democracy and/or community to come.'[55] In Derrida's question, there is also the promise of a temporal interruption of the rhythms and associations of day and night. With this embrace that is suspended in time and space, without clarity as to the time of day, the film ends as the song of longing for the beloved continues into the credits. The grief for a departed lover is intermixed with grief for an eclipsed vision of the world.

The final scene returns to a moment of embrace between two bodies, which visually and affectively overwhelms the screen and is not placed within narrative time. This moment of erotic indetermination recalls the earlier reference to the 'suspended heart' with which the film begins. The vision of this embrace haunts the barely visible landscape of Beijing under construction. As an erotic place of inhabitation, the cinematic embrace allows for histories and bodies under threat of forgetting to dwell in the gaps, where not only what is shown in bright lights but also what is hinted at in the shadows have a chance at *survivance*. Derrida relates *survivance* to finitude and 'this alliance of the dead and the living'.[56] The audience is teased with the inheritance of this cinematic archive, a wound in search of a world. Throughout the film, there are visual suggestions that the world Handong and Lan Yu find themselves in lacks lasting spaces for their queer relationship, which remains hidden in interior spaces. In the novel, in the chapter before Lan Yu's accidental death, Lan Yu and Handong share a rare moment of intimacy outdoors when they take a walk in the Western Hills. This prompts a reflection from Handong, 'In nearly a decade of knowing him, it was only the second time we had ever shared a kiss outdoors. But now, instead of darkness, we were surrounded by radiant sunlight, blue skies, and the beautiful, rolling hills around us.' In the novel and the film's shared vacillation between hope and despair, these instances of queer intimacy are never without personal and social risk but also never without desire for a world to inhabit. In this desaturated last appeal before the end, seducing the audience into a remote, resistant world that remains in the memory of touch, gesturing towards what Derrida calls, following Levinas, 'contact beyond contact' – flesh touches, virtually.[57] While the death of Lan Yu could be read as a recapitulation to a tragic narrative of queer impossibility, the final image holds on, in soft militancy, to the memory of queer caresses, embracing the audience with the seduction of another world still dimly possible, still palpably touchable.[58]

Notes

1. Luce Irigaray, *Elemental Passions*, trans. Joanne Collie and Judith Still (New York: Routledge, 1992), 84–5.
2. Luce Irigaray, *Speculum of the Other Woman*, trans. Gillian C. Gill (Ithaca, NY: Cornell University Press, 1985), 200. See Amy Hollywood, '"That Glorious Slit": Irigaray and the Medieval Devotion to Christ's Side Wound', in *Acute Melancholia and Other Essays: Mysticism, History, and the Study of Religion* (New York: Columbia University Press, 2016), 171–88.
3. See Penelope Deutscher, 'Mourning the Other, Cultural Cannibalism, and the Politics of Friendship (Jacques Derrida and Luce Irigaray)', *differences: A Journal of Feminist Cultural Studies* 10.3 (1998), 159–84. I am heartened by Deutscher's engagement with 'difference at the site of sexual difference' without assuming that the homo is necessarily the site of the self-same (180).
4. Jacques Derrida, *The Beast and the Sovereign*, vol. II, trans. Geoffrey Bennington (Chicago: University of Chicago Press, 2011), 1.
5. Ibid., 268.
6. See Cary Wolfe's argument that Wallace Stevens's poetry allows for the recognition that the world is gone for human and non-human lives, and in that discovery, 'ethics and ecological responsibility begin' in the poetic construction of the shared world. *Ecological Poetics; or, Wallace Stevens's Birds* (Chicago: The University of Chicago Press, 2020), 109.
7. See, for example, Jacques Derrida, *Cinders*, trans. Ned Lukacher (Minneapolis: University of Minnesota Press, 2014).
8. See Michael Nass's reading of Derrida's use of 'poetically' in this passage and

how 'this *poiesis* would be a making as if that leaves within the world a trace of the end or loss of the world'. *The End of the World and Other Teachable Moments: Jacques Derrida's Final Seminar* (New York: Fordham University Press, 2014), 80.

9. Cathy Caruth, *Literature in the Ashes of History* (Baltimore, MD: John Hopkins University Press, 2013), xi–xii.

10. Margaret Hillenbrand, *Negative Exposures: Knowing What Not to Know in Contemporary China* (Durham, NC: Duke University Press, 2020). See also Louisa Lim, *The People's Republic of Amnesia: Tiananmen Revisited* (Oxford: Oxford University Press, 2014).

11. Fiona Ng, 'Interview: Love in the Time of Tiananmen; Stanley Kwan's *Lan Yu*', 25 July 2002. https://www.indiewire.com/2002/07/interview-love-in-the-time-of-tiananmen-stanley-kwans-lan-yu-80279/ (accessed 20/12/2023).

12. Scott E. Myers, 'Translator's Note', in Bei Tong, *Beijing Comrades*, trans. Scott E. Myers (New York: The Feminist Press, 2016), vii–xvii (x).

13. Bao Hongwei, *Queer China: Lesbian and Gay Literature and Visual Culture under Postsocialism* (New York: Routledge, 2020), 8.

14. Bao Hongwei, 'Queer as Catachresis: The Beijing Queer Film Festival in Cultural Translation', in *Chinese Film Festivals: Sites of Translation*, ed. Chris Berry and Luke Robinson (New York: Palgrave Macmillan, 2017), 86.

15. Hongwei, 'Queer as Catachresis', 84.

16. Howard Chiang notes that '*Lan Yu* and *Beijing Story* have served as an important focus of discussion and queer bonding across the PRC and global Sinophone communities.' *Transtopia in the Sinophone Pacific* (New York: Columbia University Press, 2021), 248.

17. José Esteban Muñoz, *Cruising Utopia* (New York: New York University Press, 2009), 32. See Ruthanne Crapo Kim's reading of Irigaray and Muñoz through a method, inspired by Tina Chanter, of reading Irigaray with a 'disidentificatory lens', by 'neither assimilating nor strictly opposing her'. 'Disidentification in Irigaray and Anzaldúa: Nepantla and Sexuate Politics', *Sophia* 61 (2022), 172.

18. See Caroline Bainbridge, *A Feminine Cinematics: Luce Irigaray, Women and Film* (London: Palgrave Macmillan UK, 2008); Lucy Bolton, *Film and Female Consciousness: Irigaray, Cinema and Thinking Women* (London: Palgrave Macmillan UK, 2011); Kaja Silverman, *The Acoustic Mirror: The Female Voice in Psychoanalysis and Cinema: Theories of Representation and Difference* (Bloomington: Indiana University Press, 1988).

19. 'Kwan has been discussed as a director of "women's pictures" with an orientation "toward the feminine"'. Shuqin Cui, 'Stanley Kwan's "Center Stage": The (Im)possible Engagement between Feminism and Postmodernism', *Cinema Journal* 39.4 (2000), 62.

20. Luce Irigaray, *An Ethics of Sexual Difference*, trans. Carolyn Burke and Gillian C. Gill (Ithaca, NY: Cornell University Press, 1993), 187.

21. Bao, *Queer China*, 77.

22. Pheng Cheah, Elizabeth Grosz, Judith Butler and Drucilla Cornell, 'The Future of Sexual Difference: An Interview with Judith Butler and Drucilla Cornell', *Diacritics* 28.1 (1998), 28.

23. Irigaray, *An Ethics of Sexual Difference*, 6.

24. Penelope Deutscher, *A Politics of Impossible Difference* (Ithaca, NY: Cornell University Press, 2002), 119. See also Dorothea Olkowski on how Irigaray's argument necessitates 'a change in the economy of desire' such that 'other relations than those between man and woman are at stake'. *Gilles Deleuze and the Ruin of Representation* (Berkeley: University of California Press, 1999), 81.

25. Gail Weiss, *Body Images: Embodiment as Intercorporeality* (New York: Routledge, 1999), 82.

26. This essay refers to the version of *Lan Yu* distributed by Mongrel Media Inc. For the film's twentieth anniversary, a 4K restoration approved by Kwan and helmed by Yongning Creative Workshop, in collaboration with the film restoration laboratory, L'immagine Ritrovata and the Hong Kong company, One Cool, was released. When comparing the Mongrel Media version with the restoration, other than colour and tonal differences, there are also some differences in shot length and shot choice including with the final scene of the film.

27. Jacques Derrida, *Learning to Live Finally: An Interview with Jean Birnbaum*, trans. Pascale-anne Brault and Michael Naas (Hoboken, NJ: Melville House Pub, 2007), 52.

28. Jacques Derrida, *On Touching–Jean-Luc Nancy*, trans. Christine Irizarry (Stanford, CA: Stanford University Press, 2005), 95. Derrida engages with Irigaray's work on touch and the caress only in the footnotes of this book.

29. Irigaray, *Elemental Passions*, 95.

30. Ibid., 215.

31. Irigaray voices this suspicion of language's role in the reproduction of sameness in Luce Irigaray and Carolyn Burke 'When Our Lips Speak Together', *Signs* 6.1 (1980), 69–79. The allusions to genital lips in this work has been debated. I am following the non-essentialist possibilities of Irigaray's reading of the body as a site of non-appropriative encounter with the other and I extend this to situations of sexual, class, political and cultural constraints where two parties are not free to realise a world together. For an analysis of Irigaray's temporalisation of touch as an interval 'between the memory of flesh and the future of becoming', see Ewa Plonowska, Ziarek, 'Toward a Radical Female Imaginary: Temporality and Embodiment in Irigaray's Ethics', *Diacritics* 28.1 (1998), 68.

32. Thomas Chen, *Made in Censorship: The Tiananmen Movement in Chinese Literature and Film* (New York: Columbia University Press, 2022), 107.

33. Ibid., 100.

34. Michael Berry, 'Stanley Kwan: From Spectral Nostalgia to Corporeal Desire', in *Speaking in Images: Interviews with Contemporary Chinese Filmmakers* (New York: Columbia University Press, 2005), 454.

35. Bei Tong, *Beijing Comrades*, trans. Scott E. Myers (New York: The Feminist

TOUCH, FLESH, WOUND AND THE CARESS OF THE SCREEN **151**

Press, 2016), 121.

36. Michael Berry, *A History of Pain: Trauma in Modern Chinese Literature and Film* (New York: Columbia University Press, 2008), 316.

37. David L. Eng, 'The Queer Space of China: Expressive Desire in Stanley Kwan's *Lan Yu*', *positions: east asia cultures critique* 18.2 (2010), 462.

38. Bei Tong, *Beijing Comrades*, 232.

39. Irigaray, *An Ethics of Sexual Difference*, 187.

40. Gayatri Spivak, *Outside in the Teaching Machine* (New York: Routledge, 2009), 188.

41. Tina Chanter, *Ethics of Eros: Irigaray's Rewriting of the Philosophers* (New York: Routledge, 1995), 281. This does not mean that homosexual relations need to be excluded from maternity but that the mystery of fecundity need not be about the procreation of the child but what Chanter reads as 'the rebirth of both lovers in eros' (219).

42. Anne Emmanuelle Berger, 'Irigaray's Breath, or Poetry After Poetics', in *Philosophy and Poetry: Continental Perspectives*, ed. Ranjan Ghosh (New York: Columbia University Press, 2019), 228–9.

43. Laura Roberts, *Irigaray and Politics* (Edinburgh: Edinburgh University Press, 2019), 8. See also the Special Issue edited by Pheng Cheah and Elizabeth Grosz, 'Irigaray and the Political Future of Sexual Difference', *Diacritics* 28.1 (1998). My interest is in drawing out the nuances in Irigaray's work in thinking corporeality between two touching bodies as a force for temporal and political disruption. See also Alison Stone's on 'the possibility of rhythmically diverse bodies' in Irigaray's metaphysics, 'The Sex of Nature: A Reinterpretation of Irigaray's Metaphysics and Political Thought', *Hypatia* 18.3 (2003), 60.

44. Penelope Deutscher, '"The Only Diabolical Thing about Women ...": Luce Irigaray on Divinity', *Hypatia* 9.4 (1994), 98. See also Margaret Whitford's analysis of how Irigaray differs from Derrida's 'space of multiple sexuality, beyond male and female'. *Luce Irigaray: Philosophy in the Feminine* (New York: Routledge, 1991), 154.

45. See Luce Irigaray, *Between East and West: From Singularity to Community*, trans. Stephen Pluháček (New York: Columbia University Press, 2002).

46. Luce Irigaray, *A New Culture of Energy: Beyond East and West*, trans. Stephen Seely and Stephen Pluháček (New York: Columbia University Press, 2021), 36.

47. Irigaray, *A New Culture of Energy*, 37.

48. Irigaray, *An Ethics of Sexual Difference*, 161.

49. Irigaray, *A New Culture of Energy*, 4.

50. Marks argues for an intercultural cinema that expresses the experience of living between two 'cultural regimes of knowledge' or 'living as a minority in the still majority white, Euro-American West'. Laura Marks, *The Skin of the Film: Intercultural Cinema, Embodiment, and the Senses* (Durham, NC: Duke University Press, 2000), 1. She invokes Irigaray's question on 'How to preserve the memory of the caress' but engages more deeply with

Maurice Merleau-Ponty and Henri Bergson in her analysis (150).

51. Naoki Sakai, *The End of Pax Americana: The Loss of Empire and Hikikomori Nationalism* (Durham, N.C: Duke University Press, 2022). See also Naoki Sakai, 'Theory and Asian Humanity: On the Question of Humanitas and Anthropos', *Postcolonial Studies* 13.4 (2010), 441–64.

52. Jacques Derrida, *Right of Inspection*, trans. David Wills, photographs by Marie-Françoise Plissart (New York: The Monacelli Press, 1998). See J. Hillis Miller's reading of the deconstruction of gender binaries in Derrida's essay on the photographs in 'Preposterous Preface: Derrida and Queer Discourse', in *Derrida and Queer Theory*, ed. Christian Hite (New York: Punctum Books, 2017), 24–67.

53. The song serves as a reminder of the broader geopolitics of this film. Howard Chiang makes a convincing argument that *Lan Yu*'s relevance exceeds the politics of China, noting that 'critics have noted *Lan Yu*'s indebtedness to Taiwan, for the popularity of the film in Taiwan preceded that in China', *Transtopia*, 248.

54. Derrida, *On Touching*, 3. See Elizabeth Rottenberg on dawn and the primal scene of sovereignty's visibility in Derrida's *The Death Penalty*, vol. 1. 'A New Primal Scene: Derrida and the Scene of Execution', in *Deconstructing the Death Penalty: Derrida's Seminars and the New Abolitionism*, eds Kelly Oliver and Stephanie Straub (New York: Fordham University Press, 2020), 32–62.

55. Linnell Secomb, *Philosophy and Love: From Plato to Popular Culture* (Edinburgh University Press, 2007), 156.

56. Derrida, *Beast*, 130. See also Kas Saghafi, 'Dying Alive', *Mosaic* 48.3 (2015), 15–26.

57. Derrida, *On Touching*, 77.

58. My gratitude to Lynn Turner for her valuable suggestions on improving this chapter. The title is inspired by a writing group at Cornell University that I participated in during the 2016–17 academic year.

8

No Deconstruction Without Pleasure: Openings, Tunnels and Holes

Quinn Eades

A note on the text

Reading sometimes hurts. It is a practice of opening to the text and what it will bring, and because of that opening, when we read, we are vulnerable. Reading this text may hurt, or bring tears, or a rush of desire, or a memory pushing forwards unbidden. There are accounts of sexual violence here, and there is some explicit detail regarding the act/s I am writing from/with/about. This work has trauma in it (just like this body), but it also has love.

> [...] when you can't stop crumpling the sheets around you to make a hole in the violence to find the way out [...] I am writing with a view to waking up [...].
> (Jacques Derrida)[1]

> Many of my predecessors died and continue to die to this day, murdered, raped, beaten, incarcerated, medicalized [...] or they lived or are living their difference in secret. This is my heritage [...].
> (Paul B. Preciado)[2]

On the (dead)name

We are thinking about the many categories the many kinds many ways of writing that will give us a way. We make a careful note: we are writing this from inside The University, we are vulnerable, we worry that we can't write any of this. Here is where we think where we worry and wonder

Writing rape

We write this rape again, all ways again, just in order to say this is has will happen to transmasc people and to transmen. Never forget that we were trained, like all girls are, to lie still, to wait til it's over, to fawn, to bend. We hope we have made something like a warning sign. We what bipolar what transman what white late transitioning gay transman bipolar CPTSD birthed two babies a dyke for most of our life kinky as fuck writing is.

Before we can get to this writing we are stopped at our name. Our name, like all names, is haunted. Our name carries so many other names so many other ones how can we how could we send them all a way.

He wakes knowing he has lost his name again. In the dream the details change but what happens stays the same. He is in a crowd of people. He is asked his name. No name except his deadname comes. It comes out of his mouth and he says *no, that's wrong, my name is …* but he can't remember there is no remembering his name the name he gave himself. So his deadname stays on other people's lips.

Says again *no, my name is …* but can't find it, again again. The name he gifted he rooted himself with is out-of-bounds a slippage a stutter a tongue left blunt from scraping against the cliff edge of what is this, how is this place called again again?

Because a body is a place and he named this place and now in the dream the name is gone. Because a body is a place and often it is a place he cannot find. Because a transbody is a hidden a secret place a cavern a well a doorway a ruin a gate because a transbody is time fucked is his body fucked is learning to say an ecstatic yes.

walk as far as the night.[3] We write into the night into the throat of a swallowing man under a bushfire moon saying love is will be here in this ruin. Saying stay, love, stay.

Fucking apps

In the ends and the beginnings it is just him with a fucking app and no language to describe what he wants or what he is looking for. Guys message him and use words like *raw* and *raunchy*, like *bareback*, tell him they've *never fucked a trans guy before*, ask him to *squirt all over their face*, say *can I come over.*

he lets one of them come. Sends him a message saying my house isn't very clean and is he ok with dogs. He doesn't reply. He looks at himself in the mirror. Wants to want this. He knocks on the door he opens the door He walks straight to his bedroom. Complains that He *can't get hard with a condom on.* PrEP has changed every thing and most men he talks to on Scruff have a strong preference for bareback, as if HIV is the only thing we need to worry about.

he tells him where the gloves and lube are, says *if you're not going to use a condom you can fist me instead.* He does. he wanks while He fucks him and he comes. He puts his clothes on fast and before He leaves says *Well I've ticked that off my list* and he is numb.

he wonders if there are a lot of straight cis men on Scruff, and if they search for trans guys, search

Each name haunts all others

In the same way that we are multiplely bodied we are multiplely named.

We cannot do not leave these bodies behind we cannot do not seek to integrate our bodies or our selves we cannot do not carry our many names. We have tried it before it hurts too much we seek to leave all names but some behind.

The most powerful names are the ones we will we never say. Names call us to each other and to our selves. They will never have our secret names our quiet names the names our great love calls us in the depths of our body in a heart beat felt from the inside.

Each name carries each name bears its weight. Each name haunts all others.

We take the name of a man we never knew. We take the name of our ghostpoet grandfather, John Quinn. We take what came last and we make it first. The last time we speak to our mother she says *I can't call you that – that's my name* and we say *it's my name too.*

We take the name of a man we never knew. We take the name of our great grandfather, a man named Francis Eades. Say to our selves that 'everything impossible

'– Here, in this very place where we are …

– …where we're taking ourselves…'[4]

not even for trans guys, but for our holes, and for what they can do with those holes. Find out later that yes, there are many men like this on fucking apps, that this practice is called trawling.

he decides to try again. Thinks he has been spoilt with years of queer bent transmasc fucking, of fists and strap ons and slings and sounding rods. he runs his profile past a gay friend who is on apps all the time. He says it is good.

he can't tell you what his profile said because after the rape he deleted it.

They had been talking on Scruff for about six weeks. He has no profile picture (warning). He messages him one afternoon not long after he has moved house. *Invite me over* He says. he tells Him he is *tired* and *vulnerable. Invite me over* He says, as if he had not spoken at all (warning). he doesn't say anything. *Invite me over.* he unpacks another box, turns on the TV for COVID news because it is between the first and second wave in Melbourne the virus is churning and shedding, the virus is not coming the virus is already here. *Invite me over invite me over invite me over.* he says *ok.* he says *bring some cider let's have a chat about what we might like to do I'm not up for anything else. No problem,* He says.

The first thing he sees when he opens his front door is His baseball cap with an Australian flag on the front (warning). *Don't be closed minded* is what he thinks even will be possible' stake our lives on our name, learn that 'what was not is'.[5] Read the editor's note in *On the Name* that says *Sauf le Nom* can also be translated as *Safe the Name*.[6] Weep on a shadowed back step. Safe, the name. Name safe, name keep, keepsake, keep safe.

though he is yet to meet a patriot he likes, and he lets him in. It is dark outside. He has parked his car around the corner which later means he has no number plate, no way of tracking

Him. He sits down on his couch and they start talking. He asks him what he likes and he tells Him. *You're making me hard*, He says and takes His hand and puts it on His cock and then he goes a way (WARNING).

small hands and thick forearms are sought after he has both when D comes over with his fisting friends he sees how they display their hands and arms cocks not considered never that important for fisters he has been damaged by cocks but also by hands and arms he was a radical leather dyke and then a dyke for decades so he knows how women can hurt each other how far and hard a fist in a cunt can go not when he wants it but because he wants it like that often he goes as soft as he can he takes it but D's hands are crooked beautiful strong his arms are ropey and blue veined he makes his way in only hurts him if he wants it and he does want it often and when it's his turn when he watches his hand and arm drawn slowly in he sees D smile sees his face ecstatic looks like some kind of saint in the sling in the blood thumped dawn says *I love you* hears *I love you* back goes in in in.

No deconstruction without pleasure

'So: no deconstruction without pleasure and no pleasure without deconstruction. "It is necessary", if one wants to or can, to resign oneself to it or take it from there.'[7]

We take it from there. We spend many years turning in a cocoon of our own making, in a restless sleep, silkwrapped and shaking, a stutter nested in a scream. We go towards every broken place every part

Dead men don't rape

We Are Raped. We cannot say *were* Raped. We cannot not have this word without it being a Proper Noun a naming a calling in. We cannot not have this word without it always being in the Present Tense but the *are* is the tense that holds us in that is this three hours that ticks over and over a bomb clock in the body no coloured wires to snip it stopped no pliers in a steady hand no defusing never

NO DECONSTRUCTION WITHOUT PLEASURE

taken we stroke we lay down we let him into all of them he blind-folds he restrains he opens us he holds us he loves us in the filthiest in the most ecstatic ways.

We take it from there. We shudder under him we tunnel into him. We find bliss find the deep-est pleasure in our beings pulled a part we give our selves up to our in sides we interleave trauma with bliss-in-the-body with *jouissance*.

We laugh unbidden. We come.

I am writing a poetics of fisting. This is not abject writing. This is not disgust.

He knows he is a monster. He has questions about monsters about ghosts and veils and veilings about hiding and unhidden about being found out and found under. Wants to know what does a transperson who isn't a monster look like?

What can a transman write?

What faggot, what dyke herit-ages does he carry?

What does The University have to say about how he writes this?

What poems for his body? For his love?

What is the abject category, par excellence?

What is that category?

What is par? Are we under or over or through or beside par?

What is beside par what is under through excellence?

What pleasure?

What can he say that won't be filtered through (most of) his listen-ers' understandings and experiences of cisheterosexual masculinity?

because we also cannot say We Are Rape. We cannot say We Are Rape because then we are doing the raping as well as being done to. We Are Raped and the body is not home.

He takes our body our bodies there are so many of us in here in the honey curl in the between in the wax walled cells the wax he leaves his fucking fingerprints in. He does his hands and his cock and his quiet fucking words make leave impressions we do Every Thing to stay cured to live for a thousand years to feed his larval young to lie wordless in this length of time where time is not a line not a rope to balance on not a To Ward where time pushes down our throats and fills this pushed open tunnel side ways and long ways and In and Out where time is frothing is a spit is wipe come on his jumper In Between Acts.

Rape is not a Good Word. It is not a Care Full word. Every One prefers the words Sexual Assault this is what the websites say what the pamphlets say what the services are called. It is the Centre Against Sexual Assault that takes our phone call that takes our tremor voice that says I Was Sexually Assaulted can you can you can you help can I talk can I move can I unshake The World can I can you make time ordinary again. Can time be a thick wet rope spooling down to a rusted anchor drop can it find lichen and moss can the deep be any blacker can phosphorescence

What can't he write? What can't he speak? There is so much he can't say but can write, can't write but can say. He writes can't I write cunt we write cunt, we write. We write with a singular multiple *we*. This *we* is a revelation and so is writing in the third person – he revels in some small distance, in a breath made by *him* made by *he*.

Trauma theory has already told him he is split. That every moment trauma laid itself down in his body a part of him has stayed there, stayed at four, at nine, at fifteen, at twenty one, at twenty eight, at thirty, at thirty seven, at forty five, at forty eight. At all in-betweens he is torn a part.

He is raped in his home, violently, 5 months into the Melbourne lockdown. There is a 9pm curfew and a 5k limit. He can leave home for only three reasons. He is decimated. He is ruined. He is a ruin. He insists on survival in his ruination. He lays himself down in the ruins in the ruins of his body of his desire. Makes a home in a multiple and multiplying being. Says yes to being a mad crip gay trans mother poet.

remember us to the milky surface of the sea. Can we swim down a wet line a tunnel can we still say a tunnel when there is no space no air no any thing on the inside can we take a mirror can we hold it up broken to his rutting face can we take a piece for our own can we slice something Off Him can we say You Are Rape.

the shallows are through the first opening. Or second opening because the first opening is the opening of legs the first opening is made possible by the sling and the sling is made possible by the frame. On a play weekend if he has finished his work they set up the frame together. Black steel, machined precise, each leg made of two parts, a tube nestled into a tube with bright gold catches to stop things from sliding. Alignment is critical. Force cannot be used. It is a gentle, a soft twisting to get the holes to align to ask for the gold pin to put the pin through aligned holes so the frame stays together. It does more than stay together the frame

NO DECONSTRUCTION WITHOUT PLEASURE

when assembled is only a few feet from the ceiling of the back room transformed a back room become dungeon become play room out of time they move out of time it never matters where the sun is what hour what minute it is.

On a play weekend if he hasn't finished his work D sets up the dungeon alone. Any other time this room is the place where his oldest child plays console games and sends messages to friends and eats. Any other time this is the room they all walk through to get to the back garden to be with the fig tree who is fruiting who likes them all, even the dog. The dungeon, whether the boy is helping or not, takes shape. The sling is slung from chains so it hangs in suspension, a small leather bed with stirrups at one end and cuffs at the other. Towels everywhere. A chair placed at the stirrup end. Another chair close, holding crisco and paper towels and lube. A chest over there, near the couch, holding long thin and thick toys, black gloves embedded with tiny metal pins on the palms and undersides of the fingers, toys that can be pumped full of air toys as long as his arm, whips and paddles and canes. Ecstatic implements. Fluid drawn.

The first opening is the opening of legs. The first time they play D lies down in the sling, opens his legs, puts his feet in the stirrups, breathes, settles into the cradle of leather and steel. His hands stay uncuffed but as the boy moves his fingers into the opening D often puts both hands over his face, smiling, smiling, saying *yes.* The boy thinks he looks like some stunning gay saint, thinks of Jarman in 'Blue', sees a blue shroud a halo made from candlelight a supplicant a ritual every moment an opening a sacred a holy place had not expected visions those washes of colour the world turned golden and bright bitten red.[8]

The first opening is gentling fingers softened knuckles the way a hand can compress. They take time and turn it into a twisting a moving a going on going in. Slow is how they get to the shallows, the first place they rest. The first time his hand goes over the lip, fingers curling into the palm, fingers hand and wrist a kind of animal warm and closed quiet while they rest. D says *I love you* his hands over his face again and the boy says *I love you* and they have known each other a little less than a fortnight but they both know it they both say yes. They are 76 and 46 when they meet. The boy finds himself praying *give me 15 good years* and now, as he writes this, realises there are only 11 left.

Your gift of sex	**This story is a tunnel**
In 1922, Kafka asked himself in his diary: 'What have you done with your gift of sex? It was a failure,	It was between the first and second wave, I tell the we that is me. This I that is the me you have already

in the end that is all that they will say.'[9]

After decades of no-sex or not-what-he-wants sex he observes, then approaches, then accepts this gift of sex. He makes a home in a multiple and multiplying being. Falls in love with a man who loves him back. Realises this is the first time a lover has done that. Says yes to being a mad crip gay trans mother poet. Says this is my language these are my words they can be written but it is very hard to say them.

He is fairly convinced that his mad crip gay trans pleasure writing could cost him his livelihood, his children, his job. Does it anyway. Gambles that The University won't read him. Says yes to writing a poetics of the gay trans body of fisting of praying at the altar of each other's bodies of our in sides of how carefully we come back out.

Dust moths

How does writing come? Coming and writing, writing-to-come, how do we write the writing that is not-yet but yet and then and then and we were never amongst friends it was years it was years we went years on a couch out of the weather in the dust in the moths in the moths bedded down in the three carpeted rooms of our house.

When A was here (dearest friend, dearest love) from Utrecht they said one morning after sleep-

read is the one that will do what he can to tell the trauma story to the we that is me, that is sometimes, not All The Time, you. I remember writing and saying so many times this:

trauma is not always at the limits of language

as if insisting to others would make it true for myself, as if by writing Every Thing I could find language for some (for all, please for all, can language be capable of closing wounds) of What Happens. I have lived the blank places. I know the walls they are an old yellow the floor mined out of itself the floor dug through water table the floor below bedrock where No Thing passes. The word is impermeable. But this story has holes, is stitched and unstitching, like all stories, like all traumas.

This story is a hole.
What is a hole.
A hole is the opening to a
    tunnel.
What is a tunnel.
A tunnel is not a well.
This story is a tunnel.

A tunnel may branch. A branch may hold. A hold may open. An open may cave. A cave may close. A close may crack. A crack may broaden. A broaden may branch. A branch may tunnel.

A tunnel is not a well a tunnel does not only move from top to bottom does not always have ing in my bedroom for the third night *I don't think I can stay in your room I'm sorry this morning I watched a moth hatch and wriggle through the grey mauve under my feet* and we vacuumed and swapped rooms but they weren't just in the carpet.

They had built an underworld a net of moth dust strings running from bed base to bed leg to floor and back up and back down the dust the dust strings made from chewed fibre a hatching ground a nursery for hundreds for thousands of skittering wings and legs.

They could make a pattern and they do but I can't see the pattern I can see the multitudes I have been sleeping above an infestation they eat everything this is a hatching ground a nursery under my bed crawling through clothes so many places to fuck and lay to hatch hatch hatch.

mossy sides a slip a Death trap the rise of cold water up to armpits to base of throat to chin crease to lips to nostrils to eyes already searching the up side down.

A tunnel can be a root system a tunnel can be a taproot the throat is a taproot that pushes down then branches laterally through the body he does not accept His cock as a taproot a throat as empty as something to be filled he can spit Him out with all the force of a clench of a gag of a no. He spits Him out, eventually, but it takes an hour a life a blink of an unopened eye it takes bleeding gums a tunnel forced wide a gut burst open it takes language it makes flesh into horror it makes a haunt.

Ghosts are not light. Ghosts settle heavy in the body push into crevices make themselves a home.

It was between the first and second wave. So many words infected. Wave. Apart. Together. Transmission. Mask. Corona. Spread. Community. Tracing. Curve. Cluster. Novel. Distancing. Containment. Shelter. Home.

the depths is where the boy goes next. He moves his fingers gentle gentley and finds the next opening the next hole. It is a muscle band a tunnel a contraction a waiting a wanting to expand. The colour wash still red and eyes closed the boy eases his fingers in and around and in and over the next four years makes a place there for his whole hand. The depths are here in him where toys have been but no one else but the boy has coaxed himself this far in. He strokes D's silken insides he strokes and curls and twists he is patience and quiet he is pressure and pull back he goes in by the smallest increments and each time they play D's body remembers how far he has been in and he lets him back there more easily each place they leave from is the place they begin.

162 — QUINN EADES

This is prayer, the boy thinks. They are now both of them, one thing. And then there is no *who is out* and *who is in* and *who is on top* and *who will submit* there are two bodies intertwined so far and so deep that there is no telling one from the other and that the untwining will not happen so easily. *This is more than touch*, the boy thinks.

When it is the boy's turn he becomes baby girl and D is her Daddy and he lays her down in the sling. He has trained her to take his cock into her mouth whenever it is near. He likes her sharp little teeth, the way she bites and scrapes and makes him bleed. She chews on him while he cuffs her she is always blindfolded she is cradled with leather hung by ropes and chains there is music a dull bass her feet are in stirrups he begins. He is training her arse she is learning how to twist around him how to take him in. He has threaded toys all the way in but his hand so far has stayed in the shallows has pushed against the opening beyond it she likes it she wriggles down on him. She will not touch her clit her cock for as long as she can but at some point she uncuffs her own wrists and reaches down. She comes many times in a night in a morning in a pervert afternoon. When she squirts, which is often and far, he will come up from between her legs gleaming. When she comes like that she laughs, ecstatically.

Cocoons

He wonders if he has had enough of cocoons. If he called the moths to him in the writing of this. If he is more interested in the worm, in the silk, than in its brief container. If he can think-write through and with the brown mouthed worm 'becoming silk', with its orifice-not-orifices, its 'milk become thread'.[10] He learns from J.D. that the caterpillar's silk-producing glands can 'be labial or salivary, but also rectal. And then it was impossible to distinguish between several states [...]'.[11]

He knows he is always shuttling between and through states. Notices how the weekends he spends with his Daddy tied down

3 definitions of rape

He had been messaging him on an app that is mostly used by gay men for casual sex. No profile picture. No name. An age. 48? he did and didn't want to be on that app. he was unsure of the rules. Remembers Him asking if he liked raw and raunchy. Asking *what do you mean by raunchy*. Looking up raunchy. Finding dictionary definitions but nothing that would unhide the meaning in the context of the app of gay sex of post PrEP and PEP. Worked out eventually it had to do with fluid with expulsion with what comes from the cis male body. he looks up the word rape. Thinks about making a poem from its *seduce* and *seize*, its *cruciferous* so

A transbody at play

He and his love learn that his transbody at play, in ecstacy, shatters hetero- and homosexuality. Clothed and in the world he is/his body is 'the secret of this secret over there [...]', a matter of curiosity and maybe something to do with desire, but not these silken openings this found vocabulary for body for sex for pleasure for fucking for play.[12]

Understands, like Preciado, that 'a whole epistemology needs to be changed', and knows that this change is/was/can-be made through and between bodies, writing a story in extruded white silk before the cocoon, before thread and stitch, before flight, before death.[13]

Secretion

We know we will write a strange and silken story of many threads made from bodies-in-secretion, from bodies secreting. *'It secreted it, the secretion. It secreted.'*[14] He reads this sentence many times before he sees it. The secreted and the secret. How he is all ways a secret, to everyone and to himself.

And because he writes in/from The University, and The

close to crucified so much to work with. Realises it is already.

Going head first

Going is always has always been an option. Going first is never an option because of his two kids, birthed from his body and the dearest loves of his life; because of his grandfather who chose that way out and he saw what it did to his mother. How it simultaneously blanked and sharpened her. How as she got older the blank took over the sharp. How much she wanted to write, how much she knew she could write, how a too late bipolar diagnosis meant a lifetime of

I'll write when

but the conditions were never write. The desk was overflowing or the many canines she looked after needed walking or her partner was calling her or

She once showed him some research she'd done on her father. he offered a collaboration. he was thinking of writing a play about ghosts and memory and suicide and PTSD and mental illness and war.

This offer, the offer to write together, startled her. Not long after she asked for her notes back, for him to not keep any copies. She said it was for her to write and of course he agreed and did as she asked but the conditions

University believes it owns his language, he must work to be a secret in that place too. He is knowable in his transness but never in his laughter when he comes, slung, never in these shining threads, this writing-to-come.

were never write. he realises as he's writing that he's doing so in the past tense, as if she is already gone. She is already gone.

coming back out should be done almost as carefully as going deep in. It is an untwisting a coming apart it is gentle and slippery it is hard not to push to slide all the way all that way back in. As the boy unwinds and comes out D smiles he breathes *Am I clean?* he asks, *Am I clean?* Most times the boy's answer is *yes* and he takes paper towels wipes his love and then himself stands between D's legs and grins. When they are steady the boy walks with D to the couch covered in towels and they sit down they sink in. D always sits facing forwards one leg up one down the boy sits next to him gathers him up in his thick arms leans into his chest D can still feel where the boy's hand and fingers and forearm have been. In the low light on the towelled couch in the bass throb they hold each other D will come down by degrees. They run on their bodies not minutes not hours they run on when their bodies say *yes*, *again, more, please.*

Still

'The catastrophe had happened in silence.'[15]

He sees a photo of himself from a few months after the rape. It's not a photo it's a still. It's a still of a video, a short video for his dear friend and intimate, L. In the still his face is large and grey and cracked open. At some point he starts stuttering, can't pull anything across or down or out then places his open hand on his chest just below his sternum, pauses, starts crying, stops crying, looks away. Turns back. Hands flat pressed flat pressured flat onto flat chest presser presses turns back says a few small

To be laid out

He flies to Sydney, to the arms (he thinks) of J, but to get to them he needs to do 2 weeks of quarantine in a health run hotel because he is at risk of suicide in the wake of a violent rape.

Quarantine nearly breaks him. he can't stop thinking about stepping off the balcony.

The propulsion, even standing up to look over the edge, to calculate distance, to see if there was a drop that wouldn't kill him, but would put him in hospital for a long time. Thinking it was best to go over the edge head first. Fast, dead on impact. A ghost in front and behind him, one calling the things then *I love you*, then waves, looks down, and the video stops.

He sees a still of himself, the first frame of a video sent to L, who cared for him for many years with holding, lawns mown, dishes washed, movies watched, snow on a plate and up all night – sometimes these nights were the only times he laughed for months.

He sees this still three years later he was looking at pictures of his children his two other hearts, dearest loves, first inside then through and down then outside but all ways a part of him and parts of them him. Cells meshed many years earlier. We leave traces in and on each the other, find our way by touch and smell.

But the still. The shattering face. His attempts to hold himself. That press. He is shattered again. This rush this flooding these silted eyes all the muck from the river's bottom stirred all particles of a lone a man a man alone no matter the babies no matter the loves.

Steady

He writes the still writes a self disappearing in front of his eyes. He cries as much as any other time but perhaps the crying it does it stops sooner it stops sooner in the arms of the man who loves him back and down and between and under the luminous night says *I've got you* and *my love*, and strokes his head holds him arms around and *steady, so steady* is the first thing he

other pressing. Go over. Go head first. Fall at last.

Every time he touches his neck he is back on his back on his bed Him fucking my throat Him grinding relentless he touches his neck when he's rereading his writing. He touches his neck often. he is ground on often. The smell He left on his face. his jaw that still grinds and clenches and cracks.

he walks to his grandmother's poetry collection, finds Yeats, and later on the phone with A talks about being in love with the poet's melancholy. Being made to study Him in high school and understanding His malaise, somewhere some part of him always wanting to be laid out laid down like that, a wheelchair, a patterned rug, the slow deliverance of laudanum, sometimes ether through a steel meshed mask cloth lined for true descent for the deep the pushed under waterness of every day a blurry metronome a stone in the belly swallowed decades ago accreting calcite crystal granule grating against slowly through the stomach wall.

said the first time they hugged like this. *Looks as if he'd stagger in an August wind* is what he'd thought, misjudging the man's slenderness (only once) for frailness, because this is the only way he and any of us have been taught to think about ageing.

They play one weekend a month. He learns a new corpus, another way of naming the body: shallows, openings, depth, shrapnel, rinse, holes, fist, fist, fist. He is always frightened of writing at the edge of gay trans ecstatics of kink of age play of depth play of fisting as the sacred in their imagined profane.

It is not inevitable that the boy might compare play to birth but he finds that it is. Before hormones and surgery he birthed two babies he remembers the red wash of colour that stained everything he remembers that time when time meant no thing when everything he was was one body becoming two bodies untwining.

He knows that like birth, fisting is all about spiralling. So once they have separated a little on the couch and the boy has washed himself and D has come down by degrees they come close again they begin again they take turns until the weekend has gone until the clocks turn back on until his teenagers are about to come home to let themselves in with their keys.

They take the sling and then the sling frame down they wash and clean and wash and clean. The dungeon restored to a loungeroom again D takes himself to bed the boy to the TV where he will leave his hand on his cock and remember all the years of waiting while not knowing he was waiting.

Nightlight

Walk as far as the night, H.C. says. Night is his home so he wonders what this command means, if he has lived always in the moon's

Another fucking app

his relationship with J disintegrates because of the 1,000 kilometres because of the virus because of the rape because. *You are stagnant*

NO DECONSTRUCTION WITHOUT PLEASURE

house under the dullest of stars his grandmother quoting Wilde '*we are all of us in the gutter*', believed as she was speaking that she was stargrazed and that he was in the gutter, face down in a slurry of water and waste, barely twitching. *You must look to the light*, she'd say – another command.[17]

Well which is it? *It is many* is always the answer he gives back to himself. What this many when this many how many why multiple *we are carrying too many already* they say they sing a mad choral he wants too much it has always been too much.

How rest how retreat how cocoon?

A squinty eye

How *jouissance*, how pleasure and orgasmic practices as serious undertakings with the capacity to change the way we respond in our bodies to trauma and its inevitable dissasociations? In 'Passion', J.D. asks whether we should proceed obliquely, and in *Veils* asks us to look with 'a squinty eye'.[18]

We wonder if writing a poetics of fisting requires an oblique approach, one that doesn't produce an abject/regurgitating response to a text to come. If we write with an eye half closed or through a blindfold or in cuffs, if we write from a sling from the place where wax meets skin, from the insides of a body opened up and pulsed throughalong, we could perhaps

they say *you are stuck in a trauma loop.* They say *I am just living my life in Sydney* and *you are in Melbourne* and *I am in love with some one else* and *I have enough love for the both of you I just have two life partners now instead of one* and he leaves. he leaves because they don't have enough for both of them. he leaves because he is not stagnant he is slow moving absolutely he is crawling up the sides of the well he is stuttering and shaking all ways.

he leaves.

he decides to try another fucking app, but this time it is also a kink app. Writes a new profile. he is Very Careful about who he talks to. Writes that he dreams of a transmasc Daddy whose favourite book is *Macho Sluts*, who is gentle and clear and rough, who wants a boy naked always at his knee.[16]

A man messages him. He is 76. He likes to fist. His best friend is a trans guy and sometimes they play. On Saturday he messages Him to see if he would like to meet for a beer and a chat and He says *sorry can't do today I am out looking for birds* and he tells him *I love king parrots and magpies*, sends Him a picture of him and his brindle staghound. *Beautiful dog*, He says. *Let's keep messaging.*

When they meet for the first time He brings scones and they sit outside under a raucous fig tree and talk for three hours. The first time they play they fall in love. he seeks pleasure in his body in his pain he

write this pleasure roped pain this ecstatic afternoon those many hours of in and out and down.	is held it is warm where he is there is bliss there he lets pleasure lace his throat he knows it as his own.

J.D. says he is 'writing with a view to waking up' but the boy knows he is writing with a view to appear.[19] He knows no one who does what and how he does finds so little writing to hold his cunted faggot body that the only thing he can do is to write it for D and for him. To write past the abject to write with silk and semen 'the extruded saliva of a very fine sperm, shiny, gleaming'.[20] He has written with breastmilk and blood so now he writes with his own squirt he drenches these pages he drenches his love he is drink and drunk from he is cup and tunnel and tongue. He is 'love itself' and he was beginning to write with a view to addressing himself which he does he gives himself names he gives his names to D and D says them D addresses him with them and in this way he learns what he sounds like in the tongue in the throat between the lips of his love. He learns the sound of his name not said like a taunt he learns the sound of his names from his love.[21]

It is not that he will no longer suffer. Love is catastrophe delayed. They both know it, know death and separation comes. The body has its own time the boy could go first but it is far more likely it will be he that treads the turned earth untwined and alone, that no matter what happens D won't see him grow old. But he writes with this view to appear, he writes to address himself. He writes a ritual, a wait between plays that takes all phases of the moon. He writes open and openings he writes cradles and songs and they are both of them touch, and in this drenched silken page they are never untwined.

Notes

1. Jacques Derrida 'A Silkworm of One's Own', in Hélène Cixous and Jacques Derrida, *Veils*, trans. Geoffrey Bennington, with drawings by Ernest Pignon-Ernest (Stanford, CA: Stanford University Press, 2001), 86.
4. Ibid., 30.
5. Hélène Cixous, 'Savoir', in Hélène Cixous and Jacques Derrida, *Veils*, trans. Geoffrey Bennington, with drawings by Ernest Pignon-Ernest (Stanford, CA: Stanford University Press, 2001), 7–8.
6. Thomas Dutoit, 'Translating the Name?', in Jacques Derrida, *On The Name*, ed. Thomas Dutoit, trans. David Wood, John P. Leavet, Jr. and Ian McLeod (Stanford, CA: Stanford University Press, 1995), xiii.
2. Paul B. Preciado, *Can The Monster Speak?*, trans. Frank Wynne (London: Fitzcaraldo Editions, 2021), 59.

3. Hélène Cixous, *Three Steps on the Ladder of Writing*, trans. Sarah Cornell and Susan Sellers (New York: Columbia University Press, 1993), 65.

7. Derek Attridge, ed., '"The Strange Institution Called Literature": An Interview with Jacques Derrida', trans. Geoffrey Bennington and Rachel Bowlby, in *Jacques Derrida: Acts of Literature*, ed. Derek Attridge (New York: Routledge, 1992), 41.

8. Derek Jarman, dir., *Blue* (Artificial Eye, UK, 1993).

9. Franz Kafka, *The Diaries of Franz Kafka: 1910–1923*, trans. Ross Benjamin (New York: Schocken Books, 1965), 399.

10. Derrida, 'Silkworm', 88.

11. Ibid.

12. Ibid., 89.

13. Preciado, *Can The Monster Speak?*, 62–3.

14. Derrida, 'Silkworm', 89.

15. Cixous, 'Savoir', 6.

17. Oscar Wilde, *Lady Windemere's Fan* (Project Gutenberg e-books edition), n.p.

18. Derrida, *On The Name*, 12; 'Silkworm', 89.

16. Patrick Califia, *Macho Sluts* (Vancouver: Arsenal Pulp Press, 2009).

19. Derrida, 'Silkworm', 87.

20. Ibid., 89.

21. Ibid., 90.

9

BODIES IN E-MOTION: KOFMAN AND CIXOUS ENCOUNTERING REMBRANDT

Lenka Vráblíková

Anne Berger argues that the multiple voices of women writers of the Women's Liberation Movement that became prominent in France in the 1970s had in common a 'revolt against naturalized body of heteropatriarchy'.[1] It was motioned by an understanding of the body as a lived-in or live body, a notion she traces to Jacques Derrida's use of the phrase *corps propre*.[2] The lived-in body develops from phenomenological attempts to 'account for the uniqueness of each embodied human life in its relation to the world'[3] and Freud's theorisation of the complex and dynamic processes that produce the psyche, where the body is understood as a libidinal entity induced by 'the circuits of emotions, traces of experience and pressures of sexual excitation'.[4] Considering these phenomenological and psychoanalytical genealogies, Berger argues that the lived-in body is 'not only in motion, but each body in emotion'.[5] It is the unique experience of the self as a psychic body – or an embodied psyche – formed through relations with others that co-motions or animates the lived-in body.

This chapter emphasises the intertwined relationality and the vital potentiality of the lived-in body through the phrase 'bodies in e-motion' to explore how European painting has grappled with the discourse on the body in the heteropatriarchal political and libidinal economy. The exploration proceeds through a reading of Sarah Kofman's and Hélène Cixous's texts published in the 1990s that focus on the work of Rembrandt van Rijn. In 'Conjuring Death: Remarks on *The Anatomy Lesson of Doctor Nicolas Tulp* (1632)' Kofman provides a reading of Rembrandt's display of a 'scientific gaze' arising from a group of doctors who move attention from the corpse laid out before them to a book at his foot.[6] Cixous's text 'Bathsheba or the Interior Bible' is a reading of the painter's later work *Bathsheba at Her Bath* (1654) and opens with a rather intricate declaration: 'I've taken twenty-four steps in (the direction of) Bathsheba.'[7]

BODIES IN E-MOTION   171

My reading of Kofman's and Cixous's encounters with Rembrandt
develops from the tradition of feminist theorising that has aimed to
deconstruct any set notion of the body and its place through consideration of movement – triggered particularly by 'Choreographies', the
famous conversation between Christie McDonald and Derrida.[8] Coining
the phrase 'bodies in e-motion' emphasises one of its key aspects – the
understanding of embodiment as always expanding beyond itself. Like
email or e-book, e-motion invokes virtuality that is not constrained to
cybernetics but saturates every motion and its traces. It is, as Elizabeth
Grosz puts it, 'the space of emergence of the new, the unthought, the
unrealized, which at every moment loads the presence of the present
with supplementarity […].'[9] Contributing to such theorisations proposed by feminist deconstruction,[10] I suggests that bodies in e-motion
are not only in motion and emotion but also evoke bodies-to-come,
bodies that might come – and as they might come – in or from the future
that would be radically different from the present.

Thinking of bodies as in e-motion also implies that they are intertwined with a mode of auto-affection that is always a hetero-affection:
they are inextricably psychical *and* corporeal, material *and* immaterial, as
well as singular *and* plural. The emphasis on the aporetic yet inseparable
relationship between singularity and plurality stems from understanding
signification through the notion of *écriture* ('writing' or 'inscription') that
Kofman and Cixous share with Derrida. Signification is a process that
proceeds as scattering[11] (or dissemination as Derrida would put it), a
dispersive motion that leads in different directions and cannot be ever
fully mastered. Writing (including that of the body) allows to understand
signification as a process that is irreducible to a code or programme as it
always embodies aspects that escape such reductive generalisations.

One of the issues that signification understood as scattering makes us
reconsider in relation to embodiment is sexuation. It deconstructs what
Berger, following Derrida, calls 'sex*d*uality': 'the dual logic that underlines the traditional idea of sexual difference and sexuality in general'
and that organises sex into the hierarchical opposition of a couple 'the
one and its other'.[12] As Derrida famously professes in 'Choreographies',
deconstruction of sex*d*uality does not imply erasure of sexuality or sexual
difference but incites a 'dream' of a relationship that

> would not be a-sexual, far from it, but would be sexual otherwise:
> beyond the binary difference that governs the decorum of all codes,
> beyond the opposition feminine/masculine, beyond bisexuality as
> well, beyond homosexuality and heterosexuality which come to
> the same thing. As I dream of saving the chance that this question

offers I would like to believe in the multiplicity of sexually marked voices. I would like to believe in the masses, this indeterminable number of blended voices, this mobile of non-identified sexual marks whose choreography can carry, divide, multiply the body of each 'individual,' whether he be classified as 'man' or as 'woman' according to the criteria of usage.[13]

Bodies in e-motion also prompt reconsideration of the conceptions of space and time. As Grosz argues, embodiment and spatiotemporality are mutually constitutive: space and time are conceivable only through the body; hence, they are corporeal categories.[14] Conversely, any understanding of embodiment requires a spatial and temporal framework to provide coordinates for the renegotiation of the body and its delimitations. It thus destabilises any set notions of spatiotemporality as a discrete domain defined through a juxtaposition against what it is not as, for instance, the definition of interiority through a juxtaposition against exteriority, or presence against absence.

Understanding bodies as in e-motion also implies specific understanding of representation. Berger argues that

the live or lived-in body as such cannot be properly represented, or perhaps it can only be approached figuratively, by means of a complex tropology […] No machine, however sophisticated, no technics of exploration of the inner body, even the ones employed today and heavily relied on by contemporary neurosciences, can render visible, much less fully account for the ways in which each individual experiences or lives (through) her or his body, according to the vicissitudes of her or his story. What one calls literature may indeed be the best instrument humans have devised so far to explore the live body […].[15]

Being a scholar of French literature, Berger focuses on literary forms of writing, but it can clearly be extended to other kinds of inscriptions that use complex tropology, such as music, sculpture or indeed painting, and particularly that of Rembrandt. This painter has been praised for 'the unconventional movement of his figures' that 'works beyond their own mobility' that have 'no sources in the pictorial tradition'.[16] Rembrandt's interest in the exploration of embodied movement as a vital force is also evidenced by a statement he made about his art, where he famously professes that the aim is 'to introduce the greatest and most natural movement' (Svetlana Alpers explains, in this context, the word 'natural' is used interchangeably with the word 'lively').[17]

Finally, the question of the body is also a question of life and death. As Berger puts it

> [o]ne could consider the so-called natural body, that is, literally, the body given at and by birth – remember that the word 'nature' comes from the Latin verb *nascior, natus sum*, which means to be born – to be also a kind of dead body, that is, a body 'given' before anything happens, before history, before life (as bios rather than zoe), although of course, the eventful exposition to others and to the experience of alteration can be said to start in the womb. Still, because one starts to live (and to die) once one is born, the body given at and with birth, hence the properly natural body if there is such a thing, is a form of life before it is being lived, a still life so to speak.[18]

'Still life', an English expression that names a genre of painting that depicts an arrangement of objects that do not move comes from Dutch, where it was 'originally applied to representations not of inanimate objects but of living things portrayed in a state of rest'.[19] The way in which Berger uses the term – that is as a form of life that exists without living – and unlike the French expression *nature morte* for instance, thus aptly conveys the effort to challenge the seemingly secure opposition between life and death and destabilises preconceptions on what is natural when it comes to bodies.

I add another layer to Berger's deliberation that directly concerns the political and libidinal economy of heteropatriarchy. In her famous text 'Sorties: Out and Out: Attacks/Ways Out/Forays', where Cixous reflects on her experience as a Jewish girl growing up in Algeria under French colonial rule in the wake of the Second World War, she calls this economy 'the Empire of the Selfsame [*Propre*]'. Cixous maintains that in this 'empire' the only possible desire is a desire triggered by inequality that is put in motion by a conflict that results in destruction of the other through appropriation (as illustrated by the 'Hegelian machinery' of dialectics). Under heteropatriarchy and its logic of sex/duality, it is impossible 'to recognize each other in a type of exchange in which each one would keep the *other* alive and different'.[20] 'Death is always at work.'[21]

Heteropatriarchy generates life where, as Berger would put it, living takes shape through various forms of a still life. It is an economy where life is subjugated to the power of death, an 'economy of death' or 'necro-economy', as Achille Mbembe would put it,[22] where for some to make a life for themselves, lives of others must be reduced to precarious conditions, to the living in between life and death, to the spectrality of the living dead. The argument put forward is that challenging this violent and unjust status quo that would open a possibility of imagining ethics and politics beyond its constraints requires radical rethinking of embodiment in relation to auto-affection as hetero-affection, sex and representation. This chapter seeks to contribute to this effort by continuing the revolt against what Berger calls 'the naturalized body of heteropatriarchy' and that was initiated by the women writers associated with the French Women's Liberation Movement.

Sarah Kofman encountering Rembrandt

'Conjuring Death: Remarks on *The Anatomy Lesson of Doctor Nicolas Tulp* (1632)' is Kofman's final and unfinished text published posthumously in 1995, that is less than a year after she took her own life.[23] In this essay, Kofman examines the relationship between at least three kinds of bodies: the corpse of a human body; the book of anatomy that is laid at the corpse's feet and that represents a corpus of scientific knowledge; and the group of figures that represent the Amsterdam Anatomy Guild. Kofman interprets the scene as a deliberation on modern science and its methodology, the scientific method based on empirical observation and

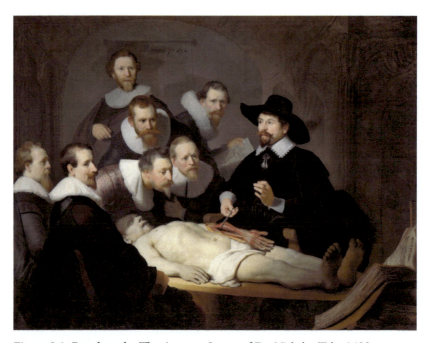

Figure 9.1 Rembrandt: *The Anatomy Lesson of Dr. Nicholas Tulp*, 1632, Mauritshuis, The Hague.

experimentation. The book of anatomy is supported by the materiality of the cadaver and its dissection. Simultaneously, the anatomy book allows the doctors to decipher the human body according to the definitions agreed upon by their scientific community.

This is suggested also through visually and linguistically generated conflation and the overlapping of various meanings of the word 'anatomy'. Like another semantically close word – 'autopsy' – that guided Derrida's deconstruction of sovereignty and particularly that of humans over animals in his seminars on *The Beast and the Sovereign*, the various meanings of 'anatomy' lead the analysis in several directions.[24] 'Anatomy' designates the bodily structure of an organism and its parts (the anatomy of the body); a scientific discipline that studies this bodily structure (the science of anatomy); as well as the treatise on anatomic science (the book of anatomy). Additionally, 'anatomy' also means 'dissection', the actual process of cutting and dividing the body (the Greek word *anatomē* comes from *anatemmein* meaning to 'cut up'); a meaning that has expanded to designate any detailed analysis that relies on the dividing for the purpose of the examination of its parts.[25] The painting also calls attention to anatomy's particular relationship to representation. As Kofman stresses, it is, after all, a lesson – a demonstration that presents anatomy as a powerful didactic instrument of how to show and see the human body, how to – 'in flesh' – generate a discourse on the body. The repetition of the painting's theme in its title then leads to deliberations on the differences between the discourses on the body generated by anatomy and painting, that is, by science and art.

The various meanings of this word that surround and permeate the scene are connected through a gaze that Kofman calls 'a scientific gaze'.[26] This gaze is motivated by a 'singular desire to learn and to know', to reveal 'the truth of life', 'the secret of life', through 'science of life and its mastery'.[27] It is both a vehicle and a result of doctors moving their attention from a corpse of a man laid bare in front of them to the book at his feet. What animates doctors' desire to know is therefore not the feeling towards the deceased man, be they feelings of compassion, pity, revulsion, or terror, but its substitution with another feeling, a feeling of a tense and concentrated attention, a fascination with the book. Kofman reads the scene as a visual rendering of displacement, an unconscious defence mechanism that is key to the formation and the functioning of the psyche. In this essay she accounts for its intricate operation with the help of the verb 'to conjure'[28] and proposes that the anatomy lesson and Rembrandt's display of it represent examples of methods and economies devised to overcome anxiety connected to the fear of death.

As others have pointed out, the formulation 'to render or make the intolerable tolerable' appears all over Kofman's corpus.[29] It 'frustrates the logic of noncontradiction'[30] as it follows a logic which is that of a magic that art, religion, philosophy or science perform for the psyche as they transform intolerable content into tolerable one through the linking of affect and representation and thus fulfil their 'pharmaceutical function'.[31] The fear of death is also connected to the fear for (and thus of) the body as a fragile and mortal entity and, as Derrida insists in his reading of 'Conjuring Death' in the eulogy for Kofman, it is also – or above all – inextricably linked to sexuation. He considers the transfiguration of the body into a book to be clearly 'a scene of men ... as long as we keep to the visibility of the scene',[32] and reads the repression of the cadaver also as the repression of sexual difference. To resist this motion, he coins a neologism '*la corpse*':

> I prefer the English word *corpse* here because it incorporates at once the body *[le corps]*, the corpus, and the cadaver, and because, when read in French, *la corpse* seems to put the body in the feminine and to become an allusion to sexual difference, if not a respect for it.[33]

I take the neologism '*la corpse*' as an opportunity to dream of the multiple non-identified sexual marks of which Derrida fantasizes in 'Choreographies' that, I propose, Rembrandt's painting makes possible by problematising the cutting of the sexed body. The phenomenon of cutting, partitioning and wounding is not only at the root of the word 'anatomy' but also, as Berger points out in her reading of 'Choreographies', of 'sex' and its lexical derivatives (like 'section' and 'dissection', the Latin root of 'sex' comes from words such as *secare, sectrum*). Sexual identity can thus be understood as referring to 'a specific incision', a certain 'imaginary and symbolic cut in and of the very fabric of each human being'. 'To belong to one sex, then in so far as one does', Berger continues, 'would mean to have a certain cut, to be cut a certain way and away from something or somebody else'. Deconstruction, a 'procedure' that questions 'the formation, logic, and decisiveness of any clear-cut distinction' – including that of the most normative and widespread strands of psychoanalytical theory where 'sexual difference ... is predicated on a certain psychic experience of castration' – does not aim to suture such clear-cuts but to rescind them. As Berger envisions it, deconstruction seeks to 'cut the cut'.[34] In doing so, it casts out any longing for wholeness, a unified 'uncut' totality, and instead emphasises both the inevitability and infiniteness of sectioning. In relation to sex

BODIES IN E-MOTION 177

specifically, cutting-through-the-cut of sex implies multiple sexes, the multiplication of sexual possibilities beyond the heteropatriarchal logic of sex*d*uality.

Guided by Berger's feminist deconstruction of sex, I read *The Anatomy Lesson* as a work that shows the tendency to arrest and formalise the sectioning strokes of sex in a 'clear-cut' attempt to delimit and separate life and masculinity from death and femininity, a clear-cut that Rembrandt's painting however further rescinds. As Kofman points out, although the doctors are 'not all looking in the same direction ... they are all inhibited by a common inner concentration ... It is the common "scientific" gaze that these men belonging to the same corporation or practicing body *form one body [font corps]*'.[35] They belong to the same corporation, which, as Derrida glosses Kofman's account, is also a 'gathering of a conspiring or a *conspiracy [conjuration]*', as one of the meanings of the French noun 'conjuration' that is no longer in use in English suggests.[36] This body formed through a secret pact of plotting men, I therefore suggest, seeks to conjure up life by conjuring away, and thus also mastering, not only death but also the body as a material entity marked by the cut of sex which, in heteropatriarchal economy, amounts to the cutting of *his* sex – castration, a sign of negative difference displaced onto femininity.

This is achieved through the contrast drawn between the group of doctors and the corpse under examination. Although all figures present in the painting are coded masculine, the dead man is not seen as a subject but a mere instrument that one of them manipulates. The deceased does not belong only to the circle of the living, but also (or not completely) to that of masculinity. Apart from representing mortality, the cadaver is also clearly associated with corporeality: except for a cloth covering the genitals, the body is laid bare, even stripped of skin to some extent. The dissection of the hand and forearm and the resulting wound is a reminder of what also is feared and must stay hidden – the inevitability of sectioning that, as argued above, in heteropatriarchal economy is made tolerable through displacement on femininity. The painting thus makes visible that the anatomy lesson and its quest to reveal the truth of life through science of life and its mastery is a masculine defence against the threat of death/femininity.

Yet, as Elisabeth Bronfen shows in her study of the use of the feminine body as a trope for castration and mortality, although such displacement permits defence (renders the intolerable tolerable in Kofman's words), it however 'lets the repressed return, albeit in a disguised manner [...] Death and Femininity both involve the uncanny return of the repressed ... [they] cause a disorder to stability, mark moments of ambivalence, disruption or duplicity [...].'[37] In *The Anatomy Lesson* such return is made evident by showing other effects of the scientific gaze: it does not only transform the body of the dead, but also that of the doctors. As noted previously, Rembrandt has been praised for the unconventional movement of his figures. The unusual rigidity of figures standing for the group of doctors, except for Tulp who conducts the dissection, therefore bears significance. The group stares at the book motionless. It is as if it was the doctors who are experiencing the stiffening of the body in death, who are in 'rigor mortis'. Although they are, and unlike the body in front of them, alive, this life is a version of yet another still life; a still life that makes the body disappear. As Kofman puts it,

> [e]ncircled by a white ruff, put into relief by it, the head stands out, detached, and rises above the rest of the body, which is covered by dark clothing. And with this dissimulation of the body, its fragility, its mortality, comes to be forgotten, even though it is exhibited in full light by the pale cadaver that is right there [...].[38]

Although the men of science try to master mortality and the material and sexed body through anatomy lesson, the scene nonetheless proliferates with bodies and body parts in various configurations with marks of life, death and sex moving through and around them in multiple and intricate ways. Rembrandt further enhances this scattering effect by self-referencing the medium of painting. The figure that manipulates the ligaments does not have to be read only as a surgeon who executes the dissection but as a painter, perhaps Rembrandt himself.[39] This reading incites deliberations on the difference that surgeon's scissors and painter's brush have for the body, and by proxy, the different 'pharmaceutics' science and art offer to render the intolerable tolerable.

Rembrandt's painting does not aim for realism.[40] Although it is a depiction of an actual event, a public lecture that took place in Amsterdam on 16 January 1632, with veritable portraits of each of the doctors and even with the known identity of the deceased (Adriaen Adriaenszoon, executed for theft the very same day), it is not a 'truthful' rendering of the events. Tulp would not have done the surgery himself (it would have been conducted by his assistant), and the dissection would not have begun with the opening of a limb but with the abdomen. In the same vein, Kofman points out that Rembrandt does not reveal the 'truth of anatomy'. Rembrandt does not 'exhibit the entrails',[41] the wound is depicted figuratively: it is '[t]he colored envelope of the painting [that] makes tolerable the sight of the flesh'.[42] According to this reading, what makes tolerable the sight of flesh is thus not the displacement of the cadaver with the book (the anatomy lesson) but its figurative representation. Through the medium of painting, Rembrandt rescinds the clear-cut that the anatomy lesson seeks to establish and thus opens a space to imagine a body that is not the naturalised body of heteropatriarchy but another body, a body in e-motion, a body that is perhaps akin to '*la corpse*' about which Derrida fantasizes in his eulogy for Kofman.

I will conclude my reading of Kofman's encounter with Rembrandt by continuing in a direction of this proliferation, an e-motion that expands the corporeal. The cut of the wound is not only repeated in the depiction of the doctors, immobilising them in a kind of 'rigor mortis', detaching their bodies from their heads as observed by Kofman. The sectioning motion also expands to the surrounding space. The wound is hollow inside with stylised ligaments forming its sides. This motif, as I read it, is repeated in the room that surrounds the figures. It appears as shallow grooves that run vertically on the columns, spreading further to the arches and the ornament that decorates the walls of the room. And this is perhaps where the scene takes place – in the inside of the fantastic body sexed otherwise, in another interiority where '[t]he entire room is flesh. Sex'[43] as Cixous writes in relation to Rembrandt's other painting that I will examine in the following section.

Hélène Cixous encountering Rembrandt

Bathsheba at Her Bath was painted more than twenty years after *The Anatomy Lesson of Dr. Nicholas Tulp* and the politics of sex and gender have been central for the interpretations of this work classified as a female nude. The painting is a rendering of a story in the Second Book of Samuel concerning Bathsheba, the wife of Uriah, General of King David's army. After being spied on by David whilst bathing, Bathsheba was summoned to the palace where David had sex with her and impregnated her. David attempted to cover the crime evidenced by Bathsheba's pregnancy but with no success and therefore ordered the killing of Uriah and married Bathsheba himself. Bathsheba then gave birth to her first child that was conceived through this rape, but the child died soon after. The second child of Bathsheba and David was Solomon who later became, as David's successor, the King of Israel.

The Biblical text, itself frustratingly ambiguous about the character of the sex act between a man and a woman in such an asymmetrical power relation, has a long and complicated history.[44] It goes from the representation of Bathsheba as a virtuous character (as 'the queen mother') to a culpable one, culminating with that of a seductress and adulteress introduced in the sixteenth century that became prominent

Figure 9.2 *Rembrandt: Bathsheba at her Bath*, 1654, Louvre Museum, Paris.

particularly in the art of the Dutch Republic.[45] Art historians generally agree that Rembrandt's rendering of the theme breaks away from this tradition, giving rise to various modes of reading, including those that are critical of the reduction of Bathsheba to a sexualised and objectified spectacle and that reflect on the viewer's complicity.[46] Cixous's 'Bathsheba or the Interior Bible' expands on such a reading. It refuses to reduce Bathsheba's subjectivity and personhood to that of an object of voyeurism but also solely to that of the victim of sexual violence. Instead, Cixous attends to Bathsheba as a singular living and feeling being who – in the face of the violence of rape and the deaths of a husband and a child – thinks, mourns, fears, protests, loves and dreams. This reading stems from Cixous's understanding of Rembrandt as 'paint[ing] what we do not see',[47] as trying to make visible the invisible. Supporting her reading with careful consideration of Rembrandt's choices with regards to the construction of the scene and the usage of pictorial devices such

BODIES IN E-MOTION   181

as composition, chiaroscuro, the colour and intertextual references, she calls this space – that is also a body in e-motion – 'the interior Bible'.[48]

The painting depicts two life-sized figures that are coded as feminine. The younger seated woman holding a letter, whose naked breasts and abdomen are in full view, but her head is bent and turned away, is Bathsheba. The model for this central figure was Hendrickje Stoffels, Rembrandt's long-time partner. The older and fully dressed woman shown in profile at the bottom-left corner tending to Bathsheba's right foot represents the servant (the identity of the model for this figure is unknown). Like *The Anatomy Lesson*, this scene is rather static – apart from the servant's manipulation of Bathsheba's foot, no visible action takes place. The quality of this motionlessness is however different. The two women are not rigid as are the doctors. In this painting, there are no bodies in 'rigor mortis' although, and as I will discuss later, death is also visually and semantically central to it. *Bathsheba at Her Bath* is thus also a kind of a still life but not because of the repression of the corporeal. Here the stillness sits in the body. Like in *The Anatomy Lesson*, the still-life effect is generated through the depicted gaze. The absence of the eye contact that the viewer expects to occur between two figures produces a strong sense of preoccupation. The women are neither 'there' (in the space and time of the scene) nor 'here' (in the space and time of its viewing, a sense that can be generated through a gaze directed to an audience); '[t]he two women withdraw from the scene thoughtfully [...] They are elsewhere.'[49] Cixous connects this elsewhere to an interiority of a psychic body (the interior Bible) that is not defined through a juxtaposition against what it is not, i.e., its exteriority.

One of the figures through which this elsewhere/interior Bible takes shape is that of embodied aporetic movement of footsteps. The essay opens with a rather intricate declaration: 'I've taken twenty-four steps in (the direction of) Bathsheba.'[50] The sentence indicates the protocol of Cixous's reading: the essay is written in twenty-four fragments that stand for steps and through poetic use of language engages in self-conscious multiplication of intertextual references and active transformation of the relationship between walking, viewing, reading, painting and writing. A proclamation 'I've taken 24 steps in (the direction) of Bathsheba' can thus be read as a counter move against the reduction of Bathsheba to a sexualised and objectified spectacle by reversing the asymmetrical relationship that is paramount to the Biblical story and reinforced by its pictorial depictions. In other words, with the walking *towards* Bathsheba, Cixous seeks to undo Bathsheba's subjugation and violation by David who, after spying on her, summoned her to come to him. Furthermore, by claiming that the steps are taken not only *towards* Bathsheba but simultaneously also *inside* her, an effect achieved with the use of parentheses, the sentence disobeys the laws of spatiotemporal ordering of presence and absence as exclusive domains.

Cixous's footsteps generate a sense of vibrant visceral landscape where – unlike in the paintings of Vermeer, where '[t]he outside knocks on the windowpanes', where '[t]he exterior enters the interior' – '[e]verything is in the interior'.[51] The idea of interiority that is not defined by its exteriority also collapses the pictorial convention that distinguishes the figure from the background and suggests interconnection between the subject and the object of her gaze. Furthermore, for Cixous, the journey to the unheard-of interiority is also inextricable from an attempt to mark – and thus generate – femininity that is irreducible to the complement of masculinity as it is within the heteropatriarchal logic of sex*d*uality. This other femininity, a mode of relation that is not restricted to women, is a whole other 'world' that Cixous moulds throughout the essay:

> This world is full of night and of golden stuff. The stuff of night is
>   a clay. A mud. It is still moving, imperceptibly.
> [...]
> It's dark here. We're down below. We're here. In the breast.
>   Immediately. Such an absence of exterior!
> The country is a room of palpitating folds.
> [...]
> The entire room is flesh. Sex.[52]

Cixous interprets the steps she has taken in (the direction of) Bathsheba as following the movements of the painter: it is Rembrandt who leads the way and who 'takes us to a foreign land, our own'.[53] A decision not to portray David is important for this journey. It is an indication of a desire to paint Bathsheba that is not defined by the hierarchical opposition of the couple 'David and Bathsheba' but another Bathsheba, 'Bathsheba in truth', an '[a]bsolute Bathsheba', '[w]ithout a man'.[54] In Rembrandt's rendering of the Biblical story, David is not there. Or, rather, as Cixous asserts further, not visibly there: it is Bathsheba 'without a "visible" man'.[55] Along the way, specifically after making thirteen steps, in the fourteenth and fifteenth fragment, the reader learns that although not visible, *he is there.* The man/David is invoked through the letter that Bathsheba holds in her hand:

> 14. The Violence of the Letter.
> At first I didn't see it. The letter.
> Little by little the letter captures the gazes.

BODIES IN E-MOTION   183

At first I looked at the body.
[...]
Suddenly I am letterstruck. And I see only it.
[...]
15. [...]
There is always a letter.
The letter, what violence! How it seeks us out, how it aims at us!
Us.
Especially women.
[...] It is David, an old tale whispers to me.
David the outsider. The outside. The arranger. Invisible.
'David and Bathsheba,' that's it: it is Bathsheba to the letter ...
The letter resounds throughout the entire painting.[56]

Scholars generally agree that the letter is a central point of the painting both visually and semantically.[57] Most commonly it is interpreted
as a message from David to Bathsheba in which he summons her to
his palace, but it can also stand for the letter in which David orders
Uriah's killing in the battlefield, or one that informs Bathsheba of
Uriah's death.[58] In any case, the letter is a sign of violence and death as it
is also suggested by a red spot in the letter's right corner that represents
a bloodstain rather than a seal (the seal would have been placed in the
middle of the letter).[59] Undoubtedly keeping in mind a story of another
famous letter and its readings – Edgar Allan Poe's 'The Purloined Letter',
and Derrida's deconstructive response to Jacques Lacan's interpretation
of it[60] – Cixous supports this agreed-upon interpretation of the letter in
Rembrandt's painting but also develops it further. The letter is a reference to David; it stands for David *as* violence and death and, vice versa,
death and violence *as* David. It is a sign of the Empire of the Selfsame
as Cixous calls it in 'Sorties', the political and libidinal economy of heteropatriarchy grounded in the logic of sex*d*uality, where it is impossible
'to recognize each other in a type of exchange in which each one would
keep the *other* alive and different'.[61]

I will conclude with a deliberation on Cixous's handling of the letter
Bathsheba holds in her hand along the reading I proposed in the previous
section. Reading Cixous's encounter with Rembrandt along Kofman's
would suggest that the event that Cixous describes as 'getting letterstruck' produces an effect (a kind of a stroke) that is akin to that of the
scientific gaze Kofman explored in *The Anatomy Lesson*. Like the book
of anatomy that captures the attention of the doctors, the letter, Cixous
says, 'seeks us out ... aims at us'. Like the doctors who moved their
attention from a corpse to the book, and in result are fascinated by it,

Cixous – although 'at first she looked at the body' – is suddenly 'letterstruck' and 'see[s] only it'. The event of 'getting letterstruck', I thus suggest, is another figurative rendering of displacement, a method and economy devised to overcome anxiety connected to the fear of death/ femininity, that represses the material and sexed body and replaces it with heteropatriarchal discourse on the body. Cixous however resists this motion. It takes her thirteen steps to get her attention caught by the letter. She does not mention the letter straightaway but calls attention to it only in the fourteenth fragment. Given its centrality to the painting and its interpretations, I consider the gesture of putting the letter aside to be significant and interpret it as a move that is meant to defer the working of the heteropatriarchal political and libidinal economy. The time and space of the thirteen steps allows Cixous to examine the violence of the letter without centring her attention to it. It postpones the moment when 'little by little the letter captures the gazes', when one 'see[s] only it' and 'no longer see[s] Bathsheba'.[62] Walking in (the direction of) Bathsheba, the processual protocol of aporetic walking that follows Rembrandt, thus enables Cixous to write what Rembrandt paints, that is 'what we do not see'.[63] In this e-motion (some)body arrives from a future that would be radically different from the present, a future that is not constrained by heteropatriarchal logic of sex*d*uality.

Notes

1. Anne Emmanuelle Berger, 'The Queer Body of MLF Literature', in *Paragraph* 41.3 (1 November 2018), 268–9.
2. Anne Emmanuelle Berger, 'Live Body: An Interview with Anne Emmanuelle Berger', interview by Lenka Vráblíková, in *Parallax* 25.2 (2019), 132. *Corps propre* is a notion coined by Maurice Merleau-Ponty. It refers to 'body-subject' or 'embodied subject' (*corps sujet*) rather than to the problematic of property, as for instance does the expression *mon propre corps* that translates as 'my own body', or Hélène Cixous's phrase *L'Empire du Propre*, the 'empire of the selfsame'. The 'empire of the selfsame' is a name Cixous gives to colonial heteropatriarchy and refers to the logic of appropriation as well as the meaning of 'proper' as 'appropriate' but also 'pure' and 'clean'. Maurice Merleau-Ponty, *Phenomenology of Perception* (Routledge, 2013); Hélène Cixous, 'Sorties: Out and Out: Attacks/ Ways Out, Forays', in *The Newly Born Woman*, by Hélène Cixous and Catherine Clément, trans. Betsy Wing (University of Minnesota Press, 1986), 63–132.
3. Berger, 'Live Body', 132.
4. Ibid., 121.
5. Ibid.

BODIES IN E-MOTION 185

6. Sarah Kofman, 'Conjuring Death: Remarks on The Anatomy Lesson of Doctor Nicolas Tulp (1632)', in *Selected Writings* (Stanford University Press, 2007), 237–43.

7. Hélène Cixous and Catherine A. F. MacGillivray, 'Bathsheba or the Interior Bible', in *New Literary History* 24.4 (1993), 820.

8. Christie McDonald V. and Jacques Derrida, 'Interview: Choreographies: Jacques Derrida and Christie V. McDonald', in *Diacritics* 12.2 (1982), 66–76.

9. Elizabeth Grosz, 'Lived Spatiality (The Spaces of Corporeal Desire)', in *Architecture from the Outside: Essays on Virtual and Real Space* (The MIT Press, 2001), 77.

10. For a feminist developments of Derrida's 'to come' (*à-venir*), see Drucilla Cornell, *Beyond Accommodation: Ethical Feminism, Deconstruction, and the Law* (Routledge, 1991).

11. See Geoffrey Bennington, *Scatter 1: The Politics of Politics in Foucault, Heidegger, And Derrida* (Fordham University Press, 2016).

12. Anne Emmanuelle Berger, 'The Ends of an Idiom, or Sexual Difference in Translation', in *The Queer Turn in Feminism: Identities, Sexualities, and the Theater of Gender* (Fordham University Press, 2014), 116. See also Anne-Emmanuelle Berger, 'Sexing Differances', in *Differences* 16.3 (2005), 56; Berger, 'Live Body', 72.

13. McDonald V. and Derrida, 'Choreographies', 76. My approach to sexual difference as a multiplying 'motion' or 'force' also follows Oli Stephano's reading of Elizabeth Grosz's work. See Oli Stephano, 'Irreducibility and (Trans) Sexual Difference', in *Hypatia* 34.1 (2019), 141–54.

14. Grosz, 'Lived Spatiality', 32.

15. Berger, 'Live Body', 121–2.

16. Mieke Bal, *Reading Rembrandt: Beyond the Word-Image Opposition* (Amsterdam University Press, 2006), 54.

17. Svetlana Alpers, *Rembrandt's Enterprise: The Studio and the Market* (University of Chicago Press, 1990), 49; Bal, *Reading Rembrandt*, 54.

18. Berger, 'Live Body', 122.

19. 'Still Life, n. Meanings, Etymology and More | Oxford English Dictionary': https://www.oed.com/dictionary/still-life_n?tab=etymology#20704124 (accessed 29/10/2023).

20. Cixous, 'Sorties', 78. Description of the heteropatriarchal logic of sex*du*ality as deadly appears also in Cixous's text 'Castration or Decapitation?' Hélène Cixous, 'Castration or Decapitation?', trans. Annette Kuhn, in *Signs* 7.1 (1981), 44.

21. Cixous, 'Sorties', 64.

22. Achille Mbembe, 'Necropolitics', in *Public Culture* 15.1 (1 January 2003), 11–40.

23. Kofman, 'Conjuring Death', 293.

24. Jacques Derrida, *The Beast and the Sovereign, Vol. I*, trans. Geoffrey Bennington (University of Chicago Press, 2010).

25. 'Anatomy, n.', in *OED Online* (Oxford University Press): https://www.oed.com/view/Entry/7179 (accessed 05/07/022).
26. Kofman, 'Conjuring Death', 237.
27. Kofman, 'Conjuring Death', 237–8; Jacques Derrida, 'Introduction', in *Selected Writings* (Stanford University Press, 2007), 4.
28. Pleshette DeArmitt, 'Conjuring Bodies: Kofman's Lesson on Death', in *Parallax* 17.1 (2011), 4–17.
29. See Pleshette DeArmitt, 'Introduction: The Lifework of Sarah Kofman', in *Sarah Kofman's Corpus*, ed. Tina Chanter and Pleshette DeArmitt (State University of New York Press, 2008), 1–8; Michael Naas, 'Fire Walls: Sarah Kofman's Pyrotechnics', in *Sarah Kofman's Corpus*, ed. Tina Chanter and Pleshette DeArmitt (State University of New York Press, 2008), 49–74; Tina Chanter, 'Eating Words: Antigone as Kofman's Proper Name', in *Enigmas: Essays on Sarah Kofman*, ed. Penelope Deutscher and Tina Chanter (Cornell University Press, 1999), 189–202.
30. Pleshette DeArmitt, 'Sarah Kofman's Art of Affirmation, or the "Non-Illusory Life of an Illusion"', in *Sarah Kofman's Corpus*, ed. Tina Chanter and Pleshette DeArmitt (New York: SUNY Press, 2008), 26.
31. Kofman, 'Conjuring Death', 239.
32. Derrida, 'Introduction', 2.
33. Ibid., 9.
34. Berger, 'Sexing Differances', 57–8; See also Berger, 'The Ends of an Idiom'.
35. Kofman, 'Conjuring Death', 237.
36. Derrida, 'Introduction', 21. For a reading of this scene in relation to Freud's *Totem and Taboo*, see DeArmitt, 'Conjuring Bodies'.
37. Elisabeth Bronfen, *Over Her Dead Body: Death, Femininity and the Aesthetic* (Manchester University Press, 1992), xi–xii. Bronfen focuses on the representation of beautiful women. For a discussion of sexual difference and death in relation to the figure of the mother, see Elissa Marder, 'The Sex of Death and the Maternal Crypt', in *Parallax* 15.1 (2009), 5–20.
38. Kofman, 'Conjuring Death', 23.
39. This is also an established reading. See Bal, *Reading Rembrandt*; Alpers, *Rembrandt's Enterprise*; Kofman, 'Conjuring Death'.
40. See Bal, *Reading Rembrandt*; Alpers, *Rembrandt's Enterprise*; Kofman, 'Conjuring Death'.
41. Kofman, 'Conjuring Death', 240.
42. Ibid.
43. Cixous, 'Bathsheba or the Interior Bible', 824.
44. See Yohana A. Junker, 'Unsettling the Gaze: Bathsheba Beyond Verse and Image', in *The Art of Biblical Interpretation: Visual Portrayals of Scriptural Narratives*, ed. Heidi J. Hornik, Ian Boxall and Bobbi Dykema (SBL Press, 2021), 11–35.
45. Ibid., 15.
46. See Alpers, *Rembrandt's Enterprise*, 65; Junker, 'Unsettling the Gaze', 18; Bal, *Reading Rembrandt*.

BODIES IN E-MOTION 187

47. Cixous, 'Bathsheba or the Interior Bible', 831.
48. For a reading of Cixous's engagement with religion and the Bible see Irving Goh, 'The Passion According to Cixous: From Human Blindness to "Animots"', in *MLN* 125.5 (2010), 1050–74; Hugh S. Pyper, '"Job the Dog": Wounds, Scars and the Biblical Text', in *Parallax* 13.3 (2007), 83–93.
49. Cixous, 'Bathsheba or the Interior Bible', 827.
50. Ibid., 820. This rendering however does not appear it the later publication in *Stigmata*. Hélène Cixous, *Stigmata: Escaping Texts* (Routledge, 1998).
51. Cixous, 'Bathsheba or the Interior Bible', 822.
52. Ibid., 823–4.
53. Ibid., 822.
54. Ibid., 820.
55. Ibid.
56. Ibid., 827–9.
57. See Bal, *Reading Rembrandt*, 227.
58. 'A letter can also be a reminisce of a letter Hendrickje received from the council of the Dutch Reformed Church summoning her to the hearing for "living in sin with Rembrandt the painter" the same year the work was painted.' Bal, *Reading Rembrandt*, 225–6.
59. Ibid., 229.
60. Jacques Derrida, 'The Purveyor of Truth', trans. Alan Bass, in *Yale French Studies* 52 (1975), 31–113.
61. Cixous, 'Sorties', 78.
62. Cixous, 'Bathsheba or the Interior Bible', 828.
63. Ibid., 831.

10

VOICE AND SEXTUALITY

Anne Emmanuelle Berger

[W]e're going to show them our sexts!
  (Hélène Cixous)[1]

About 'sexuality' and under this name – but also about sex, the sexual, sexual difference and sexual differences – Derrida never stopped writing, albeit in a 'disseminated' fashion. Many of his commentators have pointed this out. From Derrida's reading of the operation of the 'hymen' in 'The Double Session', to that of 'invagination' in *Parages*; from the writing of *La Carte Postale* to that of the 'Silkworm of One's Own' (stitched onto Hélène Cixous's veil or sail) and 'Circonfession'; from the composition of the three 'Geschlecht' (even if *Geschlecht III* is partly a posthumous reconstruction) to 'At This Very Moment in This Work Here I Am', Derrida's work, at once sexophagous and 'sexiferous', seems never to have let up.[2] Isn't it pointless then, or at least redundant, to highlight Derrida's interest in this subject? In doing so, I do not mean to content myself to take up one more time the subject of Derrida's deconstruction of what he once called 'sex*d*uality', namely the conceptual dependency of a certain idea of 'sexuality' on that of 'sexual difference' understood as a binary construct; nor do I want to limit myself to probe further the stakes of his 're-writing' of 'sexual difference' as 'sexual differ*a*nce'.[3] Rather, I aim to think about the shift from sexual differ*a*nce to what I call 'vocal differ*a*nce', or, more precisely, about Derrida's reinscription of 'sexual differ*a*nce' as 'vocal differ*a*nce'.

What does sexuality name?

But do we really know what the word 'sexuality' names (or has named) in its use and/or its mention, what it is responsible for or to? What it names in general, but also in Derrida's work in particular? What knowledge and

VOICE AND SEXTUALITY

what discourse is the reference to sexuality predicated upon, but above all, perhaps, to what extent? What historical, political, epistemological but perhaps also poetic and 'psychical' urgency commands the invocation or inscription of this word in Derrida, if indeed we can distinguish and prioritise these determinations in his work? And even if, as I noted a moment ago, Derrida spoke extensively of sexuality under this name, for example in the first '*Geschlecht*' and in *Geschlecht III*, and if he himself admits, in an interview with Christie McDonald, that his singular use of the terms 'hymen' or 'invagination' and their promotion to the rank of textual operators is indeed part of a strategy of 're-sexualisation' of philosophical discourse,[4] are we sure, to paraphrase his formula in the first '*Geschlecht*', that we can rely on its 'index'? Does Derrida's use of the word 'sexuality' and of other members of its extended lexical family (for example, the use of the neologism 'sexualisation') at a precise moment in a certain history (that is at once − but not necessarily all together − epistemological, intellectual and cultural) guarantee its conceptual grasp and unity? This is the hypothesis formulated by the philosopher and historian of science Arnold Davidson in 'Sex and the Emergence of Sexuality'.[5] Basing his argument on the epistemological rupture between the biological notion of 'sex' and the psychological notion of 'sexuality' established first by the psychopathology of the second half of the nineteenth century and then, in a much more radical way, by Freud and psychoanalysis, Davidson is confident that the diffusion of the neologism 'sexuality' at the end of the nineteenth century and its re-semantisation in this context guard against interpretative error, by fixing the meaning of its usage in the twentieth century. The epistemological rupture to which the promotion and expansion of the notion of 'sexuality' would testify is confirmed, Davidson asserts, by the way in which the word, having become a concept, now maintains regulated and regular relations with other concepts, and in which it is used in an identical and repeated manner in many discourses.[6] It would therefore suffice to note the presence of the word and its lexical family thus recomposed to be sure, if not of the overall meaning of the statements, at least of their belonging to a particular episteme with well-defined contours.

Does 'sexuality' as a concept really refer, in Derrida but also in all those who refer to it or have referred to it since its re-semanticisation by Freud, to a homogeneous and stable scientific or discursive corpus? Is sexuality as an experience lived according to a phenomenality that can be identified by virtue of its regularity? And what relationship between concept and experience does the summoning of this lexicon presuppose or promote?

Unnamable, innumerable

If neither the mention nor the use of the vocabulary of sexuality seems to me to refer to a coherent epistemological base in Derrida's work, the questions that I have just sketched arise with even greater acuity in the absence of recognisable lexical clues. In talking, above, about Derrida's interest in 'sexuality', I mentioned 'At This Very Moment in This Work Here I Am', the essay that he devoted to Emmanuel Levinas, or rather to EL (pronounced 'Elle' in French: 'She'), and published in *Psyche: Inventions of the Other*, in 1986. The essay ends or rather is (de)limited with a textual and graphic performance that mimics the intertwining of voices calling and responding to each other, 'interweaving their bodies', inviting each other to a form of carnal (and more exactly oral) consumption, according to a choreography that disrupts their alternation and makes their place of emission indistinguishable. Incestuous voices, suggests Derrida, and first of all in that they blur the limits that ensure their distinction, thus compromising their separation, which ordinary rhetoric works to maintain.[7] But on what basis did I authorise myself to recognise in this textual performance a sexual performance? If the voices that make themselves 'heard' are not clearly identifiable, if their entanglement is such that it is impossible to distinguish them,[8] if they are therefore assignable neither to 'one sex' and only one, nor even to one gender,[9] do they still belong to the scene of what has been called sexual relations, or the sexual relationship (*la relation sexuelle, ou le rapport sexuel*)? More difficult still, what is, or would be, the relationship of voice to sex, or perhaps, rather, of the voice to the sexual? Reading this kind of call-and-response song under the banner of the 'sexual' demands a conception of the sexual and of sexuality that is precisely what is at stake in my questioning.

In her excellent essay on 'The Other Sexual Difference', Peggy Kamuf underlined the difficulty of delimiting the discourse on sexuality in Derrida's work, of identifying its topos and circumscribing its theme, because of its infinite *dissemination*. What happens in the course of '[the dissemination] of "sexuality's" thematic name [...] through every other term'[10] is, as Kamuf notes, that 'the difference collapses between naming and not naming "sexuality" by whatever name it is given in a language'.[11] While the 'name' of sexuality is not pronounced by the voices that intertwine at the end of the extremely dense reading of Levinas (aka EL) offered by Derrida, the very emergence of these voices, the mutual and repeated offering of their 'bodies', the register of their dialogue (marked by the thematised affects of mourning and jealousy), and the breathy quality of their choir seem to bear witness to a certain sexual charge

VOICE AND SEXUALITY   191

accumulated during the analysis, which this alternating song serves to illustrate even while 'liquidating' it.

The difficulty of isolating the object 'sexuality' in Derrida is indeed also due to the fact that, unlike Foucault, who never departs from the position of the epistemologist or archaeologist even when his words and writings touch upon questions involving his most intimate experience, Derrida does not seem (able or willing) to limit himself to an exclusively thetic or thematic treatment of the question, whatever the lexicon used. The postscript to 'At This Very Moment [...]' is exemplary in this regard.

I have already noted that the score sung by these intertwined voices exceeded, even ignored, the binary distinction of gender, in such a way that one cannot be identified as masculine, the other as feminine. However, a certain number of clues lead us to think that the matrix of this duet – for it is indeed a duet, as indicated by the use of the pronouns of the dual interlocution 'I' and 'You' (*Tu*) – is a matrix that I will provisionally qualify as heterosexual, even if Derrida explicitly invites us, in 'Choreographies' for example, to suspend the opposition between heterosexuality and homosexuality, as between all the oppositions which feed and continue to burden (or to command) attempts to think sexuality since Freud – and despite the fact that Freud initiated a deconstruction, long before the term was coined, of the binary structure of sexuality. Even before their intertwining, two voices effectively carry Derrida's reading of EL, and these voices are clearly gendered.[12] No doubt this is a way for Derrida to mark at the level of his own language his refusal to participate in the operation of erasing the feminine that takes place in the French language under cover of the generic neutrality of the masculine, and which signs the submission to the 'phallogocentric' regime of discourse. But it is also clear that, in Derrida, the discourse on and of sexuality is almost always deployed in the context of a structure of enunciation that mobilises a grammar of sexual difference, if not sexed (*sexuée*) difference,[13] if by sexual difference we seek to name the point where the duality of the sexes (fixed or mobile, presumed to be real, symbolic or fantasized) is articulated with a certain scene of desire.[14]

Whether this structure of enunciation is presented as fictional, as in the divided step of *Pas* in *Parages* or the duet of 'At This Very Moment [...]', or as autofictional, as in the 'Envois' of *The Postcard*; whether it is allegorical (and metapoetic), as in the exchange between poetry and its reader staged by 'Che Cos'è la Poesia',[15] or embodied in the scene of the supposedly real dialogue between a (male) speaker – the man and the author answering to the name of Derrida – and a (female) speaker, it's as if the thinking (but perhaps also the emergence) of the sexual and of sexuality, were inseparable from a scenic summoning of sexual difference in the form of a duet 'interpreting' the sexual score, to use Derrida's formula in 'Ants'.[16] It was during his interview with Christie McDonald, in 1981, that Derrida found himself 'dreaming' of 'this indeterminable number of intertwined voices, this mobile of non-identified sexual marks whose choreography can carry off the body of each "individual", crossing through it, dividing it, multiplying it, whether it be classified as "man" or "woman" according to the habitual criteria'.[17] In 'Voice II', a 1982 interview conducted by Verena Andermatt Conley, but which seems to continue the conversation begun in 'Choreographies', Derrida returns to what he calls 'the dreamed-of form of [his] desire' and attempts to imagine a 'sexual difference' that is not 'dialectizable', and whose 'sublime' (but not sublimated) experience would no longer depend on a logic of opposition.[18] In 'Dialanguages', a 1983 interview with the young Anne Emmanuelle Berger devoted to the subject of 'taste', Derrida, evoking his taste for the voice, speaks of his 'enjoyment' (*jouissance*) at 'giv[ing] to be heard, in what [he] writes, a certain position of the voice', of his taste 'for what is written by tongues [*les langues*], from mouth to ear [*de bouche à oreille*], from mouth to mouth, or from mouth to lips …'.[19] In 'Ants', an interpretation of 'sexual difference' given in duet with Hélène Cixous in 1990, Derrida quotes at length Jules Michelet's description of a wedding party (*noce*) of ants, and qualifies this wild celebration as a 'festival [*fête*] of sexual difference'.[20] No wonder, then, that it is above all the female readers of Derrida, who – responding to this kind of call to the other (woman?) inscribed in the structure of the text and thematised by the discourse – set about deciphering Derrida's sexual score, whether it be Hélène Cixous, Peggy Kamuf, Ginette Michaud, Evelyne Grossman, the author of these lines, and many more in languages other than French and English.

Some years ago I analysed this structure in a short essay entitled 'Pas de deux'.[21] I am returning today in a different way to what I see at play in this Derridian 'pas de deux', a dancing duet which signifies both the two and its negation in a movement that evokes two 'differing' (*différant*) bodies.

In 'Choreographies', Derrida rejects the topos of a 'woman's place' put forward by his interlocutor, and he proposes in its place (sic) a meditation on the '*pas de femme(s)*', dance steps of certain women or stasis of a certain feminism. Suggesting a relationship between the dance step and the movement of differance (with an 'a'), he then poses a question that has already been the subject of numerous comments: 'Should we think "differance" "before" sexual difference or deriving "from" it?'[22] My question today could be this: should we think of 'sexuality' *deriving from* 'sexual difference', as Derrida seems to do on numerous occasions?

VOICE AND SEXTUALITY   193

Why should an analysis of the secondarisation of sexual difference in the order of ontological determinations, and of the feminine in the symbolic order, such as Derrida performs it with regard to Levinas in 'At This Very Moment [...]', lead to (or trigger) a love song as ardent as it is degendered? How does Derrida manage, in the first 'Geschlecht', to transform his analysis of the ontological neutralisation of 'sexual difference' by Heidegger into a reading of the sexual positivity, even the sexual power (*puissance*), of this gesture?

Geschlechtigkeit or Sexualität?

No doubt we cannot begin to answer this question without first asking ourselves, as I have begun to do with regard to 'sexuality', what Derrida is talking about or trying to talk about in the name, and under the name, of 'sexual difference', and in which linguistic, discursive, conceptual, epistemological networks the formula is caught at the moment when Derrida takes it up again and recirculates it. I have already sketched some answers to this last question in an article entitled 'Sexing Differances' and in 'The Ends of an Idiom or Sexual Difference in Translation'.[23] I underlined the apparent paradox that consists for Derrida in insistently reinscribing the motif of sexual difference even as he endeavours to deconstruct 'sexduality'. I gave two types of explanation for this, one having to do with Derrida's complex relationship to psychoanalysis and Freud's legacy in particular, the other with a certain work on the resources of language, whether it be a matter of giving some play to the notion of difference, by emphasising the movement of trans-ferential dispersion that any '(di-)ference'[24] implies, or of leading, through the handling of the adjective 'sexual', the thinking of sexual difference or differences towards a thinking (and a dream) of the sexual relation, more exactly, and to paraphrase Peggy Kamuf paraphrasing Derrida, of another sexual relation. Finally, as I have already pointed out in 'Sexing Differances', and as Lynn Turner remarked to me with great accuracy, this other sexual relation Derrida writes and dreams about doesn't involve getting rid of the duo – and Derrida's love scenes are almost always duets of sorts – so much as eschewing both the dual as an (op)positional structure and the duel in the duo, by insisting on the divisibility, hence potential multiplicity of each subject, as well as on the conceptual untenability of the very notion of 'duality'. Indeed, the ordinary understanding of both sexual difference and the sexual relation relies on a notion of the one (two ones as it were) as well as of the third (as what the two supposedly exclude) which are both contested by Derrida.

In fact, Derrida never spoke of the '*difference between the sexes*' (*différence des sexes*). It is not, to borrow a certain vocabulary from the feminist philosopher Geneviève Fraisse, the presumed empirical nature of this difference or its factuality – Simone de Beauvoir would have spoken of its 'facticity' (*facticité*) – that interest him or that he seeks to establish on whatever basis (physiological, phenomenological, anthropological, historical or cultural). It is rather, as we have begun to see it, the desire to approach a certain experience, or perhaps first of all, an (im)possibility, of the sexual – not in the primitive sense relating to the division of the sexes in reproduction,[25] but in the 'expanded' sense that Freud gave to this lexicon – that seems to orient his discourse.

But this is where the difficulties begin. As Freud himself emphasises in different ways in the *Three Essays on the Theory of Sexuality* as well as in his various essays on the topic, sexuality (*Sexualität*), which Freud gradually discovered and began to analyse, and, likewise, the '*sexual*' which relates to it,[26] have to do neither with the 'biological function' (the need to ensure the reproduction of the species), nor even with the recognition of the difference between the sexes according to a process which would transform its empirical perception simultaneously into a psychic constraint and a socio-symbolic rule. From his investigation of infantile sexuality – a sexuality which Jean Laplanche says constitutes for Freud the essence of sexuality in the sense that he henceforth gives to this term – Freud thus draws the conclusion that 'a disposition to perversions is an original and universal disposition of the human sexual instinct'.[27] We know that perversion, a major concept inherited from nineteenth-century psychopathology, was used to precisely designate all that, in sexual motion and activity, was supposed to divert the subject from the biological imperative by removing her/him from the path allegedly prescribed by this imperative (heterosexual copulation with a view to reproduction). To say, like Freud, that perversion is 'original' is therefore to say that the sexual drive, and the sexuality which testifies to it, are always already 'led astray', that they have never *as such* responded to the supposed 'call of nature' dictating the union of the (two) sexes. In 'On the Sexual Theories of Children', Freud drives home the point, asserting, on the basis of clinical observations, that if 'the existence of two sexes' (*Beide Geschlechter*) seems obvious to us adults – an obviousness whose at least partially 'fabricated' character he also underlines – children, for their part, do not make the difference between the sexes 'the starting point of their research on sexual problems'.[28] In the place of '*Geschlechtstrieb*' – a formula that is usually and inadvertently translated as 'sexual instinct' in French (*instinct sexuel*), and that was employed notably by Krafft-Ebing, one of Freud's main predecessors in the study of sexual life – Freud therefore substitutes a *Sexualtrieb*. This terminological shift represents a major epistemological and philosophical displacement,

VOICE AND SEXTUALITY

as Jean Laplanche, who supervised Freud's retranslation into French, again underlines. To speak of *Geschlechtstrieb* is to link the said sexual instinct both to the dual structure of gender and to the survival of the species, according to the semantic spectrum of the word *Geschlecht* in German, which also means, and therefore binds together (Derrida will recall this in the first 'Geschlecht') 'sex, race, family, generation, lineage, species, genre or genus [*genre*]'.[29] Freud's choice of the Latin vocabulary of sexuality, even if it is not thought out by him in a completely explicit way nor always applied with rigour[30] – and even if, for speakers of Romance languages, it refers still confusedly to the sexual partition[31] – this choice, therefore, is precisely a way of breaking this logical and ideological anchoring of sexuality to the dual structure of gender and to the law of generation. As Laplanche writes, '[t]he S*exualtheorie* is not a *Geschlechtstheorie*'.[32] And yet (*damit*), in the first 'Geschlecht' ('Geschlecht sexual difference, ontological difference'), Derrida sometimes seems to act as if, between *Geschlechtigkeit*, which is in fact commonly and indifferently translated by 'sexuality' (*sexualité*) in French, and *Sexualität*, there was no conceptual difference, as if, in other words, one could derive (*dériver*) a thinking of sexuality from a thinking of *Geschlecht*, or perhaps more exactly, as if he wanted to make the Heideggerian thinking of the *Geschlecht* drift *towards* (*dériver vers*) a thinking of sexuality, in the sense opened up by Freud.

Indeed nowhere more than in this first text devoted to the word and the motif of *Geschlecht* in Heidegger do the philosophical and epistemological stakes of the choice of words appear so clearly in their irreducible complexity, multiplied as they are by the exercise of permanent translation in which Derrida engages, between German and French, but also, between their two idioms (the singular way in which each philosopher handles his respective writing language), between Heidegger's thought and Derrida's own, even between one element of the Heideggerian corpus and another. So, let's pause for a moment to explore this essay.

At first glance, observes Derrida, Heidegger seems never to have spoken of 'sex', a term to which Derrida immediately adds three expressions, three possible glosses of it in a certain contemporary French: the 'sexual-relation' (*rapport-sexuel*), 'sexual-difference', 'the-man-and-the-woman'. To 'Heidegger's apparent silence' on sex,[33] Derrida responds, in an apparent contradiction, with a provocative move which consists in using 'sex' as the very first lexical *and* syntagmatic unit of his discourse, thanks to a particular turn of phrase in French (in this case, this turn of emphasis by anteposition and doubling of the object which is called a 'segmented construction').[34] But the opposition played out between Heidegger's silence and Derrida's displayed volubility with regard to sex will be undermined by Derrida's reading of Heidegger. Inviting us not to rely on the conceptual grammar of philosophical language, which bases the semantic charge of a speech or a thesis on the use of this or that 'noun' – for example, the noun 'sex' and the noun phrase 'sexual difference', or again, the nouns '*Geschlecht*' and '*Geschlechtigkeit*' – Derrida embarks on an extraordinary hunt for the syntactic operators which organise in an almost invisible way Heidegger's few remarks concerning the place to be granted to *Geschlecht* in the structure of *Dasein*, in order to make readable in the discourse of the latter an 'order of implications'.[35] Noting the presence in Heidegger's discourse of a number of tiny logical connectors and adverbial phrases – *damit, auch, erstrecht* – that the ordinary conception of language relegates to the rank of secondary tools, devoid of meaning by themselves and therefore without ontological weight, he shows how these in fact structure Heidegger's thinking of '*Geschlecht*' and, departing *from* the latter, of the 'sexuality' of *Dasein*. The tenuous trace of a nominal discourse on sex is thus neglected in favour of the identification of a series of syntactic micro-operations that Derrida reads as so many machines for surreptitiously sexualising *Dasein*.[36] In a sense, these (small) 'words' take revenge here on the (big) 'nouns' which are the obligatory support of 'concepts', the syntax takes revenge on the lexicon, and dissemination takes revenge on the gathering up of meaning in the noun.

This attention to 'the order of implications' established by the syntactic operators in Heidegger's sentences is the occasion for Derrida to formulate quasi-dialectically a quasi-thesis: namely that the logical neutralisation of the binary structure of the *Geschlecht* operated by Heidegger at the level of the 'existential' analysis is precisely what makes it possible to liberate *Dasein's Mächtigkeit*, its 'positivity' or its originary power. The ontic determination of *Geschlecht* as a binary structure, whether it derives from an anthropological, sociological or biological explanation, limits as such 'the originarily disseminational (*originairement disséminale*) structure' of *Dasein*.[37] Isn't all determination negation? It must therefore be denied or neutralised in turn to bring out the 'pre-dual' positivity of *Dasein*, in a movement that resembles, up to a certain point, the work of Hegelian negativity. By qualifying this pre-dual positivity or this 'disseminational' power of *Dasein* as 'sexual', Derrida invites us to think sexuality *beyond* sexual duality, both before and after the latter. In doing so, is he not anticipating the conception of the sexual that *queer* thinkers subsequently contributed to developing? Above all, does he not rediscover, where one does not expect it – in Heidegger's text and thought – the great Freudian thesis on sexuality and the '*sexual*' as fundamentally rebellious to *Geschlecht?* (i.e., to the duality of the sexes)? The surprise is all the

VOICE AND SEXTUALITY

greater since Derrida's analysis unfolds here against the background of a merciless criticism of the facile recourse to a psychoanalysing discourse as soon as the question of sexuality arises.[38]

But this reading of Heidegger could not have been proposed without the constant work of translation-betrayal to which Derrida devotes himself, starting with the first words of his essay. Whether the title – '*Geschlecht* Sexual Difference, Ontological Difference' – was devised as an afterthought or from the start, it immediately raises the question: what is the relationship between the German '*Geschlecht*' and the French phrase 'sexual difference' which immediately follows it without any punctuation? Does this juxtaposition inscribe an irreducible gap between the German and French languages, between Heidegger's idiom and Derrida's, or does it translate the one into the other, the one through the other, by postulating an equivalence between these two notions, or even, and this is not the same thing, an affinity between their respective treatments by the two philosophers? What happens when one 'translates' '*Geschlecht*', this 'noun' which Derrida reminds us means 'sex, race, family, generation, lineage, species, genre or genus [*genre*]',[39] as 'sexual difference'? And when one reads the first through the prism of the second? The question becomes even more complicated if one recalls that, as I have already noted, the Freudian intervention, beginning in the last quarter of the nineteenth century, in the epistemological domain indexed by the notion of 'sexuality' provoked a critical shift, indissociably lexical and theoretical, that set the thinking of *Geschlecht* and that of *Sexualität* off in two different directions: the traditional one, which links *Geschlecht* to its biological determination (*Geschlechtig, Geschlechtigkeit, Zwigeschlechtigkeit*), and the modern and Freudian one (*Sexualität, Sexuell, Sexual, Bisexualität*), which breaks the anchoring of sexuality in the physiological division of the sexes. Even if it is true that the 'ante-Freudian' habit of translating *Geschlechtigkeit* as '*sexualité*' in French (or as 'sexuality' in English) has persisted, and even if the old, pre-theoretical meaning of the word 'sexuality' (in the sense of the sexual division of living beings)[40] has been in use until recently in French *alongside* its modern meaning, which I have described as Freudian, it is impossible to imagine that Derrida, who constantly underlines the 'problems of translation' and the 'very subtle differentiation of a certain lexicon',[41] ignores the meaning and the effects, both pragmatic and theoretical, of these distinctions. The quasi-systematic translation of the deliberately non-Freudian and more purely Germanic lexicon of *Geschlechtigkeit* mobilised by Heidegger into the Latin and Freudian vocabulary of sexuality allows Derrida to pull the Heideggerian thinking of *Geschlecht* towards a 'Derridean' thinking of the sexual and sexuality.

With a linguistic magic trick, Derrida skips over the epistemological rupture to which the lexical divergence between *Geschlechigkeit* and *Sexualität* is supposed to testify: traction and distraction of translation. To put it another way, Derrida's choice of 'sexual difference' to translate and betray the Heideggerian problematic of *Geschlecht* allows him to wrench the motif of 'sexual difference' from a logic and a thinking of *Geschlecht* (binary structure of sex or gender), in order to reinscribe it in the orbit of a problematic of sexuality. It is by effecting a shift from '*two* sexes' (*deux* sexes) (*Geschlecht*) to '*of* sex' (*de* sexe) (*Sexualität*) – as when he writes, in a subtly playful manner: 'If *Dasein* as such belongs to neither of *the two sexes* [*des deux sexes*], that does not mean that it is deprived *of sex* [*de sexe*]'[42] – that Derrida can interpret the neutralisation of the binary structure of *Geschlecht* as a movement of re-sexualisation. And it is only on this condition that he can read the *Mächtigkeit* of the Heideggerian *Dasein as a sexual* potency.

Sexual difference, vocal difference

I have already said that the Derridian discourse on sexuality, and, even more, the direct or disseminated inscription of the 'sexual' in Derrida's language, most often unfolds thanks to this enunciative structure that I have qualified as a '*pas de deux*', though it's impossible to decide which of these two, this apparently heterosexual pas–de–deux or the attraction of the sexual question, drew the other into its dance. Insofar as the sexual moves beyond the duality of the sexes, this pas–de–deux in any case untethers the *play* of sexual difference from the (ontic or ontological, empirical or symbolic) *structure* of the difference between the sexes, as a fixed and universal structure. But it is above all a certain articulation of the sexual and the vocal – and the rise of the sexual as vocal (or the reverse) – that is striking in almost all the texts mentioned. There is not a single Derridian dialogue, real or fictional, with a female interlocutor, that does not situate the irruption of the sexual, and the reflection on it, in the vicinity of a meditation on the voice. Whether it is a question of 'believ[ing] in the multiplicity of sexually marked voices', the choral inscription of which Derrida dreams about in 'Choreographies', and of which he wrote the interlacing score at the end of 'At This Very Moment [...]'; or of 'sing[ing] [...] according to such and such a voice' 'the dreamed form of [his] desire' in 'Voice II',[43] of admitting in 'Dialanguages' that his 'preferred pleasure [*jouissance*]' is, or would be, to 'let be heard in what [he] write[s] a certain position of the voice, when the voice and the body are no longer distinguishable',[44] or of underlining the tele*phonic* origin of the duet he performs with Cixous in *Lectures de la*

VOICE AND SEXTUALITY

différence sexuelle, the voice, this lyrical organ, seems to be the privileged mode of the 'phenomenalisation' of sexuality in Derrida's work.[45]

Nowhere, perhaps, does Derrida formulate more explicitly than in 'Voice II' what separates vocal differ*a*nce as sexual differ*a*nce from genital difference, which is supposed to ground sexual difference – and attraction.[46] 'Why', Derrida asks himself and his interlocutor, 'Why are we talking about the voice at such great length when our subject is sexual difference?'[47] The three pages that follow by way of an 'answer' deserve a detailed analysis that I cannot engage in here. But I will underline a certain number of its traits, starting with the remarkable proximity between the argument (if it is one) Derrida develops here, and the reading of the Heideggerian *Dasein*'s sexual (or sexu*a*le)[48] potency (*puissance*) that he proposes in '*Geschlecht* I'.

Just as the disseminational power of *Dasein* can only be discovered and deployed by neutralising *Geschlecht* as a binary and oppositional ontic determination, so, Derrida writes, '[i]n order to be exposed to the braided polyphony which is coiled up in every voice, perhaps we must come back to a vocal *difference* rebellious to any *opposition* and which is not derived from anything else'.[49] Just as the anthropological, biological or sociological approach to *Geschlecht* does not make it possible to grasp the radicality of ontological difference as non-dual difference, so '[n]either physics, phonetics, linguistics, psychoanalysis, nor philosophy', as examples of so-called positive knowledge or discourse (Derrida would perhaps call them negative) about living beings (*l'existant*), 'teach us anything whatsoever about this essence of the voice'.[50] But on the other hand, Derrida's challenge to the empirical determinations and assignations of 'the voice' to a *single* origin and function should not lead according to him to its logocentric 'hypostasis' – fetishisation? – as 'VOICE: anonymous and asexual, having come from nowhere'. Derrida continues: 'Provided that one hears this well [*qu'on l'entende bien*]. To the contrary, it is the brutality of assignation that multiplies hypostases in order to oppose vocal difference, to turn difference into opposition, into an opposition without multiplicity, without internal spacing, the very homogeneity of a dialectic.'[51]

When it escapes both the violence of assignations of all kinds *and* its dialectical neutralisation, 'vocal difference' allows, according to Derrida, the sexual polyphony to be heard, not only, not even primarily, the sexual polyphony of the choir of women and men – which it does not allow to, or allows *not to*, be determined as such – but of each 'singular voice'. '[W]here *there is voice*' (emphasis added), writes Derrida, taking care not to identify the mouth or mouths from which it is understood to emanate and the ear or ears to which it is supposed to arrive, 'sex becomes undecided':[52] where there is not *one* or *two* voices or even *some* voices, but *some* voice (*de la voix*), the work of the cut (of sexuation, a fortiori of '*sexage*', in the sense that the feminist sociologist Colette Guillaumin gives to the neologism[53]) no longer marks the oppositional boundary between 'the one and the other' sex, nor an internal fracture or boundary, according to the old logic of sexual division from which derives, for example, the psychoanalytic notion of bisexuality.

Is it because the voice nevertheless appeals to the mouth(s) and ear(s), these non-genital organs of the oldest pleasure taken in the relation with a foreign body, even with one's own body as a foreign body, in this experience of auto-affection so often described or invoked by Derrida, that the voice becomes in his work, in such an insistent way, the organ of a pleasure that I would provisionally call sexual?[54] The voice connects the mouth to itself as to the ear of the other – what is heard in the ear always coming *from the other*, from outside, even when we hear ourselves speak. It eroticises the ducts and orifices of the body by affecting them; before the vagina, therefore, there is the ear, and for 'all sexes' ('*tous les sexes*' (sic)); before the hymen and like a hymen, there is the tympanum, as Derrida suggests.[55] But 'hearing oneself speak' also introduces, as Derrida strove to show against Husserl, division and spacing between oneself and oneself. And the voice that affects me (even if it is 'mine') is always already cut off, detached as such from its place of origin and emission: not 'ideal', like the 'white' voice that its phenomenological reduction condemns to silence, but strange if not foreign, separated as it is from the subject from which it is supposed to emanate: spectral, like writing.[56]

If I hear Derrida correctly, the 'vocal difference' does not stem from the traditional opposition between speech and writing, which on the contrary it calls into question. In fact, it is in the vicinity of this meditation on the sexiferous character of the voice, whose indefinitely broken and (re)knotted thread can be followed throughout his work, that Derrida ventures to think about the co-implication, if not the consubstantiality, of writing, at least that which he dreams of, and sexuality, in the sense in which he understands it.

It is following on from an affirmation that 'there is voice',[57] from this attempt to make heard, and to note, the 'vocal *differance*' against the metaphysical conception of the voice as an organ ensuring the immediate presence of the subject to himself in speech, that Derrida thinks 'writing' in 'Voice II'. The 'lyrical' reflection on the '"colors" of the voice' in which Derrida engages as soon as the question arises for him of thinking 'innumerable sexuality', leads indeed to a dream of writing, a dream that Derrida claims to sing while writing it – '[...] what I am writing [...],

VOICE AND SEXUALITY   201

well, the fact that I write it, I sing it according to such and such a voice [...]'[58] – a strangely familiar 'dream' (like any dream) of a 'singular writing' or rather, as he writes, a '[w]riting of the singular voice'.[59] On the grammatical level, the epithet 'singular' in the French original (*écriture de la voix singulière*) can actually refer to writing as well as to the voice, as if in each case to the 'same' phenomenon of 'differential' auto-affection. The singularity of the voice or of writing (of one for the other) would accomplish and testify to what Derrida, in *Speech and Phenomena*, calls 'forego[ing] any claim to universality', by which the writing would break vocally with the claim of the *logos* to speak the (universal) truth, to present itself as the (voiceless) voice of truth.[60] Writing, as such, would therefore always be *writing of the singular voice*: 'Writing of the singular voice. Type, since there is inscription, *typtein*, timbre and tympanum, but without a type, that is to say, without a model, without a prescriptive form, type without "type" and without stereotype.' And Derrida adds, in a joking tone that defies philosophical gravity: 'Why does one say a "*type*" for a "guy" in common French? Is there a relation?'[61]

It is also in this, or perhaps primarily in this, that writing, far from being destined to simply reproduce a type of speech and a 'typical' (guy's) speech (*de 'type'*), would be 'feminine'; but writing's femininity would be one without reference and without essence (and perhaps even without existence). Indeed, a number of feminist thinkers have reproached Derrida for this. It should be clear that the 'timbre' is not a tessitura, a vocal 'colour' that would be specific to one sex – or the other. Each time singular, strange and penetrating, the 'timbre' – this resonance of the marked, mad voice (*timbrée, folle*), which Derrida tries to make vibrate in each gesture of inscription – does not characterise a recognisable place and form of emission. And the singular, a-typical (and consequently non-reproducible) *jouissance* that writing gives, according to Derrida, is due to this. 'My' writing voice is an other.

It would therefore be wrong to interpret Derrida's deconstruction of phonocentrism – and his inaugural analysis of the metaphysical conception of 'hearing oneself speak' as the immediate presence of meaning to itself in the element of full speech, such as he deploys it in *Speech and Phenomena* – as a repudiation of 'the voice' in favor of 'writing'. The writing of which Derrida 'dreams' and whose operation he tries to translate into his 'language', is rather, on the contrary, what seeks to restore 'body' (therefore voice) to the voice, by reinscribing speech, this speech that Abrahamic religions and Western philosophy have striven to disincarnate, in the circuit, or rather – since an interrupted and resumed, divided and tangled (telephone) line does not form a circle but rather a text – in the 'context' of the mouth and the ear.[62]

The moment of 'writing' as the moment of 'sexuality'

But why and how did the question of 'writing' (as 'writing of the singular voice') and that of 'sexuality' find themselves intimately linked (not to say entangled) in Derrida's work? The short essay that Evelyne Grossman devoted in 2016 to the 'beyond' of sexual difference in the works of Barthes and Derrida, and the important opus by Eric Marty, *Le Sexe des Modernes*, published in 2021, can help us sketch an answer.[63]

According to Grossman, what connects the works of Barthes and Derrida, in addition to their belonging to the same era of thinking, is their attempt to make '*jouissance*' both a defining trait and a central issue of what the two thinkers call, by pairing them according to a movement of incestuous convergence, 'reading' and 'writing'. By blurring, each in his own way, in theory as well as in practice, the criteriology of the distinction, Barthes and Derrida have conferred on reading the dignity and strength of what I have called a 'counter-writing', drawing inspiration from what Derrida thinks and does under the name of the countersignature.[64] Thanks to this undermining of their constitutive oppositions – author/reader, activity of creation/passivity of reception, originality (and originarity) of the writing gesture/secondariness of the work of reading – they have also questioned the gendered imaginary of the writing/reading opposition, which is the product of a normative understanding of 'the difference between the sexes' (*différence des sexes*). Thus, if as Grossman writes, 'writing [...] is an act, or perhaps even an activity, beyond the opposition between the active and the passive',[65] the same can be said of the act of reading, which is neither secondary nor passive, as it is advocated and practiced differently by Barthes and Derrida. By refusing 'to ground [their thinking] in [these] undisturbed binary oppositions' (*enracinement dans [ces] tranquilles oppositions binaires*)[66] according to Grossman's formula, each of them opened up a space of writing (more exactly of reading/writing) under the sign of the Neutral. And this Neutral, to which they devoted so many pages, is precisely the condition of the deployment of a '*jouissance* of [...] textual work'[67] that is produced (or is only produced) when one ventures 'beyond sexual difference'. It is this same 'thinking of the Neutral' developed in contact with the 'transgressive power of literature' that Marty explores in *Le Sexe des Modernes*, where he distinguishes it in part from the work of deconstructing the binarity of gender initiated on the other side of the Atlantic by *queer* theorists like Gayle Rubin and Judith Butler.[68] 'The Neutral', Marty writes, commenting on a passage in Barthes, 'is what releases sexuality from sex insofar as sex could claim to constitute itself as the meaning of sexuality.'[69] And he adds shortly thereafter, in a more

VOICE AND SEXTUALITY   203

Foucauldian register, about Barthes's work on the figure of the trans-
vestite: 'The Neutral of transvestism suspends the Western structure of
sexuality which imposes sex as the truth of the representations of the
body.'[70] By releasing sexuality from sex, in other words, by suspending
the relationship between sexuality and sexual duality, by breaking with
the conceptual and ideological matrix of 'sexduality', the textual operation of the neutralisation of 'sex', which Marty ambiguously qualifies
as an operation of 'desexualisation', opens the way for a 'degenitalised',
and therefore also a dephallicised *jouissance*. 'Writing', in the sense given
to it by the Moderns, is both the name and the privileged medium of
this operation.[71]

Neither Derrida nor Barthes clings to the word '*jouissance*' to designate the work and the effects of 'writing' (or of reading/writing). Nor
do they cling to the rigorous distinction between *jouissance* and pleasure, as elaborated by Lacan in the wake of Freud's *Beyond the Pleasure
Principle* and Bataille's *Eroticism*. This is no doubt a way for them to
maintain a non-dogmatic relationship to psychoanalysis, an affinity
without affiliation. The 'impure affect', to use Grossman's expression,
that each of them brings into their reading practice, a reading that is
both naive and scholarly, and in defiance of any 'scientific deontology
of neutrality',[72] is sometimes called '*jouissance*' or 'pleasure' by Barthes
and Derrida, and by the latter, sometimes 'ecstasy'. But Derrida clearly
situates the emergence of a paroxysmal *jouissance*, inseparably intellectual and sensuous, at the point where 'the fatality of 1/2' is overcome,
at the very moment when, in and through 'writing', he touches on
the limit of the limit, and consequently has the ecstatic experience
(improbable and fleeting like a dream) of crossing it: 'Yes, yes', he
writes in 'Voice II', 'but is it not enough to *think* this law which is law
itself [he is talking about the law of the sexual partition as binary divi-
sion], in order to have the precarious presentiment, if not the proof,
of its limit and of its impotence with regard to whatever it is in me
that desires [*ce qui désire en moi*] and that keeps this *thinking* awake?'[73]
Derrida continues:

> It is enough to evoke that which, beyond the fatality of 1/2, gives
> me pleasure [*jouissance*], the *idea* of a bliss of colors [*jouissance des
> couleurs*]; at the very limit of this distribution, of this destiny to
> be divided according to the law [*nomos, moira*], at the moment
> of its victory: its failure. The experience of this limit is a pleas-
> ure greater than my pleasure [*une jouissance plus grande que ma
> jouissance*], it exceeds both myself and my sex, it is sublime, but
> without sublimation. [...]

> This is what is anticipated when I write *this*, for example, even if it is false. Quite simply when I *write it* and this ecstasy is produced which consists in thinking, in order to love it, the impossible.[74]

Grossman qualifies on several occasions this dis-proportionate *jouissance* that Derrida claims to experience in the act of writing as a 'non-anthropological *jouissance*'. She means, no doubt, that it is precisely in human experience (that of the *anthropos*) and above all with regard to human experience that sexuality tends to be conceived as 'sexduality', the binary structure that constitutes both a 'backstop for thought', to use Françoise Héritier's formula, and an organising principle of experience, a condition of its phenomenalisation. The beyond-sexual-difference would in this sense open onto a beyond-human. But this 'beyond', for Derrida, has no proper place or substance of its own. It is only reached in accordance with or as a result of the operation of neutralisation of the dual structure that I have already described in connection with his reading of Heidegger. Where Grossman, following Blanchot and Barthes in this, tends to nominalise and therefore substantialise the 'neutral', Derrida again prefers the *operation* of neutralisation (and thus the noun derived from the verb 'neutralise'), which invites us to come back to (and start from) sexual difference, in order to de-limit it and, in so doing and at the same time, pluralise and singularise it.

Grossman relies on Blanchot and on Derrida's reading of him in *Parages* in her attempt to think through what she calls 'the strange Heideggerian "neutral"', this 'sexed Neutral which is at once asexual and hypersexual [*a-sexué et hypersexué*]'.[75] Marty, meanwhile, conjugates Modernity only in the masculine gender by summoning Barthes and Derrida, but also Blanchot, Deleuze and Foucault in order to think the Neutral. But perhaps we could look towards the Cixousian 'Neutral' – recall that Cixous published a fiction entitled *Neutre* in 1972 – to grasp the significance of Derrida's 'dream' of 'liberating' through 'writing' the radical positivity of sexuality, or of the 'sexual', from the fixed strait-jacket of dual difference. Like many literary fictions of this period, this text is anomic, and it features a number of 'actors' such as 'the analyst, the Subject, the Story, the Text, Chance, Son, Thread [*Fils, Fil*]', etc.[76] Cixous refers to what she calls, in the feminine, 'Neutrality', presenting it as 'an inexhaustible source of energy, the trace of the power through which the vanished power will reappear, [...] the erased trail of writing through which reading will surface'.[77] She multiplies the formulas that evoke both the energy (inexhaustible and underground) of the Freudian libido and the *Mächtigkeit*, potency or 'mightiness' of *Dasein* (as not

VOICE AND SEXUALITY   205

gendered) that Derrida qualifies as sexual, and which constitutes for him writing's vein or resource. On several occasions in her text, Cixous gives a version of the 'Ne-uter' which is consonant with the Derridian gesture of affirmation of an 'other' sexual difference, beyond 'sexduality': 'the one is not without the other', she writes at the start of her wanderings,[78] according to a syntax whose implications her text will strive to deploy in various ways. The generality of the assertion maintains the indefinite pronouns 'one' and 'the other' beyond or short of an identifiable gender, even if it does indeed affirm the existence (performance of desire by language) of a paradoxical duo: the affirmative double negation of 'the one *is not without* the other' couples 'the one' and 'the other', whatever their sex(s) and their genders(s), not in the mode of erasing any gap, any division, in the indifference of homogeneity (the one is the other), nor in the mode of a programmed and fated complementarity (the one is with the other), but as the intimation of an always recommenced crossing through the negative and through deprivation ('is not without'), whose outcome is by definition uncertain. At the end of *Neutre*, 'the Subject rises, one can begin to read what is written of Neutre [*ce qui s'écrit de Neutre*], mixed with smooth and lunar Silk [*Soie*], with Death, and with Other self [*soi*]'.[79] As for the 'text' that the 'Subject' – caught as it is, being a good psychoanalytic (and more precisely Lacanian) concept, in the constraining threads of relations of belonging and filiation – has nevertheless allowed to form, it 'enjoys' (*jouit*) without limits, as indicated by the ellipsis. And these are its last words:

> The text, seized with envy, hilarity, resemblance, vaginates, laughs, is covered with splotches, with different sexes and with centuries' effects, and unfolds, Nil, neither the one nor the other, neither Himself [*Soimême*], but traversed, running, extraordinary, natural, neither Achilles, nor Amazon nor Hamlet father or son, but the child of all: his mother is limitless, and he enjoys it ...[80]

'Textual incest', comments Cixous, but an incest freed, at the time and place where it occurs, from the sanction which accompanies Oedipus's transgression and which ensures with a single gesture both the repression and the socialisation of sexuality.[81]

In several of his essays, all of which aim to restore to the Freudian notion of sexuality its centrality and its incandescence, Laplanche insists on the fact that the fable of Oedipus, far from constituting the originary unconscious core of human sexuality, serves rather to translate (therefore to betray) what in sexuality is untranslatable – and therefore irreducible to any communication that can be shared according to the code common to the group in which it circulates – in the socio-cultural idiom of kinship relations which define the balance of places and powers. The 'Oedipal' desire ('vanquish the father, marry the mother') is itself not 'purely' sexual, in the sense understood by Laplanche.[82] And this is why, 'from the metapsychological point of view', the 'structure' of the Oedipus complex and its constituent elements (incest, castration), is not, according to Laplanche, a matter of the unconscious but of the preconscious.[83] However, the form and the narrative dimension of the Oedipus complex testify to the fable's role in the attenuating domestication of the sexual. 'Its task', Laplanche writes, is precisely 'to help put into narrative form the – conscious-preconscious-unconscious – history of the subject, and therefore of the analysand.'[84] The Oedipus complex is a story that can be told as such; it is what Laplanche calls a 'narrative schema', which serves to ensure its cultural transmission. Its elements, Laplanche notes, 'are relatively fixed, their relations sufficiently predictable, so that it is possible to pass from one "novel" to another'. And he adds: 'The "remakes" of a film are sometimes superior and richer, sometimes inferior to the first version. There is nothing stopping each human from trying.'[85] The 'family romance' is precisely a novel (*un roman*). And the 'Oedipal' subject who is its hero or heroine is not in this sense the 'subject of the unconscious' but a social subject, indeed the subject par excellence of the social, as Lévi-Strauss understood and theorised it.

In *Positions*, when he begins to use the lexeme of 'dissemination' as an operator for the 'sexualisation' of the philosophical field, Derrida affirms that 'dissemination represents *what does not belong or return to the Father*' (*ne revient pas au Père*). It therefore also breaks in this sense with the Oedipal narrative schema according to which the son, by taking the father's place in the end, belongs and returns to him. In this same passage, Derrida offers 'dissemination' as the improper name of 'writing' and plays the 'endlessness' of 'textuality' against the closure of the narrative.[86] Deleuze and Guattari too, in *Anti-Oedipus*, called for a departure from the family narrative, believing that they were playing in this way, if not against Freud, at least against the discursive and institutional field of psychoanalysis. But in doing so, aren't all three of them approaching in reality this untranslatable dimension of sexuality of which Laplanche speaks, and which is, according to him, the heart of the Freudian discovery?

'Writing' – the writing that Derrida 'sings', that Blanchot, Cixous and Celan practise in various ways, but also, at the time of *Le Plaisir du Texte*, Marguerite Duras, Pierre Guyotat or even Philippe Sollers – does not as such tell tales (*ne fait pas de roman*).[87] Perhaps the practical resistance to the translation and transmission of unchanged cultural patterns is an untenable 'position' as such. But we can clearly see how 'writing' and 'sexuality' were able to feed each other, and how each of these notions contributes to clarifying the other. Although the play on words seems facile today, even worn-out, could we not say that by trying to think of writing as a 'disseminational' practice, Derrida gave a certain '*sextual* pleasure [*jouissance*]' its most rigorous illustration and explanation?

The disenchantment with the one ('writing'), and, with it, the retreat of a certain idea and practice of literature, perhaps triggered the decline of the other ('sexuality').

Translated by Eric Prenowitz

Notes

1. Hélène Cixous, 'The Laugh of the Medusa', trans. Keith Cohen and Paula Cohen, in *Signs* 1.4 (1976), 885 [*Le Rire de la Méduse et autres ironies*, Paris: Galilée, 2010 (1975), 54]. [Published English translations, modified where necessary, have been used for citations from French texts. References to the English editions are followed by those to the French originals. – Trans.]
2. While the first neologism, '*sexophagous*', is my creation inspired by Derrida's insistent plugging together of sex and mouth, it is Derrida who qualifies the Heideggerian *Dasein* as 'sexiferous'. See '*Geschlecht* I: Sexual Difference, Ontological Difference', in *Psyche: Inventions of the Other*, vol. II (Stanford, CA: Stanford University Press, 2008), 8 ['*Geschlecht*: différence sexuelle, différence ontologique', in *Psyché: Inventions de l'autre* (Paris: Galilée, 1987), 396].
3. Until Lynn Turner asked me for the precise reference in Derrida's text of the occurrence of 'sexduality', I was under the impression that this neologism, to which I have referred many times, played an important role in Derrida's sexual lexicon. I now realise that it is nowhere to be found in Derrida's published work. He must have coined it during a session of a seminar I attended in Paris, or perhaps I dreamed it ...
4. Jacques Derrida, 'Choreographies', trans. Christie V. McDonald, in *Points...: Interviews, 1974–1994*, ed. Elisabeth Weber (Stanford, CA: Stanford University Press, 1995), 105 ['Choréographies', in *Points de suspension. Entretiens*, ed. Elisabeth Weber (Paris: Galilée, 1992), 111].
5. Arnold I. Davidson, *The Emergence of Sexuality: Historical Epistemology and the Formation of Concepts* (Cambridge, MA: Harvard University Press, 2001), 30–63.
6. 'We should examine the word "sexuality" in the sites in which it is used [...] Typically, at least when we are dealing with an epistemological break, we will find that the concept under investigation enters into systematic relations with other very specific concepts, and that it is used in distinctive kinds of sentences to perform regular, because often repeated, functions' (ibid., 38–9).

7. Incest does not only consist in upsetting the cultural ordering of kinship ties, even less in crossing some biological barrier, but rather, *in fine*, in blurring the boundary between (the relationship to) oneself and (the relationship to) the other and, consequently, the distinction between self-love and love of the other, without which no society is possible. Claude Lévi-Strauss, *The Elementary Structures of Kinship*, revised edition, trans. James Harle Bell et al. (Boston, MA: Beacon Press, 1969), 489 [*Les Structures élémentaires de la parenté*, 2nd edition (Paris: Mouton, 1967), 561].

8. '[…] I would like to believe in the multiplicity of sexually marked voices, in this indeterminable number of intertwined voices […]', Derrida, 'Choreographies', 108, translation modified ['Choréographies', 114–15.]

9. The French language is strongly gendered and 'gendering', and what's more, in a dual mode, and yet the voices that intertwine in this incredible postscript bear no gender mark that would allow the reader (*la lectrice*) to distinguish between a feminine pole and a masculine pole of enunciation.

10. The word 'dissemination' maintains the confusion between two semes and two germs, two lexical roots knowingly intertwined by Derrida: the radical 'meaning' (seme) and the radical 'seed' (semen).

11. Peggy Kamuf, 'Derrida and Gender: The Other Sexual Difference', in *Jacques Derrida and the Humanities: A Critical Reader*, ed. Tom Cohen (Cambridge: Cambridge University Press, 2001), 89 ['*L'autre différence sexuelle*', Europe, no. 901, May 2004 ('Jacques Derrida'), 172].

12. From the outset, the 'you' (*tu*) to which the first voice of the text is addressed is identified as feminine: 'You have not been visited [visit*ée*] but just as after the passage of some singular visitor, you no longer recognize the place […]' (emphasis added), 'At This Very Moment in This Work Here I Am', in *Psyche: Inventions of the Other*, vol. I (Stanford, CA: Stanford University Press, 2007), 143 [*Psyché: Inventions de l'autre*, 159], translation modified.

13. Derrida scarcely used the vocabulary of gender to deal with the hierarchical division of masculine and feminine, even at the time when the latter began to impose itself in the field of sociolinguistic practices in France. See Kamuf 'Derrida and Gender', 82 [163].

14. Isabelle Alfandary suggests that what the notion of 'sexual difference', in the wake of Lacan, seeks to articulate is precisely the point where the desire of the other constitutes me as a feminine or masculine subject by interpellating me in these terms. See 'L'Identité entre sexe et genre', in *Revue Descartes* 95 (2019/01) ('Discours, performance et sexualités'), 33. 'Sexual difference' would thus invite us to think about the so-called difference or differences between the sexes starting from a consideration of the sexual, and not the reverse. In this sense, and contrary to what Geneviève Fraisse seems to think, the notion of sexual difference summons not so much the organic reality of sex as the process of subjectivation and, with it, the historicity of the emergence of and of the confrontation between subjects.

15. This response by Derrida to the generic question appeared for the first time in *Poesia* I.11 (1988), 5–10.

16. Jacques Derrida, 'Ants', trans. Eric Prenowitz, *Oxford Literary Review*, vol. 24 (2002), 36 ['Fourmis' in *Lectures de la différence sexuelle*, dir. Anne Berger and Mara Negron (Paris: Editions des Femmes, 1994), 96.]

17. Derrida, 'Choreographies', 108, translation modified ['Choréographies', 114–15.]

18. Derrida, 'Voice II', 164–5, translation modified ['Voice II', 175].

19. Derrida, 'Dialanguages', 141, translation modified ['Dialangues', 150].

20. See Jules Michelet, *L'insecte* (*The Insect*) (1857) (Paris: Édition des Equateurs, 2011) and Derrida, 'Ants', 31, translation modified ['Fourmis', 90].

21. See Anne-Emmanuelle Berger, 'Pas de deux', in *Cahiers Jacques Derrida*, dir. Marie-Louise Mallet and Ginette Michaud (Paris: L'Herne, 2004), 357–62.

22. Derrida, 'Choreographies', 98, translation modified ['Choréographies', 103].

23. Anne-Emmanuelle Berger, 'Sexing Differances', in *Differences* 16.3 (2005): 52–67, and *Le Grand Théâtre du genre: Identités, Sexualités et Féminisme en 'Amérique'* (Paris: Belin, 2013), 151–77.

24. The word 'difference' belongs to the rich lexical family of 'ference', from Latin *fero, tuli, latum*, which means 'to carry' or 'to transport' and behaves or relates differently according to its prefixes in French or English (pre-ference, re-ference, trans-ference, etc.).

25. The word 'sexuality' was a neologism introduced into French during the first half of the nineteenth century by botanists studying plants' modes of reproduction. In his famous dictionary (the *Grand Dictionnaire Universel*, 1866–77), Pierre Larousse defined the word as follows: 'Physiol. Sexual character, way of being of whatever has a sex. A small number of botanists have gone so far as to deny that plants have a sexuality (P. Duchartre).' (*Grand Dictionnaire Universel*, T.14, 652). All the examples given by Larousse of the use of the adjective 'sexual', of the word 'sexuality' and of the neol-ogism 'sexualism', which has since fallen into disuse, relate to botany. We measure here the epistemological leap accomplished by the invention of sexology closely followed by psychoanalysis.

26. Jean Laplanche distinguishes the adjective '*sexuel*' from the adjective '*sexual*' which he also proposes to introduce into 'French' vocabulary. The two adjectives, taken from the Latin '*sexualis*', are also abundantly used by Freud. According to Laplanche, '*sexual*' (as in '*Sexualtheorie*' which is trans-lated into French either as '*théorie de la sexualité*' (theory of sexuality) or as '*théorie sexuelle*' (sexual theory)) is 'more scholarly and more Germanic'; '*sexuell*' is 'more Latinate and more commonplace'. See his *Sexual: La sexu-alité élargie au sens freudien* (Paris: PUF, 2007), 155. It is the '*sexual*' that car-ries the properly Freudian meaning given to sexuality: the meaning furthest removed from the binary division of organs and functions in the mechanism of biological reproduction.

27. Sigmund Freud, 'Summary', *Three Essays on the Theory of Sexuality*, [1953] in *The Standard Edition of the Complete Psychological Works of Sigmund Freud* (hereafter *S.E.*), vol. 7, ed. and trans. James Strachey (London: Vintage (The

210   ANNE EMMANUELLE BERGER

Hogarth Press), 2001), 231 [trans. B. Reverchon-Jouve, Paris: Gallimard, Coll. Ideas, 1962, p. 146].

28. Sigmund Freud, 'On the Sexual Theories of Children', in *S.E.*, vol. IX, 209, translation modified.

29. Derrida, *Geschlecht* I, 7 [395], translation modified.

30. It is nonetheless clear that Freud was aware of the theoretical and epistemological stakes of his terminological choices from his remark on the subject of his choice of the Latin word 'libido' rather than the German word 'Lust' to designate the sexual drive: 'The only appropriate word in the German language, "*Lust*", is unfortunately ambiguous, and is used to denote the experience both of a need and of a gratification', in *Three Essays on the Theory of Sexuality*, 135, n.2. (Adding a comment to Freud's footnote, Strachey remarks: 'Unlike the English "lust", [the German *Lust*] can mean either "desire" or "pleasure"', ibid.). Freud makes the same remark again in a footnote to the third essay: '"*Lust*" has two meanings, and is used to describe the sensation of sexual tension [...] as well as the feeling of satisfaction', ibid., 212, n.1.

31. The word 'sex' comes from the Latin *seco, secare, sectum*, which means to cut, to sever. However, Jean-Luc Nancy proposes another etymology which paradoxically links the motif of separation, of sectioning, to that of continuity: 'Of course there is only one sex and its very name says separation, whether it is derived from *secare* (to cut) or from *sequor* (to follow) which seems more probable and which moreover entails both separation, succession and accompaniment' (Jean-Luc Nancy, *Sexistence* (Paris: Galilée, 2017), 114).

32. Laplanche, *Sexual: La sexualité élargie au sens freudien*, 155.

33. Derrida, '*Geschlecht* I', 8 [396].

34. Let us recall the first words of this essay: 'Of sex, yes, one easily notices it, Heidegger speaks as little as possible and perhaps he never did' (Derrida, '*Geschlecht* I', 7 [395], translation modified).

35. By 'order of implications' ('*Geschlecht* I', 25, 26 [413, 414]), Derrida designates the complex unfolding of Heidegger's argumentation, such that the argument about the ontological secondariness of *Geschlecht* finds itself contradicted by the logical and/or rhetorical primacy accorded to it in the order of discourse.

36. See for example his analysis of Heidegger's use of the adverb 'also' in the sentence 'This neutrality *also* indicates [emphasis original] that *Dasein* is neither of the two sexes' (ibid., 12 [400–1]).

37. Ibid., 19 [407].

38. Derrida makes clear his wariness of a certain modern discursive 'panoply' deriving from psychoanalysis that is often used to deal with any question relating to sexuality, and, even more, his wariness of silence concerning the latter: 'Where does the silence work on this discourse? And what are the forms and determinable contours of this unsaid [*non-dit*]? We can wager that nothing pauses in these places which the arrows of the aforesaid panoply

VOICE AND SEXTUALITY 211

come to pin down with a name: omission, repression, denial, foreclosure, even the unthought' (ibid., 9 [397], translation modified).

39. Ibid., 7 [395], translation modified.

40. This primary meaning of the term is mobilised by Simone de Beauvoir in *The Second Sex*, trans. Constance Borde and Sheila Malovany-Chevallier (London: Vintage, 2010), 21–49 [*Le Deuxième Sexe*, vol. 1 (Paris: Gallimard, Folio Essais, 1976)].

41. Derrida, '*Geschlecht* I', 17 [405].

42. Ibid., 14 [402], emphasis added.

43. Derrida, 'Voice II', 164–5 [175].

44. Ibid., 141 [150].

45. This phenomenality of the voice is paradoxical, since the very notion of phenomenon is organically linked, so to speak, to that of light (from the Greek verb *phenestaï* which means to appear in the light, to be visible). See *Speech and Phenomena and Other Essays on Husserl's Theory of Signs* (Evanston, IL: Northwestern University Press, 1973), 72 [*La Voix et le phénomène*, 2nd edn (Paris: PUF, 1993), 80]. Maurice Merleau-Ponty's phenomenology of perception is moreover a phenomenology of visual perception, a theory of the visible.

46. Note the choice of another language, English, for the title of this interview, a language which is also, in the context of this interview, that of *another*, of Derrida's interlocutor. '*Voice*' makes it possible to de-nominalise, to deconceptualise, 'the voice', since this word can also be understood in English as a verb, an imperious call to pronounce words: *Voice!*

47. Derrida, 'Voice II', 161 [172], translation modified.

48. The difference suggested by Freud and thematised by Laplanche between 'sexuell' and 'sexual' (in German) is similar to the distinction theorised by Heidegger between existentiell analysis (from which Merleau-Ponty's '*psychanalyse existentielle*' derives) and existential analysis.

49. Derrida, 'Voice II', 162 [173] (emphasis original).

50. Ibid., 161–2 [172], translation modified.

51. Ibid., 162–3 [173], translation modified.

52. Ibid., 161 [172].

53. Guillaumin compares the collective appropriation and exploitation of women's bodies to a form of 'esclavage' (enslavement) whereby a group of people – black, women – are appropriated by a dominant group (white, men). Perhaps one could translate 'sexage' as 'sexslavement'. See *Sexe, race et pratique du pouvoir. L'idée de Nature* (Paris: Côté-femmes, 1992).

54. Isabelle Alfandary drew my attention to the following remark by Freud in *The Ego and the Id*: love (Eros) is basically noisy (*bruyant*) or 'clamourous' ('vocal', one might say), whereas the death instincts are 'mute': 'Over and over again we find, when we are able to trace instinctual impulses back, that they reveal themselves as derivatives of Eros [...] [W]e *are driven to conclude that the death instincts are by their nature mute and that the clamour of life proceeds for the most part from Eros*', Sigmund Freud, 'The Ego and the Id', in *S.E.*, vol. XIX, 46, emphasis added.

55. Jacques Derrida 'Tympan', in *Margins of Philosophy*, trans. Alan Bass (Chicago: University of Chicago Press, 1982) ['Tympanum', *Marges de la philosophie* (Paris: Editions de Minuit, 1972), n.6, xiv [n.2, VI].
56. See Derrida, *Speech and Phenomena*, 70–87 [78–97].
57. Derrida 'Voice II', 161 [172].
58. Ibid., 164 [175].
59. Ibid., 165 [175].
60. Derrida, *Speech and Phenomena*, 78 [88].
61. Derrida, 'Voice II', 165 [175].
62. One could compare these remarks with what Lacan says in *Seminar VII*, and what Tim Dean reports. In a chapter entitled 'Lacan Meets Queer Theory', Dean meditates on the election by Freud and Lacan of the mouth and the ear as first erogenous zones, and quotes, in English, the following passage from Lacan: 'These erogenous zones, that, until one has achieved a fuller elucidation of Freud's thought, one can consider to be generic, and that are limited to a number of special points, to points that are openings, to a limited number of mouths at the body's surface, are the points where Eros will have to find his source (SVII 93)' (Dean, *Beyond Sexuality* (Chicago: The University of Chicago Press, 2000), 254). According to Dean, by taking the mouth, and not the genitals, as the model of erogenous zones, Lacan questions the privilege that traditionally attaches to the male sex as the 'reason for desire' in an androcentric gender order. He also hypothesises that it is because the mouth is also the organ of speech, that it, as well as other mouth-like bodily 'openings', 'are the points where Eros will have to find his source' (254).
63. Evelyne Grossman, 'Roland Barthes, Jacques Derrida: au-delà de la différence sexuelle', at the conference 'Rastros do impensado: A deconstruçao a literatura (De retorno a Derrida)' [Traces of the Unthought: Deconstruction, Literature (Return to Derrida)'], University of Brasilia, 2016 (https://shs.hal.science/halshs-01421410); and Eric Marty, *Le Sexe des Modernes: Pensée du Neutre et théorie du genre* (Paris: Editions du Seuil, 2021).
64. Anne Emmanuelle Berger, 'Malaise dans la lecture', in *La Littérature sans condition*, dir. Isabelle Alfandary (Lormont: Le Bord de l'eau, 2020), 229.
65. Grossman, 'Roland Barthes, Jacques Derrida', 2.
66. Ibid., 3.
67. Ibid., 7.
68. Marty, *Le Sexe des Modernes*, 25.
69. Ibid., 162.
70. Ibid., 163.
71. Marty, *Le Sexe des Modernes*, 457–62.
72. Grossman, 'Roland Barthes, Jacques Derrida', 3. And this is another border, and, with it, another criterion of distinction between writing and reading, that is undermined: the one that separates the subjective work from the objective criticism of it, the trance of the writing subject from the supposedly disaffected position from the learned reader.

VOICE AND SEXTUALITY 213

73. Derrida, 'Voice II', 164 [175], translation modified, emphasis original.
74. Ibid,, translation modified, emphasis original.
75. Grossman, 'Roland Barthes, Jacques Derrida', 9.
76. Hélène Cixous, *Neutre* [1972] (Paris: Editions des Femmes, 1998), 18.
77. Ibid., 55.
78. Ibid., 19.
79. Ibid., 172.
80. Ibid., 173.
81. Ibid., 172.
82. Laplanche, 'Castration et Oedipe comme codes et schémas narratifs', in *Sexual: La sexualité élargie au sens freudien*, 299.
83. Laplanche, 'Inceste et sexualité infantile', in *Sexual: La sexualité élargie au sens freudien*, 280.
84. Ibid.
85. Laplanche, 'Castration et Oedipe', 300.
86. 'Writing – dissemination – is it not to take into account castration [...] by putting into play its position as transcendental signified or signifier [...] the ultimate recourse of all textuality, the central truth or the truth in the last analysis, the semantically full and non-substitutable definition of the generating (disseminating) void where the text is launched? Dissemination *affirms* [...] endless substitution, it neither arrests nor controls play [...]', Jacques Derrida, 'Positions', in *Positions*, trans. Alan Bass (Chicago: University of Chicago Press, 1981), 86 [*Positions* (Paris: Editions de Minuit, 1972), 120], translation modified, emphasis original.
87. Roland Barthes, *The Pleasure of the Text*, trans. Richard Miller (New York: Farrar, Strauss and Giroux, 1975) [*Le Plaisir du Texte* (Paris: Editions du Seuil, 1973)].

Part III

Panthropology

11

THE MASTURBATING ANIMAL: THE AUTO-HETERO-AFFECTION OF THE LIVING

Nicole Anderson

[T]he movement of language does not, one suspects, have only an analogical relationship with 'sexual' auto-affection. It is totally indistinguishable from it ... sexual autoaffection begins well before what is thought to be circumscribed by the name masturbation.

(Jacques Derrida)[1]

Nothing risks becoming more poisonous than an autobiography, poisonous for oneself in the first place, auto-infectious for the presumed signatory who is so auto-affected.

(Jacques Derrida)[2]

It is in the context of an exposition and analysis of Rousseau's works in *Of Grammatology* (1967) that Jacques Derrida first raises the topic of masturbation. Thirty years later masturbation, I would argue, manifests as an auto-affective performance in his book *The Animal That Therefore I Am*. I demonstrate that masturbation, auto-affection and autobiography are analogous, and consequently the *Animal* could be described as a masturbatory book that Derrida at the same time deconstructs. What he deconstructs is the exhibitionist and auto-affective practice of autobiography *per se*, as well as himself as an autobiographical animal, all of which serves to question the ways in which autobiography and auto-affection are philosophically and metaphysically constituted and framed in opposition to non-human animals.[3] Given this, I further argue that Derrida's masturbatory, that is auto-affective, performance in *The Animal That Therefore I am* is not only erotic,[4] but 'hetero-erotic'. (As we will see masturbation, and consequently autobiography, as acts of self-othering, always already involve the other.)

The portmanteau 'hetero-erotic' deconstructs the confinement of sexuality and erotics to the human, and in the process demonstrates that all human sexual and erotic auto-affection is defined by the other, not least the *animot*.[5] And when I say 'defined' by the *animot*, I don't mean the human animal is defined specifically or necessarily by physical sexual acts with other non-human animals, despite the continuous debates about this issue made famous by Peter Singer.[6] Rather, the human is defined by the exclusion *per se* of the non-human animal from auto-affection and consequently from the notion of erotics more broadly speaking. This is because for many philosophers, following Descartes, all non-human animals are just automatons and therefore mechanistic in their actions.[7] However, I want to begin by taking a step back and reviewing, across some of Derrida's earlier works, what he means by auto-affection and autobiography so as to set the scene for examining his self-deconstructive auto-affective performance in *The Animal That Therefore I Am*.

* * *

Throughout the history of Western philosophy and metaphysics, from the Greeks to the moderns, 'time' dominates an understanding of how the self becomes self-conscious, in other words, develops its sense of self, and affects itself. In his seminar of 1964–5 entitled 'Heidegger: The Question of Being and History', Derrida shows how this philosophical understanding of time significantly marks the metaphysics of subjectivity, or the self, particularly from Kant to Heidegger. Quoting Heidegger who argues that 'time as pure self-affection forms the essential structure of subjectivity',[8] Derrida points out that this 'time as pure self-affection' (or '*affection of self by self*') is captured by Heidegger's phrase the 'temporalization of time'; a phrase or concept that seems tautological, and as Derrida also quips a concept that is somewhat 'incomprehensible'.[9] What is interesting about this phrase is the fact that most dictionaries define 'temporalisation' not as 'time' in and of itself, but as a manifestation of time in a particular physical place or situation: the abstract notion of time embodied in the *present*, so to speak.[10] This explains how auto-affection takes place in the here and now (the present of the presence); in other words, the abstract is made physically manifest. However, 'auto-affection as temporality' Derrida goes onto say, is how the self or the

> I think constitutes itself and announces itself to itself ... It is this proposition – affectivity as transcendence or transcendence as essence of manifestation – that would sum up today the history of Western philosophy, whether it be summed up in Hegel, Husserl or Heidegger.[11]

We can understand better what Derrida means here by 'affectivity as transcendence or transcendence as essence of manifestation' when turning to

THE MASTURBATING ANIMAL   219

his discussion of Husserl's notion of auto-affection a couple of years later (in 1967) in *Speech and Phenomena*.[12] There he argues that for Husserl auto-affection is characterised by the immediacy of hearing oneself speak. Hearing oneself speak creates a sense of absolute self-proximity (and transcendence) because there is no 'supposed' detour (no time delay, no spacing) between hearing and speaking. Consequently, in this metaphysical history speech is privileged over writing because it is considered to be a pure thought closely tied to interior consciousness. The self is present to itself through speech: this is 'the essence or norm of speech. It is implied in the very structure of speech that the speaker *hears himself*.'[13] That is, self-proximity is a result of a reduction of time to the present moment, the 'now', or a 'time' unrelated to spacing.[14] It is because of this perceived self-proximity, produced through speech, that the self has been considered auto-affected and autonomous: 'hearing oneself speak [*s'entendre parler*] is experienced as an absolutely pure auto-affection, occurring in a self-proximity that would in fact be the absolute reduction of space in general. In auto-affection the self is self-sufficient. It is this purity that makes it fit for universality.'[15] In summary, in Western metaphysics and philosophy auto-affection (the self, experiencing itself) is considered the 'condition for self-presence' *par excellence*.[16]

Again in 1967, Derrida extends this discussion of auto-affection in *Speech and Phenomena* to *Of Grammatology*. But it is in this latter book that Derrida makes the analogy between auto-affection and masturbation in the context of a close reading of the works of Jean-Jacques Rousseau. For instance, in the same way that writing is perceived by Rousseau, and others in the philosophical-metaphysical tradition (such as Husserl), to be 'dangerous' because it is unnatural and an extrinsic supplement to 'unmediated hearing and speaking' (auto-affective experience), Rousseau's penchant for the auto-affective act of masturbation is also perceived by himself as a dangerous supplement to the 'real' and immediate sexual act with another human, because it destroys Nature and what is, at least traditionally and normatively, sexually 'natural'.

But Rousseau is full of paradoxes! On the one hand Rousseau considers writing, like masturbation, to be a dangerous supplement, he is on the other hand mistrustful of full speech, and considers the 'immediacy' of speech to be a mirage because as Derrida points out, in 'the spoken address, presence is at once promised and refused' and so we 'are dispossessed of the longed-for presence in the gesture of language by which we attempt to seize it'.[17] Contradictions therefore abound: writing and masturbation (aligned with the dangerous supplement) are opposed to speech and sexual intercourse with another person (aligned with what is natural). What is ironic is that Rousseau privileges the auto-affection

220   NICOLE ANDERSON

that is speech (of which he is suspicious) but categorises the other auto-affectious act of masturbation as a dangerous supplement. All the while, in another irony Rousseau admits partaking of masturbation in his 'written' *Confessions*. Furthermore, and as Derrida also argues in *The Animal That Therefore I Am*, confessions are inextricably linked to the definition and art of autobiography, since the beginning of Christianity if not before.[18] The fact that Rousseau *writes* his autobiography/confessions is, according to Derrida, a paradoxical means by which he can attempt to reconstruct presence, because on the one hand 'Rousseau condemns writing as destruction of presence and as a disease of speech', yet on the other hand,

> [h]e rehabilitates it to the extent that it promises the reappropri-ation of that of which speech allowed itself to be dispossessed ... To write is indeed the only way of keeping or recapturing speech since speech denies itself as it gives itself.[19]

I'll come back to this notion of autobiographical writing, but mean-while in regards to this connection between time and auto-affection, what Derrida makes obvious across his oeuvre, and in this discussion of Rousseau's confliction about writing and speech as presence, is the domination in our history of this idea of pure presence, and thus pure auto-affection. That is, the idea of the self as self-present to itself (auto-affected), of which speech is the essence or norm. Yet as this con-flict resulting from the paradoxical and ironic twists taken by Rousseau reveal, things are not so simple. Because, as Derrida shows, what has also failed to be taken into account, this time by those influential modern philosophers Heidegger, Husserl and Hegel for instance, is the imbri-cation of time *and* space. In a deconstructive move Derrida unveils this imbrication by demonstrating that auto-affection as 'the movement of the temporalization of time' is at *the same time* spacing:

> Space is 'in' time; it is time's pure leaving-itself; it is the outside-itself as the self-relation of time. The externality of space, externality as space, does not overtake time; rather, it opens as pure 'out-side' 'within' the movement of temporalization ... we see that the theme of a pure inwardness of speech, or of the 'hearing oneself speak,' is radically contradicted by 'time' itself.[20]

A year later in 1968 this imbrication of space-time is developed through his neologism 'différance' – a neologism or 'economic concept desig-nating the production of differing/deferring'[21] so that any presence,

THE MASTURBATING ANIMAL   221

any *autos*, and auto-affection is always interrupted and haunted by self-difference: the differing from and deferring of itself, or the other within itself (and which is why literal and metaphorical masturbation can never be pure auto-affection). Derrida puts it another way: 'Speech and the consciousness of speech – that is to say consciousness simply as self-presence – are the phenomenon of an auto-affection lived as suppression of difference.'[22]

The upshot of this is *not* that there is no auto-affection (or indeed self-presence), after all Derrida argues that 'auto-affection is no doubt the possibility for what is called *subjectivity* or the *for-itself*, but, without it, no world as such would appear'.[23] Rather auto-affection is produced precisely by this movement of différance (which means that auto-affection is always already a result of the other), even despite the attempt at the suppression of difference (a suppression that is arguably an (auto)immunising reaction, and that is why Derrida suggests in the second epigraph that autobiography is poisonous for the self):

> This movement of différance is not something that happens to a transcendental subject; it produces a subject. Auto-affection is not a modality of experience that characterizes a being that would already be itself (*autos*). It produces sameness as self-relation within self-difference; it produces sameness as the nonidentical.[24]

The self is self-conscious, it is aware of its auto-affection, precisely because it is self-othering: there is something other to presence (an absent presence, or another presence), a space-time between itself and itself, and another. Consequently, there is no pure unadulterated unmediated auto-affection because all auto-affection is always already deferred and differed (différance), and therefore divided by the other within and outside itself: '[a]uto-affection constitutes the same (*auto*) as it divides the same'.[25] That is, to be able to feel the pleasure one gives oneself requires literally feeling and making oneself as other: it requires feeling the difference (différance) between receiving and the giving of pleasure to oneself. Masturbation, and thus auto-affectivity, is, as a result, constituted by the other. And therefore, returning to Rousseau, even his sexually auto-affective act (masturbation) is relational, even if that relation is the imaginary other (an image or feeling of an absent other) as well as the other in himself:

> Rousseau will never stop having recourse to, and accusing himself of, this onanism that permits one to be himself affected by providing himself with presences, by summoning absent beauties ...

Affecting oneself by another presence, one corrupts oneself [makes oneself other] by oneself [*on s'altère soi-même*]. Rousseau neither wishes to think nor can think that this alteration does not simply happen to the self, that it is the self's very origin ... If the presence that it then gives itself is the substitutive symbol of another presence, it has never been possible to desire that presence 'in person' before this play of substitution and this symbolic experience of auto-affection. The thing itself does not appear outside of the symbolic system that does not exist without the possibility of auto-affection.[26]

Now this attempted suppression of difference – which is the philosophical and political attempt to exclude everything from auto-affection, such as space, the world, the body, life and, as we will see shortly, animals, in order to secure some pure transcendental reduction or transcendental signified – is for Derrida a 'chimera'. It is also 'a pure speculation' he writes, not least because auto-affection is already constituted by différance, but because all auto-affection (evidenced by the way in which Rousseau conjures the other as an image when masturbating) has its '*passage through the world*'.[27] That is, and to repeat, to masturbate is to touch oneself as other:

> to auto-affect is to not only touch oneself but to be touched: 'the experience of touching-touched admits the world as third-party ... Within the general structure of auto-affection, within the giving-oneself-a-presence or a pleasure, the operation of touching-touched receives the other within the narrow gulf that separates doing from suffering'.[28]

This is also why Derrida argues, in the first epigraph, that if auto-affection (e.g., masturbation) cannot be simply circumscribed as a sexual act with oneself it is because it is constitutive of the living in general: it is a universal experience. And this being the case, all life or living is sexual in the broadest possible understanding: it is, in other words, *erotic*. What Derrida reveals in *Of Grammatology* and *Speech and Phenomena* then, is that all auto-affection is divided by différance: there is no auto-affection without going through the other. This otherness (différance) within, and constitutive of, auto-affection is what Derrida calls hetero-affection,[29] which is the basis of any and all auto-affection in 'the first place', because without hetero-affection there would be no self. That is, if there is no time delay, no spacing, there can be no difference/s, and if there are no differences that differentiate then there

THE MASTURBATING ANIMAL   223

is an absolute reduction. Or as Derrida puts it in *On Touching*, 'there would be some auto-affection "effects," but their analysis cannot escape from the hetero-affection that makes them possible and keeps haunting them',[30] and which is also why he makes obvious the imbrication through the word: 'auto-hetero-affection'.[31] Furthermore, in regards to the sexual and erotic, Derrida argues that 'between auto-eroticism and hetero-eroticism, there is not a frontier but an economic distribution' of multiple erotic differences.[32] This 'economic distribution' is also evident in autobiography: as we will see later in *The Animal That Therefore I Am* whatever story we tell about or to ourselves (as individuals and as a species) will always be 'economical' with the 'truth'; with 'fabulation', for political ends. And in that book this autobiographical distribution of the truth between human and other animals is eroticised in and through an animal bestiary that deconstructs the dualism between the human sexes.[33]

* * *

In the meantime, Derrida shows us in *Of Grammatology* that the desire for full presence, enabled through auto-affective speech, is like the desire to reveal, relieve, expose and present the truth of oneself: a presentation to an other, but also to oneself in an auto-affective gesture where to touch is to be touched and vice versa. This characteristic of autobiography, is in turn characteristic of metaphysics:

> *the history of* (the only) *metaphysics*, which has, in spite of all differences, not only from Plato to Hegel (even including Leibniz) but also, beyond these apparent limits, from the pre-Socratics to Heidegger, always assigned the origin of truth in general to the logos: the history of truth, of the truth of truth, has always been – except for a metaphysical diversion that we shall have to explain – the debasement of writing, and its repression outside 'full' speech.[34]

This history of the *logos* as truth can take the form of testimony or confession, such as through personal accounts of one's experiences or life (or more broadly through the testimony of the human species as a whole: through history, biology, religion, philosophy, and so on). Regardless of whether this testimony takes place through writing or speech, the outcome is the same: autobiography and auto-affection perpetuate the metaphysical belief in the autonomy of the self or the 'I think' and therefore 'I Am'. Confirming this in *The Animal That Therefore I Am* Derrida argues that in this metaphysical history of truth,

[a]ll autobiography, presents itself as a testimony: I say or write what I am, saw, see, feel, hear, touch, think, and vice versa, every testimony presents itself as autobiographical truth: I promise the truth concerning what I, myself, have perceived, seen, heard, felt, lived, thought, etc.[35]

As Derrida points out here, testimony is not only associated with auto-biography, but with an auto-affective ('seen, heard, felt') revealing of oneself that is presented as truth. And this confession/testimony, and hence apparent 'truth', is in turn associated with a metaphysical concept of nudity: here I am, this is me, and '"I am telling you the truth" without shame, bareback, naked and raw'.[36] In this sense, for Derrida, 'the autobiographical animal would be the sort of man or woman who, as a matter of character, chooses to indulge in or can't resist indulging in autobiographical confidences'.[37] Like the irresistible desire to release or relieve one's desire in masturbation, autobiography is an 'irresistible desire' to reveal, unveil, exhibit, *expose* oneself in full nudity:

'I': by saying 'I' the signatory of an autobiography would claim to point himself in the present [*se présenter au présent*] (*sui-referential deixis*) and in his totally naked truth ... By naming himself and answering for his name, he would be saying 'I stake and engage my nudity without shame.' One can well doubt whether this pledge, this wager, this desire or promise of nudity is possible. Nudity perhaps remains untenable.[38]

Why would nudity be untenable? First, as Derrida argues there is no nudity without shame and modesty (which he also associates with erection and phallogocentrism). And with shame and modesty comes a form of hiding (clothing), or to keep with the theme of masturbation, a detumescence. As Derrida argues, erection (metaphorically speaking) is the condition par excellence in the phallic history of the 'I Am':

There is a rhythmic difference between erection and detumescence. It is no doubt at the heart of what concerns us here, namely, a sentiment of shame related to standing upright — here with respect to erection in general and not only phallic surrection.[39]

Second, nudity is untenable because representing oneself will inevitably involve selection or curation (intentional or otherwise). Derrida also makes this point in *Archive Fever*, where he argues that an archive (or autobiography, the archive of the self) is structured by the choices around what we save and keep and what we don't (and what we don't keep, which like 'repression', would be no simple form of forgetting or destroying – if that were indeed possible – but an archiving form or process of ourselves). For Derrida, then, 'the technical structure of the archiving archive also determines the structure of the archivable content even in its very coming into existence and in its relationship to the future. The archivization produces as much as it records the event.'[40] It is therefore a dream to think that the archive or autobiography can accurately represent reality or truth, as if they are not always already constructed and thus mediated. While Michael Naas eloquently describes Derrida on the archive, his point is applicable to autobiography given that it is living archive: 'there is no individual without this archival selection, without an "economy of memory" that keeps some things and not others, represses some things and not others'.[41] To put it another way, to hide in full view is to archive oneself in a particular way: to hide parts of oneself by narrating what you want others to see (a form of shame and movement of erection–detumescence perhaps?).

In the metaphysical tradition there is then a contradiction: on the one hand, Derrida shows that autobiography is perceived to be associated with being nude (confession; testimony; truth, the 'here I am' figuratively associated with erection), while on the other, to be nude is associated with modesty and shame, precisely because 'man' is aware and knows itself to be ashamed of its nudity, and ashamed of shame: 'Man could never be naked any more because he has the sense of nakedness, that is to say, of modesty or shame.'[42] But in sharp opposition to this the metaphysical tradition places 'the animal' in a position of 'non-nudity because it is nude, and man in nudity to the extent that he is no longer nude'.[43] There is then, perhaps, an immodesty about autobiography. After all, if in *Of Grammatology* Derrida shows that masturbation is a particular example of an auto-affective act, and if as he shows through Rousseau's *Confessions* that autobiography is also an auto-affection, then autobiography is analogous to masturbation: a touching of oneself, or the touching-touched of oneself. As we will see now in the scene with his cat, the masturbatory performance that Derrida autobiographically undertakes in *The Animal That Therefore I Am* is like the 'rhythmic' form of an erection (visible narration or confession) and detumescence (a hiding or 'disappearance'): an archiving of the self that is like a game of peek-a-boo or 'fort/da'.[44] And it is for this reason why I have described Derrida's book as a masturbatory performance, albeit one that ironically and comically deconstructs itself.

* * *

226   NICOLE ANDERSON

The collection of essays that comprise the book *The Animal That Therefore I Am* were given as a ten-hour seminar in 1997 at the Cérisy conference on his work. Derrida chose the conference title: 'The Autobiographical Animal'.[45] As he puts it in the first essay, the title of the conference 'obliges us to cross the animal with autobiography'.[46] This begs the question: What is the result of this 'crossing' if autobiography is akin to masturbation? And what happens when you cross the non-human animal with masturbation (aka autobiography, and auto-affection), which in this history of metaphysics is attributed to the human only? The answer I would argue is in the story Derrida tells of himself ('autobiographical animal') that involves his female cat.

There is a simultaneous immodesty (sexual exhibition) and modesty (shame) about this now famous story.[47] It initially goes like this: one day Derrida's female cat follows him into the bathroom and he tells us this 'pussycat' really exists and that it is female (although that does not necessarily mean the story about this real cat is true! And he taunts us with this possibility in his discussion of the cat in Lewis Carroll's works.).[48] While he is facing his cat naked, he sees the cat staring at him, and what's more Derrida sees that the cat sees him seeing her looking at him:

> Against the impropriety [*malséance*] that can come of finding oneself naked, one's sex exposed, stark naked before a cat that looks at you without moving, just to see ... Especially, I should make clear, if the cat observes me frontally naked, face to face, and if I am naked faced with the cat's eyes looking at me from head to toe, as it were just to see, with a view to seeing – in the direction of my sex.[49]

Referring to my discussion earlier about nudity and shame, it becomes clear why Derrida says he is 'embarrassed' and 'ashamed'[50] and '[r]ather than ... chasing the cat away' attempts to dress himself quickly or 'even a little' 'to cover the obscenity of the event',[51] and in another rendition he turns his back on the cat.[52] Further on, after some theoretical discussion, he comes back to the story, and this time there is humour in this recounting, and a kind of modesty about his 'sex': 'she first follows me into the bathroom then immediately regrets her decision ... she demands to leave that said bathroom as soon as it (or she) sees me naked'.[53] The mind boggles. Is Derrida's nakedness; the look of his 'sex', really that bad that even the cat wants to leave! At least one reader of this story is now wondering what Derrida looks like naked. But isn't that the point of this exhibition? And isn't this humorous recounting in fact a false modesty? Because in recounting this story Derrida shamelessly exposes his sex to the imagination of his readers. Admitting as much he

THE MASTURBATING ANIMAL   227

later on claims that he is 'frankly and shamelessly' 'indulging in' an 'auto-biographical exercise'[54] and that 'this difficulty [*mal*]' of Derrida accepting the cat looking at him, 'does not exclude the announcement of a certain enjoyment [*jouissance*] ... but one will understand that it is also the same thing, that thing that combines within itself desire, *jouissance*, and anguish'.[55] Whose enjoyment? The reader's, the cat's, his own? In stark contrast to Descartes's view of an animal as an automaton, a sensitivity to nakedness and thus modesty and shame is not necessarily foreign to the *animot*, says Derrida.[56] Confirming this in *On Touching* Derrida argues that auto–hetero-affection doesn't have an 'anthropological limit':

> only the 'self-touching-you' (and not 'oneself') can interrupt the reappropriation or the absolute reflection of self-presence (pure life or pure death: it is always, infinitely the same thing) ... And this should be valid, *on the one hand*, for all 'animal' or 'divine' *life*; and *consequently*, *on the other hand*, make the life of the living in general a derivative concept with regard to this possibility of self-touching-you.[57]

Now to continue with Derrida's story, it turns out to have a few more twists and turns: like exposing oneself suddenly, unexpectedly, more of the same (or another similar) story of Derrida and his cat is revealed and made visible. In any case this time there is a woman in the room (a bedroom or bathroom, it's not clear). Like some kind of generally erotic *ménage à trois* that involves an animal, jealousy fills the room, and it is worth noting that the sentence preceding that which I quote below begins with Derrida saying 'that an autobiography of any consequence cannot not touch on this assurance of saying "I am a man," "I am a woman," I am a man who is also a woman'. He then goes on:

> Now this self, this male me, believes he has noted that the presence of a woman in the room warms things up in the relation to the cat, vis-à-vis the gaze of the naked cat that sees me naked, and sees me see it seeing me naked, like a shining fire with a cloud of jealousy that begins to float like the smoke of incense in the room ... besides the presence of a woman, there is a mirror [*psyché*] in the room. We no longer know how many we are then, all males and females of us. And I maintain that autobiography has begun there'.[58]

This series of stories of himself naked with his female cat, and then also with a woman, in different rooms, and therefore obviously at different times/days; this series of stories which are interspersed between theoretical discussions works to complicate and deconstruct a range of issues simultaneously: auto-affection, autobiography, autonomy, anthropocentrism, anthropomorphism, sexuality and erotics. Difficult to disentangle, let me attempt to begin with Derrida's deconstruction of sexuality and erotics.

In the description of himself naked with the cat and a woman, it doesn't matter who is jealous of who, what is revealing is that the cat/animal is involved in the jealousy and constitutes the erotised scene. There is not just jealousy between humans, but between humans and an animal. Through the mirror in this scene (a nod to the discussion of Jacques Lacan in the third essay of the book), Derrida plays with an erotic and sexual fluidity that undermines the fixed boundaries of not only human but animal sexual identities: 'I am a man who is also a woman.'[59] While there may be fluidity, Derrida is very emphatic that this fluidity does not preclude difference. I would argue that in *The Animal That Therefore I Am* there is a subtle difference between undermining the anthropocentrism of the 'I Am' by questioning the politics and ideologies that form the constructed boundaries between human and non-human, on the one hand, and attempting or arguing for the dissolution of boundaries without care for the complexity of difference in order to pursue a political cause, on the other hand. And Derrida is very careful here. He may contest the political boundaries, but he by no means abandons difference:

> I shan't for a single moment venture to contest [...] the rupture or abyss between this 'I-we' and what we call animals [...] [Because] it would mean forgetting all the signs that I have managed to give, tirelessly, of my attention to difference, to differences, to heterogeneities and abyssal ruptures as against the homogenous and continuous. I have thus never believed in some homogenous continuity between what calls itself man and what he calls the animal. I am not about to begin to do so now.[60]

This perhaps sheds light on Derrida's 'bone of contention' with the way in which all this multiplicity of differences between animals, between sexualities, between humans is grouped under two words – the 'Animal' and the 'Human' – thereby creating a political boundary between human and animal that supports a metaphysical, philosophical and everyday practiced anthropocentrism. This is why Derrida argues there is no philosopher ('from Plato to Heidegger') who even differentiates the sexualities of animals.[61] Rather *l'animot*, all of them, are 'neutralized, not to say

THE MASTURBATING ANIMAL 229

castrated' (and therefore certainly don't masturbate) by being subsumed under the homogenous category 'The Animal'.[62] And this is perhaps why animal masturbations and sexualities are not discussed along with the fact that if animals are automatons (according to Descartes) then so too must animal sex be a purely procreative automatic act. The human of course is provided with a story about the characteristics that make it human; characteristics that animals are denied, such as

> speech, reason, experience of death, mourning, culture, insti-tutions, technics, clothing, lying, pretense of pretense [*feinte de feinte*], covering of tracks, gift, laughing, tears, response, etc. – the list is necessarily without limit, and the most powerful philosoph-ical tradition in which we live has refused the 'animal' *all of that*.[63]

And yet, as Derrida argues when critiquing Immanuel Kant's notion of the autonomous self:

> If autoposition, the *automonstrative autotely* of the 'I,' even in the human, implies the 'I' to be an other that must welcome within itself some irreducible heteroaffection ... then this autonomy of the 'I' can be neither pure nor rigorous; it would not be able to form the basis for a simple and linear differentiation of the human from the animal.[64]

If there is no linear and simple differentiation between animal and human, it is not because there are no differences. There is instead a 'het-erogeneous multiplicity of the living' that undercuts and complicates 'a single opposing side' between animal and human.[65]

If there is no simple differentiation it does beg the question what degree and *kind* of interest in Derrida's nakedness is the cat taking? Of course, Derrida deliberately doesn't anthropomorphise this stare of the cat but what he does do is to question his response to the stare as a way of undermining and deconstructing his humanness and to ask himself what kind of animal he is (apart from autobiographical). The imme-diate sentences following the block quote above theoretically question the human construction of the self in the history of philosophy and metaphysics:

> the question of the 'I,' of 'I am' or 'I think,' would have to be dis-placed toward the prerequisite question of the other: the other, the other me that I am (following) or that is following me. Which other? And how will the determination of the law of the other,

of heteronomy, permit the anthropocentrism whose logic we are following to be either displaced or confirmed ...?[66]

The deconstruction of Derrida's autobiographical tale of him naked with his cat goes a long way to making this displacement, while also demonstrating that the other (différance) is what enables self-presence, autonomy, autobiography as auto-affection. In other words, the scenes he paints of himself with his cat suggests that rather than autonomy, which perpetuates anthropocentrism, there is in fact, as just mentioned, 'an irreducible living multiplicity of mortals', what he calls *Ecce animot.*[67] If the mirror traditionally is perceived to accurately represent 'an absolute specularity at the heart of the "self-touching"',[68] that is, reflects ourselves back to ourselves as pure auto-affection, then I would argue that this reflection is interrupted by the seeing eyes of his cat, who is also reflected in the mirror. In this story the mirror reflects instead the multiplicity of selves (animals and humans) so that '[w]e no longer know how many we are', or what we are (is the cat a reflection of Derrida?), or who is following or being followed.[69] A multiplicity of selves; of self-touching-selves, that operate to deconstruct this nude exhibition, this erection, and sexual auto-affection of the 'I Am', and which is encapsulated by this autobiographical scene. If there is, then, an *autos* to this biography, it is a result of a multiplicity of others. As we saw in *Of Grammatology*, like masturbation, autobiography as a form of auto-affection has a '*passage through the world*'[70] in that it involves the other (characters, situations, events), and like différance the unfolding of any story is haunted by the other.

The multiplicity of the living that haunts this autobiographical scene, then, reveals the instability of the assumed rigour of the self's autonomy and auto-affection. The hybrid erotics (cat, man, woman) shows the self as heteronomous and hetero-affective. The absolute other, that in this particular instance is the cat, is that which also enables one's auto-affection, because by being part of the eroticised scene animals (the cat) contribute to shaping the sexuality and the erotics of the human.[71] And so, just as presence is made possible by différance, so too autobiography is made possible because of the difference of the other. That is, this masturbatory (aka autobiographical) performance always already involves the other, and which is why the idea that autobiography is a true projection of the autonomous self is for Derrida a fabulation. Rather this fabulation operates as 'an anthropomorphic taming, a moralizing subjection, a domestication. Always a discourse of man, on man, and indeed on animality of man, but for and in man.'[72] What is anthropomorphically tamed, then, is not just 'the animal' but 'the human', that is, we construct a categorically confined species autobiography that does a disservice not

THE MASTURBATING ANIMAL 231

just to human and non-human animals, but to the differences internal and external to this historically constructed binary.

Alongside Derrida's autobiographical response to and exchange with his female cat, one that involves a mirror that reflects multiple selves that works to deconstruct the metaphysical *autos*, is his 'confession' that he is more than one animal, and that he has developed a bestiary across his texts to counter-act or deconstruct the fabulation of a species anthropomorphic autobiography. Derrida admits this when he says he has an 'old obsession with a personal and somewhat paradisaical bestiary', in order to avoid those metaphysical fables.[73]

But it's not obvious what animal he is following, or what animal is following him, because '[r]ather than developing that fabulous bestiary, I gave myself a horde of animals, within the forest of my own signs and the memoirs of my memory'.[74] How many animals is he? And how many is he following tracing tracking in the *Animal*? One of them is a cat: 'That is the track I am following, the track I am ferreting out [*la piste que je déspiste*], following the traces of this "wholly other they call 'animal,' for example, 'cat.'"'[75] Or is he a ferret in this instance? In being more than one animal, he is not only proliferating the differences (among animals and the animals within himself) but revealing at the same time that there can never be one autobiography of the self, never one autobiography of the human species. And in making this clear, Derrida deflates our self-congratulatory superiority over the animal and the exceptionalism we inhabit: our erection quickly moves into detumescence.[76]

If, metaphorically, the mirror is the eye of the female cat reflecting back to Derrida himself as other, and if as a result of the reflection of the mirror '[w]e no longer know how many we are then, all males and females of us', and who is male or female, animal and human, then for Derrida this is where autobiography begins (in the eyes of the other).[77] As he puts it in *Of Grammatology* when talking about the play of the mirror image to which Rousseau is subjected as it '"captures his reflection and exposes his presence"', the play of the mirror image works as a 'speculary dispossession which at the same time institutes and deconstitutes me'.[70] And so too are we, as readers, reflected in that mirror (which also happens to be Derrida). That is, we too are cats looking at Derrida naked in our imaginations. We too are partaking of that voyeuristic masturbation. We too are being sexualised as animals by Derrida's deconstructive autobiography, the autobiography of himself as one of many animals (so much for Descartes saying animals don't have the capacity for awareness or self-reflection!).[79] And so, if hetero-affection is the basis of any and all auto-affection (auto-hetero-affection), then so too is autobiography constituted by what Derrida calls 'hetero-graphy' (or an 'auto-hetero-graphy'): by the others reflected in and by the stories we tell ourselves, but also by the stories shaped by what we leave out, such as the *animot*. What indeed would happen if the *animot* was included in our species philosophical autobiography?

Notes

1. Jacques Derrida, *Of Grammatology*, trans. Gayatri Chakravorty Spivak (Baltimore, MD: Johns Hopkins University Press, 1976), 167.
2. Jacques Derrida, *The Animal That Therefore I Am*, trans. David Wills, ed. Marie-Louise Mallet (New York: Fordham University Press, 2008), 47.
3. In *Grammatology* Derrida discusses the implications of Rousseau's physical act of masturbation, likening it to the notions of auto-affection and autobiography. I extend this analogy to the *Animal* attempting to demonstrate and argue that Derrida performs a comic deconstructive figurative masturbation and exhibition (or auto-affection and autobiography). While I don't go into the cultural-sexual histories of the uses (pejorative and otherwise) of the word 'masturbation', I use the word figuratively in an attempt to show that masturbation, being a focus on oneself (auto-affection), is characteristic of the human species *per se*, hence the title 'The Masturbating Animal'. Focusing on oneself is a form of species dominance and an anthropocentrism: the 'I Am' is another term for autobiography (see Derrida, *Animal*, 88).
4. Arguments about the differing meanings of 'erotic' and 'sexual' are complicated and prolific, and by no means consistent. Because of the similarities in meaning, they are often conflated. The *OED* describes sexuality as the 'physical activity of sex', while erotics is defined as 'showing or involving sexual desire and pleasure'. George Bataille makes this distinction arguing: "Eroticism, unlike simple sexual activity, is a psychological quest independent of the natural goal: reproduction and the desire for children ... eroticism is assenting to life even in death." George Bataille, *Eroticism: Death & Sensuality*, trans. Mary Dalwood (San Francisco, CA: First City Lights Books, 1986), 11. Derrida doesn't make this distinction as he sometimes uses 'sexual-auto-affection' and sometimes 'auto-eroticism'. It seems, then, that Derrida uses the word 'sexuality' similarly to 'erotics' as defined by Bataille. Bataille's definition also seems to be consistent with Derrida's terms: hetero-affection or hetero-erotic. The distinction I make here between sexual and erotic follows Bataille.
5. Derrida coins the word: '*animot*, which, when spoken, has the plural *animaux*, heard within the singular, recalling the extreme diversity of animals that "the animal" erases' (see Derrida, *Animal*, x).
6. Peter Singer, 'Heavy Petting' (2001) at: www.nerve.com; and at: https://www.prospectmagazine.co.uk/opinions/56258/heavy-petting. Singer and others, such as Joanna Bourke, argue that actual sexual relations with animals under certain circumstances (such as the animal welcoming or initiating

THE MASTURBATING ANIMAL   233

some form of sex) is morally permissible. See Bourke, *Loving Animals: On Bestiality, Zoophilia and Post-human Love* (London: Reaktion Books, 2020).

7. Derrida, *Animal*, 76; René Descartes, *Discourse on the Method*, in *Philosophical Writings of Descartes, vol. 1*, trans. John Cottingham, Robert Stoothoff and Dugald Murdoch (Cambridge: Cambridge University Press, 1985), 140–1.

8. Martin Heidegger, *Kant and the Problem of Metaphysics*, trans. Richard Taft (Bloomington and Indianapolis: Indiana University Press, 1992), 132. Also quoted in Jacques Derrida, *Heidegger: The Question of Being & History*, trans. Geoffrey Bennington (Chicago: Chicago University Press, 2016), 181.

9. Derrida, *Heidegger*, 181.

10. For example, *The Collins Dictionary*: '1. to make temporal in time; place in time 2. to make concerned with the present life; secularize.' The *OED* definition: '1. Relating to time. 2. Relating to worldly affairs, secular.'

11. Derrida, *Heidegger*, 180–1.

12. Jacques Derrida, *Speech and Phenomena, and Other Essays on Husserl's Theory of Signs*, trans. David B. Allison (Evanston, IL: Northwestern University Press, 1973). Re-translated by Leonard Lawlor as *Voice and Phenomena* (2011). I use Allison's translation as it contains the essay 'Differance' from which I quote, and the phrasing of the translation underscores my arguments.

13. Ibid., 78.

14. Ibid., 79.

15. Ibid.

16. Ibid.

17. Derrida, *Grammatology*, 141.

18. Derrida, *Animal*, 21.

19. Derrida, *Grammatology*, 141–2.

20. Derrida, *Speech and Phenomena*, 78.

21. Derrida, *Grammatology*, 23.

22. Ibid., 166.

23. Derrida, *Speech and Phenomena*, 79.

24. Ibid., 82.

25. Derrida, *Grammatology*, 166.

26. Ibid., 153–4.

27. Ibid., 154.

28. Ibid., 165.

29. See *Animal*, 95, *Of Grammatology*, p. L, and throughout Jacques Derrida, *On Touching – Jean-Luc Nancy*, trans. Christine Irizarry (Stanford, CA: Stanford University Press, 2005).

30. Derrida, *On Touching*, 180.

31. Ibid., 292. While *On Touching* is an important book for understanding the philosophy of touch and the body in Western philosophy, the scope of *On Touching* would have made it impractical to discuss here. Bringing the three works together ('Differance', *Animal*, *On Touching*) is the task for my current monograph.

32. Derrida, *Grammatology*, 155.

33. Derrida, *Animal*, 36.
34. Derrida, *Grammatology*, 3.
35. Derrida, *Animal*, 77.
36. Ibid., 57.
37. Ibid., 49.
38. Ibid., 50.
39. Ibid., 36, see also 55, 61. In making the distinction between phallic surrection and erection in general, Derrida is suggesting that erection is a metaphor for 'standing upright' and thus for the phallogocentric dominance of the 'I Am' over animals (a dominance that goes beyond sexual difference/dualism).
40. Jacques Derrida, *Archive Fever: A Freudian Impression*, trans. Eric Prenowitz (Chicago & London: The University of Chicago Press, 1996), 17.
41. Michael Naas, *The End of the World and Other Teachable Moments: Jacques Derrida's Final Seminar* (New York: Fordham University Press, 2015), 136.
42. Derrida, *Animal*, 5. Derrida uses the word 'man' as a means of highlighting the phallogocentrism of the 'I Am' in Western philosophy.
43. Ibid.
44. Ibid., 9.
45. Ibid., ix.
46. Ibid., 37.
47. The story of Derrida's cat was in part made infamous by Donna Haraway's critique of him and the *Animal* in her book *When Species Meet* (Minneapolis and London: University of Minnesota Press, 2008), 20. For one among many responses to Haraway's critique of Derrida see Lynn Turner, *Poetics of Deconstruction: On the Threshold of Differences* (London: Bloomsbury, 2020), 106–9.
48. Derrida's questioning of the role of cats ('little black pussycat' and the Cheshire cat) in Lewis Carroll's *Alice in Wonderland*, plays with the dissimulation of the truth and lie of the story of his cat: 'Although I don't have time to do so, I would of course have liked to inscribe my whole talk within a reading of Lewis Carroll. In fact you can't be certain that I am not doing that, for better or worse, silently, unconsciously, or without your knowing' (*Animal*, 7).
49. Derrida, *Animal*, 3.
50. Ibid.
51. Ibid., 9.
52. Ibid., 11.
53. Ibid., 13.
54. Ibid., 57.
55. Ibid., 61.
56. Ibid., 60.
57. Derrida, *On Touching*, 290–1.
58. Derrida, *Animal*, 58.
59. Ibid.

THE MASTURBATING ANIMAL 235

60. Ibid., 30.
61. For more on the multitude of animal sexualities, see Kelly Oliver, *Animal Lessons: How They Teach Us to Be Human* (New York: Columbia University Press, 2009). Oliver argues how thinking the multitude can 'take us beyond the male/female sexual binary itself' (147).
62. Derrida, *Animal*, 30.
63. Ibid., 135.
64. Ibid., 95.
65. Ibid., 31.
66. Ibid.
67. Ibid., 41.
68. Derrida, *On Touching*, 290.
69. Derrida, *Animal*, 58.
70. Derrida, *Grammatology*, 159, emphasis original.
71. It would be too easy, but I think misguided, to use the story of his cat as a means of undertaking some kind of psychobiography of Derrida and his relations to animals or his cat. Rather, the auto-affective (i.e., masturbatory) performance of the *Animal* is *not* a pseudo-psychoanalysis of Derrida himself, which would take us 'toward some psychobiographical signified' (*Grammatology*, 159), as if Derrida was a single unified autonomous self (like the 'Animal' as a category), and as if Derrida wasn't deconstructing this notion of ipseity, and thus its dominant feature, auto-affection and autobiography. To undertake a psychoanalysis here would be, to use Derrida's word, an *asinanity*, because in this instance it would replicate a transcendental signified associated with traditional autobiography that Derrida deconstructs by performing an atypical or radical auto/biography.
72. Derrida, *Animal*, 37.
73. Ibid.
74. Ibid.
75. Ibid., 14.
76. I use the word erection figuratively here to represent the domination of the human species over other non-human animals and its anthropocentric exceptionalism.
77. Ibid., 58.
78. Derrida, *Grammatology*, 141.
79. Descartes, *Discourse*, 42.

12

PLAYING THE FIELD:
NON-NONBINARY PROMISCUITY

Vicki Kirby

I have a seemingly simple question, one that feels frustratingly caught up in generational differences that are difficult to translate. In brief, can I reconcile why the political assault and transformative power of what was then called 'Theory', a force that changed my life so profoundly in the 1980s and 1990s, now appears overly abstract and opaque, attracting little interest? What happened to the ideas and insights that fuelled it? Were they misguided, found to be wanting, or has the detail of that history and the literatures it inspired faded from memory, not so much rejected as overlooked or even forgotten? In short, are those ways of thinking still relevant?[1]

It seems fair to say that history is an unreliable reference point if we are hoping to plot a progress narrative of accumulated experience and wisdom, or its opposite, the failure to remember and maintain what retrospectively may have felt especially important. In view of my opening question, I am forced to begin tentatively, already a little defeated but not entirely. Because if the constant of the past is its radical *instability* – because always in translation, always reinterpretable and shifting – then perhaps there is some comfort to be had from this ongoing movement regardless of what we find. If our attempts to understand the present inevitably revivify the past in hailing the future, and this implies that political and ethical concerns are still open and under review, then it seems right to say that to some degree we remain agents of history rather than passive witnesses. Similarly, if we can't assume that a moment in time, even the one we currently inhabit, is coherent, indeed, 'one' – because the past has yet to make its presence felt in any final way – then can we take advantage of this lack of closure to open questions that might now appear answered, or even censored?[2]

It is significant that my political coming of age was in the heady days of the 1980s and 1990s. Although power and its subtleties had always intrigued me, especially the elusive nature of equity and how it might be measured, my return to university in this respect was life-changing. In the last decades of the twentieth century we became entranced by the intrigues of psychoanalysis, the relationship between language and political life, the vagaries of subjectivity, and the wild, perverse and convoluted aspects of desire. There was a growing appreciation that power is a force that does more than say 'no'; a counter-intuitive realisation that words such as 'production' and 'generativity' that seem to affirm a one-directional positive outcome can, from a different perspective, mark changes that are much more ambiguous, even destructive. Freud and Michel Foucault were just two names among myriad provocative writers that heralded a significant shift in our collective awareness.[3] What was it that made such a difference throughout those earlier years? And is a commitment to robust debate, curiosity and the airing of uncertainties, still valued?

During the 1980s and 1990s what was variously described as 'critical theory', 'French theory', 'continental philosophy', 'poststructuralism' or just 'theory'[4] changed our vocabularies, methodologies and political focus in such remarkable ways that the left, from where most of us had come, was in serious disarray. It was increasingly felt that Marxism was unable to provide a compelling account of corporeality, gender and sexuality, race, subjective 'interiority', the insidious and largely invisible politics of representation that exceeded an analysis of content, or emerging questions about the intricate and surprising manifestations of matter. In short, models that rested on a base/superstructure division, or that returned power to the either/or of domination and exploitation, felt inadequate. Importantly however, 'poststructuralism', as it was engaged in many countries, remained in active debate with Marxism. After all, what most of us wanted to better understand was power – what it is and how it works in all its materialisations. To this extent, and despite claims that poststructuralism forfeited notions of truth, rationality and a sense of shared communication, as Jurgen Habermas asserted,[5] by its very nature it could never enjoy clear air. It was constantly made to explain why its modes of argumentation were difficult to comprehend, even inaccessible, and why its vocabularies appeared obscure unless one had done their homework. Understandably, many resented the difficulty and judged it an elitist affectation that ignored the pressing realities of injustice. And to be fair – because I'm trying to better appreciate the rage that sometimes accompanied that incomprehension – from the perspective of those who saw themselves as outsiders, lacking a way in, there was a frustrated sense that you had to believe in the analytical leverage and superiority of certain critical theories before you could understand why. Clearly there were problems.

What I'll continue to call poststructuralism for want of a better word had an argumentative profile because it tarried quite deliberately with common sense and ordinary language in strikingly unfamiliar ways. Indeed, it was the political agenda in the commonplace, or 'what goes without saying', that provoked our attentions.

One influence on the changing shape of intellectual life that found value in the hidden and counter-intuitive, with its admitted difficulty, and contemporary interest in an identity politics that tends towards the obvious, is the significant restructuring of the tertiary sector. Global competition among universities now ranks institutions, faculties and courses by translating goals and outcomes into standardised metric data, rejecting 'abstract' aims in favour of vocational or market-driven ambitions that are thought to be measurable. Retirements and transfers by those whose futures under the current regime looked increasingly terminal have consolidated this direction, as business models and the need to secure employment have made resistance risky. Given the traction of neoliberal rationalisation at the administrative level, the massive casualisation of the workforce, the enormous amounts gouged in systematic wage theft that, at least in Australia, have become routine,[6] it seems inevitable that 'critical thinking' in its various guises has come off poorly. To argue that critical theory has explanatory insight, that it can acknowledge the complexity, value and even the necessity of uncertainty, that it is an asset for an informed citizenry to appreciate the subtleties of political life, will seem misguided when what counts as practical solutions and ready answers tends to eschew such considerations.

In the social sciences, my own research area, myriad examples illustrate the devaluation of difficulty and ambiguity. How often do we hear the phrase, 'evidence-based research', as if this constative utterance guarantees the superiority of its results? Relying in the main on positivist and empirical approaches, with little appreciation of the knotty theoretical and scientific questions that attend both methodologies, imbues 'evidence' with the magical power of a conjurer's invocation. What appears 'right before our eyes', captured by our senses as transparently and immediately present to us, is thoroughly mediated by the reinventions of memory.[7] I assume that I perceive what is present to my senses, and to an extent I do. However, I also sense by way of previous experiences, many unacknowledged, even misremembered, that re-present a tangle of synaesthetic impressions, psychological investments and even other people's heartfelt understandings as my own. Given the dynamic involvements of what count as experience and confound common sense, we can understand why Jacques Derrida provocatively declared, 'There never was any "perception."'[8] Further to this, students are more time-poor than in previous

PLAYING THE FIELD

decades, working long hours in employment to manage financial debts, suffering unanticipated consequences from COVID-19 shutdowns, and just trying to stay buoyant. The attraction of interpretive riddles that are never fully resolved, coupled with an appreciation that the determination of 'evidence' will always be provisional and in play, may appear as frustrating obstacles to the overworked and uninitiated, to be avoided at all costs.

Another consideration in the current environment is that students are less likely to have access to certain resources that were considered important to previous generations and to the question I want to pose here. My own history at The University of Sydney saw the establishment of Women's Studies and a significant shift in student activism around pedagogical content and delivery across the humanities and social sciences. These were exciting times that enabled the introduction of feminism and feminist philosophy, Marxism, semiotics, animal studies, Foucault and Freud, to mention just a few. We learned of Foucault's interventions against equating power with domination; the infrastructural patterns within language and representation – a largely invisible political economy thought to instantiate and exemplify wider social injustices. Course offerings across the faculty began to interrogate 'the how' of subject formation in all its manifestations. Even History and Anthropology, those disciplinary bastions that co-ordinate time and space for the rest of us, were brought up short and forced to recognise the rhetorical and writerly aspects of their practice, mediating, inventing – in sum, understanding the world and making it credible through the practice of re-presentation.[9] Where, then, did truth lie?

Together with this question, one of the most important challenges to emerge from this knowledge shake-up concerned the understanding of our own personhood, now described as 'the inquiring subject', 'the one who knows', 'the sovereign subject'. We think of ourselves as unique individuals, a word whose etymology underlines our integrity, as it means, 'can't be broken up or divided from itself'. Consequently, what we'd regarded as self-evident, namely, an individual's identity, autonomy, intentional purpose and responsibility for themselves, was now a site of considerable intrigue. The wisdom at that time was that the subject was produced through social forces that were always on the move.[10] Further to this, and what might seem especially strange for a contemporary audience, we were persuaded that the workings of this intricate 'machinery' could be largely unknown to us, indeed, so much so that the individual was no longer considered a fully responsible agent in the conventional sense, able to make decisions with complete awareness of their motivations. In sum, the proof was in that none of us could be the author of our own life in a transparent and determining way.

It is this last point that I want to focus on because it sounds so counter-intuitive in a culture increasingly fascinated by the commodification of self into ever-proliferating categories of claimed authenticity. Not unrelated, there is a much narrower bandwidth for exploring political and ethical difficulty in the academy than previously enjoyed, probably because social media can replace debate, however awkward, with summary censorship and a more fearful atmosphere of repercussion. But also, as already mentioned, because the tertiary sector's business model largely discourages the sort of scholarly research that can sit with ambiguity and remain curious about a persistent impasse and the complex subtleties of power. As an atmosphere of menace can go in either direction, I hope to explain how differences, whether those that separate personal identities, the agonism of certain political judgements, or even something as obvious as the mind/body division, might be considerably more implicated than we like to concede. To this end, I want to explore what I perceive as the dangers that attend a politics of identity that can tolerate no ambiguity, no infectious crossovers or awkward confusion with what appears to be 'other'.

An illustration of what is at stake can be found in the splintering of identity into ever finer categories of gender and sexual marginality that claim their unorthodox and more experimental expressions under the catch-all, 'nonbinary'. This more liberated and positive description of what was previously recognised as a normative demand for binary compliance celebrates personal independence and its self-expression; its ability to break with the mould that devalued its difference as a failure to measure up. To see the margin differently, and in a comparatively positive way, is to tether it to a centre that now appears in negative relief, the conservative and compliant background that effectively highlights the specificity of that margin's uncommon status. However, the 'tell' that things aren't as they seem, that this flip-flop preserves a structural complicity, is the oppositional nature of their respective identities. Certain attributes, behaviours and understandings of self are either present or absent, their difference valued or devalued. The centre, for example, is regarded as fixed, enduring and closed rather than fluid and open; it is a place of compliant, or minimally, uniform and conventional behaviours and desires, everyone much the same when compared with the diversity and potential unconventionality that now attaches to the margin. However, a presumptive (dull and entirely predictable?) heteronormativity will not provide the ballast against which 'nonbinary' identities can assert their escapee leverage. Even putting the insights of psychoanalysis aside that complicate sexual and gender identity as (always) fraught with homosexual fantasy, heterosexuality remains an illusory category of presumed coherence. Kadji Amin, in their provocative article

PLAYING THE FIELD 241

'We Are All Nonbinary: A Brief History of Accidents',[11] explains how an increasing need since the 1990s to emphasise difference as divergence actively hones and produces heterosexuality as its departure point. Recalling Judith Butler's work on the 'regulatory operations' of dominant norms, Amin reminds us that the fabrication of these norms that deny the messy incoherence of all identity and desire has an uncanny history. Determined, for example, to claim butch/femme as their own, and 'to avoid the charge of lesbian mimicry, *both categories* [i.e., lesbian and heterosexual] had to be defended as mutually unrelated, immune to any contaminating cross-identifications, fantasies, or desires'.[12]

If we insist on oppositional ways of thinking we can unwittingly recuperate an ideological chauvinism that we might otherwise contest, or at least, strive to ameliorate. The image of a seesaw is helpful here as it provides some sense that the independence and autonomy of identity – each side positioned differently – can be deceiving. From the perspective of the hinge, or fulcrum, that allows the differentiation as either up or down, one state or another, both sides exist in and as a shared horizon. To extrapolate from this, although individual identity, as already mentioned, receives considerable attention today, it is perhaps ironic that the nuance and mystery of its production, the veritable disorder and constant compromise that renders identity unstable, ambiguous and intra-dependent for all of us, is arguably more censored than explored. In sum, what have I forfeited by insisting that the claim of 'nonbinarity' *is* binarity at work? And why would it matter if this is the case?

Bringing such questions to the forefront of this meditation allows us to revisit those approaches from the past that engaged them head-on. In previous decades, binarity was also regarded as a problem. It demeans what counts as 'the feminine', or 'otherness', that broad grab-bag whose diverse contents share a comparative lack of value – more primitive, often perceived as threatening or yet to evolve, when compared with a male or white reference point. How to correct the politics of oppositional valuation when the reach of its violence is as insidious as it is ubiquitous? It is evident in the workings of language and representation and provides the interpretive frame that organises actions and behaviours into political legibility of more or less importance.[13] Understandably, as we discovered the oppressive gravitas of this gendered economy and its sticky persistence, we were keen to destabilise the identity categories we'd inherited. In short, we wanted to acknowledge the structural adhesions and delusional investments that compromise orthodox claims to an 'I am'. Indeed, the more radical possibilities of what sexuality and gender might mean, or how they might be lived and explored, were very much under review.

I recall the magical spell I was under when I first read Luce Irigaray's *This Sex Which Is Not One*[14] and *Speculum of the Other Woman*.[15] I found her analysis of phallocentrism's representation of 'the feminine' entirely persuasive, that is, as inherently deficient, emotionally overwrought, irrational and limited by the immanence of corporeality. Although there was a concession that 'the feminine' provided the necessary connecting tissue that made signification work, the passage and support for everything that appears proper – clean, complete, separate and self-defined – a *natural* incapacity, at least according to this logic, seemed inevitable. However, in Irigaray's hands the surreal absurdity of such representations wrought a suggestive counter-politics. It wasn't so much that phallocentrism's predictable denigrations were simply wrong and we could now correct the error. It was more the case that the political weighting of this economy that divides the corporeal from the intellectual, nature from culture, the feminine from the masculine and the one from the other, demanded we re-evaluate what 'the feminine' might actually involve.

Two things are important here. Although there are many ways to interpret this figure/ground (image/support, visible/invisible) reasoning, there was an understandable tendency to focus on 'the feminine' in the belief that 'this sex which is not one' more accurately evoked what was essentially unrepresentable about 'woman' and 'otherness'. Clearly, 'she' exceeded masculinism's attempts to pin her down as the absence, or negativity, that enabled his inherent (phallic) self-importance and self-definition. Consequently, 'the woman question' boiled down to 'who is she really?', and if 'she' could speak in her own voice, what would 'she' want?[16] In the main, there was no real intention to answer this question, at least not definitively, but instead to tarry with its provocation about the political economy of symbolic systems that silence difference by misrepresenting it. But here is the rub. What we might call 'the man question', potentially another opportunity to appreciate that 'this sex which is not one' might have more general analytical leverage, attracted considerably less interest. Instead, the crude simplicity and oppositional violence of what binarity dictates effected a reversal, now intent on diagnosing what was previously valued as proof of man's failures – his pomposity, the fear he confronts regarding his own embodiment, the fragility of his knowledge and the violence of his entitlement.[17]

It seems that even when we appreciate the cloying predictability and censorial aspects of identity politics regarding alterity or 'the feminine', we redeploy its hierarchical economy in our attempts to counter its effects. For example, if we acknowledge the comparative denigration of otherness within masculinism[18] and our response is to reverse this logic's seesaw binary, then what have we achieved? Man retains his identity as the purported centre of reference who requires no inverted commas, now appearing as a cartoon of control and culpability. But isn't the 'how' or 'why' of 'him' equally curious? Does 'he' really know who 'he' is and what motivates 'him' to do what 'he' does, given that masculinism's economy precedes his birth? He didn't engineer it, even if he benefits from and lends his being to its enduring repetition. Put simply, is 'he' self-defined and at one with 'himself'? Indeed, isn't what is most challenging and politically exciting about 'the woman question' that it also heralds the possibility of engaging 'the man question' with equal passion? A corollary is that any political analysis of the margin, or what seems outside or other, can similarly open an enquiry into the 'how' and 'what' of 'centering', or what seems to require no explanation because its identity is established. Regarding this quandary of how to achieve an effective critique of 'what is established' and to displace its terms of reference,[19] Derrida warns us that things are not what they seem. For example,

> The center is not the center. The concept of centered structure – although it represents coherence itself, the condition of the *épistémè* as philosophy or science – is contradictorily coherent ... The concept of centered structure is in fact the concept of a free-play based on a fundamental ground, a freeplay which is constituted upon a fundamental immobility and a reassuring certitude, which is itself beyond the reach of the freeplay.[20]

Admittedly, to explore the full measure of what this undoing of stability implies is potentially disturbing. To forfeit or qualify how we identify 'the culprit', to suggest that a shared if differentially weighted productivity somehow entangles all of us and complicates what we mean by 'responsibility' and 'the agential', might seem to tie our hands, rendering us impotent, unable to achieve a more equitable political situation. The immediate worry is the consolidation of conservatism, now further invested with theoretical sophistication and endorsing injustice as prescriptive – 'it's just the way it is!' But there is more to this story than meets the eye, more to conceding that power can be a force of domination and a dynamic that enables an enduring resistance.[21]

To clarify, the point isn't that power's perversity can accommodate both at the same time, or that 'the one' *and* 'the other' are somehow connected: such descriptions already posit two distinct entities whose constitutive ambiguity and entangled coming into being are impossible to even acknowledge. Because of this, the challenge is that the very connotation of what we mean by 'both' is 'contradictorily coherent'.

In other words, and to evoke a Derridean approach here, the genetics of *différance* confound the integrity of identity *before* the concepts of spatial relationship that locate it, whether separate, different, together, or both... and. In short, we are in a quantum problematic where the difference between separability and inseparability is, strangely, no difference at all, and yet 'difference' operates, or works, as if entities really do pre-exist the forces that produce and inform them. This confounding of common sense and our belief that a definite starting and end point can be identified has further implications for how we circumscribe desire, gender and sexuality, as well as the identity of power *as such* and how we attribute blame. At this juncture we can appreciate the resonance of Michel Foucault's challenge to the belief that power is always sovereign, central and easily identifiable, with Derrida's complication of centripetal power that questions the difference between centre and periphery. Consistent with the model of power as always located, a force of domination that we might liken to a commodity – you possess it or you don't – is the assumption that Foucault's contribution is his ever-finer attention to the microphysics of domination. However, this is far from the case.

> Power's condition of possibility, or in any case the viewpoint which permits one to understand its exercise, even in its more 'peripheral' effects, and which also makes it possible to use its mechanisms as a grid of intelligibility of the social order, must not be sought in the primary existence of a central point, in a unique source of sovereignty from which secondary and descendent forms would emanate ... Power is everywhere; not because it embraces everything, but because it comes from everywhere.[22]

For Foucault, it's not that domination and even ruthless sovereign power aren't in evidence, rather, the point he is making concerns 'the how' and 'what' of its possibility and expression. To go a little sideways here to explain this further, in *Discourse on Voluntary Servitude*[23] Étienne de La Boétie, a sixteenth-century writer who influenced Foucault,[24] succinctly captures what is at stake.

> He who domineers over you has only two eyes, only two hands, only one body, no more than is possessed by the least man among the infinite numbers dwelling in your cities; he has indeed nothing more than the power that you confer upon him to destroy you ... How can he have so many arms to beat you with, if he does not borrow them from you? How does he have any power over you except through you.[25]

And yet, despite the statement's disturbing truth its condemnation of what might appear as a wilful, moral complicity that translates into 'blaming the victim' feels unfair or misguided. Importantly, the injustice of victim-blaming concerns the accuracy of who is blamed: importantly, our disquiet doesn't extend to the notion of culpability itself as a fraught determination. Indeed, the suggestion that power is dispersed and implicated, an energy whose ubiquity complicates the notion of origin and cause, thereby involving us all, is routinely rejected before the provocation of its consequences can be unpacked. It seems that 'politics' equates with culpability, and for this we need an individual whose desires and actions are properly their own. We desire a sovereign subject, some*one* who remains in charge of their own behaviours, the author of their desires and responsible for their choices. Consistent with this, power is conceived instrumentally as 'something' we can pick up or put down. But what happens if a more general erotic of identity formation is at work in a 'scene'[26] whose transductive and intra-active desires express Life's promiscuous sexual and sexualising attractions and repulsions in/ as us?[27]

To entertain this sense of Life in the broadest sense – indeed, we might even think of Life as a 'worlding', a Subject whose 'own' ecological entanglements explain us – is to rethink what seems fixed, or given, about gender and sexuality, as well as how we understand power. Even La Boétie's sense that the sovereign can only exist as a social collective becomes a more palatable and provocative notion if we acknowledge identity's structural complicity, thereby complicating the moral adjudication that too readily identifies victim versus culprit. We will return to this suggestion which is 'contradictorily coherent'. Suffice to say at this stage that there is something perverse about how we claim our respective identities: what we might offer in all honesty as our private truth *requires* us to disavow a constitutive reliance on what we define ourselves against. Claims to nonbinary, gender diverse and experimental identities will tend to value play and fluidity over conformity and predictability. And who wouldn't prefer an identity marked by creativity to one regarded as prescriptive and unimaginative? But must we buy into this either/or cartoon? Underlining a growing impasse, Amin argues that the term 'nonbinary' is 'a ubiquitous category that could seemingly apply to almost anyone', explaining that, 'increasingly, nonbinary identity is being claimed by people who look and behave in a manner indistinguishable from ordinary lesbians and gays, or even ordinary heterosexuals'.[28] Not unrelated and as already noted, in my attempt to retrieve what felt like a positive political intervention from the 1980s and 1990s that refused the 'givenness' of identity, I failed to realise that as we championed the mystery and ambiguity of 'woman' and 'the feminine' on the one hand, there was a tendency to accept the accuracy of man's representation.

If we can appreciate that binarity is an insidious logic that assumes the independence and autonomy of two terms whose difference is something of an illusion, a denial of their actual intra-dependence, and if we can concede that perhaps this same logic survives, indeed, thrives, on the naive assumption that claims of nonbinarity are all it takes to escape its reductive violence, then we can be forgiven for wondering what strategies are available to us that might complicate this persistence. Or to put the quandary in Derridean terms, what to do if 'one always inhabits, and all the more when one does not suspect it'.[29]

For Derrida, his focus on the structure of structuration bravely engages this place where politics, ethics, indeed, everything we hold to be straightforwardly 'itself', is already promiscuously involved with whatever it refuses or has yet to encounter. His will be a very different story about identity and sexuality because it will generalise intercourse, complicate the how, what and where of reproduction, and radically reconfigure the force and energy of desire and eroticism that are their playing field. Although he will not presume to escape metaphysics, he will radically reroute its understanding to show the constitutive perversion and disavowal required to maintain sovereign identity as properly contained. It is important to appreciate that Derrida is doing more than negative critique, the illumination of an error in the hope that its mistake will be corrected (another binary). As we will see, the disruptive nature of a deconstructive strategy is its utter immersion with/as the problematic being investigated, a strategy that complicates the pragmatic call, however necessary, to 'just take a side'.

This is difficult terrain to navigate because the sovereign returns as 'one' whose (fractured) integrity is secured through the hauntological resonance of a field. It might help to think of the Sovereign Subject as Life, a 'worlding' from which nothing is excluded and whose 'own' ecological entanglements individuate and identify: even human species being is articulated by this in-habiting.[30] Importantly however, human identity in this reading is no longer an entity backgrounded or contextualised by the non-human, that is, one whose sovereign being is enclosed against its others; instead, human haecceity is born of, with and through implication. In other words, a sense of identity returns but not in the same way. We see this in Derrida's nuanced engagement with the sovereign in *The Beast and the Sovereign*.

> In a certain sense, there is no contrary of sovereignty, even if there are things other than sovereignty [...] even in politics, the choice

PLAYING THE FIELD

is not between sovereignty and nonsovereignty, but among several forms of partings, partitions, divisions, conditions that come along to broach a sovereignty that is always supposed to be indivisible and unconditional [...] A divisible sovereignty is no longer a sovereignty, a sovereignty worthy of the name, i.e. pure and unconditional.[31]

But we are left with a question: What relevance will this attention to a constitutive fragility and fracturing have for the discourse of Man and his confession of planetary irresponsibility, increasingly legible in/as the Anthropocene?

We need to move through this last part of the argument quite carefully. To return to my opening disappointment that valuable aspects of feminist work from the 1980s and 1990s have been abandoned or forgotten, one of the most problematic assumptions that focused so much of our critical energy was the Cartesian separation of body from mind, and by association, nature from culture. This sense that the site of self is locatable ('cogito ergo sum') and can be defined *against* corporeality – which can support thinking but remains incapable of it – captured the politics of engendering in phallocentric logic at its most powerful. It is no surprise that 'woman', and 'the feminine', identities which also resonate with racial and ability valuations, have been understood in terms of lack – corporeal immanence, emotional disarray and a more primordial state of being that remains closer to nature. By contrast, man is attributed with more rationality and logical focus because he is more evolved and can better transcend his biology. Although the binary is absurd it can be seen to acquire lived credibility in many respects, and it was precisely this sense that signification and the discursive, or what we used to call ideology, was somehow materialising that captured our critical attentions. We came to see that ideas and prejudices were not like a bad outfit we might choose to take off. Indeed, we began to wonder how what we considered ideational could animate and change our biology. Although this research and its implications were pathfinding, the political framework of this interrogation retained the belief that culture was a separate and agential force, capable of inscribing and transforming a passive, yet nonetheless, receptive biology. Surprisingly, exactly how biology could read and perform these cultural lessons is rarely engaged.

The phenomenon of hysteria, that 'mysterious leap from the mind to the body'[32] that includes the autographic skin, blindness, paralyses and many other psychological symptoms that are biologically expressed, made me wonder if there was any leap at all. And further, have the most politically challenging aspects of this phenomenon been understood.[33]

To provide a thumbnail sketch of the quandary, we will recall Simone de Beauvoir's iconic assertion in 1949, 'One is not born, but rather becomes, a woman',[34] an instructive example of how the mind/body question emerges as a feminist issue. The intervening years have entrenched a particular interpretation of this statement, namely, that regardless of our biological inheritance it is ideological forces, cultural beliefs and the personal perceptions that attach to social and political life that play a major role in producing our sense of self as an interpretive overlay *upon* biology. Although Beauvoir gives special attention to the exigencies of female biology, such as menstruation, maternity and reproductive concerns, her argument persuades us that biology need not equate with destiny. Indeed, the threat of biological determination is significantly displaced when culture is granted a materialising agency in the matter of what counts.

Building on this, the prominent philosopher and cultural activist Judith Butler, although in agreement with the direction of Beauvoir's position – namely, we need to question and reinterpret naturalising arguments – effectively banishes the biological altogether. By reminding us that biology is a cultural sign, Butler endorses the tenets of 'the linguistic turn' that circumscribe language and other forms of cultural mediation in such a way as to prohibit access to what they believe must be a non-linguistic world.[35] In other words, whatever we understand or experience as nature is really culture in disguise, a negative back projection whose devaluation can be contested. Nature, now under erasure, is regarded as radically outside – the other of what is specific to human achievement. And so again we see a robust and persuasive intervention into the political conservatism that segregates nature from culture and an awareness that binary logic proves both misogynistic and racialising, only to witness a reinvestment in this same economy when human exceptionalism is at risk. Must all our arguments against binarity end up repeating its 'good sense'?

Against this constant return to binarity's conservatism, a return that seems unthinking inasmuch as 'nonbinary' is the go-to tag for its critique and refusal, we might wonder about the claims of another binary identification, 'cis-gender versus trans-gender'. As Finn Enke informs us, the biologist Dana Leland de Fosse was probably the first to circulate the term 'cis' in 1994 'as a linguistic complement to "trans"'.[36] The term refers to the correspondence one feels with their anatomical identity – 'cis'; whereas 'trans' acknowledges a mis-fit. As 'cis' refers to the Latin, 'on the side of', we are given an image of cis-gender as harmoniously lining up vertically, whereas trans-gender involves a crossover that rests on the horizontal separation of mind from body. The assumption that

PLAYING THE FIELD

nature and culture are two entirely separate entities that may or may not align underpins both identity claims, as if what is 'given', and therefore outside interrogation, is the prescriptive fixity of nature/biology as mere support. In a quite brilliant exploration of the prohibitive consequences of these rigid identity divisions, Amin explores 'the consequences of an ill-conceived taxonomy that sought to, counterfactually and in an affront to the entirety of queer history, neatly sort people into cis-gender versus trans-gender'.[37] In places, Amin makes their point by paraphrasing Butler's important provocations about the fiction of normativity more generally. 'In short, are we idealizing cis-gender as uncontaminated by any gender-trouble whatsoever, just as we have idealized heterosexuality as untainted by the slightest homosexual longing?'[38] Not only does cis-gender become a suspect description in Amin's hands, but the appeal of prohibition that accompanies these adjudications is also engaged. Given the rigid either/or of 'cis' or 'trans', categories that erase myriad differences, Amin asks, 'So what has happened to all the gender variants who do not desire transition? Put differently, what are the contemporary fates of those who would have been fairies, queens, and butches in the past?'[39]

The above can only be a cursory introduction to certain conceptual difficulties that are also lived, both claimed and rejected, and in constant negotiation. To cut to the chase, my own interest concerns the politics of the departure point, what all the debates rest upon yet defend against engaging. And surely this is the biological body, which in Derrida's hands is entirely criss-crossed, diffracted and never at one with itself; a body that was never the other of the cerebral; never the mere support of ideation and cultural complexity; never a horizontal match nor a vertical mismatch. Derrida argues that 'origins' are fractured, disseminated, *différantial*, a suggestion that today might evoke a quantum space/time problematic, separate yet inseparable, 'both and... neither/nor', and this, because there is no atomic identity, or entity, that anchors the addition or refusal of a supplement. We have seen that Butler corrals the question of what matters, or where our analysis should begin, within a notion of culture whose circumscription Amin describes as a 'linguistic idealism'.[40] However, Butler is not alone, as we see similar assumptions in the work of thinkers such as Gayatri Spivak and Catherine Malabou, who, despite their deconstructionist credentials, remain, at least to my mind, cultural constructionists of a certain stripe.[41] Geoffrey Bennington makes similar charges in his scathing review essay of the re-publication of *Of Grammatology* – the fortieth anniversary edition, entitled, 'Embarrassing Ourselves'.[42] In response to the addition of an Introduction by Butler, revisions in translation and an Afterword by Spivak, he writes that the republication is 'riddled with vagueness, inaccuracies, misunderstandings, and plain errors. It does Spivak's (and, more importantly, Derrida's) work a real disservice, badly scrambling in advance the access a new generation of readers might otherwise have had to Derrida's book.'[43]

Derrida's 'writing', 'general textuality' or 'language' are not terms that try to capture a literacy that attests to what is unique in human achievement. Although there is no 'outside language' for Derrida, the implication is not one of cultural confinement but of essential entanglement and involvement that evoke Life writing itself.[44] In Derrida's hands, for example, biology is not a separate system of the corporeal that culture might write or impress itself upon, the supporting 'blank page' that the aetiology of hysteria assumes in that 'mysterious leap'. Our fear that we *are* our biology is evident when we describe biology as pre-scriptive, before writing, yet somehow rigid in its scriptural rules. It follows that we attribute the agency of contestation and change to what is not biology, thereby emphasising that culture (human consciousness) can overcome nature's dictation.

In *Life Death* Derrida engages with the geneticist, François Jacob, whose *Logic of Life* (1993) concedes the generality of the scriptural and decipherment, while still holding to the difference between the cultural and biological for reasons he can neither explain nor justify. Derrida seizes on this confusion, arguing that what Jacob reserves for the genetic programme is also apparent in what he glosses as the 'psychical, social, cultural, institutional, politico-economic, and so on'.[45] Here, at the nub of Derrida's intervention, we can proceed in two different ways. We can read Derrida's impatience with Jacob as a bid to remind the geneticist that he remains caught in the metaphysical commitments of cultural representation. In other words, the presumptive explanations of the behaviour and literacy of genes is an inevitable reflection of the language Jacob must use to represent them: the tool constitutes and contaminates the object. However, Derrida is not confirming linguisticism's cultural enclosure, but offering something much more challenging for how we understand human identity, the subject, materiality, and otherness more generally.

Can we imagine, if just for a moment, what the following citation about the mediating status of a model might imply for identity politics, whether claims to human exceptionalism, exclusionary gender and sexual identifications, ethical judgements, or the identity of power as only and always domination? What happens if we consider auto-affection, or an entity's apparent integrity – the 'I am' that all of us experience – as some-*thing* that manifests in/as entangled heterogeneity, as we see increasingly with scientific investigations into biological plasticity, and more recently,

PLAYING THE FIELD   251

the quantum aspects of biology.[46] Doesn't this imply that biology, a nature that was culture all along, constantly investigates and transforms itself? And isn't the crossing over and crossing out of a definite departure and arrival point relevant for why we might want to concede that nature is always/already in translation/transition?

> what we human beings claim to take from culture as a model, namely, discursive texts or computers and everything we believe we know and are familiar with under the name *text*, what we then claim to take as a model, comparison, or analogy in order to understand the living at its most elementary level is itself a complex product of life, of the living, and the alleged model is external neither to the knowing subject nor to the known object ... The text is not a third term in the relation between the biologist and the living; it is the very structure of the living as the structure common to the biologist, as a living being, to science, as a production of life, and to the living itself.[47]

Finally, the point isn't that we forfeit identity, or even triumph over binarity, but that we consider the processual and implicated nature of identity's appearing from Life's 'commons'. As Life 'speaks' the sovereign subject's appearing, a hauntological being, it is not an error we can refuse, but 'one' we must refuse to refuse because it involves 'the how' of materialising. Of course, how we do this is the challenge, and considering the inevitable perversity of what we claim to be and desire, this is a good place to start.[48]

Notes

1. This is a deceptively complex question. Although we know that History involves constant reinvention, we tend to assume that something substantial, a temporal in itself, pre existed its passing and forgetting. Although my introduction seems to affirm such a reading, an unavoidable heuristic, the challenge is to acknowledge that temporality's 'then' was always inflected through and as a 'now', which is also a future.

2. Freud's provocative little essay on perception and memory, and Derrida's engagement with its most foundational assumptions, prove helpful in showing that our faith in identifying and separating what comes first (here, perception – raw and corporeal) from what appears to come second (memory – interpretation, translation, a more evolved mental process) is seriously misguided. The German word, *nachträglichkeit*, captures this sense of a backwards and forwards causation where temporal direction and the sense of finality appear undone. See Sigmund Freud, 'A Note upon the

"Mystic Writing Pad"', [1924] in *The Standard Edition of The Complete Psychological Works of Sigmund Freud Volume 19*, trans. James Strachey (London: The Hogarth Press, 1961), 226–32; and Jacques Derrida, 'Freud and the Scene of Writing', in *Writing and Difference*, trans. Alan Bass (Chicago: The University of Chicago Press, 1978), 196–231.

3. Other notables included Lyotard, Barthes, Lacan, Nietzsche, Deleuze, Cixous, Irigaray, Said, Kristeva, Spivak, to name just a few.

4. The meanings of all these terms have been debated and often rejected entirely. Derrida, for example, recognised none of them.

5. For a helpful discussion of this period's intellectual frisson, see Michael Peters, 'HABERMAS, POST-STRUCTURALISM AND THE QUESTION OF POSTMODERNITY: The Defiant Periphery', in *Social Analysis: The International Journal of Anthropology* 36 (1994), 3–20.

6. In Australia, according to David Marin-Guzman, 'University wage theft tops \$159m: union tally', *Financial Review*, 5 December 2023, and the National Tertiary Education Union, since 2009 systematic wage theft is at AUD\$159 million. Casualisation rates between 40 per cent and 50 per cent, and the employment of students as course convenors (not just tutors), have eroded the value of disciplinary expertise and intellectual difficulty.

7. An important example of how faith in what appears self-evident can have unfortunate repercussions is eye-witness testimony. It is regarded by juries as the most valuable and trustworthy evidence, testament to an unarguable 'I was there.' However, it has proven alarmingly unreliable because memories are inherently plastic and creative. See Elizabeth Loftus, *Witness for the Defense: The Accused, the Eyewitness, and the Expert who Puts Memory on Trial* (New York: St Martin's Press, 1992).

8. Jacques Derrida, *Speech and Phenomena: And Other Essays on Husserl's Theory of Signs*, trans. David B. Allison (Evanston, IL: Northwestern University Press, 1973), 103.

9. See Hayden White, *Metahistory: The Historical Imagination in Nineteenth-century Europe* (Baltimore, MD: Johns Hopkins University Press, 1973); and James Clifford and George Marcus, eds, *Writing Culture: The Poetics and Politics of Ethnography* (Oakland: University of California Press, 1986).

10. For an introduction as to why 'the subject' had become problematic, see Mikkel Borch-Jacobsen, *The Freudian Subject*, trans. Catherine Porter (Stanford, CA: Stanford University Press, 1999); Jacques Lacan, 'The Mirror Stage as Formative of the Function of The I As Revealed in Psychoanalytic Experience', in *Écrits: A Selection*, trans. Alan Sheridan (London: Routledge, 2001); Michel Foucault, *The History of Sexuality Vol 1: An Introduction*, trans. Robert Hurley (New York: Vintage Books Random House, 1980).

11. Kadji Amin, 'We Are All Nonbinary: A Brief History of Accidents', in *Representations* 158 (2022), 106–19.

12. Amin, 'We Are All Nonbinary', 107.

13. We see a clear example of this during the COVID-19 lockdowns. By and large, it was the underpaid, feminised workforce that we came to rely upon

PLAYING THE FIELD   253

for our most basic daily support. Feminised, because these jobs are associated with more menial service – read corporeal – hands-on maintenance and caring work: nurses, cleaners, garbage and city workers, teachers. See Ann Game and Rosemary Pringle, *Gender at Work* (London: Routledge, 1983) for an insightful analysis of how the division of labour into gendered industries and pay inequity is conceptually justified.

14. Luce Irigaray, *This Sex Which Is Not One*, trans. Catherine Porter with Carolyn Burke (Ithaca, NY: Cornell University Press, 1985).

15. Luce Irigaray, *Speculum of the Other Woman*, trans. Gillian C. Gill (Ithaca, NY: Cornell University Press, 1985).

16. We are reminded of Freud's infamous question in a letter to Marie Bonaparte, 'What does a woman want?' which captures this sense of an enigma, waiting to be deciphered. Freud also depicted woman's sexuality as a 'dark continent', largely unknown and yet to be explored, a description with obvious reference to colonial Africa, waiting to be penetrated and conquered.

17. I am not suggesting that the direction of these arguments, namely, to make 'the feminine' an elusive and ambiguous referent while preserving the representational accuracy of 'the masculine' was Irigaray's thesis or intention. However, in the theoretical circles I mixed in and the myriad academic papers in circulation at that time, this was a favoured reading.

18. A common strategy across many disadvantaged groups that seek redress is to reverse the logic of denigration and its negative associations by actively embracing and revaluing what was previously devalued. Much feminist and anti-racism literature, for example, will argue for the importance of nature, corporeal being and emotional and intuitive life. However, although this reversal certainly shifts the value of these gendered and racial associations, it leaves the structure of binarity and the comparative identities that sustain it intact. Consequently, the body cannot reason, there can be no logic in emotional life and no emotional 'heat' in what counts as logic. Unless we displace the respective identities that allow a binary to work – the belief in the autonomy and self-presence of identity – we remain wedded to defending the containment, purity and censorship we are trying to contest.

19. For an account of why the displacement of value must accompany its mere reversal, see Jacques Derrida, 'Structure, Sign, and Play in the Discourse of the Human Sciences', in *The Languages of Criticism and the Sciences of Man: The Structuralist Controversy*, ed. Richard Macksey and Eugenio Donato (Baltimore, MD: John Hopkins University Press, 1970).

20. Ibid., 352.

21. Foucault is often read through an either/or of domination versus resistance; however, much of his work complicates the automatic faith in their apparent separation.

22. Foucault, *History of Sexuality 1*, 93.

23. Étienne de La Boétie, *The Politics of Obedience: Discourse on Voluntary Servitude*, trans. Harry Kurz (Montréal, New York, London: Black Rose Books, 1997 [1577]).

24. See, for example, Saul Newman, 'Power, Freedom and Obedience in Foucault and La Boétie: Voluntary Servitude as the Problem of Government', in *Theory, Culture and Society* 39.1 (2022), 123–41.
25. Étienne de La Boétie in Borch-Jacobsen, *The Freudian Subject*, 153.
26. I use this to evoke Derrida's sense of a 'scene of writing' from which nothing is excluded.
27. I have written elsewhere about the nuanced complications that attend Derrida's engagement with the sovereign subject. See Vicki Kirby, 'Human Exceptionalism on the Line', in *SubStance: a review of theory and literary criticism* 43.2 (2014), 50–67.
28. Amin, 'We Are All Nonbinary', 113.
29. Jacques Derrida, *Of Grammatology*, trans. Gayatri Chakravorty Spivak (Baltimore, MD: Johns Hopkins University Press, 1976), 24.
30. The relatively new research area of environmental humanities, together with related discourses such as animal and plant studies, almost routinely understand 'the ecological' as an *aggregation* of separate entities. Human identity becomes the stand-out, the recognised agential culprit and irresponsible caretaker of a passive, feminised and incapable Nature. Regardless of claims to 'queering' the ecology, a gesture intended to mix things up and credential a very different perspective, identity politics and the nature/culture split remain prerequisite. See Vicki Kirby, 'Un/limited Ecologies', in David Wood, Matthias Fritsch and Phil Lynes, eds, *Eco-Deconstruction: Derrida and Environmental Ethics* (New York: Fordham University Press, 2018), 121–40.
31. Jacques Derrida, *The Beast and the Sovereign Vol. I*, trans. Geoffrey Bennington (Evanston, IL: Northwestern University Press, 2011), 176–7.
32. Felix Deutsch, 'The Riddle of the Mind-Body Correlations', in Felix Deutsch, ed., *On the Mysterious Leap from the Mind to the Body* (Madison, CT: International Universities Press, 1959).
33. See Elizabeth Wilson, 'Introduction: Somatic Compliance – Feminism, Biology and Science', in *Australian Feminist Studies* 14.29 (1999); and my *Telling Flesh: The Substance of the Corporeal* (New York: Routledge, 1997).
34. Simone de Beauvoir, *The Second Sex*, trans. Howard Madison Parshley (London: Jonathan Cape, 1953), 273.
35. Butler is aware of the politics of conflating agency with culture and passivity with nature, however their corrective rests on the belief that both terms are linguistic/cultural. Interestingly however, when asked how biology can sign/speak through hysterical symptoms, Butler concedes that they, 'did not take account of a nature that might be, as it were, beyond the nature/culture divide, one that is not immediately harnessed for the aims of certain kinds of legitimation practices'. See Judith Butler in Vicki Kirby, *Judith Butler: Live Theory* (London and New York: Continuum, 2006), 145. Unfortunately, the concession recuperates as fact a nature/culture divide that remains consistent with a conception of power as either dominant or resistant.

36. Finn Enke, 'The Education of Little Cis: Cisgender and the Discipline of Opposing Bodies', in Aren Aizura and Susan Stryker, eds, *The Transgender Studies Reader 2* (New York: Routledge, 2013), 60.
37. Amin, 'We Are All Nonbinary', 112–13.
38. Ibid., 109–10.
39. Ibid., 112. Space restrictions prevent a more thorough acknowledgement of the many provocations in both Amin's and Enke's arguments. See also the special issue of *parallax* 25.2 (2019), and Kadji Amin, 'Taxonomically Queer? Sexology and New Queer, Trans, and Asexual Identities', in *GLQ* 29.1 (2023), 91–107.
40. Amin, 'Taxonomically Queer?', 107.
41. For an elaboration of this claim in reference to Malabou, who understands Derrida's work as a sort of history of ideas – hence her correction of the term 'writing' because it is no longer an adequate representation, see Vicki Kirby, 'Grammatology: A Vital Science', in *Derrida Today* 9.1 (2016), 47–67. And regarding Spivak's understanding of radical alterity, and what Derrida implies by the systematicity of writing, see Vicki Kirby, 'Risky Paths', in Anirban Das, ed., *Theory Practice* (Oxford: Oxford University Press, forthcoming).
42. Geoffrey Bennington, 'Embarrassing Ourselves', in *Los Angeles Review of Books*, 20 March 2016: https://lareviewofbooks.org/article/embarrassing-ourselves/ (accessed 29/01/2024).
43. Ibid, n.p.
44. Jacques Derrida, *Life Death*, trans. Pascale Anne-Brault and Michael Naas (Chicago, IL: University of Chicago Press, 2020), offers an extended meditation on this theme.
45. Ibid., 19.
46. See, for example, the work of Sonia Contera in the Physics Department at Oxford University.
47. Derrida, *Life Death*, 81.
48. I would like to thank Lynn Turner for her thoughtful editing advice as I grappled with this difficult material. The final argument, however, is mine to defend.

13

'GENE FOR GENE': CLONING, 'SEXINESS' AND THE (POST)MATERNAL IN CAROLA DIBBELL'S *THE ONLY ONES*

Naomi Morgenstern

A clone is like anyone else. *Anyone else.*
(Carola Dibbell)[1]

As if cloning began with cloning! As if there weren't cloning and then more cloning! As if there weren't a clonelike way of reproducing the discourse against cloning.
(Jacques Derrida)[2]

I. 'In the name of the singularity and *nonrepetitive* unicity of the human person'

When US President George Bush announced his intention to create a Council on Bioethics in August of 2001, his choice to head the council was physician Leon Kass, who had been serving as one of Bush's expert advisors on stem cell policy. In 1997, Kass had written and published an anti-human cloning jeremiad in *The New Republic*, in which he articulated what he called 'The Wisdom of Repugnance': 'We are repelled by the prospect of cloning human beings not because of the strangeness or novelty of the undertaking, but because we intuit and feel, immediately and without argument, the violation of things we rightfully hold dear.'[3] Kass's essay might be said to reproduce, 'in a clonelike way', the discourse against cloning, but like many a symptomatic text, the essay also contains knots of pleasure and displeasure that I will attempt to untangle in some detail in what follows. And here Derrida's account of just what is at stake in anti-cloning discourse provides us with a kind of philosophical x-ray:

> One thus objects to all cloning in the name of ethics, human rights, what is proper to humanity, and the dignity of human life, the name of the singularity and *nonrepetitive* unicity of the human

person, in the name of an ethics of desire or a love of the other – which we sometimes believe or try to make others believe, with an optimistic confidence, must always inspire the act of procreation. And, finally, one objects to cloning in the name of that incalculable element that must be left to birth, to the coming to light or into the world of a unique, irreplaceable, free, and thus nonprogrammable living being.[4]

As Derrida goes on to suggest, the very 'militance' of this most lofty set of objections, aimed at preserving what is 'proper' to humanity, has already betrayed the very figure it was conjured to protect: 'militant humanism ... actually shares with the axiomatic it claims to oppose a certain geneticism or biologism, indeed a deep zoologism, a fundamental but unacknowledged reductionism'.[5] (Militant) Humanism, in other words, requires the utmost in defence precisely because it doesn't really believe in itself – the animal and the machine (not to mention the woman) have always already encroached upon the humanist subject's sacrosanct domain. Derrida, identifying the cloning controversy as 'some metonymy of all the urgencies that confront us', calls for 'a different elaboration' of the reproductive problematic: 'The question concerning cloning will therefore never be "Yes or no?" but "How?": how to deal with difference or with the reproduction of the identical, and first of all "What is duplication?"'[6]

In her 2015 novel, *The Only Ones*, Carola Dibbell offers precisely such a 'different elaboration', an elaboration unconstrained by an always predetermined binary structure. *The Only Ones* depicts a relationship between a mother and her daughter that features a crucial twist: the daughter is her mother's clone. This conceit allows Dibbell to grapple with a range of pressing questions related to contemporary reproductive technology and feminist critique. While the technological innovation depicted is clearly the product of a dystopian, though simultaneously *realist*, neoliberal economic order, it is nevertheless not without its feminist philosophical affordances (at least in the world of fiction). Dibbell, I will argue, uses cloning to deconstruct an enduring heteropatriarchal imaginary of reproduction, thereby making a distinctive contribution to ongoing work in the field of critical maternal studies.

II. 'Not by accident is the human being the sexiest animal'

One of the many ironies of anti-clone discourse is that the identity or self-sameness of its critical target is always in question. While in Kass's

'The Wisdom of Repugnance', (human) cloning is (human) cloning and we would forget this at our peril ('A fateful question is at hand. To clone or not to clone a human being is no longer an academic question' (17)), cloning is to be feared precisely because it is not *only* itself, but also more generally representative of 'our' culture's undoing: 'Is cloning a fulfillment of human begetting and belonging?' asks Kass, 'Or is cloning rather, as I contend, its pollution and perversion ... the perfect embodiment of the ruling opinions of our age.' 'We are all', Kass bemoans, 'or almost all, postmodernists now' (21, 18).

What does it mean to be a 'postmodernist' in 1997? It is, Kass suggests, to be an individualist associated with feminism or gay rights (and thus to be 'narcissistic' and 'rootless'). It is to have no sense of the past and it is to want to control the future, such that there will be no unpredictability, no chance for surprise. But this postmodernism also disavows our very moral foundation and thus our mortality (or vice versa) via an endorsement of 'cultural construction' which, according to Kass, critically defies the determining function of the *natural*. 'What would kinship be without any natural grounding', asks Kass rhetorically, 'and what would identity be without kinship?' (21). To endorse 'cultural construction' is to defy 'natural heterosexual difference' and thus the very set of oppositions that produce and secure the human as such. It is perhaps not surprising, although nevertheless fascinating, to see so explicitly all the work that 'natural heterosexual difference' can be tasked with accomplishing in this carno-phallogocentric discussion of cloning. 'For a sexual being', writes Kass, 'the world is no longer an indifferent and largely homogeneous *otherness*, in part edible, in part dangerous. It also contains some very special and related complementary beings, of the same kind, but of the opposite sex, toward whom one reaches out with special interest and intensity' (21). Simply put, natural heterosexual difference secures the human as such by producing a tolerable 'complementarity', or otherness – an otherness one seeks neither to eat nor destroy.[7] All the same, we humans had better muster our defences, if we are to protect our idealisations from temporality and materiality. In a characteristically logocentric move, Kass pleads with his fellow humans to accept mortality, chance and futurity, but only insofar as they are subordinated to an idealised and conservative gesture of protection (thereby annulling mortality, chance and futurity): 'Today defenders of stable, monogamous marriage risk giving offense to those adults who are living in "new family forms" or to those children who, even without the benefit of assisted reproduction, have acquired either three or four parents or one or none at all' (17–18). Kass concedes that our world already 'confounds lineage and confuses kinship and responsibility for children', but it's not too late to intervene: 'I exaggerate but in the direction of truth', he proclaims, 'when I insist that we are faced with having to decide nothing less than whether human procreation is going to remain human' (22, 18).

Having digested the playbook of Western metaphysics, Kass recognises the risks associated with violating the opposition between the human and the animal; the human and the machine. And this is why it will turn out that (non-human) animal cloning, for Kass, is just fine: 'We should allow all cloning research on animals to go forward, but the safe trench that we can dig across the slippery slope [try to visualize this!] ... is to insist on the inviolable distinction between animal and human cloning' (26). This distinction also draws on a pointedly American political anxiety; cloning is proto-despotic (the cloners tyrannise the cloned), because it generates a specific form of non-consent: 'The friends of cloning are not wittingly friends of despotism', writes Kass, but their work produces individuals who never consented to their status as clones (24). And here Kass symptomatically misses something he obviously knows very well: nobody gets to consent to come into being. Every human being, if they are to be a proper human being and citizen, must arrive as, in Kass's words elsewhere in the article, 'an unbidden surprise, a gift to the world rather than the designed result of someone's artful project' (22). To be human (and American!), is to transcend mechanical reproduction as the product of mindless repetition *or* of pure (rational) intention. Hence, Kass warns us about what it would mean for human beings to be made from one's intentions as opposed to from one's being ('In clonal reproduction ... we give existence to a being not by what we are but by what we intend and design' (23)). Preserving the sovereignty of the individual human being, that is to say, means protecting each and every one of us from anybody else's desire, and the clone, paradoxically, figures an intensification of that desire ('someone else's artful project').[8] As Kelly Oliver notes, 'most philosophers engaged in debates over genetic engineering and cloning begin with some version of a liberal sovereign individual who has freedom of choice that must be protected, whether we are talking about the freedom (or lack thereof) in considering genetic engineering and embryo selection, or the future person's freedom (or lack thereof) resulting from such a process' (26). Kass is no exception. The enigma of a coming into being that would be untainted by the desire of the other is solved, for Kass, by the language of 'surprise' or 'gift', and heterosexual reproduction is the mechanism for ensuring that this gift keeps arriving. For all Kass's (American) affinity for a life that is not overly regulated by the state (private families making private choices), the heterosexual family he conjures (posing as a universal kind of family) appears wired to reproduce a certain (liberal, patriarchal) version of the state. What he seems most haunted by in his discussion of cloning is the specter of reproduction without or beyond heterosexual liberal patriarchy. Derrida would appear to be less troubled: 'What is called "the family"? I would not say without hesitation that the family is eternal', comments Derrida in a conversation with Elizabeth Roudinesco, 'What is inalterable, what will continue to traverse History, is that there is, or that there *be something of* a family, some social bond organized around procreation.'[9] Kass would hardly be reassured.

Heterosexual reproduction is decisive, for Kass, because it yokes intention and chance (the decision to procreate and the unpredictability or wildness of genetics) while also fixing them in place, eliminating any possibility of play or contamination. The 'surprise' that seals the human, for Kass, thus finds a (surprising) corollary in human 'sexiness'. If '[g]enetic distinctiveness not only symbolizes the uniqueness of each human life and the independence of its parents that each human child rightfully attains', 'sexiness' is our superpower:

> the beholding of the many splendored world is suffused with desire for union, the animal antecedent of human eros and the germ of sociality. Not by accident is the human animal the sexiest animal ... and also the most aspiring, the most social, the most open, and the most intelligent ... (22).[10]

Rather than a more traditionally conservative disparagement of sexuality that does not lead to reproduction, the pressing problem for Kass, the risk of 'our age', is reproduction that does not originate in sexual desire and binary sexual difference. And one of the privileged figures for such reproduction (and, indeed, a figure for where Kass must 'draw the line') is the clone as 'single-parent child'; the 'usually sad situation of the "single-parent child"' he laments, 'is here deliberately planned and with a vengeance' (23). The 'single-parent child', who was once the result of an 'accident' ('accidental' pregnancy outside of marriage) is now, alarmingly, the stuff of monstrous design, even as the phrase itself, the 'single-parent child', collapses the distinction between the genetic and the social and suggests that *both* nature and culture are patriarchal all the way down. Moreover, this child, the child of a *single mother*, the child who is an aberration and a social problem surely resonates with the 'tangled pathology' of the black matriarchal family as portrayed by the infamous 1965 'Moynihan Report', as well as with Ronald Reagan's 'welfare queen', site of fantastic, uncontrolled racialised reproduction that somehow escapes the mastery of white heteropatriarchy and is thus rendered abject (even as it is also conjured by and used strategically for

'GENE FOR GENE' 261

conservative, racist discourse).[11] It is the child of this demonised mother (most often a disenfranchised woman of colour) who, in an oddly intensified form ('deliberately planned and with a vengeance'), is reborn in Kass's account as the clone child. Kass's symptomatic rhetorical collapse of nature and culture in the figure of the 'single-parent child' invokes a shadowy form of matriarchal social organisation and exposes his fear of cloning as, among other things, a fear of the racialisation of the idealised white mother and child.[12] Heterosexual reproduction, human 'sexiness', as Kass puts it, protects us from this version of maternal sovereignty, even as its patriarchal version secretly endorses reproduction-as-cloning (as long as the 'clone' is the sole issue of the father).[13]

The ideal child of Kass's anti-cloning imaginary is not only a 'gift' and a 'surprise'; this child is also written into being with all the fantastic authority of a signature. Good (proper?) conception takes place, according to Kass, in the form of a mutual affirmative speech act: the consenting couple says 'Yes!' and thereby conceives a new and singular human being (24). Kass does imagine other less desirable scenes of conception, including those that result in the production of 'bastards' (22), but the consenting heterosexual couple who engage in an affirmative speech act constitute one pole and the parent with their clone child represents, fantasmatically, the other. 'Our genetic individuality is not humanly trivial', he continues, 'It shows itself forth in our distinctive appearance through which we are everywhere recognized; it is revealed in our "signature" marks of fingerprints and our self-recognizing immune system;[14] it symbolizes and foreshadows exactly the unique never-to-be repeated character of each human life' (21). Kass's figure here is curious, not only because it suggests that genetic 'writing' (merely) produces *effects* of subjectivity (making it harder to fetishise the singular individual), but also because, as any reader of Derrida will know, the signature cannot but expose us to the workings of iterability: 'effects of signature are the most common thing in the world', he writes; 'But the condition of possibility of those effects is simultaneously, once again, the condition of their impossibility, of the impossibility of their rigorous purity.'[15] I can only sign a document insofar as I can also forge my own signature, and in this sense every act of signing is an instance of cloning. In light of this, one might choose to reflect upon the illustrations that accompany 'The Wisdom of Repugnance'. The first is a (rather belaboured?) drawing of Frankenstein's monster wearing a shirt featuring (presumably) cloned sheep; more interesting, however, are the three photographs of large-eyed toddlers (probably clad in diapers, although we can only see them from the shoulders up). I'm assuming that we are not supposed to think these toddlers are clones, or represent clones, but rather that they are to serve as immediate evidence of the desirability and rightness of natural heterosexual reproduction; but how would we know? Are they self-evidently non-repugnant?

In fact, it is with its insistence on 'The Wisdom of *Repugnance*' that Kass's essay most obviously courts its own symptomatic assessment. Kass asserts that most of us, from the man or woman in the street to the intellectual, from the religious person to the non-believer, find the idea of human cloning offensive, grotesque, revolting, repugnant, repulsive, *perverse* – even if we can't articulate why this would be the case. He explains why it is right that we should respond in this way even as he wields the rhetorical clout of the sanctified and unspeakable. But does the clone really (and immediately) invoke repugnance? Surely most of us, asked to conjure a feeling associated with clones and cloning, would think of the uncanny, not 'repugnance'?[16] The uncanny registers as an experience of impurity and border disturbance (womb and/or tomb? living and/or dead? mechanical and/or animate? singular and/or multiple? same and/or different?), whereas 'repugnance' functions as a defensive reassertion of a pure and endangered opposition ('the functioning of oppositions', Derrida writes, 'always has the effect of erasing differentiality').[17] Kass's account reveals its patriarchal proclivities by focusing on reproductive decision (consent) and parenting, while entirely neglecting the surely *uncanny* liminality of gestation. It is as if 'natural heterosexual difference' operates as a screen that effaces its own effacement of the maternal affinity for the material-semiotic and a different framing of the problematics of iterability and thus of reproduction. Once again, Kass's exemplary anti-cloning position becomes readable as a mode of panic about the maternal, insofar as the maternal is bound up with the deconstruction of sacrosanct oppositions: human/animal, human/machine, repetition/difference, speech/writing, matter/meaning. The clone child, we might even say, presents (for Kass? for us?) one of the many possible faces of a post-patriarchal maternal sovereignty.[18]

III. 'My life as Ani's mother starts here'

Carola Dibbell's *The Only Ones* (2015) is set mostly in the greater New York area and New York State with forays into Vermont and Canada, although it references India and other locations outside of the United States that are part of a global reproductive services marketplace. The world depicted approaches a state of nature, characterised as it is by ongoing pandemics, all traceable back to what the narrator refers to as 'the Big One'.[19] Extreme right-wing groups (the Knights of Life – regularly referred to in the novel as 'The Knights of fucking Life' (24) – and the

'GENE FOR GENE' 263

Canadian knights of [fucking] life [!]) traverse the countryside, while some governmental structures remain, precariously, in place (a Board of Ethics, various mysterious Inspectors, some forms of public education). This is a world in which pre-existing and familiar forms of social inequality have become exacerbated: the wealthy inhabit private protective Domes – Nassau County is, for example 'all personal Domes' – and the narrator will eventually work in some of these domes as a house cleaner. She comments wryly on the folly of private solutions to public crises: 'They did not think that far ahead. They built them personal because they did not want to share. Then they saw that didn't work. Too late now' (176).

The narrative is an address recorded in 2079, although the reader won't learn the identity of the addressees until the end of the novel. The narrator, the hardboiled Inez Cissy Fardo ('The test was invasive ... I had worse' (36)), who goes by '*I*', is a resource-less but resourceful woman of colour, whose bodily products have a certain marketplace value, because she is a 'hardy' specimen, having survived numerous diseases and associated lab tests: 'I did not like sex and tried to pitch other things, like blood or urine. I got no idea what they did with it. They even bought teeth sometimes. I think they wore them on a string, for luck. They even bought fingernails' (12–13).[20] As the narrative progresses, *I*'s market value increases, because she turns out to be a particular kind of 'hardy' specimen, one with immunity to all known forms of disease. *I*'s account of employment possibilities outlines various positions in the 'Life' industry – one can be a Courier, a Subject, a Donor, a Host (or a Virgin Host), or a Client – but *I* will eventually become a 'Tech'. *I* is tough and curious (and often very funny), and she is characterised not only by her ability to stay alive, but also by her formidable narrative desire (a desire she will pass on to her daughter).

It is on a particular paid errand to a farm upstate where *I* first encounters Rauden Sachs, Doctor of Veterinary Medicine and owner of a small private operation in reproductive services, who wants to make use of *I*'s 'product' and who eventually develops a more personal and intimate relationship with her (a couple of 'sex' scenes consist entirely of Rauden and *I* working in a lab together to produce 'viables' – followed by smoking and listening to jazz[21]). After detailing a very atypical 'pregnancy' and 'delivery', much of the rest of the narrative is devoted to the story of *I*'s life with her daughter (and clone), Ani ('any', 'anyone', 'a clone is like anyone'), the true love of her life, and *I*'s 'only one'. *I* struggles as a sole parent to nurture and educate Ani and to make a 'different' and good life for her despite her 'Special Needs'. She conceals from Ani the true story of her origin, but when, at sixteen, Ani finds out about the cloning that produced her, she sets out on her own quest to find the one person who might be said to have wanted her to come into existence. To fund her effort to locate this trace of desirousness, Ani will herself go to work as a reproductive labourer, but, unlike her mother, Ani is able to adopt the role of Host and thus experiences a 'regular' – what we would call a 'surrogate' – pregnancy. Close to term, Ani asks *I* to come for the birth and asserts that she is 'still not doing intervention'. *I* tells Ani that this is 'dangerous', and Ani replies: 'Ma! It's always dangerous. Come on. How I was born it was intervene this, intervene that. I just want to see what happens if we don't. I just want to try the regular way for once' (337–8). The results are tragic.

Dibbell clearly wants to write about the work of mothering in *The Only Ones*, but why, we might ask, is she also drawn to the concept of cloning? What, in other words, do the first and second halves of Dibbel's novel have to do with one another? It seems that for Dibbell, as for Kass (and Derrida), cloning 'embodies' something about 'our age'. *The Only Ones*' clones are a product of our dystopian neoliberal contemporary, where pandemics rage, fertility is in crisis, and reproduction is commodified. Cloning in this sense stands in for all forms of neoliberal baby making, and *I* would be an example of what Krølokke and Pant refers to as 'the repropreneur'.[22] Reproduction, as we know, has been drawn further into the marketplace and, as Emma Maniere argues in her discussion of contemporary surrogacy, reproduction also plays a crucial role in the economic management of class distinction. 'The economic power differential between the wealthy and the proletariat', she writes, 'is "cleansed" ["via a contract"] and remade as an equal relation'.[23] And yet *The Only Ones* conveys no nostalgia for something right, valuable or essentially human that has been 'lost' in this transformation of reproductive possibilities. It displays, alongside its condemnation of the appalling exploitation of *I*'s body, being and labour (exploitation that treats her as both an animal and a machine), a fascination with – even an affinity for – certain aspects of this brave new world. As *I* who so markedly prefers tech to sex says, 'You are going to hear what people say about girls like me, how we are exploited, got no self-esteem or worth or none of that, the life we live. They never say it's interesting' (31).[24]

Needless to say, Dibbell's *I* does *not* find cloning to be 'repugnant' or taboo. When *I* first 'consents' to her own cloning (as contractual paid labour), Rauden (the ex-veterinarian and rogue bioengineer) and Rini Jaffur (the customer and intending mother) attempt to explain the process in a rather belaboured manner. *I* characteristically cuts through their circumlocutions, dispelling anything as conventional and prescribed as horror, and says, unfazed: 'You want to make a clone from me':

'GENE FOR GENE'   265

> So now it's like they are both stunned, like what fell on their heads
> is a heavy box. They are never going to talk again, they are so
> stunned. 'Well!' Rauden gets out. 'You can call it that if you want.
> We prefer SCNT. Somatic Cell Nuclear Transfer.' I look at both
> of them, like, that's the answer? 'You could just say Transfer', he
> goes, 'if it's simpler.' (62)

In this initial planned scenario the embryos will be created using *I*'s
'soma' and Rini's mitochondria.[25] But Ani, the child who survives this
reproductive project, beset as it is with failures (both material/physical
and socio-political), is neither genetically *nor* gestationally linked to Rini
(it will turn out, much to Rini's distress, to be impossible to 'use' her
mitochondria or uterus: "'It would not be my genes! It would not be
my womb!" She is on speaker so everybody hears. "IT WOULD NOT
EVEN BE MY MITOCHONDRIA'" (83)). There will be no (genetic)
link, then, between the initial intention to make this baby (Rini's desire
for a child) and the baby (Ani) that comes into being: Ani is (or becomes)
only *I*'s 'child' – 'gene for gene [her] living replica' (153). In other hands,
this scenario might exemplify the dystopia of meaningless reproduction,
but *The Only Ones* is too canny about origins and intentions to simply
reproduce this familiar narrative.

I is nothing if she is not a plain clothes poststructuralist feminist
theorist and de-mystifier of origins. She observes several times in the
course of the novel that 'the regular way' doesn't seem to have come
with any of the guarantees heteropatriarchal nostalgia would claim
for it. When *I* 'consents' to become a mother despite her own – and
everyone else's – plans and intentions, Henry, Rauden's identical (!)
twin brother, tells her, 'Well, I think that used to happen even the
regular way. Even when it was planned. You plan and plan and then
whoosh!' (104) (in this formulation, 'whoosh' would be the equivalent of the Derridean event). But that is not all. For Dibbell, cloning is a way to take on the metaphysical conundrum of sameness
and difference in the context of a relationship between parent and
child which itself allegorises (human) futurity. Rather than positing a
kind of alternative feminist utopia or simply decrying contemporary
modes of oppression, Dibbell explores the interruption of liberal heteropatriarchal reproduction, an interruption notably free of the par-
anoid and policing anxiety so apparent in Kass's approach to cloning.
While *The Only Ones* doesn't deploy the term 'iterability' in Derrida's
sense, I would contend that this is precisely what the novel explores
in a material-semiotic feminist mode, attuned to the processes of
reproductive bodies and maternal care.

In some ways, it would have been too easy for Dibbell to have drawn on her own lived experience and depicted a *simply* adoptive mother, and therefore a mother-child relation at least apparently without the enigmatic material traces of a prior relation (a relation before relation); instead, Dibbell chooses a riskier story. *I* is so much Ani's parent (having provided all of the genetic material as well as the only human gestational and parturitional labour) that, in this instance, the reproductive relation faces a new kind of crisis, intensified as it is up to the point of its own phantasmatic dissolution. If adoptive parents or children risk facing a crisis of inauthenticity, the child who is her mother's clone represents a kind of relational excess, the fantasy of a perfect repetition, and hence Rauden's panicked insistence during the birth scene: 'She's not the mother. Technically she's not even the birth mother. She's the Original' (95). Here, too, the way Dibbell chooses to represent gestational process and the event of birth is perfect. The clone embryos produced via SCNT are nurtured in clunky artificial wombs, or tanks, developed and used for cattle ('that cockamamie hoo-ha Lucas dreamed up' (83)) and supplemented by the 'regular': *I*'s frozen uterine tissue and her miked-in heartbeat.[26] Rauden explains to *I* the system he has designed to function as a prosthetic placenta using 'regular' blood: 'Rauden said, "The child doesn't exactly eat the product that comes in. It doesn't use its mouth. Even when it has one. It takes the product in and turns it into, ahem, itself. Herself. The product is like letters of the alphabet. She turns them into words. The words say what her body is. Well! Who knows who says what?" Everyone tried to ignore Rauden when he talked like this. It was interesting though' (88). Here Rauden articulates – and *I* shows interest in – 'being' as a material-semiotic communications system. Such passages draw on the research that Dibbell conducted for the novel, but they also invoke a decidedly material-feminist account of reproduction. In a further elaboration of the material-semiotic communications system we learn that hormones also convey 'messages' ('The hormones is a message the viables send to me, like, "I! Conk out. Breast! Hurt very bad." It worked" (88–9)), and while *I* certainly does not understand herself to be in a maternal relation to the developing 'viables' (who are very much a group project, as well as a commercial endeavour), she will remark upon the continuity of such a messaging system in her early relationship with Ani: 'Remember the hormone used to send a message, do this or do that? If a baby is dirty, she sends a message herself. The way she sends it is, hit the roof' (111).

It is not only hormones that constitute a kind of *écriture feminine*, Dibbell's novel suggests, but names themselves. Four of the five 'viables' that Rini has contracted for die in their tanks, and this includes 'Ani'

'GENE FOR GENE' 267

at twenty-six weeks. After a small ceremony that involves burning the remains, Rini extracts a promise from a resistant *I*; if 'anything happens', *I* must promise to take the remaining child. Rini disappears late in the 'third trimester' and reappears via the vid phone after the 'delivery' insisting that *I* should *deliver* on her promise, because 'something has happened ... I found Madhur' (102). Rini is in Delhi where she has found two girls who survived two different devastating viruses, and the older one is named Madhur. Rini quickly renames the younger one, so that she will be called Madhur too: 'What about *this* Madhur?' *I* asks of Rini, and Rini responds, 'I give her to you' (102). Here the word 'this' (adjective? definite article?) at once performs a very mundane function of differentiation and represents a mini crisis for the humanist subject (are all Madhurs clones of one another?). When Rini checks in to ensure that *I* has taken responsibility for the baby (and kept her away from Rauden who might sell her), *I* gives her an update on Madhur, the newborn. '"Who is Madhur?" Rini asks; "The child I want to call Madhur is not your child ... Madhur is my child."' *I* has to come up with a name for the new child, and her account of this naming also gives us a version of where Dibbell's title comes from:

> Sometimes I think Ani was the last unplanned child anyone heard of. Madhur was planned. Ani was a kind of accident. We all planned for Rini to have Madhur. Rini's baby was planned. Mine was not. So because she was unplanned, I had to come up with a name in a hurry. Ani was the only one I had. (106)

The name in Dibbell's fiction clearly functions as a technological 'supplement' in the sense that it is simultaneously 'external' and contingent even as there is no being or relation without this supplementarity. A name is a privileged example of an address (or apostrophe) misrecognised as self-sustaining and simply referential. Who is the 'Ani' that will feature prominently in the rest of this narrative? What is her connection to the first 'Ani' who died in 'utero', and what is her connection (or what are her connections) to the many Madhurs? These questions are just as pressing as the question of Ani's genetic relationship to *I*. Does Ani only come into being when *I* (re)selects her name, makes a 'choice' – when she has no options ('I had to come up with a name in a hurry. Ani was the only one I had')? *The Only Ones* invokes the titular phrase in a variety of ways, but this one is particularly poignant. 'The only one I had', refers to a kind of recycled piece of materiality – the name, the materiality of the signifier – that carries inchoate traces of desire.

I is an impoverished single mother who wants something better and *different* for her child, but she is also *any* parent (Ani's parent) grappling in an ordinary way with the otherness of any other. Although the clone in Dibbell's novel, as in Kass's polemic, is a figure for the single-parent child, neither *I* nor the novel partake of any moral panic about cloning or single-parenting: *I* is too busy making sure that Ani stays alive and marvelling in her very aliveness (the phrase 'still alive' in reference to Ani punctuates the novel). Instead, Dibbell asks us to register the intensity of mothering as something returned to us anew after – or in the midst of – apocalypse. This aspect of *The Only Ones* recalls the work of those black feminist theorists who find something resistant in the maternal legacy of enslaved women misrecognised and pathologised via the Moynihan Report. As Angela Davis writes,

> The designation of the black woman as a matriarch is a cruel misnomer. It is a misnomer because it implies stable kinship structures within which the mother exercises decisive authority. It is cruel because it ignores the profound traumas the black woman must have experienced when she had to surrender her child-bearing to alien and predatory economic interests.[27]

Nevertheless, Davis also argues that the enslaved woman 'performed the only labor of the slave community which could not be directly and immediately claimed by the oppressor ... [and thus] by virtue of the brutal force of circumstances, the black woman was assigned the mission of promoting the consciousness and practice of resistance' (5). While Dibell's racialised protagonist is in no straightforward way aligned with the legacy of slavery, the figure invoked by Kass (the clone as 'the ultimate single-parent child'), and iterated by *The Only Ones*, surely partakes of a kind of 'flickering on and off' of race and the racialisation of reproduction.[28]

At the end of her famous essay, 'Mamma's Baby, Pappa's Maybe: An American Grammar Book', Hortense Spillers refers to the enslaved woman as 'both mother and mother dispossessed'. She continues, 'This problematizing of gender places her, in my view, *out* of the traditional symbolics of female gender, and it is our task to make a place for this different social subject.'[29] It might be useful to consider this structure, as outlined by Spillers, when assessing contemporary feminist uses of the terms 'maternal' and 'postmaternal'.[30] While some feminist theorists are troubled by neoliberalism's affinity for an apparently gender-neutral (and race neutral!) subject and thus by the effacing of women's experience and labour, others are concerned with the relational limitations imposed by traditional kinship structures, structures that often bring with them the essentialising expectation that femininity or womanhood be tied to mothering. With this in mind (and noting that the periodising of feminist theory comes with its own complications and limitations), it's worth recalling Sara Ruddick's *Maternal Thinking* as a text that allows us to recognise the productively 'postmaternal' aspects of Dibbell's novel.[31]

Maternal Thinking de-prioritises 'biologism' by arguing that all mothering is adoptive: ('Even the most passionately loving birthgiver engages in a social, adoptive act when she commits herself to sustain an infant in the world ... no life can survive without mothering' (51)). But Ruddick also emphasises an at once indispensable and simultaneously supplementary *decision*: the decision to nurture (new) life. Dibbell's novel draws attention to this way of thinking about the maternal in its very structure. *The Only Ones* is divided into several sections (The Life, The Work, The Ropes, The Garden Apartment, The Education, The Heritage, Ani Fardo, and The Only Ones), but also, notably, into two parts. The move from depictions of reproductive labour that are *not* mothering to a narrative dominated by the work of maternal labour is marked by *I*'s 'decision' to become a mother: 'MY LIFE AS ANI'S MOTHER STARTS RIGHT HERE' (109).[32] *I* is characteristically blunt about the transition: 'She [Ani] was still Rauden's Project', she writes, 'She used to be my job. She's not my job now. I don't get paid' (109). When Ani later asks about her origins ('*Ma! Did you steal me?*'), *I* tries to reassure her: 'No, Ani, no. You were a gift' (324). But what we know as readers is that Ani was a 'gift' accepted or decided upon under duress: a giving that, whatever it will have been, was not in advance an indisputable good. This decision, neither 'free' nor determined (if it were determined it would not be a decision), performatively founds both the mother-child relation and simultaneously creates two different (or differing) beings: a mother and a child. While these are the plot details of a work of speculative fiction, they also posit a kind of primal scene of parenting as a model for the social as such. Hence, this scene differs in important respects from the scene offered by Kass of the consenting heterosexual partners who guard humanity (and human specificity) by managing just the right balance of conscious rational decision making and unpredictability. There is a vulnerability at play in Kass's genetic unpredictability and in Dibbell's decision that is neither free nor determined; but the vulnerability is simultaneously controlled and moralised away in Kass's account, insofar as it participates in a natural order that is only a hair's breadth away from the theological domain. The decision to care for another or others ('Ani' other), as presented in *The Only Ones*, is without any such ultimate form of protection.

The addressee of a narrative fiction is often elusive, but it is clear from the opening pages of *The Only Ones* that there *is* a specific addressee:

> Before I start, let me say really fast, Don't worry. You're not in trouble. I will not track you down or hurt you – nothing like that. I just got a few things to tell you that you really need to hear, and you need to hear them from me, not someone else. OK. That's it for now. Here we go.

Readers will eventually come to realise that this 'you' refers to the other 'clones', the other viables produced by SCNT who have gone on to live their different and similar lives, having been marketed and distributed globally. Our assumption, until the very end, is that the addressee is a singular 'you',[33] and, in some ways this singularity *is* always preserved; the addressee *is* always a singular you, suggesting a certain ethics of address: each one, or any one, may – or may not – receive the message: 'I don't know your name or address. I don't your age or who your Parent is' (347). Indeed, it is precisely this tension between something like a multitude and something like singularity that *The Only Ones* explores so pointedly via the trope of the clone.[34] *The Only Ones* suggests that it is neither birth nor genes that secure human being. *I* will explain to her addressees (every reader) that genes, like words, can mean 'two things or more': 'like the Free School was not free, and Life is not life, but also bear the child or bear the pain or bear the animal or, you know bear with me. Even mean can mean two things or more' (352). No birth has a rational foundation, *I* asserts ('All I'm saying is, why were you born? ... You were born the reason anyone was. Because you're lucky. You're lucky to be alive' (353)). What is instead suggested by *The Only Ones* is that we are secured – or maybe 'held' would be the better term – by a decision that we have good reason to call '[post]maternal'.

Notes

1. I. Kissena Fardo in Carola Dibbell, *The Only Ones* (Columbus, OH: Two Dollar Radio, 2015), 223.
2. Jacques Derrida in Jacques Derrida and Elisabeth Roudinesco, 'Disordered Families', in *For What Tomorrow ...: A Dialogue* (Stanford, CA: Stanford University Press, 2004), 38.
3. Leon R. Kass, 'The Wisdom of Repugnance', in *The New Republic*, 2 June 1997, 17–26.
4. Jacques Derrida, *Rogues: Two Essays on Reason* (Stanford, CA: Stanford University Press, 2005), 146–7.

'GENE FOR GENE' 271

5. Derrida, *Rogues*, 147. For Kelly Oliver's Derridean account of what pro-cloning (John Harris) and anti-cloning (Jürgen Habermas) positions have in common, see her *Technologies of Life and Death: From Cloning to Capital Punishment* (New York: Fordham University Press, 2013).

6. Derrida, 'Disordered Families', 38.

7. When Kass unpacks the fantastic function of heterosexuality, he reveals his affinity with what Derrida calls a 'sacrificial structure', aligned with the who-ness of the [human] subject, 'phallogocentrism', and 'carnivorous virility'. Derrida does not, of course, simply dismiss the eating of the other: 'The so-called nonanthropophagic cultures practice symbolic anthropophagy and even construct their most elevated socius, indeed the sublimity of their morality, their politics, and their right on anthropophagy' (Jacques Derrida, '"Eating Well", or the Calculation of the Subject: An Interview with Jacques Derrida', in Eduardo Cadava, Peter Connor and Jean-Luc Nancy, eds, *Who Comes After the Subject?* (London: Routledge, 1991), 114).

8. Kass seems to aspire to protect each and every human being not from cloning so much as from 'birth' itself. See Derrida on 'a birth irreducible to all ontology, to all ontological or phenomenological thinking about originarity' ('The Night Watch' in *Derrida and Joyce: Texts and Contexts*, eds Andrew J. Mitchell and Sam Slote (Albany: SUNY Press, 2013), 92). See also Elissa Marder, 'Derrida's Matrix: The Birth of Deconstruction', in *Oxford Literary Review* 40.1 (2018), 1–19.

9. Derrida, 'Disordered Families', 36.

10. In *Life Death* (trans. Pascale-Anne Brault and Michael Naas (Chicago: University of Chicago Press, 2020)), Derrida references geneticist François Jacob's account of the bacterium which, unlike Kass's human being, is 'without sex appeal', without the 'supplement' of 'sexuality and death' (106).

11. On US Senator and Diplomat Daniel Patrick Moynihan's 1965 report, 'The Negro Family: The Case for National Action', and the myth of the 'welfare queen', see Dorothy Roberts, *Killing the Black Body* (New York: Random House, 1997), 16–17. More recently see Laura Briggs, *How All Politics Became Reproductive Politics: From Welfare Reform to Foreclosure to Trump* (Oakland: University of California Press, 2017), 50–63.

12. In a very different context, Eva Cherniavsky argues that 'the black female body assumes its ironic critical privilege as the site where the contingency of generic/gender designations suddenly passes into view'. See, *That Pale Mother Rising: Sentimental Discourses and the Imitation of Motherhood in 19th-Century America* (Bloomington: Indiana University Press, 1995), 5.

13. Kass inadvertently indicates some sense of this when he cites (with disapproval) those 'John Doe Jr.'s or the III's' who must negotiate the 'burden of living up to a forebear's name' (24). See Angela Davis on the misuse of the term matriarchy when applied to enslaved people and to the legacies of enslavement in 'Reflections on the Black Woman's Role in the Community of Slaves', in *The Massachusetts Review* 13.1–2 (1972), 5.

14. Unlike Kass, who posits the 'self-recognizing immune system' with great surety, Derrida writes: 'In this regard, autoimmunity is not an absolute ill or evil. It enables an exposure to the other, to what and who comes ... Without autoimmunity, with absolute immunity, nothing would ever happen or arrive ...' (*Rogues*, 152). In the context of a discussion of cloning and reproduction, it is also well worth noting the vexed history of the relationship between dominant theories of the immune system and pregnant embodiment. See Aryn Martin and Kelly Holloway, '"Something there is that doesn't love a wall": Histories of the Placental Barrier', in *Studies in History and Philosophy of Biological and Biomedical Sciences* 47 (2014), 300–10.

15. Jacques Derrida, 'Signature, Event, Context', in *Limited Inc.* (Evanston, IL: Northwestern University Press, 1988), 20.

16. On the association between the uncanny and reproduction Elissa Marder writes: 'the more closely one looks at the act of giving birth and the event of being born, the stranger the maternal function becomes'. See *The Mother in the Age of Mechanical Reproduction: Psychoanalysis, Photography, Deconstruction* (New York: Fordham University Press, 2012), 2. Repugnance also plays a role in Ishiguro's famous novel 'about' cloning, *Never Let Me Go* (London: Faber and Faber, 2005). Notably, however, it is not the novel's readers but instead the 'humans' within the text who need to assert their difference from the 'clones' in order to brutally exploit them (and remain blind to the brutality).

17. Derrida, *Life Death*, 18.

18. In his provocative account Gil Anidjar asks us to hear, in 'solicitude', the importance of a *shaking up* of foundational metaphysical oppositions that simultaneously calls for (abandons us to?) supplementary maternal care: 'There where the mother is and carries ... there is shaking and trembling, there is responsibility and – but Derrida does not use the word here – there is solicitude. Or, to begin to make our way back to *Grammatology*, there is "maternal solicitude"' ('Solicitude', in *Derrida Today* 16.1 (2023), 8).

19. Dibbell, *The Only Ones*, 43.

20. A protagonist named 'I' poses obvious problems, but I will use '*I*' (italicised) as opposed to Inez throughout, because this proper name is far too pertinent in a novel about cloning and reproduction. Dibbell's decision to name her protagonist in this way also comments on our linguistically and grammatically shaped – if not determined – sense of subjectivity or selfhood. This version of 'pronoun trouble' is worked out explicitly in the relationship between *I* and Ani, just as it must be worked out in any relationship between a young child and their intimate caregiver.

21. We might read the absence of Kass's 'sexiness' from Dibbell's novel as confirmation of the centrality of such 'sexiness' for Kass's autonomous human subject who can reproduce other such subjects. Alternatively, we could say that Dibbell follows feminist critics like Bowlby and Yaeger who, in different ways, take up the question of reproduction without sex (or sexiness?),

or reproductive scenarios in which 'sex' is the subordinated term, either as a historical-material phenomenon which provokes representational shifts or as an alternative to a hegemonic 'copulative' imaginary. Sex is also pointedly displaced in *The Only Ones* by *I*'s narrative desire, which is aligned with a certain technophilia or proclivity for 'tech'. Somewhat more displaced in the text are the erotics of the mother-child relationship repeated by the figure of the clone and cloning: the mother-child clones figure the interruption that constitutes autoeroticism (rather than 'sexiness').

22. Qtd in France Winddance Twine, *Outsourcing the Womb: Race, Class and Gestational Surrogacy in a Global Market* (New York: Routledge, 2011), 58.

23. Emma Maniere, 'Mapping Feminist Views on Commercial Surrogacy', in *Babies For Sale?: Transnational Surrogacy, Human Rights and the Politics of Reproduction*, ed. Miranda Davies (London: Zed Books, 2017), 325.

24. Dibbell's novel and protagonist are aligned with a version of feminist theory that is critical of a binary anti-tech bias. See Donna Haraway's claim: 'I'd rather be a cyborg than a goddess' in 'A Cyborg Manifesto: Science, Technology, and Socialist-Feminism in the Late Twentieth Century', in *Manifestly Haraway* (Minneapolis: University of Minnesota Press, 2016), 90. Dibbell's novel also answers Dorothy Roberts's call for 'a new reproductive dystopia', representative of neoliberal forms of power and the shifting significance of race in 'Race, Gender, and Genetic Technologies: A New Reproductive Dystopia?', in *Signs* 34.4 (2009), 786.

25. See Catherine Mills, 'Nuclear Families: Mitochondrial Replacement Techniques and The Regulation of Parenthood', in *Science, Technology, and Human Values* 46.3 (2021), 507–27. Mills explicates and explores the legal and ideological status of MtDNA in the UK: 'MtDNA is simultaneously recognized as foundational to the reproduction of the nuclear family and cast as a frivolous extra that can be excluded from it' (518). MRT has not been legalised in the United States.

26. Dibbell references the origins of reproductive medical technology as a subfield of agricultural science and practices of animal breeding. See Melinda E. Cooper, *Life as Surplus: Biotechnology and Capitalism in the Neoliberal Era* (Seattle: University of Washington Press, 2008), 132. See also Dibbell's account of her research for the novel in her interview on Zoran Rosko Vacuum Player 03/02/2015: https://zorosko.blogspot.com/search/label/Carola%20Dibbell (accessed 22/12/2023).

27. Davis, 'Reflections on the Black Woman's Role in the Community of Slaves', 5.

28. Karen Weinbaum writes: 'blackness flickers off and on in our neoliberal present because biocapitalism is a form of racial capitalism that sublates the history of slavery by rendering it a "rationally-necessary moment of the whole", even though this rationally necessary moment must be systematically disavowed for the system to function smoothly', in *The Afterlife of Reproductive Slavery: Biocapitalism and Black Feminism's Philosophy of History* (Durham, NC: Duke University Press, 2019), 11.

29. Hortense Spillers, 'Mama's Baby, Pappa's Maybe: An American Grammar Book', in *Diacritics* 17.2 (1987), 80.

30. See Julie Stephens, *Confronting Postmaternal Thinking: Feminism, Memory, and Care* (New York: Columbia University Press, 2011).

31. Sara Ruddick, *Maternal Thinking: Toward a Politics of Peace* (Boston, MA: Beacon Press, 1995).

32. See Stella Sandford's 'What is Maternal Labour?' for an attempt to think through the 'peculiar difficulty' of the concept, in *Studies in the Maternal* 3.2 (2011), 1–11.

33. Caryl Churchill's 2002 play, *A Number* (New York: Theatre Communications Group) offers a very different account of cloning as a critique of patriarchy and fatherhood without engaging in the kind of speculation about maternity found in *The Only Ones*.

34. This 'singularity' also recalls Derrida's account of the 'signature-event' in *Limited Inc.*, although it is perhaps his later 'machine-event' ('hyphenated to mark the automaticity of the machine together with the spontaneity of the event', Turner, *Visual Cultures As … Recollection* (30)) that more effectively captures how reproductive technology and reproduction-as-technology (Dibbell's 'the regular way'), are bound up in *The Only Ones* with a fidelity or singular attachment to a one-and-only (Ani-one). *I* says to the others: 'How I felt about Ani, and she is the only one I felt that way about – I really don't think it's unique … but the way I cared about Ani, she is the only one' (352). For more on the 'machine-event', gender and technology see Lynn Turner's 'Wind Up: The Machine-Event of Tape', in Astrid Schmetterling and Lynn Turner, *Visual Cultures As … Recollection* (Berlin: Sternberg Press, 2013), 30–52.

14

EROTICS OF DECOMPOSITION: CELLS AND THEIR OCEANS

Elina Staikou

In a time of regressive sexual and reproductive politics – unfailing symptoms of general political regression – we are called to reorganise and expand our strategies, to reorient our goals and intensify our desires: to think erotics of deconstruction.

What follows will mark passages and points of transition where old and new figures of deconstruction intersect, decompose and recompose, releasing transformative and regenerative longings. Spectral figures, genealogical drifts and skipped generations, (de)couplings of friends, sisters and brothers, transient silhouettes and desires for the love of law and the right to love (and then loving beyond law and right), actions of reproductive justice, colour lines and mitochondria lineages, racialised wombs and revolutionary mothering … here are some experiments in diversity that will be set in motion. Thinking sexuality and generation de- and re-composed across matters, sexes and species along with their genetic-technological-symbolic mutations powers experiments in living, loving, knowing, mothering. 'Erotics of decomposition' names the flows of matter and energy along the entangled cyclicity of life/non-life formation, their all-encompassing and transitory intricacy. 'Erotics of decomposition' swallows up 'power and information' – to conjure Audre Lorde's use of 'the erotic' – moving to the explosion of difference that sweeps away the worn-out pathways and the decomposing figures gathered under the semantics of the old word *Geschlecht* (humanity, species, sex, race, nation, generation, family, kinship), to which Derrida devoted his famous seminar of the 1980s.

Erotics of decomposition is more than the 'love of ruins' Derrida divined in Walter Benjamin's casting of the 'figures of the violence of the law' as prefigurations of ruin in its wake and doom.[1] It is more than the blow of a pure, divine (bloodless) violence that destroys positive law and its founding myths of blood, soil and purity of filiation executed in the name of a life absolved of all life/non-life entanglement. Such an erotics is closer to the 'struggle for the deconstruction of the coloniality of power' in all its ramifications that, as Françoise Vergès reminds us, entails more than the expansion of frontiers and the hybridification of figures of law, more than the critique of biopolitics and the political significGeschlechttion of 'bare life'.[2] But to move beyond even this deconstruction and its biocentric qualification, we look to the work of decomposition and its own erotics of the forces of breakdown and diffusion, transfiguration and regeneration captured in the figure of *Eros* in ancient cosmogonies. This will lead us through the deep chemistry and bioenergetics of sub-cellar compositions, the swirls and rotations of elementary components that pass through the cell's metabolic machinery, to their expanded cultural and political significance and transformative potency. We further believe that a radical politics of reproduction (including and moving beyond the legitimation of reproductive desires, powers and rights) must pass through and be renewed by an erotics of decomposition. Our approach designates the maternal as a forcefield with multiple functions and dynamic assignations driven by the bioenergetics of mitochondria (energy generating organelles in the cytoplasm of nearly all eukaryotic cells) and the dissipation of filiation and bloodline. It is perhaps a way of pumping that 'something else entirely than blood' that Derrida calls for in 'Force of Law':

> And finally for what remains to come of or from deconstruction' [*pour ce que la deconstruction rest à venir*], I believe that something else runs through its veins, perhaps without filiation, an entirely different blood or rather something else entirely than blood, be it the most fraternal blood.[3]

Might this 'entirely different' blood without patriarchal filiation be inscribed in the maternal forcefield and its techno-genetic-symbolic mutations? Our question concerns the racial politics of reproduction (not excluding whiteness) in which the deconstruction of the maternal opens a route to radicalise further the deconstruction of fratrocentrism in Derrida's *Politics of Friendship* or the decomposition of *Geschlecht* (humanity, nation, race, family, kinship, sex) in his seminar on philosophical nationalism. The question of the mother, which Derrida always addressed within a logic of surrogacy linked directly to the new reproductive technologies in the unpublished seminar 'Who is the Mother? Birth, Nature, Nation' and in 'Disordered Families', will be revisited here at the level of the cell, the infrastructural biological unit of our material organisation and tiny enclave of the forcefield that powers the growth

EROTICS OF DECOMPOSITION

and mutability of multiplied maternal functions and their biotechnological and symbolic potential.[4] The maternal figures leading the way are the lost, racialised and aborted mothers along with their struggles for reproductive justice and praxis of revolutionary mothering. Our discussion of the microscopic mitochondria is not risking the fallacy of biologism but rather acknowledges the transformative and critical potential released by their biocultural meaning, their interlacement with maternal lineages, especially those that were broken up by the middle passage.

For all their engineering ingenuity, power and wells of information, cells do not know, of course, their biocultural significance. Our human intelligence can only grasp it by means of biotechnological, experimental and critical incisions into the cell's micro-universe. Mitochondria have a paramount place in the history of life on this planet. Thought to have lived as independent organisms over two billion years ago, they were decisively implicated in the evolution of the enucleated and more complex cell – the eukariotic, the origin of our form of life. They are vital components and energy generators in nearly all eukariotic cells apart from blood, skin and sperm cells.[5] Mitochondria are charged with the production of ATP (adenosine triphosphate), the universal energy currency of life, performing essential functions for the cell's metabolism, allowing it to breathe. They can only do their work of respiration on the condition of uniparental inheritance. Biochemist Nick Lane, in his book *Power, Sex, Suicide, Mitochondria and the Meaning of Life*, argues that their manner of passing on their 'tiny but critical genomes', through maternal inheritance, could account for the evolution of the two sexes, giving us access to the deep biological meaning of sexual difference.[6] We will enquire into the power of symbolisation generated by such interpretations and draw links with Derrida's reinscription of sexual difference in *Geschlecht I* onto the ontological plane as powerful source of all sexuality. Cellular bioenergetics host intensive sexual experiments in reproduction and reproductive experiments in sexuality evolving, (de)composing, extending across micro and macro biocultural levels. They entangle the microphysical with the biocultural in our understanding of sex as forcefield of différance, potentiality and diversity.

In their book *What is Sex?* evolutionary biologist Lynn Margulis and science writer Dorion Sagan expand on sex as a force in the physical universe, a certain inkling, 'want or desire' for expenditure manifested in the flows of matter and energy 'even before the evolution of the first life forms' up to 'the experience of sexual temptation or pleasure'.[7] Sex is an enactment of 'a cosmic breakdown more primordial than life itself, one mandated in the very meaning of the Second Law of Thermodynamics'.[8] A mandate to spend, expedite, experiment, degrade, generate disorder in

278   ELINA STAIKOU

order and vice versa. This is how we understand 'erotics': as force ready
to blast open any interpretation of biological destiny confined by the
logic of binarism or the pre-erotic composure of primordial *Geschlecht*
(sex, race, species, humanity) in the Heideggerian sense. Our approach
is more akin to Audre Lorde's powerful erotics that measures emergent
senses of self against singular feelings and embodiments or to the tremendous energy of oceanic erotics in Alexis Pauline Gumbs's ode to
multispecies loving. Getting a feel for these threads (*mitos*) and their interlacing in bio-physical-cultural knots (*chondros*) will take us from *Politics of
Friendship* and the question of *Geschlecht* via the multiple functions of the
maternal or else, the countless ways of losing your mother, to the uses
of erotics, pleasure and mothering activisms practised and tendered by
black feminist and queer thinkers.

Erotics of decomposition

Yet in a strange way 'erotics of decomposition' would be philosophy itself.
Would Heidegger subscribe to this sentence? For him *Eros* signifies the
decay of the originary *phileîn* (φιλεῖν), its degeneration to the *phileîn* to
sophón, philo-sophy. In his reading of *Was ist das – die Philosophie* in *Politics
of Friendship* and in 'Heidegger's Ear: Philopolemology (Geschlecht IV)'
Derrida retraces in the pre-Socratic *phileîn* revived in the Heideggerian
motif of *Versammlung*, the genealogical path leading up to its political
configuration in fratrocentrism and autochthonism. Philosophy arrives
late on the scene, erupting with the question of Being as tension, strife,
discord and desire (*Eros*) for what is lost, wanting and enquired after, that
is, the 'originary accord' or 'harmony' (named by Heraclitus' early word
for Being, *phileîn*):

> Thought (*Das Denken*) would have become philosophy only in
> the wake of this eroticization of the questioning around being
> (Was ist das Seiende, insofem es ist?). 'Heraclitus and Parmenides
> were not yet "philosophers".' The 'step' to philosophy would have
> been prepared by sophistry, then accomplished by Socrates and
> Plato.[9]

Phileîn is the originary pre-erotic moment in the experience of being
as gathering that the derivative and decayed types of philia, including
philosophy, have no authority to question (*erotō*, ἐρωτῶ); 'the question
form τί ἐστίν "what is?" does not hold the ultimate competence. It is
itself rendered possible de jure by the movement of φιλεῖν'.[10] The ero-
tisation of the question of being or philosophical *Eros* is experienced

EROTICS OF DECOMPOSITION   279

as tension and strife with and within *philein* for which there is longing, nostalgia and mourning: 'And with this unexpected arrival of a philosophical Eros plunged in mourning, we are not far from the question of Geschlecht.'[11] The ontological question is tightly implicated with that of *Geschlecht* as the question of sexual difference from its inception.[12] What attracts Heidegger to pre-erotic *philein* – reinstated as a consistent gesture throughout his existential analytic – is the possibility of thinking beyond all anthropological, biological, psychological, ethico-political planes and traits (his chosen example of ontic neutralisation being that of sexuality) in view of yielding the bare structure of Dasein.

Yet such indiscrimination between the different types of love and friendship (which would be degenerate figures and inadequate translations of originary *philein*) appears to resemble *aimance* as another poetic thinking word that cuts across all figures of love, eros and *philein* albeit opening onto genealogical trajectories and political prefigurations that, rather than neutralising difference, appeal to 'dissemblance, heterogeneity, dissymmetry, disproportion, incommensurability, nonexchange, the excess of every measure and thus of all symmetry'.[13] Tension, difference and strife are not foreclosed within the originary gathering, which Heidegger nevertheless would like to imagine appeased and held together in polysemic and pre-erotic tranquillity. Derrida detects therein a covert strategy for mobilising the positive and powerful source of every possible sexuality,[14] a chance of affirmation of the offspring of the most anarchic and 'irreducible poleros' ('this condensation of the political, polemos and eros') charged with possibilities that are not emptied out in existential bareness but lived in the flesh.[15] Eros (Ἔρως) with its semantic and cosmogonic alliance to Eris (Ἔρις, discord, dissonance, quarrel) would be the an-archic, pre-originary *dynamis* generative of order out of disorder (and vice versa), of organisation out of chaos (and vice versa), setting everything in motion while giving off all (trans-) formative and (de- and re) generative potential. This is the other way of understanding 'erotics of de-composition'.

'Decomposition' is a recurrent theme in Derrida's reading of Heidegger's 'Language in the Poem, A Discussion on Georg Trakl's Poetic Work' in *Geschlecht III: Sex, Race, Nation, Humanity*, and appears to catalyse the profound equivocality of all singular words and places in that text. It is the sign of a decaying and belligerent humanity but also of its slow decline towards *das Land*, the 'homecoming' to a promised dwelling where it will have disposed of its embattled and decomposed forms. Decomposition signifies the decay and corruption of nations and generations at war but also the promise of a new beginning. It is a strange text that pursues a selective reading of Trakl's poetry without apparent method, justification or context, a reading that, according to Derrida, seems 'arbitrary, capricious and doomed to improvisation'[16] but draws its coherence from the Heideggerian gesture repeated throughout the *Geschlecht* series of suspending everything ('scientific, epistemological, hermeneutic, poetical, historiographical, even philosophical') that would detract from gaining access to what is essential. Heidegger's reading of Trakl leaps from poem to poem and from line to line in the manner of 'metonymic transition' drawing out and lining up figures and places that form a passageway back to the source of the originary and recomposed *Geschlecht*.[17] We follow a procession of ambiguous figures (pre-erotic couplings of brother, friend and sister, the madman who sees through reason, the animal who is not bestial, the dead who is the unborn child) set in motion by a line from Trakl's 'Springtime of the Soul II' ('It is, the soul, something strange on earth') and led by the stranger towards the reversal of the 'decomposed form of the human'.[18] We are struck by a vertiginous scene of war and generation, from which the spectral absence of the mother seems to entail a genealogical leap, the skipping of a generation between grandfathers and grandsons and the decomposition of all figures involved.[19] All these transient figures of *Geschlecht* seem to leap out onto different interpretive trajectories and questions about humanity, species, kinship, animality, sexual difference and the double form (pre-erotic or 'polerotic') of their 'decomposition'. Bringing the wider context of Derrida's reflection on 'philosophical nationality' and 'nationalism' in the *Geschlecht* series in contact with 'femonationalism', we would like to follow the figure of the racialised mother as she leads another 'path of strangers' back to a different scene of generation and towards a praxis of revolutionary mothering.[20]

Dungeons and wombs

In *Lose Your Mother, A Journey Along the Atlantic Slave Route*, Saidiya Hartman gives this definition of the slave on the path of strangers:

> The most universal definition of the slave is a stranger. Torn from kin and community, exiled from one's country, dishonored and violated, the slave defines the position of the outsider. She is the perpetual outcast, the coerced migrant, the foreigner, the shame-faced child in the lineage.[21]

Hartman's journey along the Atlantic Slave Route takes her to Ghana, a chosen and imagined destination, dictated not by a genealogical or family trail but only by 'the path of strangers impelled towards the sea'.[22]

EROTICS OF DECOMPOSITION

281

This is a story of an impossible homecoming to a place where one can only 'avow the loss that inaugurates one's existence', where you always lose your mother.[23] The history of slavery as continued dispossession and the vision of 'racial solidarity' born by 'captives, exiles and orphans and in the aftermath of the Atlantic trade slave' has always been expressed 'in the language of kinship because it both evidenced the wound and attempted to heal it. The slave and the ex-slave wanted what had been severed: kin.'[24] Different yearnings of homecoming, different imperatives for memory and oblivion, different hopes and disenchantments shaped the experiences of generations of slave descendants. 'My generation', writes Hartman, 'was the first that came here with the dungeon as our prime destination', not 'to dodge the ghosts of slavery but to confront them' unlike the hope that had been nourished by Maya Angelou that 'if she succeeded in keeping the ugly history of slavery at a distance, then perhaps she could be something more than a stranger, perhaps she would pass as a young Ghanaian woman'.[25] There is a difference in the idioms that the confrontation with the ugly histories of slavery or conjuration of the past are expressed in, according to one's place and ancestry:

> In Ghana, kinship was the idiom of slavery, and in United States, race was. The language of kinship absorbed the slave and concealed her identity within the family fold (at least that was the official line), whereas the language of race set the slave apart from man and citizen and sentenced her to an interminable servitude.[26]

The colour line between the slave and the free separating Africans and Europeans since the sixteen and seventieth centuries had hardened with the lines of division 'between kin and stranger, neighbor and alien', which decided who 'lived and died, who was sold and who was protected' during the era of the Atlantic slave trade.[27] The first word Hartman hears, the word she is 'summoned' by when she arrives in Elmina, was 'Obruni', stranger.[28] On the threshold, there is separation of kin from stranger, the boundary that Hartman is seeking to cross but can only see slipping back throughout her reckoning with ruins and ghosts of slavery. Losing one's kin, losing one's mother, having no choice but to mould one's identity out of a history of dispossession in a 'hostile country'[29] becomes the source of dreams, of the romance of origins, promises of return and the myth of the mother.

Hartman's return to Ghana takes her back to a 'tale of creation' or yet another scene of generation where the mother is absent.[30] This event of birth inaugurated by the mother's loss assumes its Biblical dimension out of the horror it wreaks: 'Adam and Eve were created in this filthy pit.

So the British called the first man and woman plucked from the dungeon and bound aboard a slave ship, replaying the drama of birth and expulsion in the Africa trade.'[31] The 'filthy pit' is the Cape Coast Castle, which the British designed to warehouse slaves and which became the headquarters for the Royal Africa Company and its successor, the company of Merchants Trading to Africa at the end of the seventeenth century.[32] The slave-house was built underground to deter rebellion and although this 'grand design' looked more like a tomb for piling up decomposing corpses, what the British saw in 'the dungeon was a womb in which the slave was born'.[33] In fact, the British called the dungeon a 'factory', a word documenting, Hartman remarks, 'the indissoluble link between England's industrial revolution and the birth of human commodities': 'The miracle of the slave trade was that it resuscitated useless lives and transformed waste into capital [...] What Aimé Césaire later described as "walking compost hideously promising tender cane and silky cotton."'[34] This was the setting for the scene of creation that Hartman conjures at her visit at the Cape Coast Castle's dungeon, whose floor was layered with the 'compressed remains of captives – feces, blood, and exfoliated skin'.[35] She continues 'Human life sprang from a black abyss, and from dust to muck we traced our beginning. Base elements were the substrate of life. Blood and shit ushered us into the world.'[36] The waste of human life and the 'human' in decomposition pressed hard not only against stone floors but against intractable histories of endless dispossession and relentless extraction and the colonial logics and narratives that sanctioned them, this is where this journey takes her, takes us back. But it also helps us retrace another hidden or murky genealogy that brings back the figure of the grieved and bereft mother of the enslaved child and the neglected history of colonial and racialised reproductive politics, of afflicted mothers and violated wombs.

In the historiography of the slave trade, Françoise Vergès notes, 'African mothers have been overlooked, their role ignored, despite the fact that never before had a modern economic system so extensively and brutally plundered the wombs of black women.'[37] The rape and appropriation of the wombs of women, to be sure, did not first occur with the slave trade. It is the stuff of primitive myths; it fashions archaic tales about the structure of kinship and the assignation of parental functions and rights. What happened with the African slave trade, and which was without precedent, was the racialisation of and racist (and rapist) aggression towards black women's bodies and wombs, which were 'turned into the essential element of the production of a mobile, sexualised, and racialised work force'.[38] This marked the beginning of a long and ongoing history of racialised and extremely violent reproductive politics, which Vergès analyses in terms of the coloniality of power in the French Republic and

EROTICS OF DECOMPOSITION

its overseas departments, an analysis that can be extended, of course, to countless other examples and geographies.[39]

How does the figure of the racialised mother enter the scene of *Geschlecht*? Retracing her stepping in and out of the genealogical trail in her own inconspicuous manner does not aim at reinserting the question of race in the analytic of *Dasein*. That is not to say that questioning 'race' (one of the meanings of *Geschlecht*) is avoidable nor that it is not implicated in Heidegger's thought in essential and disquieting ways.[40] For all the decomposing figures of *Geschlecht* mentioned earlier are on their way to *das Land*, the imagined country of the early Western humanity. This occidental race that is said to be granted privileged access to Being does not seem to question nor even see the historical and ideological constitution of its self-entitlement. Still, Derrida sees in Heidegger's gesture of suspending all anthropological traits and relations that obstruct access to the bare existential structure of *Dasein* – reserving in it, however, a place for the 'voice of the friend' as Derrida analyses in *Geschlecht IV* – and, foremost, in the neutralisation of sexual difference, the chance of an affirmation of *Dasein* that is in its starkness the potent source of sexual diversity and a site of openness and hospitality. We sense in the figure of the racialised mother, her struggles and trajectories, the discharging of an energy that would quicken the decomposition of the old forms of *Geschlecht* while generating and activating other possibilities, desires and powers, all the eruptions of *Eros* or *aimance*, or, in Hartman's words 'a promise of affiliation better than that of brothers and sisters'.[41]

In their book *Reproductive Justice, An Introduction*, Loretta J. Ross and Rickie Solinger offer a chronicle of the racial institutionalisation of control over fertility, reproduction and motherhood in the United States after slavery to the present showing how 'over time, every pregnant woman and every baby born was racialized, marked for inclusion or exclusion' in what was seen as 'a white country':[42]

> After slavery ended and the babies of African Americans no longer automatically increased the wealth of slave-owning whites, laws encouraged the sterilization of many women, frequently poor women of color. And welfare laws punished the pregnancy and childbearing of the same women. The government has also created a variety of laws over time that separated children from their mothers. These have given the state both the power to decide what constitutes a good mother and the capacity to act against the motherhood of women defined as falling short of the standard, even when that standard might be embedded and depend on racial and class biases.[43]

284 ELINA STAIKOU

The history of the racialisation of reproduction is described as 'war on motherhood'.[44] Its assault, which runs more deeply than population control programmes, is foremost structured by race and determined by the varying demands on and value attached to racialised bodies and wombs. From aggressive public programmes for the reduction of native populations to anti-miscegeneration laws, from forced abortions and sterilisations to pro-natalist and anti-natalist strategies, to the absence of adequate reproductive health services, this is a history of reproductive nationalism that associates 'citizenship with whiteness', venerating the 'white mother's role in making the white nation', while protecting her fertility and managing her reproductive capacity.[45] This informs the context of the undoubtedly racial character of the extreme disparities in reproductive and maternal healthcare in the US as well as in Europe along with those in general healthcare, which became so strikingly manifest during the COVID-19 pandemic. Their analysis must not inform a single-issue agenda but the larger context for fighting assaults on reproductive autonomy, health and dignity and the resurgence of reactionary reproductive politics as evidenced recently. This would avoid the perpetuation of racialised violence only if it is in concert with demands and struggles for reproductive justice and requires that the history of the struggle for women's liberation be revisited from perspectives that acknowledge what Vergès calls the 'racial genealogy' of European, 'civilizational'[46] feminism or 'femonationalism' and 'put into question a universalism that ultimately masks particularism',[47] She writes

> The French feminists of the 1970s failed in their creation of a 'second wave' that would have been anchored in political anti-racism. Repressing the long history of the construction of the 'French woman' – white, deprived of human rights, but retaining privileges over racialized human beings and benefitting from colonial products that improved the qualities of their lives, the second wave opened the way to reactionary feminism.[48]

In her 1981 article 'French Feminism in an International Frame', Gayatri Spivak underscored the parochialism of an 'International Feminism' narrowly defined within a Western European context.[49] French Feminism with its double effort (*against* sexism and *for* feminism), needs to be reconsidered, argues Spivak, from a perspective that does not identify women's liberation with (women's) reproductive freedom.[50] We will come back to this but for now we want to point to its link with the deep politics of *Geschlecht*, the 'genealogism' that Derrida 'so insistently recognized in the political figures of philia',[51] and Vergès's injunction that

EROTICS OF DECOMPOSITION 285

'repoliticizing feminism means provincializing European feminisms'.[52] It means that the struggle for contraceptive freedom and abortion rights must be taken up together with the demands of movements such as the Reproductive Justice Framework, envisioned by African American feminist and queer theorists and collectives. Alexis Pauline Gumbs states in *Revolutionary Mothering*: 'In addition to fighting for birth control and abortion, equal attention must be paid to the human right to become a mother, and the concomitant and enabling right to parent our children in safe and healthy environments.'[53]

Cells and their mitochondria ...

In *M Archive, After the End of the World*, Alexis Pauline Gumbs imagines a post-apocalyptic world that has come as the result of the failure to discern the 'sustainable unit'. Not the individual body as it had been confusingly believed but the stuff of 'black feminist metaphysics', that is breathing, that is everything.[54] Everything would have been different if biochemists had 'diverted their energy towards this type of theoretical antioxidant around the time of the explicit emergence of this idea', if the 'constitutive element of individualism' had not been 'adverse, if not antithetical to the dark feminine, which is to say, everything'.[55] This confusion about 'the actual scale of breathing', which ended up making the planet 'unbreathable', was what brought about the downfall.[56] That along with the belief of some people

> that they themselves were actually other than black women, which was a false and impossible belief about origin. they were all, in their origin, maintenance, and measure of survival more parts black women than anything else. it was like saying they were no parts water. (Which they must have believed as well. you can see what they did to the water.)[57]

It is not difficult to imagine here the allusion to mitochondrial lineage, which is one of the manifold meanings of the *M* in *M Archive*, as well as to its essential connection to the cell's metabolic function of respiration, energy generation and flux capacitation. Studies on mitochondrial inheritance attempt to reconstruct maternal lines in the context of palaeoanthropology, which has traced back mitochondrial DNA to 'Mitochondrial' or 'African Eve', now thought to have lived in Africa some 170,000 years ago or in the context of their intersection with the racialised colour line, the middle passage, the histories of rape and dispossession and that other 'Eve' born out of the dungeon.[58] These quests driven by the desire or fantasy of origins, that is, the desire for and the myth of the lost mother, knot together powerful genetic-symbolic threads that raise questions not only about evolutionary and historical origins but also about the meaning of the cell's forces of composition and decomposition, the cell's entropic or erotic energies, its entanglement of microphysics and micropolitics when it comes to sex, generation, sexual difference and their mutability.

The deep history of sex did not concern genital-based sexed bodies but is said to have begun even before life appeared on the surface of the planet as a phenomenon of energy dissipation within the universe's thermodynamic structures. That there were complex, organised systems of carbon chemicals before the emergence of life has even allowed for the claim 'that there may have been the molecular equivalent to sex in this pre-biotic realm'.[59] If sex at the most basic level is defined as 'genetic recombination', 'the mixing or union of genes, that is DNA molecules from more than one source', if it is deeply a matter and process of microphysics and bioenergetics, then its primary function and significance is cosmic.[60] Sexual desire and pleasure, erotic and reproductive acts (coupled or uncoupled) in their deep and cosmic sense, as Margulis and Sagan write, reflect 'inanimate tendencies already implicit before life in the Second Law'.[61] The Second Law governs the dissipation of energy as well as all life's 'complex cyclicity' of 'energy-material flow structures' – the cycles of life/non-life entanglement – through the reduction or breakdown of gradient differences across electrochemical fields and barriers.[62] Cellular metabolism, that is, respiration, with its energy generation and diffusion mechanisms powers up the formation and decomposition of the great diversity of life forms and their evolutionary trajectories. 'The living cell is a minute universe', writes Nick Lane.[63] Its breathing enacts and contains in minuscule scale the cosmic flux.

Eukaryotic cells, the evolutionary source of larger and more complex forms of life, were the outcome of entropic and erotic experimentation in energy generation and expenditure that involved the 'permanent merging through symbiosis' of distinct life forms, an event that Margulis and Sagan have named 'hypersex'.[64] These 'hypersex hybrids', the ancestry of all cells of eukaryotic life forms, engulfed tiny organs or organelles such as chloroplasts and the (ATP) energy producing mitochondria, which were once 'free-living, oxygen-breathing bacteria'.[65] 'On Earth', Lane argues, 'large size and complexity only became possible once energy generation had been internalized in mitochondria.'[66] The internalisation of energy production enabled the appearance of eukaryotic cells some two billion years ago and inaugurated the archetypically

EROTICS OF DECOMPOSITION   287

eukaryotic 'lifestyle' of predation.[67] Gradually mitochondria lost their ability to live independently from their host cells. Lane describes this as 'a symbolic moment' that 'marked the transition from symbiotic relationship to a captive state'.[68] But it also marked the 'metabolic union between two peacefully cohabiting cells, neither of which could gain from killing the other'.[69] Thanks to their tiny captives, eukariotic cells were able to overcome the energy constraints of ancestral bacteria prefiguring an evolutionary step in the history of sex that involved fertilisation and sexual difference.

Lane's hypothesis about the 'deepest biological difference between the sexes' goes back to the mitochondria's 'new playground' in the fused cell and the conflict between the two sets of mitochondrial populations.[70] 'Today, sexual organisms go to extraordinary lengths to block the entry of mitochondria from one of the two parents. Indeed, at a cellular level, the inheritance of mitochondria from only one of the two parents is among the defining attributes of gender.'[71] With meiotic sex, after the nuclear fusion of the two gametes there needs to be a kind of clearance in the new cell's cytoplasm where only one mitochondrial population can survive. In this asymmetry, according to Lane, 'lies the deepest difference between the sexes: the female sex passes on organelles, the male sex does not. The result is uniparental inheritance, which means that organelles, such as mitochondria, are normally inherited only down the maternal line.'[72] What is concluded from this is that in the deep biological sense 'proper sexes' can be distinguished not before but through the act of sex and as an outcome of the process of nuclear fusion and the complex mechanisms of controlling how cytoplasm is shared.[73] In the context of cellular bioenergetics the separation of sexes is the outcome of the prevalence of 'female' at the expense of 'male' organelles. Mitochondria are the 'culprits' for the need to have more than one sex, Lane claims, or for that matter for any sex at all.[74] This comes down to a 'serious mix-and-match problem' in the fused cell that, if not resolved, can lead to grave or fatal malfunctions in the cell's respiratory capacity.[75] The danger of mismatch between the nuclear and mitochondrial genes in the context of a composite and reshuffled dual genome system would be 'exacerbated if two dissimilar mitochondria genomes compete', so a kind of 'purging' becomes meaningful to ensure a perfect match.[76]

Does this mean that we are bound to biologically assigned, albeit redefined, sexes and reproductive roles? 'Each of our cells', write Margulis and Sagan, 'combines our mother's and our father's nuclear inheritance. We are meiotic and sexual to the very core of our being.'[77] Does Lane's hypothesis of mitochondrial uniparentality as the deep ancestry of sexual difference in eukaryotic life forms open different pathways for understanding sex formation even beyond the 'meiotic imperative'? One thing it does is to dislodge sexual determinability from the evidence of morphological traits on the individual body (Gumbs's false unit of sustainability). 'If', Lane remarks, 'the deepest distinction between the sexes relates to restricting the germ-line passage of mitochondria, then the barrier between the sexes seems curiously shaky.'[78] What kind of interpretive potential or power of symbolisation (or 'theoretical antioxidants') does such explanation of sexual difference release?

While we cannot explore Lane's detailed explanation of the cellular mechanisms of energy flow and respiration here, we would like to make a link between the cell's forcefield (and its reliance on uniparentality) and what we understand as maternal forcefield (and its multiplicity of maternal functions). Considering the maternal (function) on the level of mitochondria is neither a biological reductionism nor does it entail a hardened, incontrovertible division of sexes. It is rather understood as *life-forming-donation-empowering-mothering*. Maternal forcefields and the microphysics of sex lead us back to the originary intricacy of 'ontological' and 'sexual difference' recast as the potent source of diverse and multiplied maternal functions in which desire and reproduction are expressed, aligned, assisted and legitimated.[79] The world or matrix of sexual différance is not composed of biologically fixed destinies but of biologically cultured experimentation in sexuality and reproduction, or else, the discharges and growths of erotics of decomposition.[80] Maternal function considered through mitochondrial donation empowers rather than arrests the play of sexual difference (which is not decided at the level of phenomenal and textbook anatomy).

The cellular folding of the cosmic flux can always surge and erupt into varied forms and acts of mothering …

… and their oceans

A high tide is swelling with the tremendous energy of the ocean … Beautiful experiments in intimacy and the rhythms of wayward lives led by young black women at the turn of the twentieth century were 'a revolution in a minor key unfolding in the city', the 'everyday anarchy' of the hood, the slum, the ghetto.[81] Saidiya Hartman's book *Wayward Lives, Beautiful Experiments: Intimate Histories of Riotous Black Girls, Troublesome Women and Queer Radicals* crafts an album of portraits and the real stories of black women living in Harlem, Philadelphia, Coney Island, reviving lives that were often depicted and outlawed as 'promiscuous, reckless, wild, and wayward' but which were animated by the fierceness of desire and passionate dreams of freedom.[82] The black women portrayed by Hartman

EROTICS OF DECOMPOSITION   289

cultivated riotous arts of living, experiments in love and freedom that, in defiance of moralistic and legal sanctions, nurtured 'flexible and elastic kinship as a resource of black survival' and radical practices of mothering.[83] In the aftermath of the brutal severing of family ties during the slave trade and cruel separation in the plantation, one had to invent new ways of making kin, countless ways of losing and finding one's mother.

> After the slave ship and the plantation, the third revolution of black intimate life unfolded in the city. The hallway, bedroom, stoop, rooftop, airshaft, and kitchenette, provided the space of experiment. The tenement and the roaming house furnished the social laboratory of the black working class and the poor. The bedroom was a domain of thought indeed and a site for enacting, exceeding, undoing and remaking relations of power.[84]

The uses of erotics and the reinvention of kinship aligned with desires for expanding '"mothering" as a queer thing'[85] are radically political in effectuating the decomposition of the old forms of *Geschlecht* (nation, sex, kinship, family, generation, and so on) and perhaps close to what Derrida invokes as 'another politics for loving, another politics to love, for love (*à aimer*)'.[86] In her preface to *Revolutionary Mothering, Love on the Front Lines*, Loretta Ross, one of the founders of the Reproductive Justice Framework, describes radical 'mothering' as 'lifeforce', gift and support to the life of others, human right, and 'survival as a form of self-love'.[87] The collection's dedication 'to all the revolutionary mothers and all the revolutions they created, because mothering is **love by any means necessary**' underlines the politically radical character and anarchic force of the love and justice of such mothering. Not by opposing love to power but by empowering love. Alexis Pauline Gumbs asks 'what it would mean to us to take the word "mother" less as a gendered identity and more as a possible action, a technology of transformation'.[88] Such technology – or else, deconstructive potential released by the maternal figure and forcefield – does not merely amount to questioning the 'ongoing exclusion and criminalization of people of colour, poor people, and LGBTQ people from the status of motherhood'.[89] Gumbs understands mothering as something that applies also to ourselves and used for self-creation and reinvention, which in turn creates contexts for others to live and 'grow past the norms they knew'.[90] Toni Morrison's novel *Sula* is accredited by Gumbs with the birthing of contemporary black feminist literary theory out of the voice of Sula, a riotous young black woman who retorted to her mother's admonitions with the words: 'I don't want to make someone else. I want to make myself.'[91]

Making oneself, one of the uses of the erotic that Audre Lorde understood as power and as 'that deep and irreplaceable knowledge of my capacity for joy' in the context of pleasure activism, is interlaced with the practices and transformations of radical mothering.[92] Spivak's reformulation of the double vision of 'International Feminism' (*against* sexism and *for* feminism) recognises that 'even as we reclaim the excess of the clitoris, we cannot fully escape the symmetry of the reproductive definition'.[93] The denormalisation of the 'uterine social organization' along with its 'phallic norm of capitalism' – the sexual, racial, national configurations of the old *Geschlecht* – could be achieved only if understood in terms of the exclusion of 'a clitoral social organisation'. Spivak writes

> One cannot write off what may be called a uterine social organization (the arrangement of the world in terms of the reproduction of future generations, where the uterus is the chief agent and means of production) *in favor of* a clitoral.[94]

We would like to extend this in the context of erotics of decomposition, the breakdown of patriarchal and parochial heteronormativity, not merely in favour of the clitoral but of every singularly lived out embodiment, its sex, its politics, its m/othering. Such uses of the erotic are hailed as transformative justice in adrienne maree brown's *Pleasure Activism: The Politics of Feeling Good*:

> We are in a time of fertile ground for learning how we align our pleasures with our values, decolonising our bodies and longings, and getting into a practice of saying an orgasmic yes together, deriving our collective power from our felt sense of pleasure.[95]

Pleasure activism happens in the crafting of relationships, in 'clearing out internalised oppression' and with the nuanced attention to black multi-ethnicity, transgender and identity intersections.[96] Joan Morgan specifies it as a liberatory and expansive black feminist project, an 'imperative' for erotic agency.[97]

How far is the way from 'politics of friendship' to such 'politics of pleasure'? From the deconstruction of fraternity to erotics of decomposition? How far have we come following the stranger or the m/other stepping out of line and into visibility in *Geschlecht's* procession and series?

From ocean to cell (tiny enclave and captor of oceanic energy) and from cell to ocean, there is the cyclical flow of revolution. It has brought us back to the ocean and off the shores of the Gold Coast where Hartman bids her farewell and pledges love and memory to those lost,

EROTICS OF DECOMPOSITION   291

whose anguish was echoed in the ocean's roar.[98] It is the ocean Gumbs is drawn to in *Undrowned, Black Feminist Lessons from Marine Mammals*. Gumbs's text is framed as an experiment in echolocation, a breathing exercise, an apprenticeship with marine mammals, what is otherwise described as a listening 'across species, across extinction, across harm'.[99] Being in company with dolphins and whales, learning from their way of making kin (for example, their 'othermothering' or 'allomaternal behaviours'), their interspecies collaborations and their technologies of breathing and navigation, makes visible shared affinities within systems of extraction (whale fat was, after all, used as the main lubricant of the plantation machinery) but also of resilience and emerging strategies for survival.[100]

Opening oneself to the guidance of 'queer, fierce, protective of each other, complex, shaped by conflict' creatures, who are 'struggling to survive the extractive and militarized context our species has imposed to the planet and ourselves' can inspire radical ways of relating with others and is not that remote from the context and the struggles of movements for black and queer liberation, racial, gender, disability and environmental justice.[101] 'Context' there concerns the scale of breathing understood as something done continually and collectively, 'beyond species and sentience' and not easily distinguished from the unfinished impact of drowning.[102] The breathing of those who survived the middle passage is 'not separate from the drowning of their kin and fellow captives, their breathing is not separate from the breathing of the ocean, their breathing is not separate from the sharp exhale of the hunted whales, their kindred also' (the breathing of whales, Gumbs notes later, is as crucial to the carbon cycle of the planet as are the forests of the world),[103]

> Their breathing did not make them individual survivors. It made a context. The context of undrowning. Breathing in unbreathable circumstances is what we do every day in the chokehold of racial gendered ableist capitalism. We are still undrowning. And by we, I don't only mean people like myself whose ancestors specifically survived the middle passage, because the scale of our breathing is planetary, at the very least.[104]

Expressions of love and gratitude for the black feminist lessons well up everywhere in this text. Beautiful experiments in living, loving, dying, knowing, breathing, undrowning, making kin (and babies) are carried through oceanic erotics and its vast energetics enfolded, captured and swirling within cells, their oceans and so far beyond.[105] One of the lessons is that 'the cell and the creature and the circle and society and the galaxy are one thing organized by scale'.[106] We have learnt to call this 'one thing' différance as life/non-life force, to trace it in the anarchic transfiguration of revolutionary mothering, and to find it in erotic uses and breakdowns, in the giftings of *Eros* in an ever-expanding DE-COMPOSITION.

Notes

1. Jacques Derrida, 'Force of Law, The "Mystical Foundation of Authority"', in *Acts of Religion*, ed. Gil Anidjar (London: Routledge, 2002), 278.
2. Françoise Vergès, *The Wombs of Black Women, Race, Capital, Feminism*, trans. Kalama L. Glover (London: Duke University Press, 2020), 8.
3. Derrida, 'Force of Law', 292.
4. Jacques Derrida and Elisabeth Roudinesco, 'Disordered Families' in *For What Tomorrow ... A Dialogue*, trans. Jeff Fort (Stanford, CA: Stanford University Press, 2004), 33–46.
5. Nick Lane, *Power, Sex, Suicide: Mitochondria and the Meaning of Life* (Oxford: Oxford University Press, 2018), 17.
6. Ibid., 337.
7. Lynn Margulis and Dorion Sagan, *What is Sex?* (New York: Simon & Schuster, 1998), 45.
8. Ibid., 46.
9. Jacques Derrida, *Politics of Friendship*, trans. George Collins (London: Verso, 1997), 241.
10. Jacques Derrida, 'Heidegger's Ear, Philopolemology (*Geschlecht* IV)', in *Reading Heidegger, Commemorations*, ed. John Sallis (Bloomington: Indiana University Press, 1993), 181.
11. Ibid., 191.
12. Derrida, *Politics of Friendship*, 241–2.
13. Derrida, 'Heidegger's Ear', 183.
14. Jacques Derrida, 'Geschlecht I: Sexual Difference, Ontological Difference', in *Research in Phenomenology* XIII.45–83 (1983), 72.
15. Jacques Derrida, *Resistances of Psychoanalysis*, trans. Peggy Kamuf, Pascale-Anne Brault and Michael Naas (Stanford, CA: Stanford University Press, 1998), 9.
16. Jacques Derrida, *Geschlecht III, Sex, Race, Nation, Humanity*, trans. Katie Chenowth and Rodrigo Therezo (Chicago: University of Chicago Press, 2020), 25.
17. Ibid., 26, 27.
18. Ibid., 43.
19. See Elina Staikou, 'Decomposing Geschlecht: Thinking Mother/Land ... with Soils', Special Issue: Sex, Race, Nation, Humanity, Derrida's Geschlecht III, *Paragraph* 45.3, 366–83.
20. 'Femonationalism' is a term coined by Sara Farris to describe the 'exploitation of feminist concepts by nationalists and Islamophobic neoliberals' and is used by Vergès alongside her term 'civilizational feminism'. Françoise

Vergès, *A Decolonial Feminism*, trans. Ashley J. Bohrer (London: Pluto Press, 2021).

21. Saidiya Hartman, *Lose your Mother: A Journey Along the Atlantic Slave Route* (London: Serpent's Tail, 2021), 5.
22. Ibid., 7.
23. Ibid., 10.
24. Ibid., 6.
25. Ibid., 41, 42.
26. Ibid., 73.
27. Ibid., 73, 75.
28. Ibid., 3.
29. Ibid., 98.
30. Ibid., 110.
31. Ibid.
32. Ibid., 111.
33. Ibid.
34. Ibid.
35. Ibid., 115.
36. Ibid., 110.
37. Vergès, *The Wombs of Black Women*, 51.
38. Ibid.
39. Derrida broaches the issue of racial and sexual violence against women in the context of the testimonies of women activists before the 'Truth and Reconciliation Commission' in South Africa. Testimony to torture and rape is recognised there as 'third wounding' that comes to be added to the original violence of racist discrimination and sexual abuse against black women activists, whose role in the liberation struggle was degraded. Jacques Derrida, *Perjury & Pardon*, vol. II, trans. David Wills (Chicago: University of Chicago Press, 2023), 115–24.
40. See Donatella Di Cesare's *Heidegger and the Jews, The Black Notebooks* (Cambridge: Polity Press, 2014) for a rigorous philosophical analysis of Heidegger's 'metaphysical anti-Semitism'. For a further challenge to an understanding of raciality as primarily a question of metaphysics, see Christina Sharpe, *In the Wake: On Blackness and Being* (Durham: Duke University Press, 2016).
41. Hartman, *Lose your Mother*, 172.
42. Loretta J. Ross and Solinger Rickie, *Reproductive Justice, An Introduction* (Oakland: University of California Press, 2017), 15.
43. Ibid., 15–16.
44. Ibid., 43.
45. Ibid., 37, 23. Undoubtedly, the lamentable state of reproductive and maternal healthcare available to black and brown mothers in the United Kingdom is part of the legacy of the racialised management of social reproduction. The MBRACE-UK 2020 report 'Enquiries into Maternal Death and Morbidity' revealed that black women are 'statistically four

times more likely to die during childbirth' while women from 'Asian ethnic backgrounds were still three times more likely to die due complications than white women'. Open Access Government, 'Is Childbirth More Dangerous for Black Women in the UK?', May 2022: https://www.openaccessgovernment.org/childbirth-black-women-uk/117437/ (accessed October 2023).

46. Vergès, *A Decolonial Feminism*, 17.
47. Vergès, *The Wombs of Black Women*, 3.
48. Ibid., 112–13.
49. Gayatri Chakravorty Spivak, 'French Feminism in an International Frame', in *Yale French Studies* 62 (1981), 164.
50. Ibid., 180.
51. Derrida, *Politics of Friendship*, 243.
52. Vergès, *The Wombs of Black Women*, 117.
53. Alexis Pauline Gumbs et al., eds, *Revolutionary Mothering: Love on the Front Lines* (San Francisco, CA: PM Press, 2016), xvi.
54. Ibid.
55. Ibid.
56. Ibid., xvi, 7.
57. Ibid., 6–7.
58. Lane, *Power, Sex, Suicide*, 365.
59. Margulis and Sagan, *What is Sex?*, 70.
60. Ibid., 17.
61. Ibid., 46.
62. Ibid., 28.
63. Lane, *Power, Sex, Suicide*, 11.
64. Margulis and Sagan, *What is Sex?*, 73.
65. Ibid., 74.
66. Lane, *Power, Sex, Suicide*, 157.
67. Ibid., 188.
68. Ibid., 322.
69. Ibid., 324.
70. Ibid., 339, 327.
71. Ibid., 336.
72. Ibid., 349.
73. Ibid., 351.
74. Ibid., 342.
75. Ibid., 385.
76. Ibid., 388.
77. Margulis and Sagan, *What is Sex?*, 123.
78. Lane, *Power, Sex, Suicide*, 356.
79. See Francesco Vitale, 'Microphysics of Sex. Sexual Differences between Biology and Deconstruction', *parallax* 25.1 (2019), 92–109.
80. Ibid., 7.
81. Saidiya Hartman, *Wayward Lives, Beautiful Experiments: Intimate Histories*

EROTICS OF DECOMPOSITION

295

of Riotous Black Girls, Troublesome Women and Queer Radicals (London: Serpent's Tail, 2021), xvii.

82. Ibid., vxi.
83. Ibid., 91.
84. Ibid., 61.
85. Loretta Ross, 'Preface', in *Revolutionary Mothering, Love on the Front Lines*, ed. Alexis Pauling Gumbs, China Martens and Mai'a Williams (Toronto: PM Press, 2016), xvii.
86. Derrida, *Politics of Friendship*, 123.
87. Ross, 'Preface', xviii.
88. Alexis Pauline Gumbs, 'M/other Ourselves: A Black Queer Feminist Genealogy for Radical Mothering', in *Revolutionary Mothering*, 23.
89. Gumbs, 'M/other ourselves', 21.
90. Ibid., 22.
91. Ibid.
92. Audre Lorde, 'Uses of the Erotic', in *Pleasure Activism: The Politics of Feeling Good*, ed. adrienne maree brown (Chico, CA: AK Press, 2019 30.
93. Spivak, 'French Feminism', 183.
94. Ibid.
95. adrienne maree brown, ed., *Pleasure Activism: The Politics of Feeling Good* (Chico, CA: AK Press, 2019), 12.
96. Alexis Pauline Gumbs, 'The Sweetness of Salt, Toni Cade Bambara and the Practice of Pleasure (in Five Tributes)', in *Pleasure Activism: The Politics of Feeling Good*, ed. adrienne maree brown (Chico, CA: AK Press, 2019), 71.
97. Joan Morgan, 'Why We Get Off, Moving Towards a Black Feminist Politics of Pleasure', in *Pleasure Activism: The Politics of Feeling Good*, ed. adrienne maree brown (Chico, CA: AK Press, 2019), 83.
98. Hartman, *Lose your Mother*, 32.
99. Alexis Pauline Gumbs, *Undrowned, Black Feminist Lessons from Marine Mammals* (Chico, CA: AK Press, 2021), 15.
100. Ibid., 161–2.
101. Ibid., 9.
102. Ibid.
103. Ibid., 2, 24.
104. Ibid., 2.
105. For current discussion on 'making kin not babies' see Adele Clark and Donna Haraway, eds, *Making Kin not Population – Reconceiving Generations* (Chicago, IL: Prickly Paradigm Press, 2018).
106. Gumbs, 'The Sweetness of Salt', 74.

INDEX

Abraham, Nicolas and Mária Török, 94
absence, 36, 38, 44, 48, 99, 128, 137, 172, 182, 221–2, 240, 242, 280
Alfandary, Isabelle, 54n, 208n
Amin, Kadji, 240–1, 245, 249
Anidjar, Gil, 131n, 272n
animals (including animality), 9, 10, 18, 20, 24, 41, 43, 82, 83, 92, 99, 100–1, 104, 116–17, 118, 120, 126, 131n, 159, 175, 217–18, 222–31, 232–3n, 234n, 235n, 257, 259–60, 262, 264, 270, 273n, 280
  and *animot*, 218, 227, 228–9, 230, 232, 232n, 234n
anus, 55, 58; *see also* hands and fisting
Aristotle, 18, 21, 32n
auto-affection, 2, 4–5, 9, 19, 22, 29, 38–9, 40, 48–50 117, 171, 174, 200–1, 217–24, 225–8, 230, 231, 232n, 235n, 250–1
autobiography, 1–2, 9, 38, 85, 94, 133n, 217–18, 220–1, 223–8, 229–32, 232n, 235n

Bao, Hongwei, 136
Barthes, Roland, 36–7, 202–4
Bass, Alan, 42, 52n
Bataille, George, 39, 203, 232n
Beatles, The, 91
Benjamin, Walter, 275
Ben-Naftali, Michal, 92
Bennington, Geoffrey, 93, 249–50
Berger, Anne Emmanuelle, 144, 170–4, 176–7, 192
Bersani, Leo, 97–8, 107n
Blanchot, Maurice, 204, 206
blood, 3, 7, 8, 113–20, 122–3, 126–9,130–1n, 156, 168, 183, 263, 266, 275–6, 277, 282
Boétie, Étienne, de la 244–5
Booth, Stephen, 101
breasts, 22, 30, 181, 182, 266
Bronfen, Elizabeth, 177
brown, adrienne maree, 290

Butler, Judith, 54, 55–7, 58, 67n, 202, 241, 248–50, 254n

Califia, Patrick, 167
Calle-Gruber, Mireille, 87
Carroll, Lewis, 226, 234n
Caruth, Cathy, 135
carno-phallogocentrism, 5, 120, 127, 258
castration, 31–2, 55, 75, 99, 122–3, 124–6, 127, 176–7, 206, 213n, 228–9
Celan, Paul, 134, 206
Chanter, Tina, 144, 149n, 151n
chastity, 2, 4, 6, 117, 122; *see also* virginity
Chen, Thomas, 142
Chenoweth, Katie, 32n
Cherniavsky, Eva, 271n
childhood (including infancy), 4, 10, 20, 22, 23–5, 37, 61, 85, 98–9, 104
  and infantile sexuality 23, 194
Cixous, Hélène, 7–8, 23, 77, 84–8, 94, 98, 99, 117, 119, 123, 127, 128, 145–6 166, 179, 184n, 188, 192, 198–9, 206
  'Bathsheba or the Interior Bible', 170–1, 179–84
  'Castration or Decapitation', 128
  'Laugh of the Medusa', 12, 126
  Neutre, 204–5
  'Savoir', 8, 84–5
  'Sorties', 123, 128–9, 173, 183
Coleridge, Samuel Taylor, 100
Conley, Verena Andermatt, 192

Dante, 100
Darwin, Charles, 55
Dasein, 196, 198, 199, 204–5, 207n, 210n, 279, 283
David, Catherine, 91
Davidson, Arnold, 189
Davis, Angela, 268
de Beauvoir, Simone, 194, 248
de Lauretis, Teresa, 136

INDEX

de Man, Paul, 98
Dean, Tim, 212n
DeArmitt, Pleshette, 186n
deconstruction, 5–7, 10, 23, 36–9, 53–6,
    57–8, 65–6, 70n, 73, 74–7, 79, 81–3,
    86, 87, 92–7, 98–102, 104, 105n, 106n,
    117, 125, 128, 133n, 145, 156, 171, 175,
    176–7, 183, 188, 191, 193, 201, 202,
    217–18, 220, 223, 225, 228, 229–31,
    232n, 235n, 246, 249, 257, 262, 275–6,
    289, 290
Defoe, Daniel, 37
Deleuze, Gilles, 55–6, 67n, 204, 206
Derrida, Jacques, 4, 10–11, 12n, 23–4, 32,
    33n, 35–7, 56, 58, 68n, 69n, 70n, 74–6,
    87, 91–3, 96, 98, 101, 107n, 114–15,
    128–9, 130n, 132n, 133n, 168, 170, 179,
    183, 202, 207n, 232n, 234n, 238, 243–4,
    251n, 256–7, 260–2; 264, 265, 271n,
    293n
  and Cixous, Hélène, 7, 8, 10, 23, 77, 84,
    87–8, 99, 123, 128, 145–6, 192, 198–9
  'A Silkworm of One's Own', 37, 162, 188
  Animal That Therefore I Am, The, 1–2, 38,
    116, 126, 217–18, 220, 223–5, 226–31,
    232n, 234n, 235n
  'Ants', 192
  'Aphorism Countertime', 94–5, 103–4
  Archive Fever, 224–5
  'At This Very Moment in This Work Here I
    Am', 188, 190–1, 193, 198
  Beast and the Sovereign, The, Vol. I, 37,
    59–60, 65, 134, 175, 246–7
  'Che Cos'è la Poesia', 191
  'Choreographies', 171–2, 176, 191–2, 198,
    208n
  'Circonfession', 120, 188
  Clang, 17–18, 25–31, 37–8, 39–40
  'Counter-Signatures', 102
  Death Penalty, The, Vol. II, 6–7, 116–17,
    122–6, 128
  'Dialanguages', 192, 198
  'Disordered Families', 276
  'Double Session', 69n, 188
  'Eating Well', 9, 271n
  'Envois', 40, 44–6, 53, 69n, 91, 191
  'Faith and Knowledge', 59
  'Force of Law', 276
  'Fors', 94
  'Fourmis', 85–6
  'Freud's Legacy', 62
  'Geschlecht I: Sexual Difference,
    Ontological Difference', 199, 210n, 277
  Geschlecht III: Sex, Race, Nation, Humanity,
    188–9, 279
  Glas, 17–18, 24–7
  Heidegger: The Question of Being and History,
    218
  'Heidegger's Ear: Philopolemology
    (Geschlecht IV)', 278, 283

Life Death, 53, 66n, 250–1
Limited Inc., 274n
Parages, 188, 191, 204
'Paralysis', 62
Perjury and Pardon, 6
'Passages – From Traumatism to Promise',
    95
'Passion', 167
'Plato's Pharmacy', 55–6
Politics of Friendship, 100, 276, 278
Positions, 206, 213n
Post Card, The, 39–40, 43, 52n, 53, 61, 188,
    191
Psyche: Inventions of the Other, 190
Memoirs of the Blind, 100–1
Monolingualism of the Other, 19
Of Grammatology, 5, 8–9, 13n, 38, 217, 219,
    222–3, 225, 230–1, 232n, 235n, 249–50,
    272n
On The Name, 156
On Touching – Jean-Luc Nancy, 37, 47, 48–9,
    52n, 80–3, 84–5, 140 147, 223, 227
Resistances to Psychoanalysis, 76
Right of Inspection, 37, 102
Rogues: Two Essays on Reason, 272n
'Signature, Event, Context', 14n, 55
Signsponge, 102
Spectres of Marx, 100
Spurs, 69n
'…That Dangerous Supplement…', 55
'To Speculate – On "Freud"', 53–4, 60–1,
    63, 65, 66n
'Typewriter Ribbon', 59
Veils, 167
'Voice II', 192, 198–9, 200, 203
Voice and Phenomenon (also Speech and
    Phenomena), 38, 201, 211n, 219, 222
'What is a Relevant Translation?', 22
'Who is the Mother? Birth, Nature,
    Nation', 276
Writing and Difference, 3
Descartes, René, 218, 227, 229, 231
desire, 21, 23, 28, 36, 37, 45, 55, 58, 63,
    73, 74–6, 78, 79, 81–2, 84, 86–7, 91,
    94, 97–9, 102, 117, 123, 134, 140–3,
    146, 148, 153, 158, 163, 173, 175, 182,
    191–2, 194, 198, 203, 205, 206, 208n,
    210n, 212n, 222–4, 227, 232n, 237,
    240–1, 244–6, 249, 251, 257, 259–60,
    263, 267, 273n, 275–6 277–8, 283, 286,
    288–9
detumescence, 65, 66, 70n, 128, 224–5, 231
Deutscher, Penelope, 136–7, 144, 148n
dialectics, 4–5, 17, 27–8, 66n, 74–6, 86, 116,
    126, 173, 192, 196, 199
Dibbell, Carola, 257, 262–9, 272–3n, 274n
Dick, Kirby and Amy Ziering Kofman, 35
différance, 36, 38, 47–50, 88, 188, 192,
    198–200, 220–2, 230, 244, 249, 277,
    288, 292

dissemination, 24, 171, 188, 190, 196, 198, 199, 206–7, 208n, 213n, 249
Dixon, Willie, 52n
dreams, 58, 61, 76, 80, 91, 95, 99–100, 104, 117, 123, 129, 154, 167, 171–2, 176, 180, 192–3, 198, 200–1, 203, 204, 225, 281, 288
Dufourmantelle, Anne, 75–80, 84, 86–7
Duras, Marguerite, 206

ears, 10, 21, 29, 33n, 35, 102, 104, 199–200, 201, 212n
  and hearing 25, 29, 36, 38–9, 43, 46, 48, 52n, 76, 79, 81, 84–5, 87–8, 91, 101, 119, 138, 140, 156, 190, 192, 198–201, 219–20, 224, 270, 272n, 281
Edelman, Lee, 10, 32n, 133n
Elam, Diane, 114, 120
Eng, David L., 143
Enke, A. Finn, 248
Erasmus, 19–22
erection, 38, 59–60, 68n, 70n, 97, 127–8, 224–5, 230–1, 234n, 235n
Eros, 82, 99, 123–4, 151n, 211n, 212n, 260, 276, 278–9, 283, 292
erotics, 3, 5, 7–8, 18, 20, 22–5, 29–30, 32, 36–7, 39–40, 42, 45, 47, 48, 50, 51n, 73, 74, 76–80, 82–8, 95, 97–100, 102, 113, 117, 134–5, 137, 140–2, 147, 200, 217–18, 222–3, 227–8, 230, 232n, 245–6, 273n, 275–6, 278–80, 286, 288–92
eyes, 6–7, 8, 11, 21, 24, 33n, 37, 77, 80–5, 87–8, 98, 104, 116, 147, 161, 165, 167, 181, 226, 230–1, 238, 244, 261

family (including 'filiation'), 6, 17, 26–7, 62–3, 65–66, 70n, 71n, 195, 197, 206, 258–60, 273n, 275–6, 280–1, 289
Feinberg, Leslie, 56–7, 58
femininity, 20, 21, 24, 28, 41, 59, 60, 62–3, 65, 67n, 69n, 71n, 82, 85, 119, 131n, 144, 176, 177, 181, 182, 191, 193, 201, 204, 208n, 241–2, 246, 247, 269, 285
Ferenczi, Sándor, 123–4
Fonagy, Ivan, 30
Forster, E. M., 99–100, 102
fort/da, 46, 54, 61–2, 128, 225
Foucault, Michel, 54–6, 191, 203, 204, 237, 239, 244, 253n
Fraisse, Geneviève, 194, 208n
Freud, Sigmund, 10, 12n, 23–4, 32, 59, 60, 66, 67n, 94, 99, 100, 116, 126, 128, 132n, 170, 189, 191, 193, 196, 197, 204–6, 209n, 210n, 211n, 212n, 237, 239, 251n, 253n
  Beyond the Pleasure Principle, 53–5, 61–5, 133n, 203
  'Fetishism', 30–1
  'Taboo of Virginity, The', 122–4, 132n

Three Essays on the Theory of Sexuality, 194–5
'Totem and Taboo', 123

Gartside, Green, 92
Genet, Jean, 17–18, 25–6, 28–31, 38, 39–40
Geschlecht, 188–9, 195–8,193, 195–9, 210n, 275, 276, 278–80, 283, 284, 289, 290
Grossman, Evelyne, 192, 202–4
Grosz, Elizabeth, 55, 67n, 136, 171–2
Guillaumin, Colette, 200, 211n
Gumbs, Alexis Pauline, 278, 285, 288, 289, 291
Guyotat, Pierre, 206

Habermas, Jurgen, 237
Hall, Radclyffe, 58
hands, 2, 4, 8, 22, 35, 40–3, 47–8, 50, 57, 97–8, 139, 142, 146, 156–7 159, 161–2, 164, 166, 177, 182–3, 242, 244
  and fisting, 154–7, 160, 166–7
Haraway, Donna, 10, 54, 56, 68n, 234n
Hartman, Saidiya, 280–2, 288–9, 290–1
Hebbel, Friedrich, 122
Hegel, G. W. F., 17, 25–8, 30, 35, 37–8, 116, 118, 126, 173, 196, 218, 220, 223
Heidegger, Martin, 35, 37, 193, 195–9, 204, 207n, 210n, 211n, 218, 220, 223, 228, 278–80, 283
Héritier, Françoise, 204
Hillenbrand, Margaret, 135
Holzer, Jenny, 117–8, 128–9, 132n
  and Lustmord, 113–14, 118–22, 126–7, 129n
Husserl, Edmund, 200, 218–20

Intimacy, 36, 40, 43, 75, 78, 79, 87, 94, 138, 141–2, 145, 148, 288
Irigaray, Luce, 2–4, 8–9, 149n, 150n, 253n
  A New Culture of Energy, 144–5
  An Ethics of Sexual Difference, 136–7, 145
  Elemental Passions, 134, 141–2
  Speculum of the Other Woman, 134, 242
  This Sex Which Is Not One, 242

Jacob, François, 63, 250, 271n
Jarman, Derek, 159
John of Wales, 20–1, 33n
jouissance, 8, 11, 24, 75–6, 79, 84, 93, 99, 157, 167, 192, 198, 201, 202–4, 207, 227

Kafka, Franz, 100, 159–60
Kamuf, Peggy, 92, 190, 192–3
Kant, Immanuel, 6, 35, 218, 229
Kass, Leon, 256, 257–62, 264, 265, 268–9, 271n, 272–3n
kinship, 206, 208n, 258–9, 268, 275–6, 280–2, 289, 291
kissing, 17, 19, 22, 37, 80, 148
Kivland, Sharon, 2–3, 8
Kofman, Sarah, 170–1, 174–9, 183
Kouloukouri, Sofia, 118, 130n

INDEX

Kristeva, Julia, 118
Kwan, Stanley, 135–6, 140–3

Lacan, Jacques, 55, 71n, 126, 133n, 183, 203, 205, 208n, 212n, 228
Lane, Nick, 277, 286–8
Laplanche, Jean, 194–5, 205–6, 209n, 211n
Larousse, Pierre, 209n
Lee, Kyoo, 131n
Leibniz, Gottfried Wilhelm, 223
Levinas, Emmanuel, 41, 46, 81, 82–3, 144, 148, 190–1, 193
Levi-Strauss, Claude, 12n, 206
lips, 2, 4, 8, 21, 33n, 80, 82, 84, 150n, 154, 159, 161, 168, 192
logos, 7, 20, 38, 201, 223
Lorde, Audre, 275, 278, 290
love, 35–6, 40, 43, 47–8, 74, 79, 82, 85, 87, 88, 91–3, 94–5, 96, 97, 100–1, 103–4, 119, 129, 137–8, 144, 147, 153–4, 156, 157, 159–60, 165, 167–8, 180, 193, 208n, 257, 263, 275, 278, 279, 289, 291

Malabou, Catherine, 249
Maltz, Robin, 56, 67n
Maniere, Emma, 264
Marder, Elissa, 71n, 98, 132n, 272n
Margulis, Lynn and Sagan, Dorion, 277, 286–7
Marks, Laura, 145, 151–2n
Marty, Eric, 202–3, 204
masturbation, 4, 6, 38–9, 97–8, 217, 219–20, 221–2, 224, 225, 226, 229, 230, 231, 232n, 235n
Mbembe, Achille, 173–4
McCance, Dawn, 66n
McDonald, Christie, 171, 189, 192
memory, 38, 62, 104, 135, 141–2, 147–8, 153, 225, 230, 236, 251n, 281
Merleau-Ponty, Maurice, 184n
Michaud, Ginette, 192
Michelet, Jules, 192
Miller, J. Hillis, 92, 105n
Morgan, Joan, 290
mourning, 28–9, 53, 62–3, 70n, 101, 133n, 137–8, 180, 190, 229, 279
mouth, 11, 19, 21, 24, 30, 192, 199–201, 207n, 212n, 266
Muñoz, José Esteban, 136, 142
music, 9, 17, 20, 28–9, 52n, 64, 79–80, 87, 91–2, 104, 146–7, 162, 172, 191–2, 198–9, 263
  and singing, 76, 97, 98, 120, 167, 198, 200–1, 206

Naas, Michael, 149n, 225
Nancy, Jean-Luc, 9, 48–9, 77–9, 80, 82, 83, 84, 103, 210n
nudity, 41, 83, 167, 179, 181, 224, 225, 226–8, 229–30

Oliver, Kelly, 259

Paris, Matthew, 46
penis, 22, 32, 58–60, 68n, 70n, 97–8, 123, 124, 127–8
phallogocentrism, 4, 24, 31, 123, 191, 224, 234n, 271n
phallus, 55, 59–60, 64–6, 68n, 70n, 127, 128, 203, 224, 242
pharmakon, 19, 75
Plato, 46, 223, 228, 278
pleasure principle, the, 10, 61, 62–5
Plissart, Marie-Françoise, 146
Poe, Edgar Allan, 30, 183
poetry, 5, 30, 57, 60, 62, 69n, 92–3, 94, 99, 100–1, 102, 104, 119, 126, 129, 149n, 157, 162–3, 165, 167, 181, 191, 279–80
polymorphous perversity, 10–11, 23–5, 29, 37, 99
Ponge, Francis, 102
Potter, Sally, 73, 81
Preciado, Paul B., 55, 63, 66, 67n, 68n, 69n, 70n, 131n, 162
  and *Countersexual Manifesto*, 53, 54, 56–8, 63
presence, 4, 7, 8, 9, 36, 38, 58, 76, 81, 83, 87, 128, 171, 172, 182, 200, 218–22, 223, 227, 230, 231, 240 253n
prosthesis, 6, 17, 32n, 42, 49, 50, 54, 56, 58, 59–60, 81, 85, 86, 266
psyche, 1, 53, 74–5, 82, 124, 170, 175–6, 227
psychoanalysis, 1, 5, 54–5, 56, 64, 67n, 70n, 74–6, 77, 94, 116, 118, 124,133n, 170, 176, 189, 194, 196, 199, 203, 205, 206, 209n, 210n, 235n, 237, 240

queer, 18, 32n, 56–7, 65, 67n, 68n, 97–8, 100, 102, 135, 135–6, 138, 142–4, 148, 196, 202, 249, 254n, 278, 285, 289, 291

rape (and sexual violence), 5–6, 113, 114, 117, 119–20, 127, 153, 156–8, 162, 164, 166, 179–80, 282, 285, 293n
Rembrandt, 17, 170, 172, 176–8, 180, 182, 184
Roberts, Laura, 144–5
Ross, Loretta J. and Rickie Solinger, 283, 289
Rousseau, Jean-Jacques, 2, 4, 6, 8–9, 10, 38–9, 48, 217, 219–22, 225, 231, 232n
Royle, Nicholas, 5, 10, 23, 92–3, 96, 100
Rubin, Gayle, 202
Ruddick, Sara, 269

Sakai, Naoki, 145
Schmitt, Carl, 41
secrets, 3, 72–7, 78–9, 80–8, 94, 100, 134, 135, 154, 163, 175, 177

300 INDEX

secretions, 26, 29, 37, 81, 85, 86, 88, 162–3, 168
Sedgwick, Eve, 56
sexual difference, 24, 28, 29, 37, 55, 59, 60, 67n, 85–6, 87–8, 117, 123, 126, 134, 136–7, 144, 148n, 171, 176, 188, 191–9, 202, 204–5, 208n, 232n, 234n, 260, 277, 279–80, 283, 286–8
sexual pleasure (including 'lovemaking'), 7, 22, 24, 35–7, 40–1, 43–5, 49, 58, 64, 72–3, 74, 76, 77–80, 87, 98, 99–100, 101, 102–3, 139, 157, 161–2, 164, 167–8, 200, 203, 207, 210n, 221, 232n, 263, 277–8, 286, 290
sexuality, 18, 22–4, 26, 30, 32, 38, 41, 54, 56–8, 67n, 85, 98, 117, 135–6, 144, 171–2, 188–200, 202–7, 207n, 209n, 210n, 232n, 253n, 271n, 275, 277, 279, 288
Shakespeare, William, 95, 100–1
  and *Hamlet*, 100
  and *Romeo and Juliet*, 96
Simon, Joan, 118, 120–1
Singer, Peter, 218
Socrates, 46, 278
Sollers, Philippe, 206
sound, 17, 19–20, 25–7, 28–9, 30, 31, 65, 78, 79–80, 85, 87, 91–2, 137–8, 140, 145
speech, 18, 19, 20–1, 22, 25, 26, 32n, 33n, 43, 44, 55, 58, 75, 79, 92, 94, 99, 119, 139, 145, 158, 196, 200, 201, 212n, 219–21, 223–4, 229, 261, 262
Spillers, Hortense, 268
Spinoza, Baruch, 55
Spivak, Gayatri Chakravorty, 5, 113, 117, 119, 129, 144, 249–50, 284, 290
Stevens, Wallace, 94, 104
Stone, Alison, 151n
supplementarity, 4, 6, 9, 10, 31, 38, 48, 49, 50, 54, 55, 58–9, 62, 86, 92, 96–7, 123, 124, 127, 131n, 171, 219–20, 249, 267 271n, 272n

taste, 18, 19, 22, 81, 192
tongues, 10, 17, 18–23, 24–30, 31–2, 32n, 33–4n, 98, 128–9, 154, 168, 192
touch (and touching), 4, 8, 18, 19, 22–3, 31, 32, 38, 39, 40, 43, 47, 49, 50, 78, 79–81, 82–3, 85, 86, 103, 117, 123, 127–8, 134–5, 136, 137, 140–2, 144–5, 148, 152n, 162, 165, 222, 223–4, 225, 227, 230
trace, the, 38, 48, 58, 134, 170–1, 149n, 204, 231, 267, 292
Trakl, Georg, 279–80
Turner, Lynn, 32n, 94, 193, 274n

undecidability, 18, 19, 25, 30, 31–2, 40, 73, 82, 95, 101, 200

vagina, 32, 57–8, 200
Vergès, Françoise, 276, 282–3, 284–5, 292n
virginity, 4, 69n, 82, 122; *see also* chastity
vision, 8, 43, 80–1, 82, 85, 87
voice, 43, 44, 46, 49, 92, 102, 104, 122, 172, 188, 190–2, 198–202, 208n, 211n, 242, 283
Volkart, Yvonne, 119–20
von Krafft-Ebing, Richard, 129n, 194

Weber, Elisabeth, 91
Weinbaum, Karen, 273n
Weiss, Gail, 137
Wills, David, 85
  Killing Time 116, 130–1n
Wilson, Elizabeth A., 67n
Wittig, Monique, 54, 56, 58
  and 'The Straight Mind' 57, 68n
Wolfe, Cary, 148n
writing, 3, 4, 20, 23–4, 32n, 43, 55, 58, 86–7, 91, 94, 98–100, 102–3, 119, 125–6, 128–9, 153–4, 157–8, 160, 162–4, 165–6, 167–8, 171–2, 181, 200–5, 206–7, 212n, 213n, 219–20, 223–4, 250, 261–2